PEIRESC'S EUROPE

Frontispiece: Portrait of Peiresc by Claude Mellan, 1637. The State Hermitage Museum, St. Petersburg.

PEIRESC'S EUROPE

Learning and Virtue in the Seventeenth Century

PETER N. MILLER

YALE UNIVERSITY PRESS
NEW HAVEN AND LONDON

Designed by Elizabeth McWilliams

Printed in China

Library of Congress Cataloging-in-Publication Data

Miller, Peter N., 1964–
Peiresc's Europe : learning and virtue in the seventeenth century
/ Peter N. Miller.
p.   cm.
Includes index.
ISBN 0-300-08252-5 (alk. paper)
1. Peiresc, Nicolas Claude Fabri de, 1580–1637.
2. Humanists – France – Biography.
3. Statesmen – France – Biography.
4. France – Intellectual life – 17th century.
5. Europe – Intellectual life – 17th century.   I. Title.

DC121.8.P4 M55   2000
944'.032'092 – dc21
[B]
00-036505

A catalogue record for this book is available from
The British Library

For Deborah,
because love *is* best

CONTENTS

Home is where one starts from. As we grow older
The world becomes stranger, the pattern more complicated
Of dead and living. Not the intense moment
Isolated, with no before and after,
But a lifetime burning in every moment
And not the lifetime of one man only
But of old stones that cannot be deciphered.

T. S. Eliot, *Four Quartets*

List of Illustrations

Between pages 80 and 81

1. Frans Francken, *Interior of a Picture Gallery* (detail) (*c.*1625). The Collection of the Earl of Pembroke, Wilton House, Salisbury.

2. Plantin's printer's mark: 'Labore & Constantia'. From Justus Lipsius, *De amphitheatro* (1585). Rare Books Division. The New York Public Library. Astor, Lenox and Tilden Foundations.

3. Peiresc's Almanac for the year 1629. MS Fonds français 9531. Bibliothèque Nationale, Paris. Cliché Bibliothèque Nationale de France.

4. The emblem of 'Conversatione'. Cesare Ripa, *Nova iconologia*. Print Collection. Miriam and Ira D. Wallach Division of Art, Prints and Photographs. The New York Public Library. Astor, Lenox and Tilden Foundations.

5. The emblem of 'Amicitia'. Cesare Ripa, *Nova iconologia*. Print Collection. Miriam and Ira D. Wallach Division of Art, Prints and Photographs. The New York Public Library. Astor, Lenox and Tilden Foundations.

6. The emblem of 'Costanza'. Cesare Ripa, *Nova iconologia*. Print Collection. Miriam and Ira D. Wallach Division of Art, Prints and Photographs. The New York Public Library. Astor, Lenox and Tilden Foundations.

7. Peter-Paul Rubens, *The Garden of Love* (*Conversatie à la mode*) (*c.*1635). Museo del Prado, Madrid.

ACKNOWLEDGEMENTS

FOR A LONG TIME I had no permanent employment. During those years I was sustained by fellowships from a number of institutions and I am pleased now to be able to acknowledge their help: Clare Hall, University of Cambridge, the Collegiate Division of the Social Sciences, University of Chicago, the National Endowment for the Humanities, and the Wissenschaftskolleg zu Berlin – Institute for Advanced Study. Additional opportunities to travel were made possible by grants from the American Philosophical Society and the Gladys Krieble Delmas Foundation. An invitation to the International Society for Intellectual History's seminar on History and the Disciplines at the Folger Library in August 1993 gave me a first opportunity to work on Peiresc. Finishing the book has been made easier with the support of the Department of History and the College of Arts and Humanities of the University of Maryland, College Park, and the Fellows Program of the John D. and Catherine T. MacArthur Foundation. Insofar as I am able to attach faces to these institutions I would like to thank Stefan Collini, Quentin Skinner, Robert Pippin, Andrew Abbott, Wolf Lepenies, Joachim Nettelbeck, Donald Kelley, Constance Blackwell, John Lampe, and James Harris.

Presenting parts of this argument in the form of conference papers served an essential intellectual, but also social, function during those same years. I am grateful to Gary Smith, Peter Reill, Robert Darnton, Herbert Jaumann, Steve Pincus, Mary Louise Roberts, Hans-Erich Bödeker, Anthony Grafton, Jill Kraye, Nicholas Mann, Jean Robert Armogathe, Jean Glénisson, and Giuliano Ferretti for opportunities to participate and speak at the Einstein Forum, Potsdam, Center for Seventeenth- and Eighteenth-Century Studies, Los Angeles, East-West Seminar, Münster,

Herzog August Bibliothek, Wolfenbüttel, Early Modern European Workshop, University of Chicago, French Cultural Studies Seminar, Stanford University, European Science Foundation, Lisbon, Internationalen Forschungszentrum Kulturwissenschaften, Vienna, Warburg Institute, London, Réunion de la société des études XVIIᵉ siècle, Paris, and the Université francophone de l'été, Jonzac.

There is no better way of understanding what a Republic of Letters actually is than by plunging into the world of one of its most illustrious representatives. In the process, I have been taught the lessons of learned sociability and been the recipient, many times over, of the generosity of other scholars working on related questions: Ann Blair, Agnès Bresson, Tom Cerbu, Jérôme Delatour, Paula Findlen, David Freedberg, Marc Fumaroli, the late François Furet, Daniel Garber, Ralph Häfner, Ingo Herklotz, Thomas DaCosta Kaufmann, Sabine MacCormack, Martin Mulsow, Paul Nelles, Bruno Neveu, Tim Reiss, Ingrid Rowland, Bill Sherman, Nancy Siraisi, Guy Stroumsa, and Richard Tuck. Jean Robert Armogathe's hospitality in Paris showed me what that of Peiresc in Aix must have been like. Those who saw this book in manuscript are owed the largest debt. Harry Ballan, William Bouwsma, Anthony Grafton and Joan-Pau Rubiés read the entire text and Lorraine Daston and Debora Shuger selected chapters. I have benefited a great deal from their criticisms, and also from those of two anonymous readers. For help in checking my translations Ann Blair, Martin Mulsow and Ronan Wolfsdorf have my thanks. All that remains to be criticized is my doing. Finally, beyond the particular debts that can be registered through citation is a more general, and deep, one to those who have made straight many of the winding ways in Peiresc studies, chiefly Tamizey de Larroque, Pierre Humbert, Raymond Lebègue, Francis W. Gravit, Agnès Bresson, Sidney Aufrère, David Jaffé, Anne Reinbold, Jacques Ferrier, Jean-Francois Lhote, and Mady Smets-Hennekinne, President of the *Fondation Nicolas-Claude Fabri de Peiresc* in Brussels.

Isabelle Battez and Claudette Almeiras at the Bibliothèque Inguimbertine in Carpentras and Michel de Laburthe at the Bibliothèque Méjanes in Aix have made my working trips to these centres of Peiresc research memorable and happy. I could not have done this without their generous help. Other librarians helped me follow Peiresc's trail across Europe: at the Bibliothèque Nationale in Paris, Biblioteca Apostolica Vaticana in Rome, British Library in London, Bodleian Library in Oxford, Universiteitsbibliotheek in Leiden, Biblioteca Nazionale Marciana in Venice, Musée Paul Arbaud in Aix and the Württembergische Landesbibliothek in Stuttgart. An especially heavy debt is owed to the librarians of the Wissenschaftskolleg: Gesine Bottomley, Anja Brockmann, Marianne Buck, and Gudrun Rhein were partners in my labour. Closer to home, I wish to thank the librarians at the Folger Shakespeare Library, Regenstein Library, University of Chicago, Widener Library, Harvard University and the New York Public Library for their help. The existence of this book, in this form, is due to Gillian Malpass at the London office of Yale University Press; her encouragement and help have been matched only by her commitment to scholarship. Having had to endure streams of queries and volleys of corrections, Elizabeth McWilliams' always smiling assistance deserves special recognition.

More conversations than I can remember have gone into this book, but some do stand out: while walking by the Cam with Joan-Pau Rubiés and Béla Kapossy, and lingering on street corners with Harry Ballan. The ones that most shaped my thinking have been with Istvan Hont and Anthony Grafton: in the darkened afternoon heat of a Roman apartment at midsummer, while darting in and out of shops during an April shower in New York, deep in the meandering bowels of the Seminary Co-op Bookstore in Chicago, and beside the Grünewaldsee in Berlin.

My father, Samuel R. Miller, died before he could see any of this. I miss him on every page. My mother, Naomi Churgin Miller, read every page, usually several times, as she has for as long as I can remember. Written over a number of years and in a variety of places, some of the happiest moments in the making of this book were spent staring out across a lake still shimmering in the morning fog; I thank Barbara and David Krohn for that view, and much more. For Deborah Krohn, I have only joy. As Flavio Querenghi explained, *a questi che mi amano io scrivo....*

Sources and Abbreviations

The following references, and their abbreviations, are found in the text:

Carp. Bibl. Inguimb.   Musée Archéologique et Bibliographique
                        Paul Arbaud Carpentras, Bibliothèque
                        Inguimbertine, Aix-en-Provence
BL Add. MSS   Additional Manuscripts, British Library, London
BN F. fr.   MS Fonds français, Bibliothèque Nationale,
                        Paris
BN MS N.a.f.   Nouvelles acquisitions françaises, Bibliothèque
                        Nationale, Paris
BN MS Dupuy   MS Dupuy, Bibliothèque Nationale, Paris
BN MS Lat.   MS Latin, Bibliothèque Nationale, Paris
BN Est. Rés.   Cabinet des Estampes, Réserves, Bibliothèque
                        Nationale, Paris
Vat. MS Barb.-Lat.   MS Barberini-Latina, Vatican Library, Rome
BNM   Biblioteca Nazionale Marciana, Venice

Frequent references are made to the following printed works:

Lettres de Peiresc   Philippe Tamizey de Larroque (ed.), 7 vols,
                          (Paris, 1888–98)
Correspondance de   P. Apollinaire de Valence (ed.), *Correspondance de*
Peiresc avec Capucins   *Peiresc avec plusieurs missionaires et*
                          religieux de l'ordre des Capucins 1631–1637
                          (Paris, 1891)

Rubens Correspondance	Charles Ruelens and Max Rooses (eds), *Correspondance de Rubens et documents epistolaires concernant sa vie et ses oeuvres*, 6 vols (Antwerp, 1887–1909)
Mersenne Correspondance	Mme Paul Tannery, Cornélius de Waard, and René Pintard (eds), *Correspondance du P. Marin Mersenne religieux minime*, 17 vols (Paris, 1939–88)
Briefwisseling	*Briefwisseling van Hugo Grotius*, P. C. Molhuysen, et al. (eds), 15 vols (The Hague, 1928–)
Works	*The Works of Francis Bacon*, James Spedding, Robert Leslie Ellis, and Douglas Denon Heath (eds), 7 vols (London, 1857–59)
Vita	Pierre Gassendi, *Viri illustris Nicolai Claudii Fabricii de Peiresc senatoris aquisextentis vita*, 1641★
Mirrour	Pierre Gassendi, *Mirrour of True Nobility and Gentility* (English translation of above, 1657)★

★Because pagination in the English translation is discontinuous, references to the first five books of Gassendi's biography will include the year as well as the page, for example, 'year 1632, p. 211'. Those to the final, non-annalistic, book will read simply 'bk 6, p. 211'. The English translation also includes as frontmatter both Gassendi's original dedication and that of the English translator, and as endmatter Jean-Jacques Bouchard's Roman funeral oration, 'Prayse of Peireskius' and a series of letters memorializing Peiresc. These will be quoted by author and page number (for example, 'Naudé to Gassendi, p. 255').

★   ★   ★

All references to works divided into books, chapters and sections will take the form of bk, ch., section; for classical sources I follow convention and cite as, for example, *De Officiis* 1.ii.7.

TEXTUAL NOTE

All translations are mine except as indicated. Quotations from early modern sources preserve the orthography, and are silently modernized only when absolutely necessary for comprehension or when citing from editions in which this has already been done.

Peiresc's country home was in a hamlet whose name he spelled variously: Belgentier, Boysgency, Beaugency, etc. For consistency's sake it is referred to throughout as Belgentier.

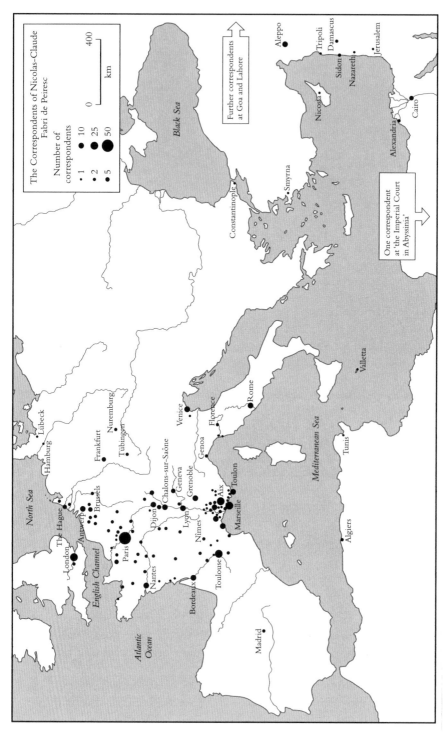

Fig 1. Map of Peiresc's correspondence. Adapted from Françoise Waquet and Hans Bots, *La République des Lettres* (Paris, 1997). Courtesy of Editions Bélin.

INTRODUCTION

UMBERTO ECO'S DESCRIPTION of an unnamed 'local gentleman' from Aix-en-Provence who was 'versed in every science, possessor of a library rich not only in books but in art objects, antiquities, and embalmed animals', aptly captures the fate of the man it refers to, Nicolas-Claude Fabri de Peiresc (1580–1637).[1] In his time, Peiresc was one of Europe's most famous men though soon after his death he was all but forgotten. His story offers us a seventeenth-century vantage point on a series of complex issues: the meaning of individual excellence, the changing shape of social life, the character of political argument, the relationship between learning and religion, and the importance of history for life.

Peiresc was educated by the Jesuits in Aix and Avignon and destined for a legal career and the family position in the Parlement of Provence. A trip to Italy (1599–1602) was designed by his uncle and father to further his legal education though the young Peiresc used it to introduce himself to the world of Italian scholars. His formal education was completed at Montpellier and Aix, culminating in a doctorate of civil law (1604). Peiresc travelled extensively through Parisian, English, Dutch, and Flemish learned circles on the northern leg of his interrupted scholarly peregrination (1606). The friends he made on these trips were the foundation of his intellectual and social life. Upon the death of his uncle on 24 June 1607, Peiresc took the family seat in the *parlement* and occupied it for exactly thirty years (he died on 24 June 1637). For seven of them (1616–23) he lived in Paris in the entourage of his patron Guillaume du Vair, then Keeper of the Seals, and saw at first hand the workings of a baroque court. After returning to Provence in 1623, he never left. For the last fourteen years of his life Peiresc was able, from this provincial headquarters, 'to unite all Mankind, through the whole World, by the Commerce and Correspondence of Letters'.[2] And so, for example, when some scholars wished to protest against the imprisonment of Galileo it was to Peiresc that they turned, hoping that his close personal relations with Pope Urban VIII and Cardinal Francesco Barberini would succeed where others had failed. He warned Cardinal Barberini that failure to reverse the verdict 'would run the great risk of being interpreted and perhaps compared one day to the persecution of the person and wisdom of Socrates in his country, so condemned by other nations and by posterity itself'.[3] Peiresc's death in 1637 was marked by an outpouring of comment across the learned world, including an extraordinary memorial meeting in Rome attended by ten cardinals and dozens of antiquaries and philologists, publication of a volume of elegiac poetry in over forty languages (which was still being celebrated one hundred years later by Samuel Johnson), and the most important biography of a scholar written in the seventeenth century, by the philosopher and astronomer Pierre Gassendi.

The 100,000 pages of letters, copies of letters, memoranda and reading notes that survive preserve a rich sample of the intellectual interests of the seventeenth-century Republic of Letters. In these pages we are plunged headlong into the world of an early modern antiquary. Like the great contemporary entrepôts in which the goods of the world were laid side by side, we can find here information about the range of issues driving the learned and political world of the first decades of the seventeenth century. Peiresc's correspondents in Europe and the Ottoman Empire served as his foreign service and he, sitting in Provence, gathered their reports and forwarded them to the most appropriate destination. For three decades he was one of the chief junctions of European intellectual life, bundling discrete bits of information into knowledge that could be examined in a more sustained fashion by experts living across the Continent. Peiresc's 'out of the way', provincial headquarters was not a liability in an age just before the emergence of modern capitals like Paris and London made the term 'provincial intellectual' an oxymoron. On the contrary, proximity to Avignon was the foundation of his close contacts with princes of the Church and from his home in Aix (near Marseille) and country estate near Toulon, Peiresc bestrode the Rhône and Mediterranean ports that connected France to Italy, North Africa, and the Levant.

In the Peiresc archive we learn of his discovery of the first nebula ever seen, in the constellation Orion, in 1610 while repeating his friend Galileo's observations of the moons of Jupiter (the 'Medicean Planets'). Peiresc rediscovered the Great Cameo of France, the so-called *Gemma Tiberiana*, in the Sainte Chapelle in 1620 and then identified many of its figures. He was behind the acquisition, in Smyrna around 1624, of the 'Marmor Parium' – one of what came to be called the 'Arundel Marbles' due to Peiresc's agent being briefly imprisoned and Lord Arundel's, hot on the trail, having swooped down to spirit them away to London. Peiresc's correspondence contains one of the first, if not *the* first, descriptions by a European, on the basis of a conversation with a traveller recently returned from Persia in 1628, of the trilingual inscription carved at Bisitun on the order of Darius the Great in 518 BCE. To correct sailing maps of the Mediterranean, Peiresc organized a series of eclipse observations whose results could be used to recalculate longitudes. It was in connection with this project that he commissioned from a visiting artist the first mapping of the moon, executed in his home observatory in 1636. Three hundred years later a crater on the moon was named Peirescius in honor of this achievement.[4] We also learn of his love of cats, which did not, however, preclude the occasional barter of kittens for antiquities, as well as his passion for gardening: his orchards contained over twenty species of citron, some dozen kinds of orange, and, astoundingly, sixty types of apple. He grafted olives to make new varieties (including *olives cannellé!*) and bottled the wine of the malvoisie grapes grown on his property which he then gave away to friends and acquaintances. A later seventeenth-century Botanist Royal commemorated this passion in the name of the most ancient phylum of succulents: *Pereskia*.[5]

It was with all this in mind that Pierre Bayle declared 'that never did anyone render more services to the Republic of Letters than he' and hailed Peiresc as its 'Procureur Général'. And yet, Peiresc's fame in life was more than matched by an oblivion in death so swift and so complete as to elicit from Bayle, who did not forget him, the judgement that the name of Peiresc was unknown, even to some Frenchmen of his own time.[6] He had already become Eco's nameless 'local gentleman'.[7]

Why then should we now be interested in him? Because Peiresc was an extraordinary figure who typifies, in the extreme, features of Europe's late humanist culture. Michelet went so far as to call him 'l'homme de la civilization'.[8] In our time, Arnaldo Momigliano described Peiresc as the 'archetype of all antiquarians', Hugh Trevor-Roper called him 'the dynamo which drove the machine of intellectual discussion throughout the Continent', and Marc Fumaroli designated him 'the prince of the Republic of Letters', while Alain Schnapp explained that 'no one, without a doubt, better embodies this type of humanist than Peiresc', adding that 'at the same time, nothing is more difficult than to reconstruct his activity'.[9] Peiresc was among the best known and most celebrated inhabitants of an intellectual continent long since sunk from view. The historian sees the rapidity with which Peiresc was forgotten – while friends like Marin Mersenne and Hugo Grotius were not – as a clue

that something dramatic must have been changing in European intellectual life during Peiresc's own lifetime and just after. But to understand
this change, one that defined central features of the modern age such as
the New Science and the state, we need to know what it changed *from*.
How could someone like Peiresc have been so famous in the first place?
That is the question I am trying to answer here.[10]

Peiresc's celebrity is evidence of what other citizens of the early
seventeenth-century Republic of Letters thought worth celebrating. The
structure of the book follows from this insight. Its initial chapter intro-
duces the man and the intellectual and social virtues for which he was
praised. Subsequent chapters then show these virtues — and therefore
their possessor, the exemplary man — in action, as he lived and worked.
Chapter Two explores the relationship between Peiresc's ideal of civility,
shared widely among members of the Republic of Letters, and the earlier
Italian and later French discussions of how best to live in society. Chapter
Three looks at Peiresc and his friends in their capacity as political actors,
typical servants of the ancient constitution and immersed in the contemporary debates about the relationship between Crown and Church
and between centre and regions. Chapter Four focuses on the antiquary's
theology. What was Peiresc's religion? and how did he accommodate
a commitment to intense and wide-ranging inquiry with belief in a
revealed, sacred history? One of the difficulties faced by anyone studying figures like Peiresc is that it is so hard to make sense of the motives
behind these vast gatherings of facts. The fifth and final chapter tries to
plumb the sensibility of those who found something deeply satisfying
about studying the past. Viewed from a different angle, the book's organization could be described as a series of reflections, in which the life
of Peiresc provides the matter, on the question 'What is a scholar?', on
the relationship of a scholarly life to sociability, politics, and religion, and,
finally, on the question, '*Why* be a scholar?'

Peiresc's way of living reflected what his English admirers called 'the
Peireskean virtues' and which they sought to inculcate through their
translation of Gassendi's *Life*. In a culture shaped by the norms of classical rhetoric, as was the seventeenth century, education was done by
illustration.[11] The value of studying history was, precisely, that it was 'philosophy teaching by example'. The history of an individual life, if well
chosen, could do the same. Peiresc's friends thought him a 'great Heroe,
which all learned men ought to admire'. Gassendi had 'set forth to Posterity a genuine example of polite Literature, and plentiful grounds of
emulation to the learned World'.[12] The celebration of the 'Peireskean
virtues' was, then, a celebration of an ideal of intellectual and social excellence in a society that was constituted by its choice of hero. For us, the

praise of Peiresc opens a window on to seventeenth-century notions of what the 'best' life looked like.

Peiresc's oblivion is also instructive. For he failed to publish just at that moment in European history when the printed word became an essential vehicle of memory.[13] His omnivorous curiosity fell victim to the rising walls of disciplinary borders and the experts who policed them. His quiet, rational, minimally doctrinal faith seemed out of place in a world no longer polarized into fanatics and believers but believers and atheists. His fascination with the past and philosophically inspired indifference to fashion marked him out with the scarlet *A* when being an ancient implied betraying one's contemporaries. And, finally, he was a proud provincial at the beginning of a long period in European history in which this came to be associated with the opposite of everything desirable. In sum, Peiresc offers us not a reflection of a world we have lost, but something much sharper: the very mirror image of the one we still inhabit.

In his lectures on the history of philology, delivered at Basel in 1871, Friedrich Nietzsche pointed to a gulf separating the generations of Joseph Scaliger and Claude Saumaise. Peiresc straddled this divide, a young friend of the former and an older one of the latter. And when Wilhelm Dilthey sought to describe the new spirit of late Renaissance Europe he singled out the achievements of three men, Scaliger, Galileo, and Grotius, all close friends whose inspiration Peiresc frequently acknowledged with indebted gratitude.[14] This generation that came of age *circa* 1600 – Peiresc's generation – also included Caravaggio, Ben Jonson, Marin Mersenne, Claudio Monteverdi and Peter-Paul Rubens (in fact, both Peiresc and Rubens, unknown to each other, were present at the celebration of Marie de' Medici's wedding to Henri IV in Florence in 1600). Theirs was a Europe stretched across a series of tensions that had not yet exploded. In political thought, pulled between the ancient constitution and new theories of absolutism; in political geography, between regions and centre; in religion, between Protestants and Catholics, national and universal churches, revelation and nature; in moral philosophy, between universal principles and conventional norms; in culture, between the authority of antiquity and the power of the 'moderns'; in the history of scholarship, between an age of polymathy and one emphasizing 'specialization'; in society, between the old nobility and the new gentlemen. Each of these themes has been the subject of much close study, and yet the life that was lived across these gigantic fault lines remains elusive. Only by reacquainting ourselves with the intellectual and moral landscape of people like Peiresc, who sprawled across the world of learning in his own lifetime, can we hope to understand him and, by

extension, those like him. The obscurity and, perhaps worse still, unin-
telligibility, of antiquarian pursuits reflects the resistance of this world to
the analytical tools and categories which the succeeding one – ours –
imposed on the world of learning.[15]

The subject of this book is Peiresc and his circle. If we wished to set
about reconstructing its membership we might best begin with the
picture gallery that Peiresc himself assembled over the course of a lifetime. Many scholars, beginning in the Renaissance, collected or commissioned paintings to hang in their studies. What distinguished Peiresc's
collection was that, first, it was composed of friends and, second, they
were scholars rather than more universally 'great men'. The content of
the gallery, as it has been reconstructed by P. J. J. van Thiel and David
Jaffé, is Peiresc's representation of his world. Included, as titular deities,
are the kings of France Henri IV and Louis XIII, and the ancient counts
of Barcelona and Toulouse. Cardinal Richelieu was present, as well as his
brother, Peiresc's close friend, the Archbishop of Aix and then Lyon. Pope
Urban VIII, whom Peiresc knew and befriended as Maffeo Barberini, was
accompanied by his nephew Cardinal Francesco Barberini and other
princes of the Church, including Jacques Davvy Du Perron, Giovanni
Francesco Cardinal de'Bagni, and Scipione Cobelluzzi, the Cardinal of
St Susanna. Older, learned role models are represented by portraits of
Baronius, Jacques-Auguste de Thou, Joseph Scaliger, Isaac Casaubon,
Justus Lipsius, Giovanni Battista Della Porta, William Camden, Guillaume
du Vair, Giulio Pace, Gian Vincenzo Pinelli, and Marcus Welser. Peers
whose portraits were solicited include Pierre Dupuy, Lorenzo Pignoria,
Girolamo Aleandro, Lucas Holstenius, Hugo Grotius, Galileo Galilei,
François Malherbe, Cassiano dal Pozzo, John Barclay, Claude Saumaise,
and, most famously, Peter-Paul Rubens, whose self-portrait (now in Canberra) for Peiresc was one of only two painted entirely by his own hand:
the other lucky recipient was Charles I of England.[16] Friends whose portraits he did not solicit include Paolo Sarpi, whom he met when a visiting student at Padua, Tommaso Campanella, who stayed *chez* Peiresc
when fleeing Rome for Paris, Athanasius Kircher, whom he met in
Avignon and whose sponsor he became, Marin Mersenne, who dedicated to Peiresc a part of the *Harmonie universelle*, and Gabriel Naudé, a
correspondent of his last years, whose letter eulogizing Peiresc was
reprinted in later editions of Gassendi's biography.

One or two of these names might be familiar to a general reader,
many more to scholars of seventeenth-century intellectual culture and
some only to the most specialized of specialists. But if Peiresc recognized
that the fame of Galileo would endure, many of his close friendships and
working relationships were with men whose names are often all that is
known of them. Yet, they were important for him and hence are impor-

tant for reconstructing his life. If posterity's verdict has condemned most of Peiresc's circle to an eclipse only somewhat less total than Peiresc's, his own *fortuna* ought to be caution enough about presuming that fame stands somehow outside of time. Who now would even think of comparing Montaigne with Flavio Querenghi (assuming one knew the name)? Yet this is precisely what the latter's friends suggested – and if they intended to flatter, they certainly did not aim to provoke laughter. Indeed, if we could imagine an inventory of seventeenth-century intellectual correspondence it would be filled with the letters of men obscure to us, but prominent in their respective worlds. To ignore this fact and focus on those whose fame has endured, or even grown, in the intervening centuries is to make Fortuna, and not Clio, the muse of history.

The geography traversed in this book also follows the contours of the social reality and intellectual agenda of Peiresc's Europe. It was shaped by friendships, many made during those youthful travels in Italy, England, and the Low Countries. But there were always three poles, Paris, Rome, and Provence (fig. 1). The surviving register of out-going mail covers the years 1623–32 and shows an equal attention to correspondents in Paris and Provence, and a greater focus on Rome than on the other French provinces.[17] Peiresc maintained the closest of relations with the Barberini and even described himself as a 'particulier serviteur de la maison de Barberin'.[18] In this household lodged some of his closest friends and intellectual collaborators, including Aleandro, dal Pozzo, Holstenius, Jean-Marie Suares, and Giovanni Battista Doni. The Cabinet Dupuy, another of the great intellectual clearing-houses of early modern Europe, was his Parisian headquarters. Du Vair had brought him into the circle of Jacques-Auguste de Thou and he remained closely tied to de Thou's continuators Pierre and Jacques Dupuy, and to de Thou's ill-fated son, François-Auguste, killed by Richelieu for complicity in the conspiracy of Cinq-Mars in 1642.[19] The Dupuy brothers kept him abreast of goings-on in Paris, and forwarded letters to friends in northern Europe. The sweep of Peiresc's long-distance correspondence tends to overshadow the local, often face-to-face relations with Provençaux that constituted the bulk of his intellectual life. Proximity to Avignon, for example, gave him ready access to the papal nuncios, several of whom, upon their return to Rome, became useful contacts, including Cardinals Bentivoglio, de' Bagni, Francesco, and, of course, Maffeo Barberini, later Pope Urban VIII. Peiresc seems, however, to have had few contacts across the Rhine, even fewer over the Pyrenees (one of whom was a Fleming) and none in the far north – he sought out Ole Worm's *Fasti Danici* through an intermediary while Worm, for his part, knew little of Peiresc and that only indirectly.[20] On the other hand, through the Marseille merchants who dominated the French diplomatic and commercial communities in the

Ottoman Empire Peiresc was able to develop multiple channels of information in Egypt, Lebanon, Syria, and Turkey.[21] Because he kept copies of out-going as well as in-coming letters, this is probably the most substantial private archive of correspondence to and from the Ottoman Empire extant for the first decades of the seventeenth century. One last observation on the map of his relationships should be made: Peiresc's is probably the first great European epistolary network to have been constructed in the vernacular. There is the odd Latin letter, but we find him using French or Italian with Germans and Englishmen to whom Latin would have made more sense (Peiresc himself confessed to having small German and less English).[22]

Peiresc studied many things but loved the past most of all. Of his four great, unfinished projects, three were historical: studies of ancient weights and measures, the Roman calendar of 354, and the past of Provence; the other was a 'commentary' on the moons of Jupiter. His study of the ancient world through its fragmentary textual and material remains belongs to a tradition of scholarship that goes back to Petrarch in the fourteenth century, Cyriac of Ancona in the fifteenth, and of course, the giants of the immediately preceding generation whom he knew well, Isaac Casaubon and Joseph Scaliger (Justus Lipsius died only months before Peiresc's arrival in Louvain).

If we speak of a 'rise of antiquarian research' we are referring to a sixteenth-century phenomenon whose center was Rome, but which was promoted as 'new' learning also in Vienna, Uppsala, Paris, and London – in short, wherever there were rulers wishing to wrap themselves in the authority of a glorious national past.[23] Antiquaries were characterized by an almost obsessive devotion to reconstructing the material culture and imaginative forms of the ancient world – 'to wake the dead', as Cyriac described his calling. Their most decisive contribution to the way the past was studied was in emphasizing the value of non-literary sources and developing rules for using them. Three sorts of intellectual practice were typical: collection, observation, and comparison. Objects of all sorts, from flora and fauna to texts to gems, became the quarry of collectors and began to fill up shelves and purpose-built display cabinets across Europe. The next step was to observe closely and then describe these materials. This fascination with objects is reflected in a literary style that itself rarely rises above the level of description. Only after having amassed a large enough collection and examined it carefully could the antiquary compare pieces and learn something.

The most important interpretation of early modern antiquarianism, the 'heroic age' of the antiquaries, is that of Arnaldo Momigliano. In a series of essays stretching over nearly forty years and interspersed within a far larger *oeuvre* he called attention to their methods and influence on the study and writing of history.[24] The more recent work of historians of early modern scholarship (Anthony Grafton), archaeology (Ingo Herklotz and Alain Schnapp), collecting (Krzysztof Pomian), science (Paula Findlen, Michael Hunter), theology (Bruno Neveu, Simon Ditchfield), and, especially, art (Elizabeth Cropper, David Freedberg, Francis Haskell, and Ingrid Rowland) has helped show just how thoroughly antiquarian this culture actually was.[25] Precisely because he was not travelling on the high road to the new science or to the modern state, Peiresc's friendships with those who were, such as Mersenne, Galileo, Grotius, and Naudé, enable us to understand much more clearly the differences, as well as the striking similarities, of new and old in early seventeenth-century learned life.

Insofar as antiquaries of Peiresc's generation did things differently from those living a generation earlier, it was due to an extraordinarily expanded access to information. Antiquaries like Peiresc inhabited a world made bigger by discovery. 'Who ever heard of th'Indian Peru?' asked Spenser in 1590. At the same time, travel eastwards brought Europeans into closer contact with the Ottoman world; flowing west were raw materials, but also native informants who made the grammars and trained the linguists who then studied the manuscripts that followed close behind and wrote the histories that reshaped the world of knowledge. More material from which to draw conclusions by comparison, and much greater facility with the languages needed to study them, separates sixteenth- from seventeenth-century antiquarianism.[26] To be sure, this was only a difference of degree and the work of men like Sigonio, Scaliger, and Saumaise would continue to be argued with – surely the greatest demonstration of continuing worth – long into the nineteenth century.[27]

In addition to the information brought back to Europe by travellers over sea and land was that dug from under foot. 'Haile bold Researcher! With thy rich returnes / From the darke coasts of Monuments and Urnes', proclaimed one seventeenth-century Englishman. Another actually placed the antiquary at the confluence of exploration and archaeology: 'As one therefore that has coasted a little further into former times, I will offer unto you a rude Mapp thereof; not like those of the exquisite Cosmographers of our latter ages, but like them of old, when as neither Cross Sails nor Compass were yet known to Navigators.'[28] Travel through space and time gave Europe's antiquaries a richer and more complex past. To the study of ancient pagan Rome was now added the late antique Christian capital, and from a fixation with the Roman Empire scholars now looked back to the Hellenistic East and forward to the early medieval West. The impact of America and Asia on the study of the past was even more complex. Perhaps most important was the discovery that one could gain access to the European past by looking at the non-European present.

Peiresc was no Scaliger, yet Anthony Grafton has described Peiresc's as the 'true continuation' of Scaliger's work.[29] Why? First, because he worked to expand the varieties of evidence from the textual to the material. Scaliger is recorded as having said that if he had more money he would have spent it on travel, not books. Peiresc not only travelled as a young man, but when older he sponsored and outfitted what we ought to call 'expeditions', dedicated shopping trips by learned explorers who were briefed by Peiresc before departure, de-briefed afterwards, and equipped with lists of questions to ask, places to see, and things to buy – all of which were destined for his working collection or those of other scholars. The great triumph of this approach to the study of texts alongside objects was in joining theory to practice. By contrast, Saumaise once explained to Peiresc, 'the majority of our learned men, having worked in only one of these parts, are content with what they can learn from books, which is not at all worth what the things them-selves teach us, once we look at them, handle them and hold them in our hands'.[30] This sort of close encounter with the world of objects is the subject of one of Frans Francken's glorious interiour scenes from around 1625 (plate 1).

Second, Peiresc recognized that Scaliger's work on chronology sug-gested the possibility of constructing a new history of Europe that inte-grated the ancient Egyptian, Israelite, and Phoenician worlds of the eastern Mediterranean with the Greek and Roman civilizations of the western. Tools developed by Renaissance humanists for understanding ancient Greek and Roman society were, over the course of the seven-teenth century, used to study the history and literature of the ancient Near East. It is the expansion of the historian's repertory of evidence, geography, and chronology in the direction of what we would identify as archaeology, anthropology, art history, and social history that represents the fulfilment of the historical revolution that Scaliger foretold.

Thomas Smith, the late seventeenth-century biographer of William Camden, who was perhaps Peiresc's closest English friend, described anti-quarianism as 'a sort of Learning, that was then but just *appearing* in the world, when that heat and vehemence of *Philosophy* and *School-Divinity* (which had possess'd all hearts and hands for so many hundred years) began to cool'.[31] This reminds us that the rise of antiquarian research lay in 'the last interconfessional generation of Renaissance scholars', an early seventeenth-century golden age that Gaetano Cozzi, Hugh Trevor-Roper, Marc Fumaroli, Enrico de Mas, and R. J. W. Evans, among others, have done so much to illuminate.[32] Between the wars of religion in

France and the Thirty Years War in Germany lay a period of relative calm and extraordinary intellectual fruitfulness. The Paris of Henri IV and the Prague of Rudolf II were the capital cities of this dream of political and cultural renewal. The Republic of Letters united far-flung political centres like London, Paris, Vienna, and Rome with regional hubs of culture such as Leiden, Padua, Breslau, Heidelberg, and Aix through letters positively fizzing with the excitement of scholarly discovery and the latest political developments. This was Peiresc's Europe. Its flourishing marks a period of extraordinary openness to learning and an equal confidence in the ability of reason to solve whatever problems – political, theological, or philosophical – this kind of intellectual endeavour generated.

The renewed conflict that brought this 'golden age' to an end also marked a crisis of public life. If politics, writ large, seemed now to afford few comforts, many obligations, and great risk, smaller, select communities of like-minded individuals offered the prospect of a welcome haven of friendship and sodality. Pierre Gassendi's biography of Peiresc presents him as the ideal member of just such a society, the Republic of Letters. Chapter One looks closely at the examined *Life* in order to show how antiquarian knowledge and the antiquarian personality converged in a model that taught the virtues of constancy, conversation, friendship, and beneficence. These were, not coincidentally, also celebrated in three earlier books whose tremendous continuing popularity, attested by multiple translations and re-editions, reflects the resonance of these ideas across Europe: Stefano Guazzo's *La civile conversatione* (1574, 1579), Justus Lipsius' *De constantia* (1584), and Michel de Montaigne's *Essais* (1580, 1588).[33] Peiresc also had before him the living examples of Pinelli in Padua, de Thou in Paris, and Camden in London whose combination of erudition, charisma, and decency had created intellectual communities within the larger political one and extending well beyond its borders.

The tremendous importance attached to friendship during this period reflects both its role as a haven in a stormy world and its privileged status as a rational relationship.[34] The proliferation of venues where friends could gather, whether academies, *salons*, coffee-houses, or clubs, reflects the desire to found communities of shared interest and presumed equality.[35] Surveying conditions of civil life in Italy, France, and the Empire *circa* 1600, A. M. Battista, Nannerl Keohane, and R. J. W. Evans have commented on the centrality of these miniature civil societies.[36] Their role in the history of European political thought is now being intensively studied, but up until recently[37] the most influential histories of the origins of 'civil society' have focused on the later seventeenth and eighteenth centuries. These frame the outer limit of my argument but it

is in the earlier part of the seventeenth century, in the Republic of
Letters, that many of the ideas about how a civil society ought to function were first elaborated. This is the subject of Chapter Two.

Civil communities, and these new ways of evaluating what it meant
to be a good member of them, began to flourish around the time when
recognizably modern states began to emerge. It is striking that 'Societies
of Antiquaries' grew up at the same time in the last two decades of the
sixteenth century in both France and England. Though the Parisian
group never obtained a formal title, the scholars gathered around Pierre
and François Pithou, like those who surrounded Camden, were dedicated to the intensive study of national geography, customs, and laws.[38]
The formal standing of antiquarianism in these two countries reflects an
early sense of the national identities that their scholarship helped shape.
The relationship of antiquarianism to the rise of the modern state is not
coincidental: scholars often served as advisors and officials whose knowledge of national history was essential at a time when dynastic origins
served as the first ground of legitimacy. The importance of 'ancient constitutions' in the making and remaking of national political institutions
put a premium on the medieval history of the modern polity and on
those able to mine surviving archival material. Similarly, the creation of
a civil service, especially in the German states, led to the institutional-
ization of antiquarian learning. Daniel Morhof's famous textbook, the
Polyhistor (1688), is an example of the way in which a learned education
became a civil service qualification.[39] Antiquaries made useful bureau-
crats in an age when policy-makers looked into the dustiest archives for
ammunition in present battles. Moreover, the most widespread languages
of political discourse in the seventeenth century were antiquarian. Arguments framed in terms of Europe's 'ancient constitution' and those that
invoked the 'interests' of the states of Europe were actually interpretations of medieval and contemporary national history. Even Europe's
growing imperial project depended upon antiquaries; it was, for example,
their knowledge of the history of religion that Spanish governors in Peru
drew upon in order to recognize the survival of the pagan gods in the
practice of their new, and barely, Christianized subjects.[40] Chapter Three
examines these issues through the prism of Peiresc's own political activities over the course of thirty years' service to France and Provence.
A *parlementaire* in Aix but also a devoted servant of the Crown, Peiresc
not only studied France's ancient constitution, he lived it. The tragedy
of being pulled in opposite directions was not only his, but a whole
generation's.

When Justus Lipsius, the famed Netherlandish humanist, proclaimed,
'I have made philosophy out of philology' ('Ego e Philologia
Philosophiam feci') he was boasting about how his editions of Seneca

and Tacitus provided the raw materials for a moral instruction emphasizing 'constancy' that has since been called 'neo-Stoicism'.[41] His *Constantia* was a service ideal that proposed to men of state the virtue of Roman legionaries able to stand fast under attack, and also taught how to remain free in the mind while serving in the world, the subject of Lipsius' other best-seller, *De politica* (1589).[42] Under conditions of war and financial duress rulers invoked necessity at will, making teachings that stressed rational detachment as 'a buckler against adversity' – as the English translation of a book by Peiresc's mentor du Vair (*De la constance*, 1594) was entitled – more than likely to find a receptive audience among those whose proximity to rulers made them especially vulnerable.[43] 'Neo-Stoicism', in short, taught the educated, lay aristocrat burdened by worldly cares the strength of mind required 'to be philosophical' – as we still call it – in the midst of it all. Gassendi had stressed both Peiresc's curiosity and his faith. Chapter Four explores the relationship of neo-Stoicism to the problem of the Christian's accommodation of pagan wisdom. Many of those who saw common ground between European Christian and Chinese Confucian beliefs drew upon the same 'optimistic' anthropology that was articulated by the Stoics and neo-Stoics. The scholar's theology, then, points us towards a central theme in early seventeenth-century religious thought.

For the sixty years that roughly coincide with Peiresc's own life, from 1580 to 1640, this Christianized, aristocratic, eclectic, stoical, and sceptical philosophy of living was the fashionable intellectual language for educated Europeans from Seville to Danzig and from Jutland to Lower Austria.[44] Neo-Stoicism never displaced Aristotle in university faculties and its diffusion was through the vernacular languages read by non-philosophers.[45] If, as Lipsius suggested in his edition of Tacitus, 'the theatre of today's life' made the history of the early Roman Empire seem immediately relevant, the same conditions of war, conspiracy, and corruption explain the renewed interest in ancient philosophers like Seneca and Epictetus who taught an art of living that emphasized self-control and serenity.[46]

The eclecticism that accounts for the popularity of neo-Stoicism has also obscured the extent and shape of its diffusion. It is simply very difficult to pin down a set of doctrines and say these and these alone constitute neo-Stoicism, and this became even more difficult as the didactic presentations and the ideas themselves were accepted and absorbed into the philosophical 'background' of ordinary discussion. Neo-Stoicism in the seventeenth century is hard to study, and in the eighteenth exceptionally so, because it no longer stands out as new, the way the Italian Renaissance stared out from the walls of Fontainebleau in the middle of the sixteenth century, or as a geographically isolated phenomenon, like the Italian city planted on the Ukrainian Marches in the late sixteenth century at Zamość. It is to overcome the difficulties that can arise from trying to study things that a society understands immanently and therefore has no need to discuss that this study of an ideal of individual excellence has been undertaken from variety of angles, some more oblique than others: from biography first of all, and then from the perspectives offered by art, literature, philosophy, scholarship, and politics.

History was a great resource for those seeking equanimity because it helped keep everything 'in perspective' – another echo from the seventeenth century. How better than by immersing oneself in the broken, obscure fragments of ancient glories? In a culture fascinated by the idea of philosophy as an art of living, the study of antiquities, in addition to its other appeals, contributed to that philosophical exercise. The characteristic shape of the late humanist culture founded on this link between the antiquarian and the eirenic was described by Evans in terms of a 'Pelagian ethic' or a 'Lipsius paradigm'.[47] Peiresc was no philosopher but his scholarly practice – and, by extension, that of his admirers – made him philosophical.[48] In Chapter Five we confront directly the question of the relationship between antiquarianism and neo-Stoicism and the place of history in the moral economy of those who devoted their lives to the study of its broken remains. Why study the past?

This is not a biography of Peiresc. Nor can it offer a satisfyingly comprehensive treatment of any of the great intellectual tributaries of modernity whose winding courses it traverses: the history of antiquarianism, the meaning of 'civility', the relationship between philosophy and theology, and the changing meaning of individual excellence. However, ranging across this terrain and drawing together strands of argument that are closely related but which have rarely been brought into the same conversation is necessary if we wish to put these parts back together again – as they were actually lived.[49] My purpose here has been to use Peiresc to summon this lost but whole world back to life and, having done so, to suggest that its story cannot be told without recognizing the place in it of men like Peiresc. Nor is this story in its broader outlines so distant from 'the theatre of today's life'; any reader of Richard Hofstadter's remarkable *Anti-Intellectualism in American Life* will recognize in the seventeenth-century relationship between learning and virtue lived by men like Peiresc the target of the American cultural revolution that began in that same century. Finally, in focusing on Peiresc as an example of excellence I have deliberately left to one side a raft of fascinating issues about his practice as an antiquary. How he worked and, in particular, how he went about studying other cultures, like those of the ancient and contemporary Near East, forms another part of this project. Peiresc's archive helps us understand how what came to be called 'oriental studies' developed out of late humanist antiquarian practice and suggests a striking continuity, that I hope to explore, between early modern antiquaries and their heirs, modern cultural historians.

A person's questions, rather than his answers, often best bear witness to his turn of mind. In this book I have tried to recover the questions that shaped intellectual conversation at a crucial moment in the history of thinking about the relationship between learning and living. In the seventeenth-century words that drive this story we come closest to the perceptions of those who lived this life. I have tried to draw out their insights and amplify their questions. If I approach these issues as a historian I necessarily draw on literature, philosophy, and the arts, just as someone interested in the same questions from one of these disciplines would need the knowledge of the others, as well as his or her own. An acute assessment of the challenges posed by this kind of study was advanced long ago by Erwin Panofsky:

> It lies in the nature of the thing, that the investigation had to proceed, here and there, in the domain of purely literary-historical, and even text-critical discussions. No single science can be ready with answers to all the questions that a sister-discipline, from its completely different intellectual context, can direct at it. And when the historian of images sees himself led to specific textual problems, he cannot expect to find exactly these problems – which from the standpoint of a philologist or literary historian are often not visible at all – already completely solved, but he will have to help himself, as well as he can.[50]

1

Peiresc

Free Mind and Friend

PEIRESC IS NOT AN ENTIRELY OBVIOUS CHOICE as a seventeenth-century hero of learning and letters. Unlike Bacon and Galileo he did not present himself as the founder of a new science nor, unlike Descartes and Hobbes, has he been claimed as a revolutionary ancestor by a grateful posterity. In a lifetime of reading and writing he published nothing (though, to be sure, there are many 'finished' essays and memoranda in manuscript). There are scattered references to him in the published works of friends, generally acknowledgements for having made documentary material available to them. A full sense of his role in the learned world must, therefore, be reconstructed by the historian before his exemplary status can be grasped. There are two major sources on which to draw. The first, the remains of Peiresc's prodigious correspondence, enables us to survey his activities through the very instrument that he himself used to define the horizon of his interests and community. The second is the biography of Peiresc written by his close friend and occasional intellectual collaborator, the philosopher and astronomer Pierre Gassendi – Eco's real-life 'Canon of Digne'. He had access to all of Peiresc's papers, an undetermined portion of which have since been lost, as well as the supreme advantage of having lived in his house and worked alongside him. Comparison with the documents on which he drew demonstrates Gassendi's fidelity; his desire to emphasize the exemplary gives us a contemporary's view of the virtues thought worth celebrating.

Because his fame was earned by how he lived and by the letters that he wrote but which remained unpublished, Peiresc could not have served as an example beyond the, albeit wide, circle of that correspondence network had it not been for the publication of Gassendi's *Viri illustris Nicolai Claudii Fabricii de Peiresc senatoris aquisextiensis vita*. He began work soon after Peiresc's death in 1637 and the book was published in Paris in 1641, and then reprinted in The Hague in 1651 and 1655 and translated into English in 1657 with the title *The Mirrour of True Nobility and Gentility*.[1] The later editions included the funeral oration delivered by Jean-Jacques Bouchard at the memorial meeting held in Rome at the Academia degl' Umoristi in December 1637, the long letter of consolation sent by Gabriel Naudé to Gassendi upon hearing of their mutual friend's death, an anthology of references to Peiresc in texts published subsequent to 1641, and the catalogue of Peiresc's manuscripts prepared by Pierre Dupuy.

Gassendi's Peiresc was a model of sound intellectual method and learned sociability. What is distinctive about this picture is the combination in one man of these two distinct kinds of virtue: there were greater scholars and greater patrons, but few who knew enough to talk to scholars as equals and few of these who possessed the broader ambition, let alone the wherewithal, to further the learning of others. Peiresc was exceptional in recognizing that in a collective enterprise like scholarship the virtues of sociability were essential. This unusual combination of learning and virtue is the ideal that Gassendi presented to the Republic of Letters.

Biography, the vehicle chosen by Gassendi, was perfectly suited to this task. Because of the rhetorical injunction to teach by example, so potent in an age whose pedagogy and even organization of knowledge was shaped by rhetorical norms, *Lives* were conceived of as extended exemplary presentations. From the Renaissance onwards, the 'illustrious' subjects of *Lives* were heroes whose story was to provide matter for inspiration and imitation.[2] E. R. Curtius identified the hero as the embodiment of the 'basic value' of nobility and therefore the 'model for emulation'. The hero was 'distinguished by an abundance of intellectual will and its concentration against the instincts'.[3] The typical manifestation of this strength was martial and some theorists of history, like Francesco Patrizi, doubted if private life could provide appropriate subjects.[4] The seventeenth-century idealization of the scholar as hero reflects, therefore, a changed view of the social importance of the trained mind and its accomplishments. For an 'abundance of intellectual will' was here the result of strengthening the mind through study rather than the body through drill. Seneca's image of the great man as the phoenix, which was adapted as praise of Peiresc and also of his older friend Paolo Sarpi, makes the connection between reason and heroism and helped redefine the older ideal of nobility.[5]

But it is Francis Bacon, in *The Advancement of Learning* (1605) [trans. and expanded as *De dignitate & augmentis scientiarum* (1623)] who supplied the decisive argument in transforming the hero. He conceded that though his age had few rulers to compare with antiquity, 'yet there are many worthy personages (even living under kings) that deserve better than dispersed report or dry and barren eulogy'. All that was wanting were the 'silver swans' described by Ariosto which Bacon adopted as a metaphor for the biographer.[6] Gassendi's biography takes Bacon's point of view and documents a widening horizon of cultural ideals – itself a lagging indicator of the social transformation that had begun to make a civil out of an aristocratic society (see Chapter Two).[7]

To those who objected to the choice of such an unconventional subject, a scholar rather than a general, Gassendi replied, in an echo of Bacon, that 'those men deserve abundantly to be commended, whom though fortune has not raised to the greatest Wealth and Dignities; yet bear the greater minds, are of a more generous Virtue, and undertake far greater Designs, than any man could expect from men of their Condition. And such an one', Gassendi pronounced, 'was Peireskius'. But because Peiresc was not a public figure like 'a Scipio or a Maximus' the biographer had to have recourse to different sources – private correspondence instead of public inscriptions, and the history of scholarship rather than warfare.[8] Because it was, in part, the life of a mind that he narrated, Gassendi's access to the private man – 'far from witnesses' and 'without any Mask or Vizard' – allowed him to 'discover a man, and shew his inside'. But Gassendi made a further observation. This intimate vantage point better served the cause of imitation since in it we also 'find some tokens of our Infirmitie' that make us feel that the great figure was human, and therefore within reach of our own feeble efforts at emulation.[9] Gassendi's declared intent was to paint the picture of a life worth emulating.

This was not lost on the work's first reader. Jean Chapelain, in a letter to his friend Guez de Balzac in January 1640, explained that he had spent the previous eight days reading Gassendi's manuscript as a favour to the author before it went to the printer.[10] He had not seen a work 'so clear, so pure, so varied, and of such great edification' in a long time. Balzac himself, he commented, would be lucky to have such a biographer (he wasn't).[11] Not long after, Chapelain passed along his final comments to the author himself. He praised Gassendi's choice and disposition of material, his candour, and his style. 'You have given in this work the perfect idea of a hero of letters', he wrote, 'and, in doing justice to your friend, you have instructed the world in a thousand curiosities'. The 'century to come will partake of this utility and bless this good work'. But 'the principal fruit' will be that such a glorious example proposed to all time will not leave the virtue of this great person without imitators, and will be like the seed of new *Mécenes* of Letters, and future promoters of the Sciences; in this way one could say that you will do more than Mr de Peyresc himself, who could only excite to this enterprise those who saw him or lived in his time, while in prolonging his life through the effort that you have made to write it, you could call yourself the author of all the good inspiration that will come to great men to favour the Muses by his example.[12]

But Chapelain's esteem for the example of Peiresc and for Gassendi's prodigious labour did not blind him to the work's greatest drawback. In an earlier letter to Balzac he praised a narrative that did not collapse under the weight of material that was rarely of an exalted nature.[13] But in another Chapelain reported that he shared the view of their – and also Gassendi's – mutual friend François Luillier who wanted to meet with Gassendi and 'cut out many things that he found too extended, if not superfluous' ('trop estendues, pour ne pas dire superflues').[14]

What makes detail 'superfluous'? The difficulty that these well-disposed and well-educated readers had with Gassendi's text alerts us to the fraying of the shared assumptions about the ends and means of historical narrative, a precise indication of a changing taste in the style of scholarship. For these same criticisms, prolixity, interminable digressiveness and the inclusion of irrelevant material, would be levelled at the antiquarian.[15] The biographer, like the antiquarian, shared the goal of reconstructing a lost world in its entirety and thus was equally vulnerable to the charge of failing to discriminate between useful and superfluous facts.[16] Chapelain's discomfort with Gassendi's style reflects an increasing discomfort with antiquarian explanation more generally in that circle of men whose intellectual and social loyalties were to the new worlds of the *salon* and Cartesianism.

Daniel Morhof acknowledged that *Lives* of scholars was a new intellectual genre by including a chapter entitled 'On the Writers of Lives' [De vitarum scriptoribus] in his mighty *Polyhistor* (1688), an encyclopedia that doubled as a how-to guide for would-be members of the Republic of Letters. He acknowledged the fundamental – and by the end of the century deeply problematic – link between antiquarianism and biography by beginning the chapter with a defence against the charge – shared, as we have just seen, in Gassendi's own circle – that biographies of scholars were marvels of disorganization and superficiality because of their profusion of micro-histoires. Morhof saw inclusiveness and even digressiveness as the genre's great virtue since it provided even more matter for exemplarity.[17] From the arcana of a scholar's life Morhof believed that one could learn a general prudence valuable 'in all affairs'.[18] In the lives of rulers it was understood that little things and 'unexpected circumstances' often had disproportionate importance. These quotidian details were not 'indecent', in the words of Agostino Mascardi quoted by Morhof, but rather necessary for the reconstruction of 'time, mode, occasion and other circumstances'. 'It is for this reason', Morhof concluded, 'that I value the Life of the great Peiresc written by Gassendi, which in all parts digresses and branches out, that our man [Maresius] condemned as a *micrologion*'.[19]

For Morhof, Gassendi's *Vita* held pride of place among all the modern biographies of scholars. The book was well written and contained 'varia memorabilia' on a wide range of subjects as if heaped together. He thought it unlikely to be surpassed because of its combination of fascinating subject and brilliant biographer. The other *Lives* that he singled out as influential were Paulo Gualdo's of Gian Vincenzo Pinelli (1609) and Fulgenzio Micanzio's of Paolo Sarpi (1646).[20] Peiresc was a fixture in Pinelli's academy during his stay in Padua in 1600–01. It was there that he met Galileo and Sarpi and established lifelong friendships with Pignoria, Gualdo, and Aleandro. Peiresc's 'heroism' was even likened to Sarpi's by Chapelain.[21]

But it was Pinelli who provided the closer model. His biography, written by Peiresc's friend Gualdo, and explicitly intended as exemplary, named Peiresc as Pinelli's successor and delineated the three tasks that were to be his inheritance: the restoration of letters, the collection of valuable books, and the support and encouragement of scholars.[22] Peiresc's praise of the *Life of Pinelli* for having succeeded in 'bringing to life [his] merits, heroic virtues and other qualities and perfections' and exciting readers to admire and imitate them could also apply to his own *Life*, written thirty years later.[23] Gassendi himself linked the two men and, by extension, the two biographies. Pinelli had 'delivered his Lampe to Peireskius' who had, in any event, 'so moulded himself according to the manners of Pinellus . . . that he might justly be thought to have inherited his heroicall virtues'. As if to stress that this was not his retrospective view only, Gassendi proceeded to cite in his book some passages in Gualdo's that proclaimed Peiresc Pinelli's successor.[24]

The problem facing the biographer was the inverse of that facing the antiquarian: he could not sacrifice chronology to achieve thematic coherence but had to find a way of accommodating synchronic observations into an inexorably diachronic structure. Gassendi addressed this problem by writing the life (bks 1–5) in chronological order. He acknowledged that this was an 'imperfect' form of history similar to 'antiquities' and described his work as 'Commentaries' organized 'as loose materials, after the way of Annals'. Others, if they wished, could 'polish' it into a 'history'.[25] Book 6, however, was organized synchronically, enabling Gassendi to paint a portrait of the scholar as man, or, as he describes it, 'the habit of his Body, the manners of his mind, and the studies in which he exercised his Wits' ('corporis habitum, animi mores, & ingenii studia').[26] It is here that Gassendi surveyed Peiresc's intellectual activities and described in detail his reading practices, note-taking technique, and filing system, as well as his moral persona.[27] It was this part that 'principally touched' Chapelain and which he thought would be 'the most useful and the most esteemed'.[28]

Earlier humanists had written *res gestae* – the 'life and times' – of political and military heroes. Gassendi did this for a scholar ruling an intellectual republic.[29] The 'times' of Peiresc amounted to nothing less than an intellectual history of Europe in the first four decades of the seventeenth century. A few years later Gassendi wrote a biography of Tycho Brahe in the same six-book format.[30] A reader who began with the life of Brahe and kept reading through that of Peiresc would have been exposed to a history of the new thinking in Europe from Brahe's maturity in the mid-1560s to Peiresc's death in 1637. Was this intentional? We cannot be sure, but in 1655 the publisher of these *Lives*, Adriaan Vlacq in The Hague, brought them out in identical quarto formats and at least one set was bound together, creating this continuous history.[31] We tend not to associate antiquarians with astronomers, and they now seem almost antithetical figures, the one an emblem of the ancients and the other of the moderns. Yet, from Gassendi's point of view they both stood as worthy representatives of the new thinking.

In the first part of the chapter we will try and understand how it was that an antiquary could have seemed like a hero of the New Science. In the second, we will turn to the scholar as an example of learned sociability and to Gassendi's *Life* as an important source for understanding the ideal of individual excellence that developed in the learned world and then spread to other civil societies later in the century.

WHAT KIND OF KNOWLEDGE IS ANTIQUARIAN KNOWLEDGE?

If the antiquary could be paired with the astronomer as heroes of the New Science it is because both were closely identified with observation. 'No man', Gassendi wrote of Peiresc, 'made more observations, or procured more to be made, to the end that at last some Notions of natural things more sound and pure, than the vulgarly received, might be collected'. His 'care in the observation of the Heavenly Bodies, was of all others most remarkable, and his Discourses which he had thereof with *Mathematicians* and other Learned Men. Whence it came to passe, that no man was better acquainted with the new *Phaenomena*, no man laboured with greater ardency and constancie [*ardentius & constantius*] to know the same'. An almanac for the year 1629, almost certainly drawn up by Peiresc, preserves his observations on memorable meteorological conditions (plate 3). At the end of such careful investigation Peiresc 'knew as much thereof, as it was possible for any mortal man to know'.[32] This was necessary because, Peiresc wrote, it was 'certain that two or three really exact observations are able to change a good part of the old foundations of astronomy and, consequently, of geography'.[33] Peiresc's own observations were responsible for the discovery and naming of the first nebula in the constellation Orion and the first map of the moon.[34] His effort to mobilize friends from Paris to Tunis to Alexandria to Aleppo for a simultaneous eclipse observation in the hope of establishing longitudes and using this information to correct maps of the Mediterranean is a monument to his commitment to observation and collaborative scholarship.[35] To ensure the reliability of observations made by many people with different kinds of training Peiresc, along with Gassendi, formulated a common protocol which they circulated among the observers in order to standardize practices and, therefore, results.[36] He had earlier overcome this problem in his own household, training his domestics to be astronomers, from 'the simple gardeners, to the simple librarians, bookbinders, to the masons and other artisans less amenable, it might seem, to such tasks'.[37] Peiresc had no doubt that of all the remains of antiquity the most noble were the astronomical observations of Hipparchus of Samos 'which have given us the steps for climbing, if one could say it, into the heavens'.[38]

Gassendi could hardly have more clearly linked Peiresc to the New Science than by suggesting that Francis Bacon was his inspiration. Peiresc 'admired the Genius, and approved the design of the great Chancellour of England Sir Francis Bacon, often grieving that he never had the happinesse to speak with him'.[39] Peiresc was, actually, instrumental in the French translation of Bacon's *History of Henry VII*.[40] He also possessed copies of the *Instauratio Magna*, *De augmentis scientiarum* (which he referred to as Bacon's 'libro del progresso'), and the essays on 'Religion' and 'Superstition' that were suppressed in the Italian edition of the *Essays*.[41] Peiresc's English translator recognized this kinship and repeatedly used the phrase 'Advancement of Learning' to describe Peiresc's motivation.[42]

In *The Advancement of Learning* Bacon had insisted that men 'have withdrawn themselves too much from the contemplation of nature and the observations of experience'. Bacon had condemnend those who 'disdain to spell and so by degrees to read in the volume of God's works'.[43] Mon-

taigne, thinking about 'Educating Children', had proclaimed 'I want it' –
what he called 'this great world of ours' – 'to be the book which our
pupil studies'.[44] It was Galileo, most famously, who explained that this
book of nature was written in the symbolic language of geometry. Peiresc
also relied on this metaphor. He urged Father Célestin de Sainte-
Lidivine in Aleppo, the brother of the great Leiden orientalist Golius, to
pay close attention to the natural landscape since 'the book of nature is
the book of books'.[45] Peiresc proclaimed to Cassiano dal Pozzo his great
love 'for the knowledge of the true natural philosophy which can be discerned in the book of nature sooner than in any other one'.[46] Their
mutual acquaintance, Tommaso Campanella, offered some of the most
precise uses of the term; it was he who declared that 'I learn more from
the anatomy of a plant than from all the books in world'.[47] Peiresc
acknowledged learning this lesson from Campanella himself: 'Because this
[nature] is the true book of philosophy, as old man Campanella reiter-
ated to us at every moment'.[48] Peiresc thought that men would be condemned to a condition of 'perpetual ignorance' if they did not 'research
the causes, or at least the most exact effects, in experience and in the
book of books, which is that of nature itself, where is found many things
different from those seen in more ordinary books'.[49] He used the word
'mortification' to describe his feelings about discussions of natural phenomena that were not based on observation.[50]

'This same course he took, touching all the wonderful things of
Nature.'[51] Peiresc studied human as he did natural antiquities. So did
many others, like the later seventeenth-century English antiquary John
Aubrey, who explained that he was always 'mixing Antiquities and natural
things together', and all those late eighteenth-century Englishmen whose
Fellowships in both the Royal and Antiquarian Societies led to the
coining of the acronym 'FRAS'. What Peiresc insisted upon, in all cases,
was careful observation and close attention to detail: where were things
found? in what climate? at what time? what did they look like? what
was their age?[52] Nor are his questions so unusual; his great contemporary, Ole Worm, asked the same sort in a letter to the Bishop of Sta-
vanger in 1638.[53] Gassendi was sure that there was 'no wonder of art,
nor rare worke of nature which he heard of, which he did not carefully
view, as Aedificies, Rare works, Engins, Plants, Animals, Metals, and other
things dug out of the Earth. In a word, all things which were worthy of
observation.'[54] Peiresc's surviving archive documents this fascination with
looking closely and describing carefully. He supplemented literary
accounts with detailed drawings of animals and objects of human manu-
facture.[55] Many of these were produced by the artists who dwelt under
his roof for longer or shorter stretches.[56] His letters include many requests

for sketches and casts and Peiresc even provided the instructions as to
how these could be made so as to ensure the greatest fidelity at the least
risk to the original.[57]

Travel was part of this education in looking. On his trip to Italy he
kept a journal 'and was resolved', so Gassendi informs us, 'not so to travaile right on from City to City, but if he heard of anything worthy
observation here or there, he would turn out of his rode and go
thither'.[58] One of these side trips, when visiting Naples, was remembered
by John Evelyn in his *Discourse of Sallets* (1699). He cited Gassendi's
account of how 'the curious and noble Peiresky [*sic*]' investigated the
local custom of cultivating mushrooms in wine cellars.[59] Many of
Peiresc's manuscripts include drawings of objects or copies of inscriptions that he encountered *en route*. More than twenty years later, when
returning from Paris to Provence, he kept in readiness 'pen, paper, ruler,
compasse, wax, brimstone, and such like implements; to draw, exscribe,
adumbrate, in Seals and Transcripts, whatever they should meet with,
worthy of observation'.[60] Peiresc viewed travel as an integral component
of scholarship and asked his correspondents 'to see with your eyes all
kinds of things that I can not go and see for myself'.[61] In an echo of
Scaliger's assertion that if he were wealthy he would travel rather than
buy books, Peiresc explained that it was from travelling that 'I have drawn
my greatest and principal advantages'.[62]

For Peiresc not only travelled himself, he organized, sponsored, and
promoted the travels of other scholars. Here, too, Scaliger's model was
crucial. His forays into Europe's most ancient history had led him to
observe that Greek and Roman history began in Phoenicia and Egypt
and to try and glean as much information as possible about the ancient
Near East from the contemporary one. Peiresc followed Scaliger's lead
on both points and, characteristically for a period in which philology
broadened into archaeology and anthropology, they ran together in his
practice. Peiresc's central role in the European rediscovery of the Samaritans and the discovery of Coptic – the birth of a scientific Egyptology
after a couple of centuries of Egyptomania had still not entirely run its
course – reflects his recognition that Scaliger's insight into the origins of
European civilization needed to be followed up. But in this as in his
other scholarly ventures, Peiresc believed that no single person's work
was adequate to the Herculean labours needed to advance learning. And
so, he turned the existing network of Provençal merchants who dominated French commercial and diplomatic establishments in the Ottoman
East into his personal procurement service. Through them manuscripts
and artifacts documenting the region's ancient and living inhabitants
found their way back to Aix-en-Provence and, thence, thanks to Peiresc's
extraordinary generosity, to those scholars elsewhere in Europe who

could derive greater benefit from these materials. For special tasks, when
he preferred not to rely on others, he twice sent to the Levant his own
agent, Théophile Minuti, a monk of the order of Minims, who would
later administer Peiresc's last rites, with lists of things to buy, questions
to ask, and people to see. It is in this labour, piecing together a history
not yet written from materials that were themselves often unwritten, that
we can see why Gassendi thought Peiresc such a hero of the advancement of learning.

Over and against the new thinking lay the old, which Peiresc rejected
'as being too obscure and imaginary, built more upon tricks of Wit, than
experiments of Nature'. The contrast between knowledge based on
observation and experiment and what was produced by purely verbal
analysis runs through Gassendi's account. Peiresc was 'wont to frown, and
look with a very discontented countenance' when reading books that
had more 'subtilty than solidity' and engaged more with 'words and trivial
distinctions, than employed in penetrating into the nature of the things
themselves, whose very surface was still unknown'.[63] We can catch here
echoes of the 'degenerate learning' of the schoolmen that Bacon condemned.[64] 'Logical and Metaphysical niceties' ('Dialecticas illas meta-
physicasve argutias') were said to preoccupy fine minds at the expense
of knowledge about the world.[65] Gassendi commented that Peiresc 'could
not endure, that men should seek out subtilties, to establish the old opinions of the Schools, contrary to evident demonstrations and observations,
as if that time could teach nothing, and that experiments were not to
be preferred before dark and cloudy reasonings'.[66] Peiresc loved mathematics precisely because it could not be made into a weapon of ideo-
logical or personal warfare. It had, moreover, a therapeutic utility since
it 'so accustomed the mind that being used to such truths as were made
clear by demonstration, it could not easily be deceived with the bare
appearance of truth'.[67]

Like many of his elder colleagues, but unlike some of his younger
ones, Peiresc's love of mathematics did not displace his historical framework and commitment to observation. An exchange of views with Marin
Mersenne, Descartes' collaborator, makes clear Peiresc's priorities and sets
in stark relief the differences between two different versions – or generations – of the new thinking. In a letter acknowledging receipt of
Mersenne's *Harmonie universelle*, one of whose parts was dedicated to him,
Peiresc declared, 'but all my studies have had a very different purpose
than yours'.[68] In 1634, Peiresc had turned to Mersenne for help in
decoding the meaning of a triangle inscribed within a circle. Mersenne
proclaimed it a musical symbol. Peiresc replied that the ancients
used symbols like this to represent philosophical concepts.[69] Mersenne
repeated that the triangle was a musical figure, representing chords. 'I do

not at all know', he added, 'what other mystery one could find there'.[70] Perhaps exasperated by their miscommunication, Peiresc made explicit what lay behind his query. 'I seek there only to learn what the Ancients believed about it, in order to judge the foundation of their beliefs and superstitions' which, in turn, 'could aid in the understanding of the mysteries of pagan religion'.[71] What mattered was understanding what had been taken seriously in the past – not whether the ancients ought to have taken such matters seriously. He was guided by what he had learned in decades of close looking. 'I have found, I say, occasions to greatly admire the precision of the Ancients that is much greater than is believed by those who race post-haste, so to speak, and don't want to look that closely'.[72]

An emphasis on precision runs through Peiresc's antiquarian inquiries, both human and natural. Letters to far-flung correspondents were often so filled with requests for detailed information that Peiresc felt the need to apologize for his 'excessives ponctualitez'. Not only was it his 'nature' to be precise, or so he claimed, but some forms of inquiry were worthless if not exact.[73] Astronomy and metrology were two such fields of study. Gassendi presents Peiresc's astronomical observations with an extreme emphasis on the precision with which they were undertaken. They are recounted complete with measurements of days, hours, minutes, and seconds.[74] Peiresc's belief that the ancients were so 'industrious that they made no vessel, which did not contain a set measure, and a certain weight' inspired his own studies.[75] Gassendi's discussion of ancient weights and measures is so detailed, down to accounts of exactly how Peiresc went about measuring and what the actual amounts were, as to facilitate repetition by the motivated reader.[76]

Ought we to be surprised, then, that Peiresc and Gassendi, who spent so many nights staring through telescopes and days peering into microscopes, seem to have devoted an almost equal amount of energy and attention to the strange and the marvellous? In the course of recounting Peiresc's story, Gassendi manages to tell us about a man at Livorno with coral growing out of his head, a Neapolitan woman frozen into a trance-like state for over twenty years after taking the Eucharist from Pope Gregory XIII, a town near Geneva whose inhabitants were possessed by the devil, and a French woman pregnant for twenty-three months.[77] In Peiresc's letters, we find the mature scholar following with great interest the latest plot twists in the story of a man with a bush growing out of his stomach. He asked for, and received, attestations backed by the 'solemn' seals of bishops and archbishops, as well as the leaves and flowers that sprouted from the poor man's abdomen.[78]

The century of Peiresc, from around 1580 to 1680 was, in fact, the great age of marvels. Sober-minded and critical contemporary scholars like Cardano, Mersenne, Boyle, Newton, and Leibniz all saw, heard, and repeated things that are today the province of 'tabloid' journalism. Peiresc explained his willingness to believe the unbelievable, such as the possibility of seeing through walls, because he had himself 'seen things, so incredible without having seen them, that I am, in faith, almost disposed not to be surprised by any other'. The microscope and telescope had undermined so many commonsense observations that Peiresc thought the most prudent intellectual position was to evaluate every report on its own merits. 'This is why I try to neglect nothing until experience opens the way for us to pure truth.'[79]

This same century of Peiresc was, however, also the age of the European witch craze. Numbers vary, but around 100–200,000 people, mostly women, were tried as witches and about half were executed. As a member of the Parlement of Provence Peiresc participated in the trial and execution of a priest accused of witchcraft, Louis Gauffridy, in April 1611. Du Vair, Peiresc's mentor and at that time President of the Parlement, defended the trial and its verdict to his Parisian correspondents. An unpublished account of the case mentions 'Nicholas Fabry Sr de Peiresc' as one of the *parlementary* interrogators of the young woman whom Gauffridy was accused of bewitching and upon whose testimony the case rested. Although he never discussed this experience – or, perhaps, his discussions do not survive – Peiresc did keep a file on 'Rantings, Sorcery' that not only contained a copy of the *arrêt* against Gauffridy, but also eyewitness accounts of other witch-hunts in Flanders (1612), Toulouse (1614), and Loudun (1634).[80]

On at least two occasions, though, this close encounter with witchcraft resurfaced in his correspondence. The context in which it appeared, and the tone with which Peiresc discussed it, is highly revealing. In a letter to Dupuy in 1632, Peiresc reported the news of a spirit that appeared in a nearby town after the death of a woman and persecuted the vicar and one of her sons. The Archbishop of Aix was on his way to investigate and Peiresc promised to forward a 'more exact report' upon his return, but in the meantime he was sending copies of two letters containing the latest news. It was in this same place, Peiresc concluded, that Gauffridy claimed to have learned magic from his uncle, the previous vicar. The tone is thoroughly matter of fact and it is as if Peiresc was reporting on a volcanic eruption or celestial phenomenon: eyewitness reports were being collected and a more detailed expert judgement would follow.[81] Three years later, in response to a letter of Mersenne's that included, for its part, an account of the examination of a suspected witch and the search for a 'mark', Peiresc replied simply that he was impressed by its size since Gauffridy's 'were no larger than a lentil'.[82]

It was these 'senseless scars', according to Gassendi, that had persuaded
Peiresc. But the account of this episode in the *Vita*, written nearly thirty
years after the event, shows Gassendi at pains to distance Peiresc from it
as much as possible. He acknowledged that Peiresc was 'very much
busied' in the affair and even wrote 'the whole History thereof at large'.
'And for a time', Gassendi observed – and this is where the account gets
interesting – 'indeed he was in the same opinion with the common
people'. All along Gassendi had shown how Peiresc's commitment to
observation had enabled him to puncture popular myths, but in this
instance it had led him to the same conclusion. Yet 'afterwards', Gassendi
continued, 'he began to doubt whether in the whole businesse there was
not some secret imposture or dotage' ('stupor animi'). Indeed, when
another case came to his attention, even though no 'marks' were discovered and the man was set free, Peiresc's trained scepticism was aroused.
Peiresc 'did call the matter so much the more in question' when he heard
of the same story making the rounds in Flanders three years later and
compared the two accounts. He was of the opinion that these crucial
stigmata could just as easily be 'natural' – the signs of a disease like 'Ele-
phantiasis' – or have been inflicted by the accused upon themselves.[83]
In Gassendi's hands, this episode becomes a case study in the inadequacy
of observation alone – as if this were ever possible – as a guarantee of
truth.

However much we might shudder to think of the lengths to which
the investigators in Aix had to go to get their information, or of
Peiresc's participation in these inquisitions, it seems clear that for him the
possibility of witchcraft, like that of coral growing from a human head
or a bush from a stomach, was something that had to be examined
and evaluated as a natural phenomenon before it could be dismissed
as impossible. The testimony of his own trained senses would be
decisive. This is emphasized in Gassendi's narrative of Peiresc's two
encounters with witchcraft. His approach, using observation alongside
comparison, illustrated the way in which the boundaries of the natural
could be determined and a framework for evaluating such claims be
established.

In Peiresc's commitment to this kind of suspension of judgement, there
is also the imprint of Bacon's natural history. For, as Lorraine Daston and
Katharine Park have argued, Bacon saw the marvellous as a means of
understanding the normal. By focusing on the domain of phenomena
between the commonplace and the miraculous, and then trying to show
that these exceptional events could be explained, but not in terms of the
categories used by Aristotelians, Bacon hoped to reform natural history
and eliminate the category of the preternatural altogether. Peiresc, like
Bacon, admitted wonders but only as prompts to further inquiry, not

as pleasurable diversions. Wonders were the beginning of knowledge, not entertainment. Natural history was to be 'a discipline for the mind, a slow and meticulous exercise in self-restraint'.[84]

Another way in which Gassendi presented Peiresc as an emblem of the new thinking was by narrating his critical analysis of the legends, dreams, prophecies, and tall tales that were popular 'among the common people, whose credulity is awakened and cherished by every slight occasion' – especially those linked to religion.[85] Portentous dreams and astrological predictions offered competing theories of explanation and Gassendi warred with them in his account of Peiresc.[86] Of a dream foretelling exactly how, where, and when he would purchase a Roman coin Gassendi observed that 'Peireskius was not the man that would conclude, that this dream did therefore proceed from any preternaturall cause'.[87] Of another, in which Peiresc foresaw his own death on the eve of his final illness, Gassendi explained that 'I call such like stories as this, which are commonly related, Fables because, if they be not altogether false, yet are they drawn in by the head and shoulders, upon some slight occasion, and happen rather by meer chance, then [sic] any intention of Nature'.[88] Peiresc's role in transmitting an astrological prophecy of Henri IV's assassination to du Vair and thence to the King afforded Gassendi an opportunity to proclaim that 'as for the vanity of Astrologie, it is needlesse for me to speak anything in this place'.[89] The witch that put a hex on the two-month-old Peiresc was explained away by childhood illnesses, the comet of 1618 was stripped of prophetic value because a naturally recurring phenomenon could not be defined as a portent, and reports of visions in the sky were simply dismissed 'seeing the same credulous & humane frailty was the cause of those other fragments. Tis truly credible, that if not all, yet very many such tales, related in Histories, have proceeded from the same Original, and deserve no greater credit.'[90] As for the alchemist's ambition to turn switches of holly into gold, Peiresc scoffed that it was 'the most ridiculous thing that could ever be imagined'.[91]

The prominence Gassendi gave to Peiresc's unravelling of two popular fables shows how a precise practice of observation and comparison could establish facts.[92] Red rain that was said by 'country folk' to have fallen in July 1608 was believed by Peiresc to be 'meer conjecture' from the start, but he was only able to solve the mystery when a worm that he happened to be keeping in a box metamorphosed into a butterfly and flew away, leaving a red ball. These butterflies were common at the time and Peiresc realized that the sticky red moult was the rain that the peasants reported. He then examined houses in the area where the rain was reported and discovered that the red splotches were always found on the underside of rocks, or in hollows, not on the flat surfaces that would

have been exposed to raindrops. Having solved this mystery Peiresc
realized that it also explained the red rain that was said to have fallen at
that same time of year on various auspicious occasions in the Middle
Ages.[93]

The supposed discovery of a giant's body in 1613 in an ancient tomb,
the public show of bones and fragments, and the subsequent
identification of the figure with a mythical Teutonic King 'Teutobachus'
afforded Gassendi another opportunity to show Peiresc exercising the
antiquary's powers of demystification. Without at first denying that bones
had been found or that they might belong to a giant, Peiresc pointed
out that the purported Latin inscription and brick tomb could not be
reconciled, while the failure of the discoverers to make public the
inscription and any bones other than the skull was suspicious. 'For the
hatchers of this fabulous story seemed to fear', Gassendi interjected, 'lest
by diligent inspection thereof, and comparing the same with some dead
mans scull [sic], the truth might have been more easily found out'.[94]
Peiresc's extremely close examination of an elephant as it passed through
Toulon on its way to Paris in 1631 enabled him to confirm that Pliny
had erroneously stated the number of its teeth. Comparison with another
supposed giant's tooth, sent from Tunis, helped him solve, many years
later, the riddle of the bones of old King Teutobachus: they belonged to
an elephant. 'Nor did he any longer admire', Gassendi concluded, 'why
so few of the Teeth of the Gyant aforesaid, were shewn'.[95]

But observation and comparison required ready access to materials.
Hence the importance of the third characteristic of antiquarian practice,
collection. For the greater the quantity of objects collected, the greater
the number that could be compared and the more precise the comparison. Peiresc offered some insight into this aspect of his work,
explaining, in a letter to Mersenne, that 'to be a good judge of the ancient
and the modern it is necessary to have seen and handled as well the one
as the other'. In Rome, at the markets in the Campo dei Fiori and Piazza
Navona, he had seen so many ancient medals and modern forgeries being
sold that they were strung together like beads and so many ancient vases
– of which he had taken home a goodly number – that rather than being
swamped by sheer quantity he had come to discern the differences
between the good, the bad, and the faked. The metaphor that he invoked
to introduce the value of comparison was typically earthy: some people
preferred to eat salty foods, like well-salted ham, when they were thirsty
in order to sharpen the contrast and heighten the eventual pleasure of
drinking.[96]

Peiresc's 'Treasury and Shop of Antiquities' ('Antiquariorum Gazo-
phylacia & Ergasteria') was celebrated by contemporaries, though no
more so than his willingness to make his hard-gotten gains available to

colleagues.[97] Peiresc contrasted his behaviour with that of others 'who only recover books in order to confine them in impenetrable prisons where they fall into a sort of darkness among others the most obscure'.[98] These collectors suffered from 'a sickness of the spirit', a jealousy 'that easily goes beyond the bounds of reason'. By implication, Peiresc's collecting was not an unruly passion. 'I praise God', he concluded, 'to be spared this evil'.[99] Gabriel Naudé, in the letter of consolation that he sent to Gassendi on Peiresc's death in August 1637, and which was subsequently reprinted with Gassendi's biography, also emphasized that Peiresc 'did not gather all this Treasure for his own delight, or to delight his study, that they might ly [sic] there . . . but that Peireskius made this Law to himself, that if he knew any learned men that might be assisted by his Counsels, Wealth, Books, Statues, or Marbles, he would not stay till with importunate intreaties they should desire the same'.[100]

Peiresc's was a working collection. He had little patience for the rigours of collecting as a form of social display. He described the daily visits of the 'galants hommes' who would try 'to pick up the fine observations they could learn' as 'a *divertissement* capable of consuming a lot of time' and interfering with scholarship.[101] Peiresc is here responding to the new phenomenon of gentlemanly travel and dilettantish collecting announced by Henry Peacham in his *Compleat Gentleman* (1634). His summary account of the kinds of antiquities that would be encountered in Italy ('Of Antiquities') came complete with a crib to the abbreviations found in classical epigraphy to help the gentleman give an impression of erudition.[102] Baudelot de Dairval's *De l'Utilité des voyages, et l'avantage que la recherche des antiquitez procure aux sçavans* (1686), while in the tradition of Peacham, nevertheless made a crucial distinction between a mere taste for the antique and serious erudition. He divided the 'curious', whom he likened to 'birds of prey', from those who were motivated by 'love of the sciences', whose work he called 'Recherches' and whom alone he intended by the term 'antiquaries'.[103] La Bruyère's essay 'De la Mode' described the fashion for collecting objects independent of their intellectual worth as a late stage of curiosity gone unchecked. 'They prefer to know more than to know well.' Equally to be condemned were those who plunged so deeply into a particular subject that they no longer addressed themselves to anything useful.[104] Collectors search 'for what is rare and unique, for what one has and others have not'.[105]

One of the antiquary's tools that has, generally, been less appreciated, is imagination. No attempt to reconstruct the past, whether by Petrarch, Cyriac of Ancona, or Peiresc, was possible without the capacity to envision the broken and fragmentary made whole again. It is this act of the imagination that lies at the heart of the antiquary's reconstructive ambition. The fabrications of Pirro Ligorio and the visions of Piranesi offer

extreme examples of how fantasy and history offered mutual illumina-
tion.[106] Details were studied with attention because the more precise the
information to hand, the more the imagination had to work with. Meric
Casaubon, son of Peiresc's famous friend Isaac, wrote 'that Antiquaries
are so taken with the sight of old things, not as doting upon the bare
forme or matter (though both often times be very notable in old things)
but because these visible superviving evidences of Antiquity represent
unto their minds former times, with as strong an impression, as if they
were actually present, and in sight, as it were'.[107] Writing for gentlemen
about statues, inscriptions, and coins, Henry Peacham explained that their
'lively presence is able to persuade a man, that he now seeth two thousand yeeres agoe'.[108]

Describing the young Peiresc wandering around Rome, Gassendi
wrote that as he walked 'he would fain know, as much as might be, where
stood the Temples of the Ancients, their Chap-Schooles, Libraries,
Amphitheaters, Theaters, Wrastling-places, Horse-race-places, Places to
represent Seafights, Fields, Musick-Rooms, Markets, Faires, Granaries,
Armories, Baths, Hotbaths, Waters, Bridges, Collosuses, Spires, Columns,
Statues, and a thousand other things which in his reading of Authors he
had observed, and noted into Books which he carried around with
him'.[109] The walk through Rome is an old topos. Petrarch described such
a stroll in his *Familiar Letters* and Poggio Bracciolini, nearly a century
later, began his *On the Inconstancy of Fortune* [De varietate fortunae] with
the account of another. In both cases, the encounter with the place in
the present made it easier to *imagine* what it was like in the past. Peiresc
acknowledged as much. In a letter to the brothers Dupuy about the
travels of the young François-Auguste de Thou, Peiresc noted that his
father, the great historian, insisted on travel 'in order to be able to speak
as if an eyewitness, given the great difficulty that there often is in imag-
ining to oneself things as they are' without having actually seen the places
one was writing about.[110]

Nietzsche perceptively singled out the complex relationship between
historical learning and imagination in an appreciation of the antiquary
that is, unfortunately, generally remembered for its unkind comments. By
attending to 'the small and limited, the decayed and obsolete' the antiquary preserved the past 'and so he serves life'. Nietzsche presents with
great sensitivity the claim that knowledge of the world was necessary if
one was to be a citizen of it. 'The history of his city becomes for him
the history of his self; he understands the wall, the turreted gate, the ordi-
nance of the town council, the national festival, like an illustrated diary
of his youth and finds himself, his strength, his diligence, his pleasure, his
judgement, his folly and rudeness, in all of them'. With a 'We' that
bridged 'the wide, obscuring and confusing centuries', the antiquary saw

past 'the ephemeral, curious, individual life' of every day. He possessed the 'power of empathy and divination, of scenting an almost cold trail, of instinctively reading aright the past however much it be written over, a quick understanding of the palimpsests, even polypsests'.[111]

Yet, while Peiresc's study of inscriptions and attempt 'to supply such words or Letters as were eaten out, and to restore such as were in manner desperate' was a triumph of imagination and reconstruction both,[112] one of his own correspondents suggested that antiquaries often saw 'figures more by imagination than by reason'. Others saw this as worship of antiquity for antiquity's sake.[113] John Earle, in his character book *Micro-cosmographie* (1629), observed that the antiquary had 'the unnatural disease to be enamored of old age and wrinckles, and loves all things (as Dutch men do Cheese) the better for being mouldy and worm-eaten'. He was a great admirer 'of the rust of old Monuments, and reads only those Characters, where time hath eaten out the letters'.[114] The nephew of 'Veteranno the Antiquary' in Shackerly Mermion's extended parody, *The Antiquary* (1641), describes his uncle as 'grown obsolete' and adds that 'they say he sits / All day in contemplation of a statue / With ne're a nose, and dotes on the decays, / With greater love, than the self-lov'd *Narcissus* did on his beauty'.[115]

Gassendi replied to the antiquary's critics with an anecdote. He recalled how one day, while looking through a magnifying glass at paper and coins whose characters were small and worn with time, Peiresc was challenged by a visitor who hurled at him Seneca's condemnation of one 'who spends the greatest part of the day poreing upon rusty plates of brasse' − in other words, the very contemporary association of antiquar-ianism with vanity. Peiresc's answer, repeated in the first person, is meant to be taken as a reply to critics of the antiquarian enterprise. 'I am not ignorant that many laugh heartily at these studies as neither honourable to my self, nor useful to others.' But only those whose learning was truly 'vain' and whose antiquities were acquired as interior decoration and for 'no other purpose, but that it may be said, that they have such things' deserved to be censured. The others, whose learning and collections were dedicated to better 'understanding of good Authors' or Histories 'and do not vainly spend their time' were, rather, to be hailed.[116]

The defence of the antiquary turns on the interpretation of vanity. For both critic and exemplar agreed that there was such a thing as vain learning, only they differed about what it referred to. In *De la sagesse* (1601), Pierre Charron, the influential synthesizer of Montaigne and Lipsius, had declared that 'Vanity is the most essential and innate quality of human nature'.[117] It was able to dominate because of another 'natural' human attribute, the weakness that made it difficult to choose well and to know oneself. The restless hunt for the curious whose trophies men heaped up in their *Kunst- und Wunderkammern* at the expense of the 'true and essential' was evidence for the power of vanity in the world of learning.[118] In Chapter Four of the *Petit Traicté de sagesse* (1610), Charron went still further and declared that the scholar's knowledge was a congeries of 'fantastic opinions' and 'nothing but vanity and lies'.[119] His vanity was reflected in an obsessive fascination with the visible, external world. Charron's attack reflects the still powerful momentum of Augustine's late antique link between vanity and curiosity. In *De la sagesse* Charron sharply contrasted what he saw as the scholar's pedantry with the sage's learning for life, a critique that follows Montaigne's essay 'Du Pédantisme' and is echoed by Bacon's attack on the vanity of scholars in book I of *The Advancement of Learning*.[120]

John Donne, a contemporary of Bacon, Charron, and Peiresc, extended Charron's indictment of learning as vanity to show how far it led an individual away from the more important quest for self-knowledge. 'Thou know'st thy selfe so little,' Donne wrote in the second *Anniversary*, 'as thou know'st not, / How thou did'st die, nor how thou was begot' (ll. 254–5). Fundamental questions about living remained elusive: 'Thou art too narrow, wretch, to comprehend / Even thy selfe: yea though thou wouldst but bend / To know thy body' (ll. 261–3). What follows is a litany of questions – where kidney stones come from, how blood passes from one side of the heart to the other, how phlegm finds its way into the lungs – showing how little men understand themselves. 'What hope have we to know our selves, when wee / Know not the least things, which for our use bee?' (ll. 279–80). And yet, much as Charron complained, people spent hours, watching, starving, freezing, and sweating (l. 283) to find out about 'unconcerning things, matters of fact' (l. 284) such as 'what Caesar did, yea, and what Cicero said' (l. 287). The antiquarian ambition to reconstruct the past was vitiated by the unfamiliarity of the subject, object, and foundation of the inquiry itself, the human being. Hence Pascal's judgement that 'La curiosité n'est que la vanité'.

But if interpretations of the antiquary split on the question of vanity, at the heart of this exchange, as Pascal reminds us, lay a disagreement about the value of curiosity.[121] For the Peirescs of early modern Europe, curiosities, whether monsters or medals, were prompts to investigation and, therefore, part of learning's necessary progress. Curiosity was also dynamic, a passion that had learning as its object.[122] Others, who might have accepted Bacon's project in principle, simply could not conceive of valuable knowledge issuing from the study of bric-à-brac. These remained for them impractical and therefore vanities.

In his commentary on Samuel Pufendorf's celebrated *Duty of Man and Citizen* [De officio hominis et civis, 1673], the historian of philosophy, Jean Barbeyrac, suggested a tripartite division of learning into useful, curious, and vain that helps make sense of the problem broached by Gassendi. The real issue, as Barbeyrac's account makes clear, is whether, like Peiresc, one believed that close study could extract knowledge from curiosities or whether, like Pascal, one believed that nothing useful could come from things so dismayingly trifling. Even Barbeyrac's own, excruciatingly precise definition of curiosities shows the strain of a category pulled in opposite directions: 'not of such use that without them one lives less socially and less easily, but which serve only to satisfy an innocent curiosity and adorn our spirit with pretty and agreeable knowledge'.[123] Is this condescending to vanities or acknowledging that human beings are driven by more than a narrow conception of utility? The uncertain legitimacy of the antiquary's labours is a reflection of the disputed status of a learning whose usefulness was not immediately obvious. A generation later, the answer was all too clear. The opening sentence of Voltaire's *Philosophy of History* envisioned a history 'written by philosophers' that contained 'nothing but *useful* truths' [emphasis added]. The contrast was with the antiquary's painstaking labour of reconstruction – these were simply dismissed as 'useless errors' and the 'ruins of ages'.[124]

Yet, like the *vanitas* painting that mocked the permanence of worldly goods by heaping them up in the most extravagant fashion, collections of artifacts could also serve as prompts for self-examination. Gassendi's portrait of Peiresc was a lesson in how to chain the passions, conquer opinion, banish dogmatism, and eradicate vanity through scholarship.[125] In short, if Peiresc could have seemed to others the incarnation of Charron's vain, narrow pedant, Gassendi tried hard to present him, often in his own words, as rather like the living embodiment of Charron's sage.

Micanzio's attempt, in his *Life* of Sarpi, to absolve his hero from the sin of vanity may shed some light on one of the vexing questions about Peiresc, his failure to publish. Why did Sarpi never publish the fruits of his nearly eight hours of daily reading? Because publication was for glory and glory was vanity.[126] Micanzio, like Gassendi, acknowledged that 'science' tended to make people proud, but claimed that it had this effect only on seekers of 'vain and superficial' knowledge. 'Consummate and profound' learning, 'on the contrary, was the machine to destroy all proud thoughts'. But this raises still another important issue: what was the relationship between learning and moral excellence? According to Micanzio, Sarpi's studies were directed 'not towards ostentation, but to the true science, the cultivation of his own soul, and to humility'.[127] Micanzio called the first of Sarpi's unpublished volumes the 'Medicine of the soul' since it was designed to do for the soul what medicine did for the body, 'to order many singular means to produce tranquillity'.[128] In his *Pensieri Medico-Morali*, a combination of medical philosophy with the teachings of Seneca and Epictetus, Sarpi urged constancy in one's interior life but flexibility in all things that lay beyond one's control. 'Above all', Sarpi concluded, 'flee that rigour that is called virtue, for that Catonian virtue is a pestiferous vice' and only a pretext for ambition and ostentation.[129]

Sarpi's learning, according to Micanzio, shaped how he lived. And Sarpi himself explained that the 'best' life was one that took living seriously because 'the most illustrious of your actions is to live'.[130] One catches here another echo of Montaigne's repudiation of Cato in favour of Socrates whom he hailed in the last of the *Essays* as proof that 'the most beautiful lives' – or teachings – were also the most human.[131] For Sarpi, as for Montaigne and, as we shall see, Gassendi too, Socrates was the 'perfect example' of the sage.[132] His greatness was in being an example of a 'natural man' who could be happy playing quoits with children.[133] The *Pensieri* conclude with a series of anecdotes about Socrates, many preserved by Seneca.[134] Sarpi's utterly Epictetan judgement – one that was shared by a whole generation and community – was that what lay beyond an individual's control was worth neither worrying about nor desiring. 'Le cose nostre', he concluded, all lay within.[135]

WHAT KIND OF MAN IS THE ANTIQUARY?

Gassendi's portrait of the scholar as hero, like Micanzio's, rests the celebration of erudition upon praise of moral strength: 'his sagacity was wonderful by reason of his constancy'. Peiresc appears as the early modern 'happy man' who exchanged benefits for gratitude, creating friendships nurtured by conversation, and preserved by a self-governance in which reason ruled the passions.[136] But he also stands as an example of the early modern sage, that otherworldly creation of those taken with neo-Stoicism. For Peiresc's lifetime coincides with the peak of interest in the late Stoic philosophers, especially Seneca and Epictetus, as they were presented to early modern Europeans through the work of a group of influential popularizers, and none more so than Justus Lipsius. In a series of works that attained wide renown and even readership, including his edition of Seneca's *Works* (1606) and his own self-help manual *De constantia* (1584), Lipsius made Stoicism fashionable. Strength of mind, self-control, and patience, all virtues that had been extolled through other sources, like the Church, over previous centuries, were now brought together in a sparkling pagan package that war-weary aristocrats could not seem to get enough of. These teachings shape the portrait of Peiresc down to its very details.

One would not read the *Vita* as an essay in 'neo-Stoicism', but the parallel between Peiresc and the ideal of the sage is striking. For Roman Stoicism, as it was revived and repackaged in the influential works of

Justus Lipsius, provided the source for this early modern art of living designed to make one philosophical. The 'Peireskean virtues' of friendship, constancy, self-control, beneficence, and conversation were none other than those made popular across Europe by those greatest of late sixteenth-century self-help books, Stefano Guazzo's *La civile conversatione* (1574, 1579), Montaigne's *Essais* (1580, 1588), and Lipsius' *De constantia*. The importance of Seneca during Peiresc's lifetime is unquestioned. The popularity of his rough-and-ready guide to life under a single ruler, *De Beneficiis*, is a reminder that while the community of citizens was held together by law and justice the society of friends was sustained by acts of beneficence and conversation.[137]

The *leitmotif* of neo-Stoicism was *constantia*, the strength of mind required to persevere on the right course despite the blows of adversity and the seductions of success. As Micanzio wrote of Francis Bacon, 'I call good estate his Constancie of mind, which is the true good'.[138] Gassendi believed that the universal scholar could, like Peiresc, 'have his mind so tempered as to enjoy the greatest tranquillity possible, and consequently, the greatest good'.[139] This well-tempered soul was what Peiresc's friends recognized in him. Rubens described him as 'the example of a well-composed soul, imbued with true philosophy' and Girolamo Aleandro, in Rome, invoking Seneca's ideal, called Peiresc 'the greatest and most happy man in the world'.[140] Peiresc himself singled out as most important – and therefore most painful to be deprived of – 'the tranquillity of the soul and the sweet conversation of our friends'.[141] This vision of a best life that was expressed in constancy, conversation, and friendship will be explored in the remaining part of this chapter and its wider implications in the one that follows.

Gassendi's portrait of Peiresc's strength of mind, or constancy, was sketched against the backdrop of his physical weakness. Gassendi suggested that physical problems bred a high tolerance for pain, but added that 'his custom of suffering was perfected and assisted by Reason which told him that what cannot be avoided, must be suffered patiently and gently'.[142] Self-control, with Peiresc as with so many of his generation, was worshipped almost as a good in itself. Jean Chapelain explained to Peiresc that he drew 'a great consolation from the force with which I observe that you support' these infirmities. It would teach him a lesson in a 'moderation' not found among 'the great part of men who are slaves to their desires' and who think only of the pursuit of pleasure.[143] Peiresc's life, Gassendi wrote, demonstrated 'that nothing could be more desirable than so great moderation of mind'.[144] He related that Peiresc often repeated that he learned 'to rule his passion' by the chance observation through a microscope of a fight between a louse and flea. The blood pulsing through the louse led him to marvel at 'how great a

Commotion of Humors and Spirits, and what a disturbance of all the faculties, anger must needs make and what harm that man avoids, who quits that passion'.[145] Peiresc attributed his own survival to philosophy: 'time and the maxims that I have practised during my hard illnesses and other adversities have prevailed and re-established my stability'.[146]

Peiresc governed his personal life according to this learned rule. Gassendi explained that while he 'affected cleanliness in his Diet, and all things about him', he nevertheless 'desired nothing superfluous, or costly'. While concerned that his clothing never appear 'unsuitable to his dignity; yet he never wore silk'. This same sense of proportion was evident in his diet. He drank ordinary white wine, heavily watered down. The one food which he consumed to excess, though he justified it to himself as med-icinal, was melons — of Cavaillon, perhaps? — and the one peculiarity of his cuisine was the use of spring water for cooking as well as drinking.[147] Behind Peiresc's sober life stood an ideal of freedom from the tyranny of excessive wants become needs. There are here echoes of Luigi Cornaro's sixteenth-century best-seller, *Della vita sobria*, but also of a more explicit reliance on an older vision of a simpler time.[148] Copied out in Peiresc's hand on a small, undated, scrap of paper is a speech of Philosophia from Boethius' *De consolatione philosophia* book 2. 'How happy', she began,

> . . . was that earlier age
> When men content depended on the trusty land,
> And not yet sunk in idle luxury
> Sated their hunger only at their need
> With acorns gathered with ease.

In this speech, Philosophia laments the passing of a simpler world when men had few wants and fewer needs. 'Would that our present times / Would now return to those good ancient ways!'[149] Boethius' reminder of the difference between things essential and indifferent provided Peiresc with ancient authority for a daily practice.[150]

But the single most important influence on Peiresc's self-fashioning was not a text but a person, Guillaume du Vair, the leading French expo-nent of a modern, Christian Stoicism. In a series of works written at the height of the civil wars in the 1580s and 1590s, du Vair presented a highly rational Christian philosophy of endurance and excellence. He drew on ancient Stoic philosophers, especially Epictetus, whose *Enchiridion* he translated into French. Peiresc met du Vair when he began his *parlemen-tary* service and worked as his secretary until the older man's death in 1621. This was how Peiresc acquired 'such knowledge of the virtue of monsieur du Vair'.[151] Du Vair's close circle of friends included, in addi-tion to Peiresc, the great writer François Malherbe, who had himself translated Epictetus and Seneca and whom Peiresc claimed to love as his own father.[152] With this kind of formation it comes as no surprise that when forced into a long confinement in the country at Belgentier by urban revolt in Aix and an outbreak of plague, Peiresc spent some of his time copying out from Malherbe's translation of Seneca, 'which did no harm to my consolation in our little solitude'.[153] Du Vair, in turn, had hailed Peiresc's companionship in a letter that dates from the beginning of their association as 'truly sweet' and 'the principal consolation that I have here'.[154]

The importance of consolation for public men in difficult times was a teaching that Peiresc made his own. 'There is no good in the world that is stable', Peiresc wrote to the brothers Dupuy, and that was why 'one must content oneself with enjoying the goods that God gives us, while, and for as long as, it pleases Him to leave them to us, and the children, parents and friends he gives to us, and to praise Him for those that He leaves us, which He could have taken away from us as easily as the others'.[155] Peiresc was moved to these particular reflections upon the theft of his gems and coins.[156]

Loss of health demanded *constantia* even more than the loss of antiquities.[157] A series of consolations preserved in Peiresc's papers, some of which may have originated with du Vair, reveal more of Peiresc's 'practical' Stoicism.[158] They reflect his 'common saying' that he 'was not so much troubled at the evils, whereunto he was subjected, as he rejoyced that they were not more grievous as they might have been'.[159] Peiresc dealt with reverses, according to Gassendi, by telling himself 'that there was more reason to rejoyce in behalf of that which good Fortune had left behind; than to grieve for that, which hard hap had taken away. Wherefore he was wont frequently to say, that who ever seeks after the uncertain good things of this World, should think and resolve, that he gathers as well for Thieves as for himself.'[160] In one of these consolations, we read that when the pain of adversity was great 'we must employ our strongest efforts not to be at all surprised and arm ourselves against all its assaults with an assured constancy, impenetrable shield, Queen and Mistress of all the virtues and so highly esteemed among all our ancients'.[161] Patience was the other, different sort of weapon at an individual's disposal. In the midst of the storm, 'patience is the true port of all our miseries and the only antidote for repelling our troubles'.[162] Not all of Peiresc's friends could tolerate this message; Rubens, for example, rebelled against its severity.[163]

Peiresc believed that it was necessary to study philosophy 'in order to be prepared with the constancy and patience needed for the obstacles that are encountered in even the most favourable affairs'. With it he had 'conquered unequalled difficulties'.[164] The perspective that he had gained through his studies was the ability to 'suspend judgement' that Pierre Charron had identified with the sage: 'to examine all things, to consider them individually, and then to compare together all the laws and customs of the world that can be known, and to judge them in good faith and dispassionately, at the level of truth, reason, and universal nature'.[165]

When Gassendi emphasized the 'constancy' and 'indefatigability' with which Peiresc pursued his researches he borrowed from the neo-Stoic's language of moral comportment to describe his scholarly excellence.[166] The convergence of Stoic *constantia* and scholarly *Sitzfleisch* led Erasmus to reserve the adjective 'Herculean' for scholars,[167] and, a century later, one of Archbishop Ussher's correspondents announced that he had begun studying Arabic 'and hope[d] (labore & constantia)' to progress.[168] 'Labore & Constantia' was the motto in Plantin's famous printer's mark and one of the early icons of European neo-Stoicism (plate 2). In his funeral oration, Bouchard claimed that Peiresc exceeded all the heroes of antiquity in his 'continual and almost incredible labour and rare industrie, to attain the knowledge of all great and excellent things, all Arts and Sciences'.[169] Gassendi too spoke of a 'rarely industrious' man possessed 'of a diligence invincible'.[170]

The combination of Stoicism and sociability was designed to create a model of individual excellence within the European Republic of Letters – as Morhof recognized. It also allowed Gassendi to use Peiresc to make a point in the European debate about whether arms or letters made the gentleman. We are told that when aged fifteen Peiresc was forced by his uncle to learn how 'to handle Armes, ride the Horse, and exercise his limbs with dancing'. But he made no effort to master these explicitly courtly skills 'so much the better did he account it, to be alwaies reading, writing or hearing some point of Learning'.[171] Charles Perrault, writing after the passage of fifty years of further refinements in aristocratic sociability, picked out this very passage in his *éloge* of Peiresc as a distinguishing chracteristic.[172]

Peiresc's much-praised practices of sociability – his beneficence, conversation, and friendship – are the outward expression of the Stoic's sense of priorities. The leading and most commented upon of the Peireskean virtues was beneficence.[173] In the dedicatory letter Gassendi proclaimed that 'I never read or heard of a man, that was more earnestly sollicitous, or made it more his constant business, to benefit Man-kind'. While there were many who had more wealth, 'yet no man could exceed him in the prudent manage of what he had, and in willingness to do good'. There was never, he concluded, 'a more generous Maecenas and Patron of the Muses'.[174] In the dedication of the *Life* Gassendi commented on Peiresc's extraordinary efforts to advance learning 'with a munificence towards all learned men, which was perfectly Royal, and Princely'.[175] '[W]ho is there', wrote Gassendi, 'that knows not how much he was inclined to Beneficence? Doubtless there was never man gave more chearfully, liberally, or frequently'. Peiresc's models were none other than God and Nature, 'who do not lend, but freely give all things'.[176] In his memorial address, Bouchard proclaimed that Peiresc was driven by a 'perpetual and constant desire to adorn and set forth learned men'.[177] It was this that Bayle may have had in mind when commenting that 'never has any man rendered more service to the Republic of Letters'.[178]

Like *De beneficiis*, which began with the assertion that 'what we need is a discussion of benefits and the rules for a practice that constitutes the chief bond of human society' (I.iv.2), Gassendi's *Vita* is a guide to virtuous giving and the society that it created. The learned and deserving were given gifts in order to support activities that promised great benefit to the world, and the poor were given charity with no expectation of recompense. A day in which Peiresc failed to exercise this liberality he accounted lost.[179] Gassendi reports that Tommaso Campanella was so overwhelmed by Peiresc's beneficence as to declare that 'he had before, so much constancy [*satis constantiae*], that he could refrain from shedding teares in the middest of most cruel torments: which now he could not do, being moved with contemplation of so magnificent a Gentleman'.[180] Peiresc's practice of generosity was so well known that it literally served as credit: a Maronite stranded without means in Livorno was transported to France without charge by a Marseille merchant because he carried a letter for Peiresc, who later paid his freight.[181]

But beneficence, as Seneca emphasized, worked in concert with gratitude. It is 'gratitude', Peiresc himself wrote, 'that secures and defends the bonds of human society'.[182] It was precisely for this reason that nothing angered him more than ingratitude. Only this was capable, he admitted, of making him 'forget' his philosophy.[183] In its classical and early modern forms, beneficence was perceived as the mortar keeping individuals together. Ingratitude, by contrast, chipped away at these ties.[184]

Since nothing, according to Gassendi, gained friends 'so much as Beneficence and friendly Offices; it is no wonder that he had so many, so good and so illustrious, all the world over'.[185] Peiresc 'made' friends by performing services and kindnesses; as Seneca claimed, 'from benefits friendship arises'.[186] But, in line with Seneca's dictum, he never sought his own profit but acted only 'for his friends' sakes'.[187] In *De tranquillitate animi* Seneca had declared that 'nothing delights the mind more than the happiness of a faithful friendship'.[188] Because of its firm foundation in reason, the loyalty of friends could be seen as an exemplification of the *constantia* that was a mark of excellence.[189] Friendship offered a haven in an age of lacerating social conflict. Mersenne, for example, thought that the friendship of Peiresc and Gassendi, 'cor unum et anima una', was a model that could stop Christians from fighting each other.[190] William Barclay, the father of Peiresc's close friend the poet John Barclay, even used Lipsius' *De constantia* as his *album amicorum*. He explained in an introductory inscription that he chose this book because it 'is always in my hands' and 'because CONSTANTIA, which is the spirit and strength of the other virtues, is the soul of friendship'.[191] These were concepts that found their way into autograph books all across Europe.[192]

Friendship allowed for the exercise of virtue, a worthwhile practice for even the morally autarkic sage, and also provided a means of self-improvement as vital as the disciplining of the passions.[193] 'Associate with those who will make a better man of you', Seneca declared; 'welcome those whom you yourself can improve. The process is mutual; for men learn while they teach'.[194] Already as a young man Peiresc had identified himself with the nobility of the friend. ' "I would lay violent hands upon my self", saies he, "if I might be justly accused of the least neglect of my duty to my friends" '.[195] Peiresc's later correspondence was full of protestations of friendship, but no action spoke louder than the special pleading he undertook with one friend, Francesco Barberini, for the liberty of another, Galileo, out of 'the duty of a friend'.[196]

The same sense of duty bound Peiresc never to accuse his friends.[197] Of course, sometimes this was a challenge. After responding angrily to a provocative letter from a friend, Peiresc enclosed it, unsealed, along with another to the Dupuy brothers and asked them to destroy the first letter if it seemed to them intemperate 'because I do not at all intend to lose his friendship, being resolved to love my friends with all their humours, just as I would not want to lose the use of roses for the thorns that are mixed among them'.[198] He tolerated his friends' idiosyncrasies with the knowledge that they tolerated his own – and that sometimes he benefited from this open-mindedness, as in his acquired taste for mustard.[199] 'Being all men', he wrote in another letter, 'we must get along with one another'.[200]

This was the rule by which he governed the Republic of Letters. He insisted that the learned not fight amongst themselves, nor 'give out uncertain things for certain', criticize others rather than be creative themselves, or drag others down in order to exalt themselves. He urged scholars to be grateful that others 'have broken the ice [*quod illi glaciem secuerint*], and have at least endeavoured to make a very rough way smooth' and, most importantly, 'to remember that they also themselves are men, and apt to be mistaken, and should by that means merit pardon, if they showed themselves gentle to others'.[201] Peiresc's views were born of the painful experience of trying to mediate conflicts among his friends: Holstenius and Suares in Rome and Campanella, Naudé and Gassendi in Paris. He urged young scholars to respect their elders, and older ones to show some 'temperance' when provoked into polemics by the younger ones. He, for his part, kept well clear of the popular transalpine learned sport of taking pot-shots at the works of Cardinals Baronius and Bellarmine.[202] Over-production of acidic commentary was a natural by-product of scholarship: 'the diligence of study', he wrote, 'makes this world more austere and more savage than it certainly should be'.[203] But the learned world, like the wider society, needed all sorts and one had to take the bad in order to get the good.[204] Recent descriptions of the practice of the Republic of Letters reflect the continuing importance of this effort at getting along.[205]

Late sixteenth- and seventeenth-century writers suggested that conversation was a complement to the giving of benefits because it established an affective context for the exchange of gifts and services. It required, as Stefano Guazzo put it, knowledge not only of oneself but also of the world since people of different backgrounds and natures needed to be spoken to differently.[206] Daniel Morhof, a century later, recognized the importance of knowing how to converse and so provided his students with a series of rules to help them navigate the shoals of learned sociability.[207] The literature on conversation followed from the well-established guides to correspondence that had proliferated from the later sixteenth century.[208] *Salon* culture, in turn, as Marc Fumaroli has argued and as we shall see in Chapter Two, marked the extension of this style of interaction from the learned world to the polite.

Peiresc viewed conversation as an intellectual tool. In a letter of 1629 to Lucas Holstenius in advance of a trip the latter was planning to the Levant, Peiresc sought to brief him on the medals, manuscripts, and monuments he might come across. 'But', he concluded, 'it is not easy to explain their meaning by writing alone; it is necessary to see them and talk face to face'.[209] As much of his intellectual life as was committed to paper, another part of it and, from this letter, perhaps the more important one, was lived in the face-to-face encounters in Aix and Belgentier – and is, therefore, more or less, lost to posterity. According to Gassendi, Peiresc delighted more in conversation 'than any other thing in the world'.[210] The description of Peiresc's practice amounts to a set of rules for the aspiring conversationalist. He first ascertained the interests of those he was with and then proceeded to discuss only those things about which they had some knowledge in order to avoid making them feel uncomfortable. With scholars or travellers he asked detailed questions about their work and experiences and then shared some of his own learning with them.[211] The prudence that Peiresc displayed in managing his conversation illustrated Seneca's precept that the giver gauge his benefits appropriate to 'the when, wherefore, and where of the gift'.[212] If the great gift giver could not bear ingratitude, the supreme conversationalist could not tolerate small talk, braggadocio, or lying – all ways of distorting the social space.[213] This was, Gassendi wrote, 'the only passion of his mind, which he could not bridle'.[214]

Gassendi explains that Peiresc 'could not endure the company of such as loved only to hear, and speak, of vulgar and trivial matters', such as whether it was hot or cold, the sky clear or cloudy, the air healthy or not. 'And for this very cause', Gassendi continued, 'he shunned the society of women because he could hardly get any good [conversation] thereby; and he must be forced to talk to them only of toies and trifles'.[215]

Does this reflect Peiresc's considered judgement of women? The most categorical pronouncement was made by Bouchard, one of the least reliable and least reputable in Peiresc's circle. Visiting Peiresc at Belgentier on his way from Paris to Rome, he wrote that 'Monsieur de Peiresc hated and had a low opinion of women his whole life'. It has been suggested that during Bouchard's stay Peiresc was simply exasperated because he was then hosting his brother's glamorous, pampered wife and their five daughters.[216] His correspondence is, otherwise, full of indications of respect for women: he was sorry to have missed Barclay's mother in Paris; he wrote with seriousness to Barclay's widow about the effort to obtain for her a French pension, and sympathized with a newly widowed woman who deserved better from fate.[217]

Peiresc did not, of course, marry. When pressed by his father to accept a good match, with the daughter of the President of the Chambre des Comptes of Provence, he explained that he 'could not care for a wife and children, and be free to follow his studies and patronize learned men'. His marriage to 'Pallas and the Muses' appears to be the only one he consummated.[218] He seems, even, to have equated celibacy with constancy. Opposite his bed hung a grisaille of the part of the Del Monte (then Barberini; and now Portland) Vase showing a woman he identified as Achilles' prize Briseis. He interpreted the serpent between her legs as a defence against Agamemnon's unwanted advances and also as an allegory of chastity.[219] And, in a letter to Paris reporting on the complex domestic arrangements of an acquaintance marrying for the second time, Peiresc explained that 'these are the inevitable consequences for those who cannot absolutely master themselves'.[220]

Gassendi's presentation of Peiresc's death amplified his virtue in life. The genre scene of *The Death of Seneca* was among the most popular in the seventeenth century, depicting the Stoic sage still dictating to the students surrounding him while his life flowed out into the already drawn bath. Micanzio, in his *Life* of Sarpi, also emphasized that his hero's manner of dying upheld his way of living and therefore 'merited being better known'.[221] Peiresc endorsed du Vair's deathbed declaration that 'one ought to think of dying well as the closure of the comedy'. He added that these words 'accord well with all his writings'.[222] Montaigne's early declaration – later modified – that 'to philosophize is to learn to die' looms over this discussion. Gassendi's long account of the great suffering endured by Peiresc, first from the kind of urinary tract problems that were so common in the seventeenth century and then from the fever and acute pain caused by the disintegration of his bladder, make for exceedingly gory reading. But that only worked to enhance the dignity with which Peiresc bore his end and 'authenticated' his philosophy.[223]

This view of death as freedom was a contemporary commonplace. In his *Monarchie of Man*, written in the Tower of London *c*.1632 where he had been imprisoned for his part in the tumultuous conclusion to the 1629 session of Parliament, and where he received from his – and Peiresc's – friend Sir Robert Cotton a gift of Lipsius' *De constantia*, the MP John Eliot explained that 'there wee anchor in securitie without the distraction of new troubles, there without danger or hazard doe wee ride'. In the 'boisterous and tempestuous sea of life' fully exposed to change and misery 'there is no refuge or retreat but to the porte of death'. Only there can be found 'a calm-nesse & tranquility'.[224] Moreover, he added in an echo of the Stoic trope made famous by Montaigne, since 'the whole life is but an exercise of dying, & all the changes & vicissitudes of nature, death, in a measure & degree: why then should death be thought soe terrible?'[225] If death was natural, why was it to be feared? Eliot recalled Seneca's advice to Lucilius to examine his own fears; at bottom, Seneca suggested, in words echoed nearly 1,900 years later by Franklin Delano Roosevelt in his First Inaugural Address, that 'there was nothing so terrible as fear itself' ('nihil terribile nisi ipsum timorem').[226]

Gassendi's Latin *Life* received its first complete French translation in 1992 (there was a partial version in 1770). Its only contemporary vernacular edition was the reliable English translation of 1657. The fact of its publication might strike the historian of scholarship, and of English scholarship in particular, as important. For the cultural historian its importance lies in extending the exemplary value of Peiresc from the narrower world of learning to the wider one of gentlemen, those who read Peacham and would read Baudelot de Dairval. Just as the virtues praised by Gassendi and adopted for the learned republic had come out of much narrower aristocratic circles, so these, in turn, were now extended to a less learned, but more gentle society. The book's new English title, *The Mirrour of True Nobility and Gentility*, made explicit the purpose for which it was designed. The further divulgation of the Peireskean virtues in Britain would be the work of the third Earl of Shaftesbury and essay journals like the *Spectator*.

The English book was a project of the 'Invisible College', the remarkable circle of practical and utopian humanists that clustered around Samuel Hartlib and Benjamin Worsley c.1646, reminding us again that the link forged by Gassendi between the virtues of learning and sociability was part of a much broader European phenomenon. Hartlib was called 'the great Intelligencer of Europe', 'hub of the axletree of knowledge', and 'Master of Innumerable Curiosities'. He, too, like Peiresc, believed strongly that knowledge had to be freely communicated if it were to serve its end, the public good.[227]

Like Gassendi, Peiresc's English supporters saw him as an example; the title page bore the legend 'Virtue lives after death' ('Vivit post Funera Virtus'). William Rand, the translator, was set to work by Hartlib and Worsley in 1646, and dedicated the finished product to John Evelyn whom he proclaimed 'the only man I ever heard of in England, whose *Peireskean Vertues*' merited the dedication.[228] He claimed that Evelyn's father's 'civility' to him and the hospitality of one of Evelyn's relatives – Rand is clearly straining here – reminded him of Peiresc. 'No man', he concluded, other than Evelyn 'is more fit effectually to recommend him to the acquaintance of our English gentry'.[229] Indeed, as Michael Hunter has observed, Evelyn's residence in Paris from 1649 to 1652 and close association with the survivors of the Cabinet Dupuy, Gassendi, Naudé, and La Mothe le Vayer, enabled him to serve as an intellectual bridge between contemporary French and English learned culture. Moreover, during this period the two books mentioned most frequently in Evelyn's commonplace book were favourites of Peiresc as well: Grotius' *On the Truth of the Christian Religion* and Bacon's *Advancement of Learning*.[230]

In only one respect were Evelyn and Peiresc incomparable and this, according to Rand, redounded to the Englishman's credit. Acknowledging that this 'most considerable' difference fell into the category of what Epictetus classified as things indifferent, he contrasted Evelyn's married state with Peiresc's lay monachism. Rand allowed that 'the scholding Humor of his [Peiresc's] Mother in law [sic], and the shallow Impertinencies of the Gentlewomen of that Countrey and Age' might have influenced his decision. Evelyn had, by contrast, made the happy choice of a woman who was 'a meet Help' in his 'most manly concernments'. And while recommending Peiresc to her he also commented that '*Peireskius*, were he now living, would count it no time lost, to be in her Company, and enjoy her ingenious converse'.[231] This entire passage is a key document of the shift in the centre of gravity of civil life in seventeenth-century France and England from aristocratic, Latinate, erudite, and male 'academies', to the mixed-gender and explicitly non-erudite *salons*. In 1657 we are not at all in the England of the *Spectator* or *Fable of the Bees* but the crucial step in liberating learned examples of living well from their original context for use in a non-learned society had already been taken.

The English translation of Gassendi's *Life of Peiresc* was an explicit intervention in an ongoing debate about the education of the 'Compleat Gentleman'.[232] Rand hoped that the life of Peiresc would teach Englishmen 'that knowledge, which is the highest perfection of Man, by which he differs from Beasts, must needs be the principal accomplishment of a Gentleman'. In drawing an explicit contrast between the subject who hunted and hawked and the one who learned, Rand used Peiresc to make the argument that letters, rather than arms, was the proper calling of the excellent man. He described hunting, a typical display of martial virtue, as breeding 'an humor inclinable to Tyrany [*sic*], like that of Nimrod the mighty Hunter, and *Proto-Tyrant* of all mankind'. From Peiresc, the 'English Gentry' would learn a better use of their leisure and become more fit to serve 'the Commonwealth in the most weighty concernements thereof'. Elaborating on the contrast between tyranny and commonwealth – surely no idle antithesis in a work achieved during the years of civil war and Interregnum – Rand argued that a society of men engaged in a life of civil conversation was the best preservative against tyranny. The gentry had become fodder for tyranny, and England engulfed in war, precisely because of their intellectual dependence. Forced 'to see with the Eyes of others', they served others' 'Interests, Factions and Trades, instead of following their own well-informed, unbiassed and generous understandings'.[233]

The opposition between hawking and hunting on the one hand, and more worthy pursuits on the other, is a main theme of another book from this period, Izaak Walton's *Compleat Angler* (1653), subtitled 'The Contemplative Man's Recreation'. It begins with a 'conference betwixt an Angler, a Faulkner, and a Hunter'. Fishing, here, occupies the role of studying in this contrast between leisure activities for the gentry.[234] The freedom of the angler, defined as freedom from the snares of desire, is the running theme of the Angler's songs interspersed in the text.

> Who Hawks, lures oft both far and wide;
> Who uses Games shall often prove
> A loser; but who falls in love,
> Is fettered in fond Cupids snare:
> My Angle breeds me no such care.
>
> Of Recreation there is none
> so free as Fishing is alone;
> All other pastimes do no lesse

Than mind and body both possesse:
My hand alone my work can do,
So I can fish and study too.[235]

Walton's text, so resonant with the themes associated with Peiresc's ideal of comportment nevertheless marks the development of these ideas in a different direction. For if the distancing from the world that so appealed to men in Peiresc's circle was necessary because of their continued involvement in worldly causes, in Walton there is an explicit move towards an actual withdrawal from the world: to be an angler one had to separate oneself physically from the court.[236] The tension between service and freedom that informs the 'Peireskean virtues' and Peiresc's circle no longer animates this later – but not that much later – ideal of the good life.

Rand urged Evelyn to further the education of the next generation of Englishmen by recommending Peiresc's life 'to the Imitation and worthy Emulation of our English Gallants'.[237] Evelyn, in turn, did just that, advising a friend travelling through the Mediterranean a year later to make a pilgrimage to Belgentier because even 'though the curiosities may be much dispersed since the tyme of the most noble Peireskius, yet the very genius of that place cannot but infuse admirable thoughts into you'.[238]

What was Peiresc's nobility? When late medieval Italians debated the question they proclaimed that *virtus* was the *vera nobilitas*. Peiresc's English translators defined this virtue in terms of learning. By trying to reshape the character of gentle society on the model of this hero of the Republic of Letters, they suggested that the virtues developed for scholarly life could be of use in wider society. In making Evelyn the intermediary, and incorporating his marriage into the ideal, Rand was adapting a model of the man of letters for the mixed conversation of the later seventeenth century. This same trajectory from the aristocratic to the learned to the polite is essential for understanding the relationship between changing ideals of individual excellence and social life in the century after Peiresc.

2

Constancy, Conversation, and Friendship

The 'Civil Life of Private Men'

TO ASK THE MEANING OF 'TRUE NOBILITY' in any society is to ask after its ideal of the best man. Dante, for example, in *The Convivio* (1304–7), summarized three contemporary definitions, wealth, ancestry, and his own favorite, virtue.[1] To assert that virtue was the 'true nobility' was to argue that nobility could be earned on merit and did not depend solely on accident of birth.[2] The tensions of political life in the Italian communes of the late Middle Ages are reflected in the pervasiveness of this question. Its importance in late sixteenth-century France, in the form of a debate about the priority of arms or letters in the education of a young gentleman, alerts us to the existence of similar social tensions.[3] And so, for Gassendi to proclaim Peiresc 'the most noble' ('Nobilissimum') and for his English translators to render the title as *The Mirrour of True Nobility and Gentility* was not only to suggest that the old mirror-for-princes literature could be applied more generally, in the same way that the subject of the *Life* was a scholar rather than a king, but also to intervene in that debate about arms and letters and propose Peiresc's virtues as a new definition of *vera nobilitas*. The chapters that follow explore this proposal, and Peiresc's celebrity, from the vantage points afforded by the different realms he commanded – in society, politics, religion, and scholarship.

Gassendi's presentation of Peiresc as a hero of learned sociability draws on an older way of talking about social life. In fact, this portrait can be situated precisely in time and space: at the crucial moment when earlier Italian discussions of comportment and civility were naturalized north of the Alps.[4] Viewed from one perspective, an archaeology of the Peireskean virtues lays bare the mechanics of cultural transmission that also characterizes the Renaissance as a European phenomenon. Viewed from another, these virtues of learned sociability appear as the basic building blocks of civil society.

For Europe's Republic of Letters was not only a network of scholars, it was also a laboratory in which ideas of civility were elaborated and lived. In the self-conscious discussions of individuals who felt themselves belonging to the same community – and acted accordingly, for better and worse – we can overhear the meanings contemporaries attached to terms and practices that later became pervasive, but were no longer talked about. Historians of the rise of civil society have looked to late seventeenth- and early eighteenth-century England and France, but the story they are interested in begins earlier in the community of scholars. My approach here is to sketch out the main lines of this trajectory – from sixteenth-century Italian academies to seventeenth-century cabinets of scholars and *salons* and, finally, to wider eighteenth-century polite society – by looking closely at a series of key texts. These include French translations of seminal Italian treatises on civility and important treatments of this theme that emerge from within the Republic of Letters and were written by scholars at a lesser or greater remove from Peiresc.

But looking at discussions of sociability through the lens of Peiresc not only gives new depth to the familiar genealogies of the modern age, it lets us see clearly what was lost, and maybe had to be lost, in the broadening of these ideas from the narrower community of the learned to the wider one of the 'gentle'. For how else could a set of values hammered out in select communities of the like-minded be made to work in increasingly larger and heterogeneous circles, whether Parisian high society or the nation? The commitment to sociability as a practice of moral excellence that complemented the life of learning could hardly be extended much beyond the world of neo-Stoics and monkish scholars and so was dropped. What remained was what we might term the 'momentum' of the practice but not its meaning: constancy without self-mastery, conversation without improvement, and friendship without philosophy. This, too, is part of the history of civil society.

The figure of Peiresc helps us recognize that ideal and trace its communication and transformation over space and time. The same changes attendant upon its wider dissemination were also his personal undoing. For the emphasis on brilliant talk and social flair that was the norm in seventeenth- and eighteenth-century *salons* made erudite conversation seem pedantic. This revolution of style against substance broke out in Paris in the 1620s and was marked by the opening of a *salon* in which Latin and learning were equally discouraged and which was dominated by worldly values of the sort that Corneille represented in his early comedies. The success, albeit *de scandale*, of the writer Guez de Balzac is a measure of how authoritative this new cultural circle had become. Why this happened in the 1620s is a significant unresolved question. The spread of *politesse* as an ideal, and its interaction with the new science, is a theme of capital importance. For our purposes, 1623–24 marks a key turning point: Peiresc left Paris for the provinces and Balzac published his *Premières Lettres*.

A defining aspect of this world, which contemporaries identified by the shorthand 'civil conversation', was that it possessed its own standard of excellence. Inherited with classical letters was the belief that the excellent man and the citizen were one and the same; it was disinherited with this shift of authority to vernacular sociability. The vogue for civil conversation across Europe in the seventeenth and eighteenth centuries culminates in the late eighteenth-century identification of the free man with the represented citizen that is so important in the wave of revolutions that brought down the *ancien régime*. Not participation in politics – citizenship in the old style – but friendship mattered most. Just as the crisis of the Hellenistic world first created an interest in understanding friendship, the breakdown of political community during the civil wars of religion that racked Europe in the century after 1560 created a context in which those earlier discussions had renewed appeal.[5] The world shaped by friendship offered an explicit alternative to the insistence on the priority of a public life that now seemed unappealing, if not downright dangerous.

This early modern discussion was guided by the writings of Seneca. Friendship emerged as a central social relation because it was rational – unlike the world 'outside' – and presumed an equality that was elsewhere elusive.[6] Friendship was rational before it was passionate and its pleasures were those of the mind.[7] The sociability of friendship was linked to a philosophical project: 'Associate with those who will make a better man of you', Seneca wrote. 'Welcome those whom you yourself can improve. The process is mutual; for men learn while they teach.'[8] This association was made concrete by beneficence, a doing good without any expectation of recompense, and endured because driven by mind.[9] A relationship that 'regards convenience only and looks to the results', Seneca concluded, 'is a bargain and not a friendship'.[10]

Writing with the experience of having been tutor to Nero, Seneca declared that 'if the state is too corrupt to be helped' the wise man ought not to struggle in politics with no chance of success. Just as he 'will not enter upon a course for which he knows he is unfitted', or go to sea in a leaky boat, a wise person tries to 'establish himself in a safe retreat before he experiences any of the storms of life'. In this place he would 'devote himself to the liberal arts' and 'cultivate the virtues' that could still be cultivated in retirement. While the wise man remained under the obligation to benefit his fellow-creatures, this referred to the 'many if he can, if not a few, if not a few, those who are nearest, if not these himself'. Even giving benefit to the few, or to himself, Seneca declared, was engaging in 'public affairs'. In this extraordinary passage, Seneca tried to redeem the society built on the virtues of friendship and self-perfection from the accusation of *otium*, a complex notion that could mean leisure, idleness, or repose. It was precisely this claim, it has been argued, and the declaration that there 'nowhere' ('nusquam') existed the state in which the wise man could live, that holds the key to understanding Thomas More's 'utopia' ('nusquam').[11]

Seneca also helped shape the first and most influential early modern presentation of this theme, Petrarch's *De vita solitaria* (*c.*1340). He argued that withdrawal from society was necessary to achieve the tranquillity of mind that was 'something great and veritably divine'.[12] This tranquillity, in turn, was identified with the creative freedom of the poet and philosopher. 'It is not so much the solitary recessses and the silence that delight me as the leisure and freedom that dwell within them.'[13] Only under these conditions could man pursue the cultivation of the mind.[14] This 'solitude' described the select sociability of the like-minded.

In book 1, Petrarch defined this 'solitude' that was not solitary. He explained that he was not 'so inhuman as to hate men' and sought only to escape from the crowds in which bad men outnumbered good.[15] Nor ought the value of solitude to lead anyone to 'despise the laws of friendship', he wrote. 'I bade them fly from crowds', Petrarch added, 'and not from friends'. Solitude was meant to be 'modest and gentle, not rude', 'tranquil, not savage', and definitely not 'barbarism'. Petrarch explicitly described his position as 'the middle of the road between the two extremes' of men who can only live in a crowd and those – though utterly inconceivable – who preferred isolation.[16]

Yet even in book 2, otherwise devoted to praise of monastic peace and quiet, Petrarch identified 'solitude' with the society of friends.[17] This redefinition of 'solitude' leads immediately into praise of friendship as the sweetest human pleasure. 'It will never', Petrarch wrote, 'be my view that solitude is disturbed by the presence of a friend but that it is enriched. If I had the choice of doing without one or the other, I should prefer to be deprived of solitude rather than of my friend.' Declaring that in 'embracing solitude I do not reject friendship', Petrarch went even further.[18] You 'will be not only a support to my peace but, if I may somehow express what is in my mind, my very peace, not only a comfort in my solitude, but in a way the very soul of my solitude. When I am with you I shall think myself truly solitary.'[19] Solitude filtered out all that hindered the free life while sociability of the like-minded, as reflected in the notion of friendship, only furthered its pursuit.

The importance of *De vita solitaria* is that the poet's quest for freedom to create led him to articulate a series of arguments about the social and psychological preconditions for living well that later, in the period we are examining, became central. (Whether or not they derived directly from reading Petrarch or were mediated – and through what? and by whom? – are interesting questions though not essential for our purposes.) And although his pronouncements in book 2 enabled later commentators to reject Petrarch's notion of solitude as unsociable and therefore inhuman, his categorical defence of sociability had an even more significant, if less obvious, importance. For Petrarch's formulations provide a benchmark against which we can study early modern discussions of civility – a term of art not available to him – and of the excellence of individuals living in that space between the hermitage and the senate.

The persistence of Seneca's, or Petrarch's, philosophical ideal and its perpetuation through the early modern literature on civility is a crucial theme to which I cannot do full justice. But if we wish to understand Gassendi's *Life* of Peiresc, and its important role in shaping and reshaping ideas of individual excellence in the seventeenth century it is, nevertheless, to this Franco-Italian literature on civility that we must turn.

La Vie civile (Paris, 1557) was written by one 'Mathieu Palmier, gentil'homme Florentin'. Its translation and publication belong to the decade of intense Italianization that also saw the publication of Du Bellay's *Defence et illustration de la langue français* (1549) and *Antiquitez de Rome* (1558). In his dedication to a young woman the translator explained that because there was no one in France to teach her proper behaviour she had been forced to travel to Italy. He had therefore decided to translate an Italian book to spare future Frenchwomen and men the need to make pilgrimages to Italy in order to learn how to live with style.[20]

This courtesy text is, however, none other than Matteo Palmieri's *Della vita civile*, published in 1530 but written a century earlier in Florence and circulated in manuscript. According to Hans Baron, *Della vita civile* gave 'full expression to a Florentine civic attitude' that had transformed humanism 'from a classicism unconnected with the citizen's active life to civic Humanism'. Baron argued that Palmieri's book was intended to do what Coluccio Salutati, Chancellor of the Florentine Republic, failed to accomplish: answer Petrarch's *De vita solitaria* from the point of view of the citizen. Baron claimed that 'if Salutati's work had been completed, it would have occupied the place in the history of civic Humanism which was to be filled, two generations later, by the *Della vita civile* of Matteo Palmieri, a disciple of Bruni'.[21]

That a text which has in the twentieth century been viewed as a classic formulation of Renaissance republicanism was read, in the later sixteenth, as a guide to the education of young ladies, might lead us to rethink our notion of republicanism. The book's purpose was to describe the nature of the good life and the means necessary to attain it. The citizen had first to be made a man; only then could he rule and be ruled in turn. But whether an emphasis on man as a sociable creature – and seeing this as an 'answer' to Petrarch first requires us to read Petrarch with blinkers on – is a sufficient description of republicanism is doubtful. Indeed, the formation proposed by Palmieri the humanist was moral before it was political, and aristocratic before it was republican. Hence the ease with which it could be, and was, adopted in France and elsewhere in a Europe dominated by monarchies and aristocratic culture.

According to Palmieri, the most serious obstacle to making correct, that is to say moral, choices was posed by man's own constitution, since an inability to govern the passions made it impossible for him to take the decisions necessary for a moral existence.[22] Because life posed so many complicated choices it was difficult not to err.[23] So book 1, ostensibly devoted to the category of the good (*honestum*), and shaped as a piece of pedagogy, actually offered a primer in self-control. The sign of a 'well-composed soul', Palmieri wrote, using the very words that Rubens would employ to describe Peiresc two centuries later, was the ability to remain firm and steady in its beliefs.[24] For Palmieri, as for classical authors, this rested, inevitably, upon self-knowledge.[25]

Palmieri's account in book 1 focused on choice as the essence of moral life and on the measures needed to overcome the natural obstacles to choosing well. This led him to invoke the legend of the young Hercules choosing at the crossroads. This story, first told by the sophist Prodicus, had the young hero wandering out to a solitary crossroads where he was confronted by two women, Virtue and Pleasure, and one choice between the hard climb to glory or the appealing descent into ease. The tale, whose early modern iconographic history was reconstructed by Erwin Panofsky, was an allegory of the challenge of choosing well and living well.[26] Hercules demonstrated the strength of mind that Palmieri lionized. The story offered a model for the teacher of moral education. Having made a choice, Palmieri insisted that one had to 'constantly persevere'.[27] Only after giving instruction in how to find one's way did Palmieri turn to a more conventional account of the cardinal virtues.

Constancy plays a central role in Palmieri's definition of fortitude as the 'fermezza insuperabile d'animo costante'. In a further specification of its meaning, Palmieri suggested that this *fortezza* was expressed by self-mastery, 'se medesimo vincere'. The strength of an 'animo forte & in se stesso costante' was needed to ward off the temptations that led so many to seek after the wrong goal.[28] Long before Lipsius had seized upon constancy as a code-word for Stoicism it had, as this disussion shows, been used to denote the purposefulness associated with self-control. The strength of mind shown by the young Hercules who chose the hard path of virtue when confronted at the crossroads with the more appealing shape of pleasure was also found in biblical figures like Job and Samson, and classical ones like Attilius Regulus, Scipio, and Mucius Scaevola.[29]

The insistence on the rigorous training of the mind that was the pre-requisite for wise choice – the essential moral act – had necessarily to come before any description of the virtues that it made possible. We find the same philosophical orientation in Stefano Guazzo's *La civile conversa-tione* (1574; expanded 1579) which was translated into French almost immediately – twice! – and published in 1582. It was easily the most important text on civil life published in the second half of the sixteenth century.[30] The 150 years that separated the writing of Palmieri's and Guazzo's books, and the nearly forty-five years that separated their pub-lication, were collapsed into twenty-five years between the appearance of their French translations. What was written as a guide to the forma-tion of young citizens was translated, and read, as a training guide for the 'finishing' of young aristocrats. The 'print revolution' and the trans-lation boom of the late sixteenth century enabled these texts to speak to each other as if participating in the same conversation.

Guazzo was a native of Casale, in northern Italy, who had travelled in Italy and lived for six years in France (1549–55) before returning home and writing a book that adapts the tradition of rhetorical instruction for the world of aristocratic-academic sodality.[31] The remarkable success of a book written by a provincial gentleman of no reputation can be explained only by its timeliness. 'Civil conversation' represented a model of social interaction that provided both a venue – the academies sprout-ing all over Italy – and an ideal of living – friendship, self-control, and improvement – for people moving in a space called 'civil' because it was between court or government on the one hand, and family on the other.[32] The line from Guazzo to seventeenth-century French treatises on sociability and thence to polite society is paralleled by a reception of Guazzo's teaching of civility among scholars concerned with the art of living in the Republic of Letters.[33] We will examine each of these in turn.

In the preface written by one of Guazzo's French translators, Gabriel Chappuys, conversation was defined as another means of pursuing excellence.[34] He interpreted Seneca's warning about the 'conversation of the many' to refer only to the dangers of mixing with indiscriminate company for all but the most 'marvellously resolute and constant' of men, and not as encouragement to 'pursue solitude and live alone'.[35] Flight from the multitude ought to take one into the company of those who made one better. Chappuys built on Seneca's view of conversation as a means of mutual self-improvement designed to complement reading.[36]

The first of the four books, 'On the Benefits of Conversation', opens with the character named Guazzo complaining that he was afflicted with the illness of melancholy and was seeking a cure.[37] Although employed at court and therefore required to 'be conversant' with all sorts of persons, he did it 'against the heart'. Only when able to 'withdraw myselfe into my lodging either to read or write, or to repose my selfe: then I recover my libertie'.[38] His interlocutor, Annibale, rejected this approach, 'For thinking to receive solace by meanes of a solitarie life, you fil your selfe ful of ill humors', and urged him 'to cast off solitarinesse' in exchange for 'companie'.[39] Petrarch's 'solitary life' was singled out by Annibale as having informed Guazzo's narrow interpretation of solitude, but this, as we have noted, can refer only to the Petrarch of book 2 and not book 1. Indeed, later in the dialogue Annibale pointed out the defective interpretation of Petrarch advanced by the proponents of solitude. 'I am sure you are not ignorant that Petrarch, notwithstanding all the prayses he attributeth to the solitary life, was not to learne, that without Conversation our life would bee defectuous.' By using the expression 'civil conversation' Guazzo could avoid the difficulty that Petrarch had created for himself, and his readers, by relying on a term, 'solitude' that was so ambivalent.[40]

'Conversation' stood for the complex demands and satisfactions of the bonds that existed between the unrelated, unconstrained, and unequal members of modern society. This is the realm between pure privacy (isolation) and pure public life (politics).[41] Where Castiglione addressed himself to a narrow world of aristocratic courtiers, Guazzo's theme was

> how to behave our selves towardes others, according to the difference of estates, for that it is our hap to come in companie, sometime with the young, sometime with the olde, as soone with Gentlemen, as soone with the baser sorte, now and then with Princes, now and then with private persons, one while with the learned, another while with the ignorant, now with our owne Countriemen, then with straungers, now with the religious, now with the secular, now with men, then with women.[42]

This is why Guazzo's younger contemporary Pierre Charron contrasted solitude not with politics but with 'la vie civile ou sociale'.[43] Where Petrarch had no alternative to 'solitude' when he wished to emphasize the autonomy of the creative life, Guazzo successfully introduced a third term, 'civil conversation', between the political and the solitary, the active and the contemplative lives. The conversation and sociability that Annibale proposed as the solvent of melancholy was identified by Trevor-Roper in his examination of seventeenth-century melancholy as having as its goal self-improvement and rationality.[44]

Guazzo, the character, could bring himself to endorse conversation only *a posteriori* – for the 'ignorant and careless' who so feared being alone with themselves that they preferred any kind of sociability to the occasional moment of solitude.[45] But Annibale consistently emphasized the higher purpose behind conversation. Because someone who left civil society 'putteth upon himselfe a brutish nature', there arose 'the common saying' (actually a distortion of Aristotle, *Politics*, I.i.9) that the solitary person was either beast or god.[46] Even the learned, most likely to live the solitary life, did so only 'for lacke of their like, with whom they may be conversant'. This conversation is defined as 'the giving and taking of the fruits which they have gathered with long travaile'. The scholar's flight was, therefore, only from the ignorant and the irritating, not from humanity as a whole. 'Wherefore I conclude', pronounced Annibale, 'that if the learned and students love solitarinesse for lacke of their like, yet they naturally love the companie of those which are their like'. This was then defended as 'the grave opinion of the Stoikes'.[47] Conversation, Annibale concluded, was 'the full perfection of learning' because it added to one's own that of others.[48]

Conversation as a means to perfection or, in Trevor-Roper's terms, self-improvement and rationality, shapes Guazzo's notion of 'civility'. 'To live civillie', Annibale argued, 'is not sayd in respect of the Cittie, but of the qualities of the minde'.[49] In this one sentence Guazzo has distilled the essence of a reorientation of the notion of excellence away from the necessity of political participation that had made the 'citizen' the exemplary man. 'So I understand civile conversation', Annibale continued, 'not having relation to the Citie, but consideration to the manners and conditions which make it civile'.[50] The city is defined as a space created not by its form of government but by the 'manners and conditions' of its inhabitants.

That this was a new presentation of civil life was acknowledged in the dialogue. Classical authorities were, indeed, of little help for this subject. But, echoing Erasmus' pioneering defence of the legitimacy of the modern age in the *Ciceronianus* of fifty years earlier, Annibale insisted that the truly authentic was that most in keeping with its time. The philosophers who set forth the ancient ways 'if they were living at this daie, woulde in manie thinges reforme their writinges, and conforme them to the customes of the present time'. So it was necessary to leave the 'auncient path, and take the waye which is beaten at this daie'. Hence the focus of conversation on matters 'which in my opinion, are necessarie of the present time'.[51]

Conversation filled the space between friends, but also that between those who could not be friends. The appeal of 'civil conversation' lay in its flexibility, since it offered the like-minded a medium for the pursuit of individual excellence and the unlike a tool for finding common ground. At one extreme lay the academy, peopled by those who, 'agreeing in like studies, and like affections, . . . cannot but take pleasure in one another, and reduce themselves, from the number of many as it were indeed to one united bodie'.[52] At the other lay the city, populated by men of different backgrounds living in the same place for different reasons and having no predisposition to agree. 'Where at this daie', Annibale asked, 'are these true friendships to be found?' In the city, he continued, 'those with whom we are conversant [are] rather well willers than true friends'.[53] So, while civil conversation offered the republic of friends an ideal of easy communication, of the sort later described by Gassendi, it also provided the 'ceremonies' of *politesse* necessary for societies held together by ties of utility and necessity rather than perfect friendship.[54]

The English translator of Guazzo's *Civil Conversation*, George Pettie, actually presented it as an intervention in the discussion of individual excellence that that was conducted as a debate about 'arms *versus* letters'. 'Those which mislike studie or learning in Gentlemen', Pettie begins, 'are some fresh water souldiers, who think that in warre it is the bodie which onlie must beare the brunt of all, not knowing that the bodie is ruled by the mind, & that in all doubtfull and dangerous matters, it is the mind only which is the man'. The image of the soldier whose heroism was of the mind was found in Seneca and animated Lipsius' exactly contemporary *De constantia*. 'Alasse', Petite continued, 'you wil be but ungentle Gentlemen, if you bee no scholars' and 'will do your country no good . . . if you bee no schollers'.[55] The English translator of Guazzo, like that of Gassendi eighty years later, used his publication as a platform from which to urge his (gentlemanly) readers to turn themselves into men of learning. 'Therefore (Gentlemen)', Pettie concluded, 'never denie your selves to bee schollers, never be ashamed to show your learning . . . for it is it which honoreth you, it is onelie it which maketh you men, it is onelie it which maketh you Gentlemen'.[56]

The translation of the *Civil Conversation* into French in 1579, English in 1581, Latin in 1585, and German in 1599 maps the diffusion of these ideas across Europe.[57] Emilio Bonfatti has studied the reception of Guazzo in Germany. Like Annibale, the translator of the first Latin edition (Cologne, 1585) felt constrained to defend civil life against those critics who would use the Bible and Seneca to claim priority for the solitary.[58] In 1602, the second translator, a resident of Amberg and servant of the Calvinist Elector Palatine, situated the book in the context created by the publication of Lipsius' works on government and self-government, *De Politica* and *De Constantia*, both of which had, in the meantime, appeared in German (1599). Heinrich Salmuth suggested that Guazzo's book did not teach speaking only, but the 'precepts of that divine philosophy' which showed each person how to live appropriately to his status and condition.[59]

According to Bonfatti, Salmuth belonged to the social and intellectual world of Stoicism and service with which Lipsius was identified. He contributed celebratory verse to the translation of Lipsius' *Politica* (*Von Unterweisung zum weltlichen Regiment*, 1599).[60] It was the influence of *De constantia*, which begins with a younger character beset by woes and thinking of flight (travel filling the role of solitude), that allowed Salmuth to see a similarity in the opening of Guazzo's book, in the appeal to solitude being answered by an attack on melancholy. The struggle Lipsius presented was between reason and the passions and it is this continuity of theme that Salmuth the translator of Guazzo had recognized. Furthermore, he explained that Guazzo's book also taught how to judge true and false, an 'art of thinking' useful for governing not only the self but also others.[61] As the art of judgement, conversation 'could not improperly be said to be the kernel of moral philosophy'.[62] The *Civil Conversation*, from this point of view, described the social world inhabited by men like *Langius*, the author's spokesman in *De Constantia* and the one who rejected flight, solitude, and melancholy (just like Annibale).[63] If Guazzo had opposed the domain of civil conversation to solitude, this was not to rehearse the old classical dichotomy. For solitude was truly the property only of beasts or gods and was not to be equated with the Petrarchan world of conversation.[64]

Chappuys, who translated Guazzo into French, also translated G. B. Giraldi Cinthio's *Tre dialoghi della vita civile* (1565; Paris, 1583). The French title emphasized, as had Palmieri's translator more implicitly, that it was the early education in civil life that was the most useful for gentlemen and women: *Dialogues . . . touchant la vie civile contenans la nourriture du premier age: l'instruction de la Ieunesse & de l'homme propre à gouverner soy mesme* (1583).[65] The reference to self-governing repeats Palmieri's nod to self-control.

Giraldi's English translator, Lodovico Bryskett, also stressed that this was a book destined for 'all the young Gentlemen of England'. But he specifically distinguished between civil and political excellence. The 'civil' in *A Discourse of Civill Life: containing the Ethike Part of Morall Philosophie* was kept separate from the 'Politike part of Morall Philosophie' about which he claimed to have prepared a separate treatise.[66] In the text, Giraldi explained that the discussion was not about rulers but was only concerned with the 'vita civile, di huomo privato', 'la vie civile, de l'homme privé' or, in Bryskett's words, 'the civill life of private men'.[67] As with Guazzo and Charron, 'civil' was intended to refer to a social world that was neither wholly political nor utterly private. The civil life of a private man, then, related to man as a social, *but not political*, creature. This is precisely the domain that comes alive in Gassendi's history of Peiresc.

In the final dialogue, Giraldi argued that friendship and conversation were the central features of this civil part of a private life. For friendship described the elective relation that drew individuals together in subpolitical organization, while conversation described the medium, or the mortar, that then held them together.[68] 'Civil happiness' demanded both. One could live without a variety of 'external things', like wealth and, perhaps, even health, but not without friends.[69] The distinction between friends and 'secondary' goods explains why friendship was so praised at this time. Its rational and virtuous foundation was contrasted with love's passionate transports and, by extension, with all other passing fancies. The bias in favour of the rational control of the passions could hardly have seemed better expressed socially than in friendship. Giraldi even proposed friendship, rather than politics, as the alternative to the solitude of beasts and gods.[70]

Another Italian treatise on civil life and self-perfection that was published in 1579 (in Venice) and appeared in French translation in 1582 was Paolo Paruta's *Della perfezzione della vita politica*.[71] This is a work of much greater, and more explicit, philosophical sophistication than the others we have examined; if they looked back towards Castiglione this one evoked Machiavelli and Aristotle. Paruta was a Venetian who belonged to the generation of 'young men' (*giovani*) who undertook to reorient Venice towards a more aggressive defence of her internal and external interests.[72] His treatise is well known as an example of Venetian republican writing. And yet, the dialogue form allowed Paruta, who later came to be of two minds on the matter, to present powerful justifications for a life in which self-perfection no longer required political participation.[73] If Guazzo's Annibale clarifies the relationship between pure solitude and conversation, Paruta's dialogue defines, at the other end of the spectrum, that between conversation and politics. We can locate the views of Guazzo in favour of isolation from humanity and Paruta's ambassadors' view in favour of total commitment to public life at the extremes of this discourse.[74]

In the dialogue the central confrontation was between the Bishop of Ceneda, who emphasized the precariousness of public life and therefore the danger of making it a necessary and sufficient means to excellence, and the two ambassadors, principally Suriano, who feared the social consequences of *not* stressing the primacy of public service. Thus, when Ceneda suggested that the moral perils of life lived in the public eye made it difficult 'to cultivate our soul', Suriano replied that this was opening the door to *otium*, ominously called 'the soul's death'.[75] This fear of idleness was inherited from ancient writers. Ambassador Dandolo – his title, like the Bishop's, adumbrates his position in the debate – even argued that the good legislator had to use all the means at his disposal to extirpate *otium* from the city, whence grew all its troubles.[76] Ceneda, in turn, defended the 'secure port of the honest *otium* of a private and virtuous life' to which all those engaged in public affairs, and therefore exposed to the 'high seas driven by winds', would gladly fly. Suriano, in response, denied the very possibility of a virtuous life separate from the city.[77] Even tranquillity was said to be attainable only in political society.[78] Ceneda replied that this necessity of public service made for the 'servitude of the self which is a perpetual companion of civil life'.[79] Public service, in short, meant private slavery.[80]

The most interesting reply to Ceneda's vague Stoicism was put into the mouth of the other cleric, Filippo Mocenigo, Bishop of Cyprus. He adopted the Augustinian position that unassisted human reason was incapable of finding its own way to virtue.[81] Political organization was necessary, though without intrinsic excellence, and the sage could not, therefore, be obliged to devote his best energies to its maintenance.[82] From this perspective it could even be affirmed that there was nothing more contrary to felicity than political service and that the sage was much better off minding his own business and trying as hard as possible to be self-sufficient.[83] In this dialogue Paruta had introduced three perspectives on the relation of politics to self-perfection: the republican for whom it was essential, the Stoic for whom it was harmful, and the Augustinian for whom it was necessary but fundamentally irrelevant.

These were the views of civil life outlined in the important Italian treatises that were translated into French in the years just after Peiresc's birth. They provided Frenchmen of the early seventeenth century with a conceptual vocabulary for describing an ideal lifestyle. Gassendi drew on this literature in writing his book and he could rely on its familiarity to his audience of readers. This Italian approach, which had such a rich northern European history, was also disseminated through an image:

Cesare Ripa's representation of Conversatione in the second edition of his famous, and many-times reissued, *Iconologia* (Rome, 1603). In it, we can see how the themes of friendship, conversation, and constancy already cohered *circa* 1600.

Conversatione is figured as a young man of smiling, buoyant countenance, wearing green, crowned by a laurel wreath, bearing in his left hand a caduceus of myrtle intertwined with flowering pomegranate topped by a pair of tongues and in his right hand, extended in greeting, a banner with the motto 'Veh Soli' (plate 4). Ripa explained as follows. Conversation describes the way in which friends interact familiarly ('l'uso domestico'); but since friends are not family they do not live together, leading us to understand 'domestic' in contrast to both household and 'public'. He is male because conversation was more appropriate to men and was depicted as a youth because Aristotle declared that young men made the closest friendships since they most delighted in living together ('vivere insieme') and judged nothing according to the standard of the merely 'useful'. In the last edition to which Ripa contributed (1625), he affirmed that 'conversation is human society and through such gratifying interaction minds are refreshed'.[84]

Conversation helped human beings express what was beautiful about life. The green garment evoked the colour that made birds sing, just as conversation moved the soul to happiness and virtue; hence the laurel wreath. The myrtle and pomegranate growing together were signs that from conversation came union and 'true friendship': these plants were mutually beneficial and in the wild would grow towards each other from a great distance. The plants growing together are also figured in Ripa's emblem of friendship (plate 5) which, in turn, drew on the emblem of constancy (plate 6) and expressed the strong relationship between these two ideas. Ripa explicitly contrasted the natural sociability of mankind that was manifested in friendship with the attitude of the world's Timons who denounced the unsociable nature of human beings. Finally, the tongues that crowned the caduceus signified that nature gave tongue to man so that he could express his feelings to others and bring forth society. The man's bent knee and outstretched arm were a sign that conversation bred good manners and behaviour. The motto of King Solomon from Proverbs damned those who preferred to be alone.

In crafting his *Life*, Gassendi relied on this repertoire of ideas by, of, and for aristocrats. But his presentation was also shaped, and in its detail perhaps more so, by discussions of how to live that emerged from within the scholarly world itself. The decisive feature of Gassendi's account, the link between sociability and learning on the one hand, and between these and a philosophical disposition inspired by neo-Stoicism on the other, put the emphasis on issues raised by other scholars in their discussions of the relationship between learning and virtue.

Peiresc's close friend, Girolamo Aleandro, for example, used the language of civil life and the courtly setting to sketch an ideal of scholarly comportment. In a discourse 'Of the way in which the sages and *letterati* of the Court must hold themselves so as not to be transformed by the Court (as if by a new Circe) into the semblance of beasts' we see how stoicizing self-control and learned sociability could be drawn together in the portrait of a scholar – an Italian illustration of Evans' 'Lipsius paradigm'. Aleandro explained that the 'marvellous herb' eaten by Odysseus to inoculate him against Circe's magic was nothing else 'if not self-knowledge' since without it men lapsed into bestiality.[85] Those who pushed others to their ruin, or who hated the idleness they nevertheless indulged, or who spent their efforts 'to buy the wind', or who served diligently and uncritically were all in different ways chasing a 'vain happiness' that made each the architect of his own misery.[86]

Self-knowledge and knowledge of the world ('il conoscimento e di se stesso, e delle cose') were the keys to liberation. Only because the scholar-sage understood 'the secret force of ambition' and the way it insidiously bound with 'chains of desire' could he remain free from those 'insane appetites'.[87] The practice of learning made the scholar able 'to weigh himself with the goldsmith's scale' and so remain free from the feelings of vanity and privilege that were invariably worked upon by manipulative rulers.[88] The claim that erudition could promote self-knowledge was a basic tenet for all those who praised scholars – and was echoed loudly by Gassendi. Like Seneca's great man who was able to live with amphorae of clay as if silver, and those of silver as if clay, only someone at ease with himself, according to Aleandro, could live amidst the clamour of a public life.[89] Rational self-control offered a way to enjoy 'a sweet tranquillity amidst the perturbations, a clear sky amidst the clouds, a secure place amidst the storms'. The wise man was content to know that the greatest honour given to man 'was to know how to rule and govern himself'.[90]

Agostino Mascardi, like Aleandro a humanist secretary, and best known for his *De arte historica* (1636) – which Peiresc praised highly in a letter to him of 7 March 1637 – also took the theme of the scholar at court for a series of academic discourses.[91] The political man could not be 'master of himself' ('padrone di se stesso') – hence the importance of having learned, well-read men at court who could provide the ruler with the education he had no time for.[92] Mascardi called this group an 'academy', and described it as a 'well-stocked arsenal' from which the ruler could find whatever he needed 'to defend against the blows of adverse fortune and to fight against the rebellion of the passions'.[93] A group, or 'accademia', was more useful than a single man because of its diversity of experience and knowledge.

Mascardi's fellow Genoese, Anton Giulio Brignole Sale, described the academy (in real life they were both members of the Accademia degl'Addormentati) as an essential instrument in preparing young nobles for a life of governing by purging 'their passions of all vice'.[94] He characterized this political education in terms of a self-control that aimed at moral improvement rather than heaping up erudition. As opposed to those who wanted to know how many oarsmen propelled Ulysses' boat, or whether Homer wrote the *Iliad* before or after the *Odyssey* – the kinds of questions that Donne parodied in the *Second Anniversary* – Brignole Sale explained that 'we study to become better, not more learned' ('studiam noi di divenir miglior non più eruditi').[95]

In a fascinating analysis of Aristotle on tyranny (*Politics*, bk 5), Mascardi had asked why tyrants were scared of academies. What was there so to fear from a group of learned men?[96] Academies were the embodiment of wisdom, friendship, and courage, as was expressed by the ancients who assembled under the tutelary guidance of Athena, Mercury, and Hercules. Tyrants feared that these gatherings would generate those 'most noble twins, generosity and friendship' – precisely what Gassendi had praised most effusively in Peiresc. 'Friendship', Mascardi wrote, 'is conceived, born, and grows in academies, which is as much to say, civil life reaches its perfection in academies'.[97] Because tyrants followed the precept *Divide & Impera*, institutions that bred solidarity appeared to him as threats. The advantage of the modern academy over the learned feasts of antiquity – *symposia*, *convivia* – was that it rested upon a common intellectual foundation and was not called into existence by the presence of food and wine. Hence, it was in academies that one found the 'true friendships that were otherwise so rare'.[98] The academy's strength was its unity in diversity. Mascardi called it 'a rich market of virtue' where individuals exchanged the 'goods of the intellect' and so enriched each other. The 'sequestered life' – the *vita solitaria* strictly construed – could not match these reciprocal advantages of intellectual exchange.[99]

The philosophical foundation of this view of the scholar as a member of a civil society emerges as the key concern of Flavio Querenghi. He was Professor of Moral Philosophy at the University of Padua and a nephew of the more famous poet and papal secretary, Antonio Querenghi. He published Latin commentaries on Aristotle and also an Italian *Discorsi morali politici e naturali* (1644).[100] His circle of friends overlapped with that of Peiresc but there is no indication of any contact between them. The seventy years that separate Guazzo from Flavio Querenghi show no diminution in the appeal of the model of a community of friends drawn together by a shared desire for self-perfection. If Guazzo emphasized more the role of speech in this space between household and court, Querenghi stressed self-knowledge. In this book, civility is presented as a pursuit of excellence definitively relocated from the sphere of politics to that of select sociability. The book's content, a series of essays on subjects that range from control of the passions to benevolence to the lamps found in ancient burial caves, is bracketed by an extraordinary printed correspondence that presents the reader with a ready-made reception history (many of the essays had circulated in manuscript for some time) designed to echo the author's arguments.[101]

The themes of the *Discorsi*, adumbrated in its lead essay 'The Alchemy of the Soul's Passions or, The Way to Convert our Regrets into Delights' ('Alchimia delle passioni dell'animo overo Modo di convertire i nostri dispiaceri in diletti'), are the ones we have already encountered: the excellence that was characterized by self-control, rational coping with adversity, friendship and the attenuated relation of political action to individual worth. The examples of emotional turmoil are prompted by the common disasters: death, especially of friends, and betrayal in interest-laden court intrigue, especially by friends. Querenghi explained that his study was, in fact, drawn from life and not books.[102]

The echoes of Montaigne are everywhere in this book from its title – the same as Montaigne's in the 1590 Ferrara edition – to its endmatter. In the preface to his readers, Querenghi explained that he was publishing these essays that had long circulated among his friends in manuscript because of their demand to have something of him to preserve

> so that my fate is not like that of fish who leave no trace of themselves after passing through water. And if the men of letters have no need for my discourses, at least my dear friends desire a portrait of me from nature before my impending departure. It is for those who love me that I write . . . We are, indeed, happy to have many friends.[103]

In the notice to *his* readers Montaigne had explained that he published for 'the private benefit of my friends and kinsmen so that, having lost me (as they must do soon) they can find here again some traits of my character and of my humours. They will thus keep their knowledge of me more full, more alive.'[104]

After the last of the *Discorsi*, Querenghi printed letters from friends commenting on the work. These made direct reference to Montaigne. The famous historian, Enrico Davila, who had lived in France, wrote to Querenghi in 1620 that he had 'perfectly imitated' the style of Montaigne. 'I knew Montaigne', Davila continued; he 'had a bit of learning, but nothing profound. He had his own style, but it was plain. He was, in the end, more soldier than learned. But you, who bear learning and letters from all of the sciences, who aid nature with art, surpass him by

a great distance.'[105] Another correspondent, in returning an Italian translation of Montaigne's *Essays* to Querenghi, hedged the comparison just
a little: 'I predict that our descendants, considering the conformity of
your genius and that of this worthy writer, will say one day: either
Montaigne Querenghizes or Querengo Montaignizes' ('O Montagnes
Querengheggia, ò Querengo Montagneggia').[106]

The printed letters reflect the importance attached to friendship as the
prized social expression of the well-composed soul. What characterized
this interaction was the same 'readiness of spirit' ('prontezza della
volontà') that drove beneficence. Neither friend nor ruler could ever be
satisfied by actions that did not emerge 'dall'interno del cuore'. Those
who acted for reasons of utility were suitable servants of tyrants but no
friends. Beneficence could not accommodate itself to the thought of
making a commerce of men as of sheep, creatures who had no end but
to be used by others. Like Gassendi, Querenghi described the uncondi-
tional giving of benefits, in emulation of God, as the mark of true
friendship.[107]

The sentiment of friendship and attendant obligation fills the book
and reflects its central place in the civil world of sodality.[108] When a
friend who was leaving Padua for Rome asked for a copy of the *Discorsi*, Querenghi sent along the text accompanied by a letter suggesting
that during their separation 'you could, though the exchange is unequal,
converse with my writings instead of me and take counsel, at times, with
them'.[109] The *Discorsi* were, in short, 'a portrait of me drawn from life'
which represented the 'humours of my brain', 'my ideas about civil life',
and 'the duties of good friendship'.[110]

The friendship and conversation that characterized Querenghi's *vita
civile* offered a world of consolation to compensate for, if not balance,
the reality of change. He took up Montaigne's insistence on change as
the only constant and, like Montaigne, located this inconstancy within
man himself. 'But man, too, is naturally mutable, wherefore what need
has he to await external changes if he is changeable in himself and is
seen to be constant in nothing else than in changing ideas'.[111] If disturbed by the world, Querenghi suggested, it was time to return to the
'anticamera' (Montaigne's famous 'arrière boutique') and remind oneself
of how things really worked.[112] Expecting permanent felicity only
doomed one to disappointment. Reflection showed that 'you have not
lost anything because from the beginning things were as they are now,
but you didn't notice'. The connection between understanding and happiness was mediated by the self-knowledge that Querenghi expressed, as
did his great Spanish contemporary, Baltasar Gracián, by the term *desengaño*. 'To be dis-illusioned even once is not without usefulness' and could
even 'be counted amongst the happiest of successes', since until one

learned this 'one will not know how to accommodate one's soul to the change in this friend, or that prince'.[113]

Knowledge of the world's nature banished fear and slavish servitude to convention in exactly the same way that the antiquaries' research into the origin of the pagan gods was the best possible unmasking of their human origin.[114] The understood world was a demystified world and, to that extent, relieved the individual of the sensation of being the particular victim of a malevolent fortune: scorpions, after all, were supposed to sting.[115] Nature, Querenghi wrote, was like a coachman in whose hands a rider placed himself. 'He who gets on should not think, or hope, to get off, or decide where to stop in this life. He should simply say: "I come".[116] That this essay was written to console himself for the death of a friend highlights its very practical character. The wisest man, the Duke of Urbino wrote to Querenghi, was the one who 'voluntarily accommodated to the necessity of nature'.[117]

Self-knowledge was, however, only a first step towards the self-control that was truly heroic. Nothing else in this world was so worthy of praise. 'If one has the ambition to be a ruler, why not command the passions, which are powerful – and rebellious – vassals?'[118] Without the ability to dominate the passions the individual, like the ruler of a kingdom, would lose control. The solution offered by Querenghi was not to extirpate the passions, which would be 'a Stoic cruelty' – note the echo of Montaigne's and Sarpi's 'pestiferous' Catonian vice – but to use the passions to do the bidding of reason, a suggestion offered by other representative neo-Stoics such as du Vair, Charron, and John Eliot.[119] Indeed, Querenghi argued that since 'commercio humano' was most insulted by 'the haughtiness of the rich, perfidy of false friends, jealousy and ill will', the only way to triumph over them was to play at being rich with the wealthy, astute with the perfidious, and malevolent with the malign.[120]

Like Lipsius and Montaigne, Querenghi offered a philosophy of consolation for those committed to a worldly life and so at risk from the world. He rejected the stark dichotomy of active and contemplative, sociable and solitary. Life 'in Villa', he wrote, referred to a mixture of action and contemplation not too distant from the world of exchange and civil comforts.[121] This harked back to Petrarch's notion of 'solitude'. Like Guazzo, Querenghi suggested that a society of men that gathered together should be called civil conversation. Because not everyone had the time to devote to these sorts of studies, or the ability to take advantage of them – as Aleandro had asserted – Querenghi sought, as he explained to Cardinal Capponi, 'to formulate a compendium of compendia and with two short and simple precepts to instruct men in *commercio* and *conversatione civile*'.[122]

Querenghi's highly personal evocation of the 'civil life of a private man' illuminates the relationship between *constantia*, conversation, and its lived practice in a circle of provincial friends, aristocrats and scholars all, in the middle of the seventeenth century.[123] Peiresc's learned sociability was formed in one such circle, that of Pinelli in Padua *c.*1600, and lived in similar ones in Paris, Aix, and Belgentier. Querenghi follows one line of a tradition about civil life whose key text is Guazzo's *La civile conversatione* and which was sometimes elaborated in great detail, as in Gassendi's *Life* of Peiresc.[124]

This brief survey has, I hope, shed light on the sources and themes available to be drawn upon by Gassendi. But if we wish to understand something of Peiresc's *fortuna* and of the fate of the ideal he embodied we need to look at a different application of civility and its practice that crystallized in the last decade of Peiresc's life. Its inspiration came from Castiglione and was oriented to forms of external display rather than internal application. Lipsius' contemporary, Edmund Spenser, who explained that the purpose of the *Faerie Queene* was 'to fashion a gentleman or noble person in vertuous and gentle discipline', located this education in courts.

> Of Court it seemes men Courtesie doe call,
> For that it there most useth to abound;
> And well beseemeth that in Princes hall
> That vertue should be plentifully found,
> Which of all goodly manners is the ground,
> And roote of civill conversation.[125]

Spenser's genealogy bypassed the learned world and this account, made famous by Elias' link between a 'civilizing process' and 'court society', has influenced the most recent histories of civility in Europe. By the late 1620s, in France, the process Spenser described had been achieved. The appeal of conversation-as-courtesy overtook the ideal of learned sociability and the death knell had been sounded for the scholar as an example of individual excellence.

This clash of ideals can nowhere better be observed than in the Paris of Louis XIII, the European capital of talk. Its poles were the Cabinet Dupuy and the hôtel de Rambouillet. The Cabinet Dupuy, which Peiresc frequented when in Paris and with which he became, after his departure in 1623, a 'corresponding member', stood for the 'old' France of Henri IV, both politically and culturally. Here, the high parliamentary magistracy and the learned exchanged grave conversation in the spirit of Jacques-Auguste de Thou, the *genius loci*. This was an entirely male world that despised courtliness and was deeply wary of politics because so enmeshed in it. In short, it was the very image of being *un*fashionable;

in an age of chic the most unforgivable of offences. John Earle, in his exactly contemporary caricature of 'The Antiquary' (1629) mocked this conspicuously bad taste, complaining that the antiquary's dress was that 'which is the eldest out of fashion'.[126] Indeed, one of the most striking features of Frans Francken's *c.*1625 painting of a conversation between a couple of aristocrats and a scholar is how differently they are dressed.

The world of the *salons* was the antithesis of the Cabinet Dupuy. Courtiers, writers, *beaux esprits* and, most importantly, women, frequented the gatherings held in the blue bedroom of the palace of Mme Rambouillet after 1620. Here, the social composition was mixed, women actually took leading roles, and there was an express emphasis on *not* being too learned. Everything was about being *à la mode*, a fashion for being fashionable that Rubens – who knew this world at first hand – captured perfectly in his dazzling *Conversatie à la mode* (or, *The Garden of Love*) (*c.*1635) (plate 7), recently described as 'a modish group of people in fashionable social interaction or engaging in agreeable and easeful interchange or discourse, with women as the center of interest'. Nicolas Faret's many times reprinted and adapted *L'Honnête Homme* (1633) is the Baedeker to this society.[127]

What makes the contrast between the Dupuy and Rambouillet circles so illuminating is that in both the emphasis was on friendship, conversation, letter-writing, and civility, yet these signified very different things. Few people – Jean Chapelain was an exception – moved in both. The differences crystallized in the *querelle* triggered by the publication of Guez de Balzac's *Premières Lettres* (1624). Lines were drawn separating the culture of the old France (Henri IV) and the new (Louis XIII). Peiresc and Dupuy paid close attention to the *querelle* and Jacques Dupuy furnished intellectual support to Balzac's antagonist, Dom Jean Goulu, for his *Lettres de Phyllarque* (1627).[128] They, like others who opposed Balzac, were disturbed that culture had become entertainment, all 'about recreation and pleasure'.[129]

This same word appears in the subtitle of Faret's *L'Honnête Homme*: *l'art de plaire à la court*. Of course, others, like Gabriel Naudé, a humanist secretary, frequenter of the Cabinet Dupuy and a friend of Peiresc, also thought about the formation of the *honnête homme*. He composed a reading list that included the greatest hits of the neo-Stoic revival: Seneca's *Letters*, Marcus Aurelius' *Meditations*, Montaigne's *Essais*, and Pierre Charron's *De la sagesse*.[130] But there is no way that an *honnête homme* raised on this intellectual diet could have conceived of his training as the art of pleasing. And yet it is perhaps too quick to suggest that the difference between these two groups lay solely in the contrast between improvement and entertainment. There is also a different notion of improvement at issue. The members of the Dupuy circle followed the traditional, grave, stoicizing view that emphasized sociability as a means to self-perfection, while those who met at the hôtel de Rambouillet made the perfection of social forms itself the purpose of social life.

Comparison of Faret and Naudé can be carried still further. Each of them published proposals for establishing what we might call an 'institute for advanced study' independent of the university structure and dedicated to higher learning – and both were successful. Naudé's *Avis pour dresser un bibliothèque* (1627) suggested the most effective way of mobilizing humanist book learning. Then the librarian of M. de Mesmes, royal councillor and president of the Parlement of Paris, he was to become librarian of the Bibliothèque Royale under Cardinal Mazarin. Faret's *Projet de l'Académie, pour servir de préface à ses status* (1634) sketched a model academy for the *honnête homme* which institutionalized exactly those differences that separated the *salon* from the Cabinet Dupuy. Faret distinguished between the learned, who were to be systematically excluded, and those possessing an appropriate genius and art of speaking. His proposal formed the basis of the Académie française.[131]

Where in this landscape do we find Peiresc? What was his attitude to court life? His descriptions of Belgentier as 'ce desert', or 'cette solitude champestre', must be balanced by the frequent protestations that he was swamped by parliamentary business.[132] While not an important public figure – though Peiresc certainly took seriously his job as a *parlementaire* – he obviously did not live a private, solitary life. When Peiresc described himself as living in an 'exile', cut off from all 'commerce and communication' as profoundly as if surrounded by 'the sands of Libya' and therefore all the more dependent on the regular correspondence of the Dupuy brothers in Paris, we need to remember that this was a highly rhetorical means of expressing his gratitude to them. Their letters enabled him 'to be transported in a moment' into their midst, and even into the King's Louvre. But – and this is very important – the provincial life with its drudgeries and danger of isolation was his choice. He preferred to have 'a great tranquillity of the spirit' even if it meant relying on others for news.[133] The letters from Paris made it possible for him to live in peace while remaining a spectator of 'the theatre of the Court, as if the acts playing there were going on in front of our windows'. What is more, for *intermezzi* they offered him 'all of the most worthy things happening in England, the Low Countries, in Germany, and in almost all of Europe, without our moving from our cabinet'.[134] In another letter he described this drama of the court as a 'tragedy' and quoted du Vair's regret that he could not continue viewing court life at a distance, from Provence, 'like a comedy much more agreeable to watch from afar than when one finds oneself caught up in it'.[135]

When it came to courts, Peiresc knew whereof he spoke. In a series of letters to Bouchard and Claude Menestrier in Rome, he provided a 'how-to' guide to being a courtier that was just as sharp-eyed as Aleandro's or Mascardi's. Necessary at all times, he wrote, was 'a marvellous reserve' because 'one could not know how to march too softly when it is a question of insinuating oneself into the good graces of these men'. To whatever sort of employ Bouchard was summoned he ought to accept 'with all the honour and reverence possible'. Above all it was necessary not to be too trusting so that 'other, more artificial, men not take too much advantage of you'. In the face of hostility, competing self-interests, and disappointments Peiresc counselled caution, prudence, and even, sometimes, dissimulation.[136]

Peiresc's correspondence also offers valuable evidence for the existence of these separate worlds in which *constantia* and *la mode* represented extremes. Maurice Magendie drew on some of this in his enduring study of 'politesse mondaine' in the first half of the seventeenth century in France. In one letter Peiresc remarked on the ignorance of the *beaux esprits* who gravitated to the court, in another he noted that his friend Gassendi 'was not brought up on the air of the Court in order to acquire that courtesy in which they excel there', and in another, worried that once someone had got used to 'the ceremonies essential among those men of court' it would be extremely difficult 'to get him to relax them the least bit'.[137] Yet, even Peiresc recognized that the force of fashion was such that 'one must, sometimes, in matters indifferent', 'accommodate a little' and so when sending letters to M. and Mme de Sourdys and to Mme la Mareschale de Roquelaure he inquired of their colour preferences in order to wrap his letters in the right shade of silk![138] Similarly, the changing fashion in hats from long and pointed to low and round served him as a metaphor for precisely those things indifferent to which one could accommodate without damage to principles.[139] Peiresc's high praise of Barclay's novel *Argenis* – he described himself as 'ravished and transported' by it – reflected a thorough familiarity with the courtly world to which it constantly and covertly referred.[140] Peiresc used the terms 'honnêteté' and 'douceur de conversation' and invoked the term *honnête homme* – even using it to describe Nicolas Faret himself, whom he had met in Paris.[141]

Peiresc's reaction to Théophraste Renaudot's importuning that he serve as a regular correspondent to his *Gazette* highlights the differences he perceived between learned and polite society. Peiresc noted that his own letters contained for the most part nothing but 'nouvelles de livres ou curiositez d'anticailles' – not the sort of stuff he thought Renaudot's audience would want to read.[142] He explained that 'I have become indifferent to news of the world, my dominant passion having always been for news of books and other curiosities as much of nature as of antiquities'.[143] It was only when Renaudot threatened to stop sending him the *Gazette* because he had not written and then, as Peiresc suspected, withheld the issue reporting on the verdict of the Inquisition against his friend Galileo that Peiresc exploded. Renaudot was trying to impose a 'tyranny' on his correspondents and tried 'to sell his trifles too dearly, whose price he himself lowers in debasing and vulgarizing them as he does, with his addresses to the "little" people'.[144]

If Peiresc was not interested in serving Renaudot and his audience, he also found himself on the other side of the decisive schism that separated the supporters and defenders of Guez de Balzac. Reporting on breaking developments in April of 1627 Jacques Dupuy explained to Peiresc that 'these books are not at all to your taste; that is why I have not wanted to send them to you without your advice'. 'These men', he continued, referring to Balzac and his supporters, were puffed up with 'vanity' and given to 'hyperbole and extravagant ways of speaking'.[145] Although Peiresc admitted that he was 'hardly curious about these sorts of books', for the fame of Balzac alone he wanted to have a look.[146] Peiresc approved of P. Goulu puncturing 'the arrogance of his Antagonist'.[147] 'Ordinary simplicity', Peiresc wrote, 'is worth thirty times more than affected language'.[148]

Peiresc's critical view of Balzac was reciprocated. In a letter to Chapelain of 1 May 1637 Balzac announced that he never understood 'the extraordinary merit of this Mr de Peiresc' and that Chapelain was 'the first who valued him to me at such a high price'. Their mutual friend, the writer François Malherbe, had spoken of him as an 'extraordinarily curious man, a great lover of relations and news, a great researcher of medals and manuscripts, a great possessor of knowledge about foreign lands, a great admirer of all the doctors of the Academy of Leyden'. But all this, Balzac concluded for emphasis, 'does not make a great man'. As if to turn the knife further, he observed that there was a difference between 'heroic' virtues and those of ordinary people, between 'glory' and 'good reputation'. The former belonged to Peiresc's mentor de Thou, the latter to Peiresc himself.[149]

Alone among leading cultural arbiters Balzac abstained from the general lament occasioned by Peiresc's death. In a letter to Jean Chapelain of January 1640 Balzac remarked that 'Monsieur de la Rochefoucauld had never heard spoken of your Mr de Peiresc, and perhaps other men who are neither so barbarous nor ignorant do not know him any better'.[150] It was in reply that Chapelain posited a distinction between Paris' two cultural worlds. It was no surprise that M. de la Rochefoucauld had not heard of Peiresc, he noted, because he had nothing in common with Peiresc, who was 'a true and solid savant' and who would have regarded La Rochefoucauld's works 'as amusements rather than occupations useful and worthy of a serious man'. For all that Peiresc was unknown to this sort of man, he 'did not cease to be a hero of his kind', suggesting that at least the most perceptive contemporary critics recognized that one could now speak of two distinct cultures.[151] The later 'Quarrel of the Ancients and the Moderns', which was to have such a devastating impact on the cultural prestige of the antiquary, is adumbrated in these differing perceptions of Peiresc.

The growth of *salons* represents the triumph of a different sort of civil conversation. The philosophical dimension stressed by Guazzo, Peiresc, and Querenghi was diluted to make these ideas suitable for a social context in which civility served either as an end in itself or as an instrument for the achievement of worldly success. 'Pedant' stood for those unable to make the kind of conversation that could hold the attention of the worldly. In the shift away from the learned academy the purpose of like-minded sociability, namely the improvement of the mind and perfection of the person, was displaced and the scholar knocked off his pedestal. *Honnêteté*, redefined as *savoir-faire* (or, if you will, Faret rather than Naudé), served as an answer to questions about *vera nobilitas* without requiring much by way of erudition.[152] As Balzac himself wrote, conversation could 'make one an *honneste homme* without the aid of the Greeks or the Romans'.[153]

The power of this French cultural invention is one of the basic facts of modern European history and paved the way for the lasting appeal of French clothing, French food, and, above all, the French language. In England taste-makers like Richard Steele and Joseph Addison presented this new style of 'polite' living in their essay journals the *Guardian*, the *Tatler*, and the *Spectator* and explicitly acknowledged their desire to broaden the audience for these French mores: to bring philosophy 'out of the Closets and Libraries, Schools and Colleges, to dwell in Clubs and Assemblies, at Tea-Tables and in Coffee-Houses'.[154] Their Scottish contemporaries, meanwhile, learned the lesson that a life of virtue – albeit less severe than Peiresc's own practice – was possible within commercial society and independent of the worlds of business, politics, and fashion.[155] The third Earl of Shaftesbury viewed conversation as the source of a self-improvement that was defined, in very 'Peireskean' terms, as a 'freedom from our passions and low interests'. While having much in common with other theorists of a content-free politeness, Shaftesbury's Stoic stamp could not be effaced.[156] Similarly, an emphasis on the perfecting power of conversation is retained in Germany where, as Wilhelm Kühlmann has shown, French *honnêteté* was modified by the Spanish ideal of the *discreto* so as to exclude both the desiccated university professor and the foppish *galant*.[157] The spread of the values associated with civil conversaton led Eric Auerbach, in the decade before the Second World War, to see in the *salons* of Louis XIV the creation of the same public that Jürgen Habermas, in the decade after, would discover in the coffee-houses of Restoration London.[158]

In 1765 Father Cesare Orlandi commemorated this new world in the second volume of his celebratory edition of Ripa's *Iconologia*. Among the new emblems that Orlandi commissioned to maintain the work's time-liness was 'Conversazione Moderna' (plate 8). It depicted a young couple, both in white, dressed to kill, and standing in a handsomely appointed *salon*. The woman is being helped on to a throne by the man, and holds a sceptre in her right hand topped with an all-seeing eye. In his left the man holds an open pouch that is spilling coins. They are depicted as young and attractive, Orlandi explains, because 'modern conversation' was practiced by the young and was stimulated by appearances. The regal clothing represents the power of conversation in the world and the throne indicates that in this realm women ruled and men were born to serve. The white garments signified honest joy, integrity, and modesty, 'a virtue universally necessary for noble, civil conversations'.[159] The sceptre was another mark of royalty, and the eye indicated that conver-sation demanded wisdom and prudence. The pouch spilling money signified that vast sums were poured out on account of this social prac-tice. The final detail is telling. The disused and damaged books lying about showed the contempt in which the practitioners of modern con-versation held learning, whether of the 'sciences' or even of the noble arts ('arti cavalleresche') – a dying echo of the 'Arms versus Letters' debate. Modern folk, Orlandi suggests, gave up their studies for a life of consuming.

Orlandi's 'modern conversation' refers to what Addison had described, half a century earlier, as 'a very great revolution' in manners. Addison singled out 'unconstrained Carriage, and a certain Openness of Behav-iour'; Orlandi wrote of the practice of nobles and the 'more polite and distinguished citizens' to meet in mixed company early in the evening to pass several hours 'in games, or balls or other similar merriments'. 'Most powerful' were the reasons that led him to wish 'totally to condemn' this practice – these can be inferred from the caricature. He was deeply uncomfortable with the dominant role of women and the decline in learning's fortunes. Still Orlandi equivocated. 'But upon reflecting on the just reasons by which it was established, and the good things that were derived from it and ought to be derived, I find myself constrained not to base my conclusions on this.'[160] Since the primary purpose of sociability was 'to tame men given over entirely to bloodshed, to make gentle the uncouth and to take profligate youths from their infernal noctural intrigues' – in short, the same task of educating gentlemen that inspired the generation of Montaigne, Guazzo, and Lipsius – he could do no less than defend 'modern conversation' against those Timons who wanted to preserve the earth for beasts.[161] 'Le doux commerce', the civilizing impact of polite and female conversation, it is implied, might actually outweigh the benefits of a learned society whose golden age at the beginning of the seventeenth century had nevertheless failed to bring about an end to civil war and religious persecution.

3

THE ANCIENT CONSTITUTION AND THE ANTIQUARIAN

Peiresc in Politics

WRITING THE HISTORY OF POLITICAL THOUGHT

IN THE PALACE OF TEMPERANCE there rose a tower that 'likest is unto that heavenly towre, / That God hath built for his owne blessed bowre'. In the tower's three most important rooms lived three sages, 'the wisest men, I weene, that lived in their ages', whose 'task was to counsel faire Alma, how to governe well'. The first of them could see into the future. He lived in a room painted with shapes of things 'such as in the world were never yit, / Ne can devized be of mortall Wit'. The second sage advised on matters present. The walls of his room were covered with pictures 'Of Magistrates, of courts, of tribunals, / Of commen wealthes, of states, of pollicy, / Of lawes, of iudgements, and of decretals; / And artes, all science, all Philosophy'. Finally, in 'th'hindmost room', 'ruinous and old', sat the third man, old, 'halfe blind, And all decrepit in his feeble corse, / Yet lively vigour rested in his mind, / And recompenst him with a better scorse: / Weake body well is chang'd for minds redoubled forse'. He *was* history. 'His chamber all was hanged about with rolles, / And old records from auncient times deriv'd, / Some made in books, some in long parchment scrolles, / That were all worme-eaten, and full of canker holes.' The old man sat amidst the rolls 'Tossing and turning them withouten end'. The visiting knights examined the 'Antique Registeres' and chanced upon two books, one called *Briton moniments* and the other '*Antiquitie of Faerie* lond' from which they began to read.[1]

Canto IX of book 2 from Spenser's *Faerie Queene* reminds us of the crucial place of antiquarian scholarship in late sixteenth- and early seventeenth-century political thought. Knowledge of the past was deemed essential for good government and the dominant discourses of political thought in the seventeenth century, ancient constitutionalism and reason of state, both reflect this antiquarian bias. The former looked backward to medieval legal history while the latter developed from the antiquary's comparative approach to politics and society. The prominence of these ways of arguing politics makes sense of Peiresc's repeated explanation that his work on antiquities served the common good. There is, of course, another, more personal, side to the sensibility about the value of deep past to lived present, whose familiarity Spenser assumed but which now requires some explanation, and this will be provided in the book's concluding chapter.

Here, the focus is on the practical side of antiquarianism and on Peiresc as an illustration of what antiquaries did when the subjects of their research and the needs of the moment converged. In this, as much as in his study of antiquity, we see how representative a figure Peiresc actually was. He possessed a vast collection of historical documents, many of which related directly to contemporary political affairs. Behind the assembling of this collection lay a commitment to law and the sovereignty of the state that was shared with other politically motivated scholars in Venice, France, the United Provinces, and England. Much of this discussion circled around the history of Europe's representative bodies and the relationship of regions and centres since the Middle Ages. Peiresc was himself a *parlementaire* and put his erudition to work as a political secretary and servant of the Crown. Because Peiresc's 'Antique Registeres' are, for the most part, still surviving we can follow his activities across this wide but typical range, and so reconstruct something of the antiquarian shape of political thought in the early seventeenth century.

There is nothing novel in this approach. Forty years ago, John Pocock published *The Ancient Constitution and the Feudal Law*, a study of the political uses of medieval English history in the seventeenth century. By locating the antiquarian heroes of his book, such as Henry Spelman and John Selden, in the history of history that had been sketched out a few years earlier by Momigliano in 'Ancient History and the Antiquarian' Pocock implied that seventeenth-century political thought ought to be understood as an antiquarian practice. And if political thought in the seventeenth century was argued by means of historical scholarship, then an adequate history of seventeenth-century political thought needed to be a history of that scholarship.[2] Pocock's book helped create a new way of studying the history of political thought. But this central claim seems to have gone unnoticed, or at least uncommented upon.[3]

It is with more recent work inspired by interest in the practical aspects of humanism, such as collecting and reading, that some of the gulf grown up between the histories of political thought and scholarship has been bridged. Study of Sir Robert Cotton, for example, Peiresc's friend and another antiquary who published nothing in his lifetime, has stressed the relationship between his learning and library on the one hand, and his political action on the other.[4] Collections like his, or Pierre and Jacques Dupuy's in Paris, were centres of political activity because they were repositories of documents that held keys to power and whose copying out constituted a political activity. Contemporaries understood this power: the arrest of 'Veteranno the Antiquary' and the seizure of his collection in Mermion's eponymous parody (1641) is believed to be a veiled reference to the arrest of Cotton and the closure of his library ten years earlier.[5]

What might be thought of as purely past-oriented (antiquarian in the modern sense) learning actually served very present needs. Lipsius' editions of Roman military treatises, for example, fuelled the military reforms of Prince Maurice of Nassau.[6] One of Peiresc's correspondents, the jeweller Vermeil from Montpellier, brought them with him to Ethiopia where he trained the army in this modern Dutch, ancient Roman strategy.[7] Post-Lipsian studies of antiquity, like those of Matthias Bernegger in Strasbourg, for example, established the canon of a *political* science in the German lands.[8] Pierre Dupuy's unpublished survey of 'the laws, customs, and forms of government of the estates, kingdoms, republics, and empires of the world' included a section on commerce and money that could have been written by someone like Peiresc (it probably was informed by his learning) whose volume on 'Actes et Memoires pour le faict des Monoyes' survives to this day.[9]

Peiresc thought that even the study of ancient coins, perhaps the archetypal antiquarian pursuit, had a present utility. A proclamation of Henri IV re-establishing the value of gold after it had inflated led Peiresc to argue 'that it was scarce to be hoped that any stop can be put to so growing a mischiefe'. Peiresc warned that 'no constant Rule' – or exchange rate – 'could be set' because wars would always provide occasions for intentional inflation, and managed trade offered similar opportunities for beggaring one's neighbour. Peiresc supported his claim with a detailed history of the debasement of Roman currency. Later, in taking up this same problem from the point of view of tax collection he suggested that fixed assessments be calculated in kind so as to avoid the long-term consequences of creeping devaluation.[10]

But the most profound political impact of antiquarian scholarship was on the important issues of the day: 'high' constitutional politics. The great conflicts that convulsed the seventeenth century, pitting crowns against estates, regional against central authorities, and ecclesiastical against political establishments, were articulated through historical argument. Their formulation depended upon the labors of antiquaries. If wars are won on battlefields, in early modern Europe there were many who believed that they were also won in the archives. The picture of the English parliamentarian, William Prynne, sifting through mouldy parchments in the Tower of London during the English Civil War searching for proofs of the pre-eminence of Parliament might be particularly striking but is not atypical.[11]

The search for historical precedent to justify contemporary policy led deep into the national past. Peiresc, for example, thought that an edition of ancient inscriptions (Gruter's *Inscriptiones antiquae totius orbis Romani*) that presented its contents by nation would 'serve the knowledge of the origins of our country'.[12] In this endeavour antiquaries were responsible for creating what was at the time one and the same: national and medieval history. Sometimes the quest for a documentable past merged with the northern European desire to acquire a classical one. If epics like Spenser's *Faerie Queene* offered fantastic allegories of national foundation myths, antiquaries provided true (though often no less strange) accounts of origins, whether of Saxons in England, Gauls in France, Visigoths in Spain, Goths in Denmark, or Batavians in Holland. These learned projects were justified as essays in national history and set in the 'dark' ages after the fall of Rome.[13]

A national history can presuppose, or create, a nation. The researches of the Society of Antiquaries in London (1586–1607) led by William Camden, and of its informal French counterpart that coalesced around the brothers Pithou in Paris during these same years, reflect a new focus on the nation. It is no coincidence that this occurred in the polities with the most developed sense of national cohesiveness, just as in 1630 Gustavus Adolphus established the Riksantikvariat (Royal Antiquarian Office) on the eve of Sweden's great imperial gambit, the invasion of Germany.

But Europe's ancient constitutions did not exist in a vacuum. Alexis de Tocqueville's discovery that if one went far enough back in time one would find a common origin for distinct national laws was no discovery to scholars like Peiresc, who excavated medieval national traditions from their archival resting places.[14] As Robert Cotton explained about the office of Constable, 'if we curiously will looke into the roots of this question we must travell out of our owne country'.[15] Comparison, in political thought as in the study of antiquities, provided a scholarly means of recovering a common history obscured by more recent developments. Peiresc was, for example, an avid reader and collector of the series of *Respublicae* published by Elzevir in Leiden that included modern France,

Poland, Scotland, Venice, and the Hanseatic cities, as well as ancient Rome and Israel. He made clear that he was 'principally' interested in the discussions of existing states.[16]

From Peiresc's surviving manuscript archive we can see that his comparative framework took nothing less than 'Europe' as its unit of measurement. Individual registers are devoted to the histories of England, Scotland, France, Germany, the Low Countries, the Holy Roman Empire, Switzerland, Scandinavia, Italy, Hungary, Transylvania, Muscovy, and the Ottoman Empire.[17] Much of Peiresc's collection were *relazioni*, or political reports and analyses of events. Some contained 'raw' data, like reports on events in Palermo from a Genoese galley captain, or on the Dutch capture of the Spanish treasure fleet off Cuba, while others were more thoroughly researched reflections at only one remove from the contemporary genre of discourses on ancient authors like Tacitus.[18] It was out of these comparative analyses of political institutions that the seventeenth-century literature on 'the interests of the states of Europe' emerged. Few other private individuals in Europe would have possessed this much information about contemporary events and the historical documentation necessary for putting them into a longer-term perspective. How many others, for example, would have collected 1,000 pages on the Valtelline crisis? This is an extremely rich hoard that presents a snapshot of early seventeenth-century European politics as it appeared to an observer living at that time.

But perhaps the most striking instance of how the expanding horizon of antiquarian research enriched the conceptual language of political thought in the sixteenth and seventeenth centuries was the use of philological research on ancient Judaism to articulate a model of politics, the *Republica Ebraeorum*. Renaissance humanists' recovery of ancient Greece and Rome had led to the recovery of their political concepts, as well, and enabled Europeans to learn the lessons of that history. This same sequence now repeated itself in the case of Israel. The first examples of this genre were produced by Cornelius Beltramus (Geneva, 1574) and Carlo Sigonio (1582). But the most important discussions, those of Hugo Grotius (1603), Petrus Cunaeus (1617), and John Selden (1655), all fall on the other side of the intellectual revolution that can be dated to 1572 and the appearance of Benito Arias Montano's volume of apparatus to the Antwerp Polyglot Bible. His studies of Hebrew words, biblical geography, chronology, weights and measures, ritual utensils, sacred priestly garments, and the topography of Jerusalem were gathered and reprinted under the title *Antiquitates iudaicae* (1593). In the following decades there was an eruption of antiquarian work on the ancient Near Eastern context of the Hebrew Bible that treated it as another ancient civilization and applied to it the same philological techniques developed for use on Greek

IVSTI LIPSI

DE

AMPHITHEATRIS

QVÆ

EXTRA ROMAM

LIBELLVS.

In quo Formæ eorum aliquot & typi.

ANTVERPIÆ,

Apud Chriſtophorum Plantinum.

cIↃ.IↃ. LXXXV.

1 (*above*). Frans Francken, *Interior of a Picture Gallery* (detail) (*c.*1625). The Collection of the Earl of Pembroke, Wilton House, Salisbury.

2 (*left*). Plantin's printer's mark: 'Labore & Constantia'. From Justus Lipsius, *De amphitheatro liber* (1585). Rare Books Division. The New York Public Library. Astor, Lenox and Tilden Foundation.

3. Peiresc's Almanac for the year 1629. MS Fonds français 9531, Bibliothèque Nationale, Paris.

CONVERSATIONE.

VEH SOLI

4. The emblem of 'Conversatione'. Cesare Ripa, *Nova iconologia*. Print Collection. Miriam and Ira D. Wallach Division of Art, Prints and Photographs. The New York Public Library. Astor, Lenox and Tilden Foundation.

AMICITIA.

5. The emblem of 'Amicitia'. Cesare Ripa, *Nova iconologia*. Print Collection. Miriam and Ira D. Wallach Division of Art, Prints and Photographs. The New York Public Library. Astor, Lenox and Tilden Foundation.

COSTANZA.

6. The emblem of 'Costanza'. Cesare Ripa, *Nova iconologia*. Print Collection. Miriam and Ira D. Wallach Division of Art, Prints and Photographs. The New York Public Library. Astor, Lenox and Tilden Foundation.

7. Peter-Paul Rubens, *The Garden of Love* (*Conversatie à la mode*) (*c.*1635). Museo del Prado, Madrid.

Conuersazione Moderna

8. The emblem of 'Conversazione Moderna'. Cesare Ripa, *Iconologia*, 1765 edition. British Library.

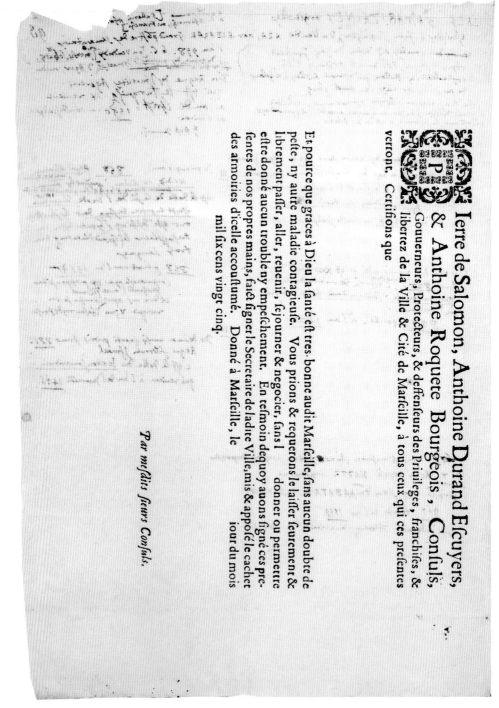

9a and b (*facing page*). The broadside of the Marseille town consuls on the back of which Peiresc recorded the circuitous path by which the Samaritans' letters to Joseph Scaliger of 1590 finally reached him in 1629, as well as brief histories of four Samaritan pentateuchs that he had retrieved. MS Latin 9340, Bibliothèque Nationale, Paris.

LES SAMARITAINES originelles
escriptes à feu Scaliger, du lieude AZA, par ELEAZAR Grand p̃stre des Samaritains
~~trouvoit~~ toubes es ~~iunte~~ mains du feu^r Guebrard
et puis de feu m^r Pollturault Argence de d'Aix
et seruteur de m^r Bollon qui les auoit bailleez à m^r Galaup
de qui je les ay eües. en Aoust. 1629.

Celle de la synagogue d'Egypte est antérieure à celle du
Grand Prestre Eleazar, en la mesme anne de l'Azyre ~~que~~ 998.
qui ont auée en automne, et est du XI. Octobre.

+ qui il nomme [Sultanii fit.
à farmacsii, ou Francsij fit.

l'an 998. le 6. Iou Vendredy ~~Vendredy sabati~~ ~~Schats~~.
~~Du regne des enfans d'Ismael filij d'Azar, ou bien~~
~~Hy en a~~
Du Regne des Ismaelites Agarens
qui est le Turquey. ~~&~~ reuient
à l'an de Christ. 1550. au calcul de scaliger.
ou enuiron.

* il est Ianuarij.

I. In mense quarto ~~se~~ definente Anno 624. regni Israel
la datte mise au bas des benedictions, et bons vœux
proferez ~~fault~~ à la fin de l'Exode du grand
pentateuq Samaritain en trois Langues.
c'est l'an 1226. au calcul de scaliger pag. 145.

II. In XIIII. die mensis saudi quiest XXIII mensis Tamus
Anno 827. ~~Annohdig~~, c'est la dernière datte du
pentateuque Samaritain tout à la fin
du volume
827. tombé à l'an 1423.

III. In principio anni 858. Regni filiorum
Kedar, ou Kedar qui est fils de Babylone
~~ou~~ ~~Regni K'AZAR~~ l'an ~~qui est fils de Christ~~ 1030.
c'est la datte de la fin de l'Exode Samaritain
escript en papier de soye dont les feuilles
ont este deschirez et y est entrelassé
En supplêant le Grand Pentateuq en
trois Langues.
858. ~~s~~ reuient ~~aue~~ l'an 1454 m.
Constantinople ayant este prinse par sultam
Muhamed l'anée 1453 aure.
Et dix ans après la mesme fut l'an
vainquit Vsun Chasan roy de Perse

IV. Die decimo mensis quarti prioris Anno 881.
Regni filiorum Israel
c'est la datte du Lexicon Samaritain.
qui reuient à l'an de l'incarnation 1476.

~~967~~ In mense Almuharan Anno ● septimo, sexegesimo nongentesimo
967. Regni populi NAOTZ. in testimonio
scripsit eam seruus dei HABATAA. In DAMASCO
967. tombe en l'an 1559.
C'est du dernier Pentateuq Samaritain, du si̇ de l'Isle.

Accipe iussis

Carmina cœpta tuis

ait poeta. Ego uero, Peiresi Amplissime, non carmen, sed librum tibi mitto, tuo hortatu
tuisque auspiciis cœptum. Adde quod ipsa hæc mea in Gallia habitatio
non parum tibi debet, quo conciliante in uirorum maximorum notitiam perueni:
ita ut hoc quoque titulo siquid inde fructus, nascitur id a te possit uindicari
Si dicam magno mihi dolori esse quod tuo conspectu, tuisque colloquiis
frui non licet, dicam quod uerissimum est: sed huic damno solatium aliquod
adhibet V.N. frater tuus, frater sane, non natura tantum, sed & morum humanitate: qui litium tractandarum molestiam iucundissimis amicorum
colloquiis et inter eos Rubenii etiam nostri diluit. Tu, quem summis
iudiciis suis tantæ Galliæ portio præfecit, etiam de hoc libro iudices
rogo: sedita ut in exsilio scriptum memineris. Si ad hoc postulatum ut
amare me pergas bonitati et constantiæ tuæ iniuriam fecero. Vale uir
candidissime.

T.X. obseruantissimus

H. Grotius.

ALIA MELIVS PINGETVR IMAGINE VIRTVS.

11 (*above*). Finsonius' 1620 portrait of du Vair, commissioned by Peiresc. The motto ('Non alia melius pingetur imagine virtus') is visible on the frame. Bibliothèque Méjanes, Aix-en-Provence.

10a and b (*facing page*). The copy of *De iure belli ac pacis* that Grotius presented to Peiresc, in Peiresc's binding and with his monogram, and the letter that accompanied the book which Peiresc bound into it. Musée Paul Arbaud, Aix-en-Provence.

14 (*above*). 'Tempus edax rerum': motto of Thomassin de Mazauges. Bibliothèque Inguimbertine, Archives et Musées de Carpentras.

12 (*facing page top*). 'The Angler's Song' from Izaak Walton, *The Compleat Angler* (1655). Rare Books Division. The New York Public Library. Astor, Lenox and Tilden Foundations.

13 (*facing page bottom*). Nicolas Poussin, *Blind Orion Searching for the Rising Sun* (1658). The Metropolitan Museum of Art, Fletcher Fund, 1924. (24.45.1).

17 (*above*). Poussin, *Et in Arcadia Ego* (1630). Devonshire Collection, Chatsworth. Reproduced by permission of the Duke of Devonshire and the Chatsworth Settlement Trustees.

15 (*facing page top*). Peiresc's Indonesian *kris*, reproduced on the last page of Lorenzo Pignoria, *Imagini delli dei de Gl'antichi* (1647). Rare Books Division. The New York Public Library. Astor, Lenox and Tilden Foundation.

16 (*facing page bottom*). Hermannus Posthumus, *Tempus edax rerum* (detail) (*c.*1536). Collections of the Prince of Liechtenstein, Vaduz.

18. Jean Baptiste Siméon Chardin, *Le Singe antiquaire* (1743). Musée des Beaux-Arts, Chartres.

and Roman texts. This was fuelled by the constant flow of new materials brought back from the Levant or from the equally – to that point – unexplored world of rabbinic literature.[19]

Discussions of the Hebrew Republic could now be conducted with the same degree of accuracy and seriousness as the more familiar debates over Greek and Roman government. If Hugo Grotius' juvenile comparison of Holland and Israel, De republica emendanda (?1603), only hints at the possibilities of this type of inquiry, Petrus Cunaeus' De republica Ebraeorum (1617) is the mature product. Cunaeus was Professor of Law at Leiden and was close to both Grotius and their mutual friend G. J. Vossius. His text marks an epoch in this genre because of its reliance on post-biblical sources.[20] When Peiresc first encountered the book, reprinted in 1632 in the Elzevir series of Respublicae, he wrote to Pierre Dupuy, 'the pleasure that I had in seeing the very nice observations of the author did not allow me to put it down until I had finished reading'.[21]

The most thorough and learned description of ancient Israelite religion and government was produced by John Selden, Peiresc's friend, in a series of works stretching from De diis Syris (1617), which Peiresc received from the author via Camden and which he enthusiastically read, to De successionibus in bona defuncti ad leges Ebraeorum (1631) copies of which Peiresc actively sought after, to the posthumously published De synedriis & praefecturis iudicis veterum Ebraeorum (1650–55).[22] Peiresc was himself deeply committed, especially in the last decade of his life, to promoting oriental studies and though he left no manuscript on ancient Israelite government there are several on Hebrew coins, weights, and measures.[23] This half-century of 'sacred philology' from Montano to Selden is surveyed in the great Prolegomena of Bishop Brian Walton to the last of the early modern Polyglot bibles, produced in London (1653–57) and, later, in the thirty-five volumes of Blasius Ugolini's Thesaurus antiquitatum sacrarum (1744–67), which was itself modelled on the twelve of Graevius' compendium of sixteenth- and seventeenth-century 'classical' learning, Thesaurus antiquitatum Romanarum (1694–99).

PROVENCE

Peiresc may have described his house in Belgentier as 'ma petite solitude' but it in no way resembled Petrarch's in nearby Fontaine de Vaucluse. It was located near the port of Toulon, and his townhouse in Aix placed him but a few hours' journey from Marseille, then, as now, France's Mediterranean metropolis. Neither, in turn, was very far from Avignon, still an extra-territorial Roman outpost, and the Rhône, highway to Lyon and beyond. Peiresc's home was an obligatory rest stop for learned travellers plying the route connecting Italy and the strongholds of northern erudition, Paris, Leiden, and Oxford. Leaving aside the crucial role of personality, these facts of geography contributed a great deal to the role Peiresc was able to play in the Republic of Letters. The centre of the learned world was moving northwards across the Alps during Peiresc's lifetime and its course led directly through Provence. The visit paid him by Cardinal Francesco Barberini, for example, when he dined *chez* Peiresc *en route* to and from Paris in 1626 – the most high level of the various delegations and individuals who stopped by to break bread with him and tour the horizon of learning – illustrates the advantages of his situation.[24] Peiresc amplified them still further by using the good offices of his friend, Alphonse du Plessis de Richelieu, then Archbishop of Aix and brother of the Cardinal-minister, to establish a regular postal service between Aix and Lyon so that a resident of Aix 'might hold also a weekly intercourse with the Parisians'.[25]

The institution of the post dramatically improved Peiresc's connection to Paris and enabled him to communicate speedily by way of Pierre and Jacques Dupuy to the rest of northern Europe. This change stimulated him, according to Gassendi, to commensurately upgrade his links to the extra-European world. 'For from this time forward', Gassendi continued, 'he kept a more frequent correspondence than ordinary, with the Consuls and Merchants resident in all the Eastern parts'.[26] We can, thanks to the surviving register of out-going correspondence, date this fairly closely: on 23 May 1624 Peiresc begins to mark letters to Paris as sent 'par la poste' (occasionally he refers to this service as 'le Parisien'; the Avignon–Rome courier remains simply 'l'ordinaire').[27] Through Marseille and Toulon he had direct access not only to the latest news and goods to flow in from the Levant, but to the far-flung network of Provençal merchants who garlanded the Mediterranean coastline from east and south to north and west. Many of his acquisitions came through these merchant connections, perhaps most spectacularly the long-lost replies prepared by the Samaritan priests in Gaza for Joseph Scaliger in 1590 but lost at sea on their return voyage. On the back of a broadside printed by the municipal government of Marseille and cannibalized for scrap paper, Peiresc recorded the recovered letters' circuitous path to him: from a M. Genebrand they went to Paul Hurault, then Archbishop of Aix, who passed them on to a M. Billon who gave them to Peiresc's friend François Gallaup de Chasteuil who delivered them, finally, to Peiresc (plates 9a and b). From the consuls, missionaries, and merchants in Cairo, Alexandria, Upper Egypt, Jerusalem, Sidon, Aleppo, Smyrna, and Constantinople he obtained information about diplomatic affairs in the

Ottoman Empire, Persia, and India, as well as the more familiar commerce in cats, chameleons, manuscripts, and marbles.

Several of the longer *relazioni* preserved in his files address the strate-
gic situation in the western Mediterranean. Peiresc shared the vision of
those who were able to recognize the importance of Provence because
their horizon extended beyond its narrow confines.[28] Two were prepared
by Savary de Brèves, the former French ambassador to the Sublime Porte
and the Holy See, whose interest in Turkish policy and the fate of Eastern
Christianity have earned him an important place in the early history of
French oriental studies.[29] Another report, prepared by Peiresc's brother-
in-law, the President of the Cour des Comptes Henri de Seguiran, 'Sur
le commerce et la defense des cotes de Provence' (1633), acknowledged
the primary importance of topography, demography, and climate.[30] Its
integration of political, military, and commercial considerations suggests
in narrow compass the development that led from Giovanni Botero's *Le
relationi universali* (1596) to the Duc de Rohan's *De l'Interest des princes et
des estats de la Chrestienté* (1638) to Samuel Pufendorf's *Einleitung zu der
Historie der vornehmsten Reiche und Statten so itziger Zeit in Europa sich
befinden* (1682), a work of recognizably familiar political science and the
progenitor of a new genre of books on the 'interests of the states of
Europe'.

The place of Provence in Peiresc's map of Europe is reflected in his
historical scholarship and in his political action. Gassendi felt little need
to comment on the depth of Peiresc's patriotism. 'What need I speak
anything in this place, of the love he bore to his Native Country, when
as it is clear enough from what has bin already recounted, that he was
wholly taken up in adorning the same?'[31] Yet, in the next sentence he
illustrated the ambiguity of 'patriotism' in an age of regional consolidation and state-building by implying that 'Native Country' referred to
both France and Provence, which was described as 'his chiefest care'.
Recall that the Counts of Barcelona and Toulouse, along with Kings
Henri IV and Louis XIII, looked down on Peiresc from the walls of his
study.

The importance of this homeland for Peiresc's intellectual life is
reflected in Gassendi's lengthy description of a project that Peiresc never
completed, a kind of 'total' history of Provence that reflects the ambi-
tiousness of the antiquary's reach.

> For to that end, he took so much care and pains, that he might pick
> an History out of the Ashes and Dust as it were, of the Earls thereof;
> and give light to its most noble Families; using to this end, not bare
> Tradition, sleight Arguments, uncertain Authorities; but Authentick

Records, as Wills, Mariage-Contracts, Transactions of business, Law-deeds, Priviledges; also Statues, Tombes, Inscriptions, Pictures, Scutcheons, Coines, Seals, and other such like things: which that he might discover, and get into his hands, he spared no Cost, Pains or Industry; perusing himself, or causing to be perused, all Acts and Monuments, which could be found in the Treasuries and Records of the Princes, Bishops, Abbots, Chapters, Monasteries, Nunneries, Nobles, Gentry and private persons whomseover: Also in the Statutes of Churches, their Registers of Burials, and Kalenders; causing to be drawn out, whatever thing of great Antiquity was shadowed, pour-traied, engraven, or expressed in Books, Vestments, Glasse-windows, and Buildings, sacred or prophane.[32]

Even in outline, this reliance on texts and images, ritual artifacts, and ephemera of everyday life suggests the 'perfect history' that was the elusive goal of so many early modern antiquaries. It also reminds us that there is a history to the attempts of many modern cultural historians, from Burckhardt and Huizinga through Warburg and Benjamin, to recover the past as lived and thought.

Peiresc's surviving historical output, though focused on Provence, is more traditionally political. The *Abrége de l'histoire de Provence*, recently published from a complete, surviving manuscript, is a history that begins in the high (for Provence) Middle Ages and continues down through the civil wars of the sixteenth century. It is chronological in format and follows the shape of political and ecclesiastical conflicts. A set of notes, still unpublished, for a history of the wars of religion in Provence offers careful, and sometimes eyewitness, accounts of battles and debates from the end of the sixteenth and beginning of the seventeenth centuries.[33] Their attention to detail bears close resemblance to Peiresc's own des-criptions of objects, excavations, and natural phenomena, suggesting a methodological unity that has been found in the work of other anti-quaries who studied both historical and natural antiquities, such as Ole Worm or John Aubrey.

As his historical output demonstrates, Peiresc was a keen student of medieval Provence and its cultural *koiné*. He sought out materials from Toulouse and Montpellier as well as from Barcelona, once even recruit-ing Cardinal Francesco Barberini to plumb the manuscript archives of the Monastery of Poblet when in Barcelona on a diplomatic mission in 1626. The history of Genoa was another special subject of research.[34] He conceived of the importance of this region on a grand scale. When du Vair's reading of de Thou's history led him to contemplate writing a history of Provence, it was Peiresc who drew up a prospectus compar-ing its history to that of ancient Greece.[35] His own history of Provence grew out of an unfinished draft of an account of Gaul and its subdivisions that began from the Roman Conquest but by the fifth century had become an institutional history with the focus narrowing to Provence and its late antique conciliar government before breaking off.[36] The difficulty of documenting Provençal history led Peiresc to ask a correspondent at the Monastery of Cluny for anything that 'could well bring lustre and light to the history of this province'. He emphasized an interest in the early Middle Ages. 'But what is earlier than the year 1200 cannot fail to be greatly useful for the understanding of the history of those centuries which were so barbarous and so dulled in simplicity, and above all that which is from the year 900 until to the year 1100.'[37]

The end of the ancient world was responsible for many of the linguistic changes that Peiresc discussed in long letters to his like-minded friends.[38] But the problem facing historians of the Middle Ages went much deeper. In a letter to Gassendi of 1633 Peiresc spelled out the difficulty of writing about a period for which sources were few and generally unreliable. These were centuries of 'great simplicity' during which people allowed themselves 'to be persuaded a little too easily of all sorts of possible things, without any proof other than simple conjectures about what might have been'. That history as fantasy was much more readily appreciated than history as fact was shown by the persisting vogue for the songs of Charlemagne and Roland, and the difficulty of convincing people that they were fiction.[39]

THE ANTIQUARY AND THE EARLY MODERN STATE

To the knowledge acquired in the archives Peiresc added that gained through personal experience. The discretion that he had singled out to Bouchard and Menestrier as the hallmark of the courtier was something that he himself possessed. It is easy to forget, amidst all his other endeavours, that he was also a secretary, that characteristic seventeenth-century figure.[40] Because he lived in du Vair's household there is little written record from this crucial period of his life. Some scattered letters testify to their familiar relations and the presence of copies of du Vair's papers in Peiresc's hand in Peiresc's files is evidence of their close working relationship.[41] There are also accounts of political goings-on as they occur, whether the ouster of du Vair, the complaints of the Queen Mother against Louis XIII, or the description of a royal entry at which Peiresc was present.[42] Peiresc also used his access to du Vair, then Keeper of the Seals, to promote others' scholarly projects.[43]

Peiresc knew his way around the bureaucratic apparatus of the early modern state. He managed Menestrier's request for naturalized citizenship of France, and made a chart of the Roman bureaucracy with descriptions of the scope of each office.[44] When it came to Roman affairs Peiresc felt confident, declaring that 'I know their humour'.[45] This same *savoir-faire* is displayed in Peiresc's decision to remove the approbation granted by Parisian theologians from twenty-seven of the 150 copies of (then) Cardinal Maffeo Barberini's book of poetry lest it prove disagreeable to the Romans.[46] But it was in his handling of the Galileo affair that Peiresc's knowledge of Roman politics – and the politics of writing – was displayed at its most astute. When asked by Gassendi about how to communicate with the imprisoned Galileo, Peiresc replied that he should frame his letter carefully 'so that there would be a means of understanding a good part of your intentions without the literal sense being so precise'.[47]

If the Galileo affair was the defining event of Peiresc's maturity, the Venetian Interdict Crisis was that of his youth. Several of Peiresc's early role models, such as de Thou and Casaubon, supported Venice and Sarpi against Rome. They defended the priority of civil over ecclesiastical jurisdiction in temporal matters, strong sovereignty coupled with a commitment to a wide sphere in which things indifferent to government (*adiaphora*, to borrow the appropriate theological term) were left to individuals to decide for themselves, and to constitutional and consultative, rather than absolute and arbitrary, government. In their personal morality these men tended to the modern, Christian Stoicism of Lipsius and du Vair, to the scepticism of Charron and Sarpi and to the belief, exemplified by Scaliger and de Thou, that the exercise of reason led to truth. For them, there was little difference between different persecuting religious establishments such as 'the tyranny of the ministers of Geneva', which, Peiresc wrote, 'leaves hardly any more liberty to the world than the Spanish Inquisition, although in the contrary fashion'.[48] This was the world of Gallican *parlementaires*, Dutch Remonstrants, and English Arminians.[49]

Paolo Sarpi was famous for his defence of Venetian civil sovereignty against the Pope and was an outstanding representative of this transnational community of interest. His close contacts with Gallican and Protestant circles that included both de Thou and Casaubon have been amply documented.[50] Peiresc met Sarpi in the circle of Gian Vincenzo Pinelli.[51] Though their correspondence was limited to a hurried letter of farewell that Peiresc sent from Montpellier in 1602 it reflects a degree of intimacy and familiarity. Peiresc explained that he had gone to the Monastery of the Servites 'three or four times' to say farewell in person. He described his new course of study and promised to be of service in any way, in recognition of favours that were so fondly recalled that he would sooner forget himself.[52] Sarpi remained an important figure ror

Peiresc and his own commitment to freedom of thought may have served as a model. At least one well-placed contemporary thought so; Jean Chapelain described Peiresc in a letter to Balzac: 'en son genre c'est un fra' Paolo'.[53] Peiresc was also one of the first Europeans to lay hands on Sarpi's *History of the Council of Trent*, having been sent copies by Camden (it was published in London). He described it as 'a very beautiful work, capable of a great effect and having a great run'.[54] His correspondence with the brothers Dupuy records continuing attempts to acquire copies of other treatises by Sarpi relating to the confrontation between civil and ecclesiastical establishments.[55]

Sarpi's *History of the Council of Trent* and the polemical pieces defending Venice against the Roman Interdict made him the European spokesman for the idea that the civil government was sovereign in its territory and independent from Rome. Was it just a coincidence that Peiresc followed a discussion of the authorship of Sarpi's *History* with a plea for the necessity of finally assembling a collection of pieces concerning 'the liberty of the Gallican Church'?[56]

A manuscript draft of a 'Project d'un livre que Fra' Paolo avoit envie de faire et le sommaire de tous les chapitres' under which Peiresc wrote 'Livre posthume de fra' Paolo' survives in Carpentras and in Paris.[57] In this prospectus, Sarpi presented in summary form the view of church government that had been developed in his Interdict-era writings and the great *History*. He began by acknowledging that society was instituted by God (ch. 1) and government created to preserve public tranquillity (ch. 4). God gave 'absolute power to the prince over the life and death of men' (ch. 5) and any diminution of this was nothing less than 'a sin' (ch. 6). The 'principal care' of the prince was the Church (ch. 8). Sarpi devoted an entire chapter to a definition of that Church for which the prince was responsible (ch. 9). The authority of the Church was the subject of another chapter (ch. 10). Marking the long and difficult to defend boundary between civil and ecclesiastical authority occupied the remaining twenty-five chapters. Sarpi paid detailed attention to the authority of the prince over the Church (ch. 15), the responsibility of the prince to enforce religious truth (ch. 16), and to punish crimes against the Church (chs 18 and 19). He explicitly denied that the Church could legislate without the approval of the prince (ch. 26), and gave the prince power to license congregations and religious (chs 27 and 28) and even to ensure that they acquitted their obligations (chs 29, 30 and 31).[58]

To the historian of political thought this appears to be the skeleton of a work which, had it been written, would have looked very much like another text read in Peiresc's circle, Hugo Grotius' *De imperio summarum potestatum circa sacra*, written between 1614 and 1616 and circulated in manuscript before being published posthumously in 1647.[59] It, too, is an examination of church government that contains no discussion of dogma and was destined by Grotius for inclusion in the volume of his projected *Opera Omnia* containing 'Politica' – in other words, it is religion from a political point of view. Like Sarpi, Grotius began (ch. 1) by declaring 'that Authority about sacred things belongs to the highest powers'. That sacred and civil were separate domains and the former subordinated to the latter was the point of Chapter 2. Chapter 5 discussed 'the judgement of the higher powers in sacred things' and Chapter 6 the 'manner of using this authority rightly'. Subsequent chapters discussed synods (ch. 7), legislation for the Church (ch. 8), the extent of ecclesiastical jurisdiction (ch. 9), election of pastors (ch. 10), other church offices (ch. 11), and the powers that remained in lower authorities (ch. 12). Scholars have long pointed to the conceptual links between the views of Sarpi, Charron, Grotius, and Thomas Hobbes on scepticism and civil authority in religion.[60] To the resemblance of Sarpi's plan to Grotius' finished work, whose English translation appeared in 1651, could be added that of both of them to Thomas Hobbes' argument in parts III and IV of *Leviathan*, also published in 1651.[61]

Peiresc's own view of civil authority seems very close to this Erastian model. In the *Vita* Gassendi explained that Peiresc did not insist on conformity as long as 'the Statutes of Religion; and Laws of the Countrey were not meddled with'.[62] The strong state was the minimal state, able to demand absolute loyalty only in matters concerned with security and able to obtain it only because of these narrow claims. In the broader realm of things indifferent to the state's survival, individuals could be left to govern themselves and their families as they wished. This was the solution that European thinkers of the first rank, like Charron and Hobbes, devised to prevent resumption of the wars that had broken out in the sixteenth and seventeenth centuries over attempts to enforce a vision of religious conformity as essential to national security.[63] 'In the observation thereof', Gassendi continued, 'consisted the safety of the Commonwealth; so that such [laws] as are not very just, may be more useful for publick good, than juster, provided they be religiously observed'.[64] For Peiresc as for Sarpi and Grotius, *salus populi*, as determined by the sovereign, was the measure of justice.[65] This idea lay behind Sarpi's description of the Jewish Torah as the ideal civil law, and Grotius' development of natural law.

If historical claims could be disputed or controverted and religious ones no longer seemed universally binding, society had to be put on a new and common footing. Grotius' minimal, anti-sceptical theory took self-preservation as the foundation that could support a natural law. Moreover, at a time of international conflict, natural law could be invoked as the only possible restraint on sovereign states, which by definition were without superiors to judge them. *De iure belli ac pacis* (1625) was an immediate success. Gustavus Adolphus even rode into battle with his copy so that he could use it to justify attacking belligerent neutrals.[66]

Peiresc befriended Grotius after his flight from prison to Paris. A letter to Barclay of May 1621 in which Peiresc praised his friend's novel, *Argenis*, mentions, *inter alia*, that Grotius had dropped in on him while he had the first pages of the book in hand and read them 'with such great evidence of pleasure and admiration for your style and of the beauty of your conceptions'. For our purposes what is so interesting is that Peiresc and Grotius were already on such familiar terms that unannounced, casual visits could occur. In the same letter Peiresc recounts the famous story of how Grotius escaped from the Loewenstein prison in a coffer of books.[67] He described the sentence against him as upheld contrary to 'the forms and against the fundamental laws of the state' in order 'to establish a tyranny and snuff out public liberty'.[68] And in his subsequent letters Grotius never failed to recall Peiresc's kindnesses.[69] Peiresc seems also to have played a significant role in the publication of *De iure belli*. Grotius proclaimed that posterity would thank Peiresc for having helped and encouraged him to complete the work.[70] Bound into the copy that he sent to Peiresc, now in the library of the Musée Arbaud in Aix-en-Provence and sheathed in Peiresc's monogrammed red Moroccan, is the letter that accompanied the book (plates 10a and b). It has never been published, although a portion was cited by Gassendi. It commended the book to Peiresc as 'judge' and celebrated his 'goodness and constancy'.[71] The volume is relatively free of marginalia, though where Grotius declared that Christians could have recourse to violence in time of necessity Peiresc pencilled in an insistence on the fine line between legitimate self-defence and the fuzzy domain of dissimulation and fraud.[72]

That Grotius' natural law, like Lipsius' earlier theory of self-preservation, emerged from a philologist's knowledge of ancient texts – recall that it was Lipsius, the student of ancient Rome, who proclaimed that he had made 'philosophy out of philology' – is clear enough from the range of subjects touched on in his correspondence with Peiresc. Following up what seems to have been an interrupted conversation about the origin of the Latin language, Grotius supplied Peiresc with a long list of Greek roots of Latin words.[73] In 1628 they discussed Grotius' annotations to Tacitus (only published in 1640),[74] in 1629 Arabic books brought back from the Lebanon by their common friend Jacob Golius, and an epitome of Greek historians retrieved by François-Auguste de Thou,[75] and in 1636 the Book of Enoch that one of Peiresc's agents found in Upper Egypt.[76] A manuscript in Peiresc's collection concerning Dutch commerce in the North Sea and Atlantic and Indian Oceans

bears witness to Peiresc's respect for Grotius' knowledge of Dutch political economy. It is described by Peiresc as 'Corrigé par M. Grotsius'.[77] As
Galileo and Campanella would become for him a decade later, Peiresc
saw Grotius as a martyr – this time a Protestant defying other Protestants – for his belief in a minimally doctrinal religion, *adiaphora* and civil
supremacy. He observed to Cardinal Bagni in 1623 that 'the edict against
Grotius is certainly tyrannical and unworthy of persons who have made
such a fuss over the restoration of liberty of conscience'.[78]

PARLEMENT

The Gallican-Arminian defence of civil sovereignty emphasized the
role of national institutions, like the Church, as well as representative
political bodies. Parliaments and parliamentarism united Peiresc with
many of his closest associates. His first great patron, du Vair, was the President of the Parlement of Provence and his second, de Thou, was President of the Parlement of Paris. Peiresc's English friends, Cotton,
Camden, Spelman, and Selden were all either Members of Parliament or
advisors to politicians. Sarpi was famous for his learned defence of Venetian political claims. Grotius had been advisor to the Advocate of Holland
Johan van Oldenbarnevelt before he was sent to prison and his patron
to the block.

Peiresc clearly belongs to Pocock's world of legal antiquarianism. Like
his friend Sir Robert Cotton (from whom he borrowed the Cotton
Genesis for Fronton le Duc), Peiresc assembled a library and manuscript
archive to support his own intellectual projects and those of his many colleagues. It is not surprising that it was with his English friends that Peiresc
consulted most closely on the history of parliaments.[79] But, and it needs
to be noted, these discussions emerged out of an effort to understand a
characteristic and enduring *medieval* institution, though at a time of conflict
between King and Parliament historical research and present need cannot
be easily distinguished. For example, in a long letter to Camden, author
of *Britannia* and Clarenceux King at Arms, prompted by a reading of an
ancient text on the Order of the Garter, Peiresc asked if the word *estal*, as
in a newly elected knight who was said to be 'mis en son estal', meant the
same thing as *estat*, as in a knight who died prior to 'la Pleine Possession
de son Estat'. He wanted Camden to examine ancient English registers
and charters to see whether these words were interchangeable.

Peiresc's next question to Camden shows the antiquary moving
smoothly between what are now considered the separate domains of
social and political history. He asked whether the places of the prelates
and barons on either side of the King in Parliament were ever called

'estalles'.[80] He then suggested, through a series of questions about the early history of the English Parliament, that this might preserve a lost name for the ambulatory courts that once existed in England and France. Peiresc thought that English history could provide clues to French history because the English had so 'religiously maintained' the 'ancient forms' that had fallen into disuse in France.[81] This sort of inquiry, he opined, 'would give us a great opportunity to penetrate to other things that are hardly known to us this day, in the absence of knowing the etymologies and origins of words from the northern languages that remain in ours'.[82] Peiresc believed that ancient French history could be studied through its terminology and that, in this context, the humanist ambition to understand a text in its historical context meant exploring related languages, like English, whose meaning might have changed less over the same time because of a different political history. It is this belief that language constituted a rich sediment for the historian of culture that also explains the unwavering encouragement Peiresc offered Sir Henry Spelman in his study of medieval Latin and Saxon, the *Glossarium archaeologicum* (1626).

Spelman and Peiresc had been introduced by Camden and Peiresc, in turn, brought Spelman's project to the attention of his erudite Parisian legal friends Nicolas Rigault, Jerome Bignon, and Jacques de Maussac, all of whom became staunch supporters. Spelman acknowledged their assistance, and especially that of Peiresc, in the book's preface.[83] Pocock took Spelman as representative of the antiquary's comparative practice, and his account of medieval parliaments would later serve as the starting point for a series of increasingly politicized historical arguments in the years preceding the Glorious Revolution.[84]

Though there is no indication that Peiresc and Spelman ever discussed Parliament or the *parlements*, we do know that Peiresc asked to see the 'cahiers' in which Spelman wrote about 'Assises' and 'Pairs', the ostensible subject of the letter to Camden.[85] Moreover, we know that Peiresc was sent 'un cayer d'epreuve' of the *Glossarium* in 1618 and in a letter to the brothers Dupuy in 1629 wrote that 'the author had sent me the first twenty quires more than ten years ago, from whence I learned of the marvels of these northern languages and the origins of old words descended from them'.[86] It cannot be certain, however, that Peiresc read Spelman's entries 'Parlamentum' and 'Mallus', since these were not published in the 1626 edition of the *Glossarium* (A–L only), and he certainly could not have read Spelman's English essay 'Of Parliaments' which was composed after his own death in 1637.

In that letter to Camden of January 1622, however, Peiresc put the history of parliaments in a comparative European context that followed from the linguistic observations. He asked if Camden knew of any

English parallel to the French *assemblées des Trois Estats*, an institution roughly the same as the English *Grand Parlement*, though with one crucial difference. In the French *Estats*, as in the Dutch *Staten* and German *Stenden*, Peiresc wrote, the third estate had no 'voix delibera-tive'. In asking if there was an English version of this particular institu-tion Peiresc was acknowledging that the modern English 'Parliament' had diverged from the French because its third estate had acquired this 'deliberative voice'.

Peiresc's questions reflect an interest that grew out of his own politi-cal experience. They hint at issues that must have been important to him when composing an undated draft essay on *La Vraye Origine des parlements, conseils et aultres cours souveraines du royaulme du France.*[87] Peiresc began by defining the meaning of 'Parlement' and tracing its etymology back to the Saxon 'Mallus' and the *Lex Salica.*[88]

The bulk of the essay documented the different kinds of consultative bodies, courts, and councils that existed in France from their origins in the seventh century, as well as their function, membership, and powers. Peiresc was careful to distinguish between France's different ruling families (Merovingian, Carolingian, Capetian, Valois, Bourbon) and their impact on the history of the institution. Though the Normans did not invade and conquer France as they did England, raising the much-debated spectre of a 'Norman Yoke', Peiresc did attribute to the 'raids and invasions of the Normans and the imbecillity of some princes' the disruption that enabled great magnates to install themselves as hereditary rulers – no less than the origin of feudalism. Peiresc argued that this social change altered the balance of power between King and subject and transformed the *parlements* into organs of the local authority. In France, Peiresc wrote, the 'parlements Generaulx du Royaume' were only con-voked by the King 'pour les plus grands necessitez de l'Estat'.[89] The change in the history of the institution followed that of its social com-position. Peiresc devoted several pages at this decisive point in his story to an analysis of the great 'Pairs et Prelats'.[90]

The shock waves from this fracturing of the political nation into its constitutive parts had linguistic as well as social and institutional conse-quences. It was then that the variety of Latin names of the assembly were dropped in favour of the vernacular 'Parlement'.[91] This alteration was first registered in Louis IX's decision to call a grand assembly of prelates, barons, and notables *c.*1254 prior to leaving France on Crusade. The four responsibilities which came to be exercised by the *parlement* namely, 'Iugement', 'Concilia', 'Inquestae', and 'Arresta', were designed to ease the King's judicial burden. Peiresc then offered a careful account of when and where the first *parlements* met in the thirteenth and fourteenth cen-turies. The proliferation of these institutions through which the King's sovereignty was administered nevertheless made for conflicting claims that were adjudicated by a newly created Conseil d'Estat. The essay concluded with descriptions of the many councils and offices that had sprung up around the King as he ruled more and more independently of the *parlements*, down through the reign of Henry IV.[92]

Because the regional *parlements*, like those of Languedoc and Provence, were vestiges of an autonomous past the description of their development over time simultaneously documented the creation of the modern French state. In Peiresc's hands the history of the institution of *parlement* shed light on wider French history. Spelman's essays, by contrast, tend to focus more narrowly on the legal documents and, especially, on the antiquity, constitution, and function of Parliament itself. Spelman's work is given shape by his strong sense of chronological development. As he moved from Saxon England to that created by the Norman Conquest, he explained that 'I go forth from darkness into dusk' and when he reached Magna Carta proclaimed triumphantly that 'From dusk we come now into light'.[93] Both Spelman and Peiresc recognized that the advent of feudalism in the person of William, Duke of Normandy marked a turning point.[94] Most important for Spelman, however, was to show that the old form of the *parlement* 'is different enough from our Parliament' because of the rise of the Commons which he unlovingly called the 'novus Leviathan'. This was a concern in England but not, as Peiresc had observed to Camden, in France.[95] Spelman's institutional history showed that the English Parliament, like the French *parlements* studied by Peiresc, began as an arm of monarchical government. The consultative role of the ancient *Magnum Concilium Regis* (Spelman) or *Regia Curia Francorum* (Peiresc) was, according to Spelman, the 'Archetype of Government'.[96]

Another of Peiresc's friends, Pierre Dupuy, also composed a brief essay on the Parlement of Paris that was published in 1655. The tract is also written in the antiquarian style, with documents cited at length and used to present political arguments that the author would rather not make *in propria persona*.[97] He claimed that the term *parlement* was not used before St Louis and its institutional form – when and where it met and who presided over it – was not yet fixed during the reign of his son, Philip. But the real point of Dupuy's essay, more like Spelman's than Peiresc's, was to provide a historical counterweight to the attack on the *parlements* orchestrated by Richelieu and Louis XIII. Unlike Peiresc's essay, at least so far as we can tell, this was intended as ammunition for a cause. Like the contemporary English definition of sovereignty as 'King-in-Parliament', Dupuy declared that the importance of the *parlement* had always been great because 'the authority of the Prince seemed to reside in it'. Moreover, because the *parlement* embodied royal dignity, 'if anyone sought to find the Royal Majesty in any place, he could not discover it but in this Company'. This was what gave force to the *parlement's* judicial authority. Conversely, those who denigrated parliamentary authority were attacking the King.[98] It was only in recent centuries that kings transformed the *parlement* into, almost exclusively, a vehicle for registering laws (the *lit de justice*), for 'their predecessors used them differently'.[99]

Peiresc, unlike Dupuy, was more circumspect in his comments about Louis XIII's expansion of power at the expense of the institution that his historical account had placed at the heart of French national political identity. Further from Paris, and, perhaps, too trusting, Peiresc identified the *parlement* as an arm of royal government and not as its opponent. 'I think that in serving the King we must make as little noise as we can, and rather seek out the remedies for our disorders, than make public our disgrace.'[100] His concern was to maintain the dignity of the *parlement* and not compromise its future authority by rash actions.[101] He was, however, aware, as one who had lived through the last of the civil wars of religion and the rule of favourites during the Regency of Marie de' Medici, that a society of ranks governed by a series of parallel and overlapping institutions could easily dissolve into anarchy.[102]

Peiresc preserved the draft of an entire speech animated by this desire to maintain the authority of the *parlement*. Internal references reflect an atmosphere of discontent bordering on outright rebellion to which Peiresc might have been referring when he wrote to the brothers Dupuy in 1628 that he had 'great difficulty in calming the rebellious and greatly altered spirits'.[103] Peiresc's opening words seems designed to cool them. 'We lack the force through which the State remains secure.' The lack of captains, fortresses, money – 'which is the nerve of war' – and popular support vitiated any recourse to a proof of force.[104] Having criticized the views of others, Peiresc offered his own suggestions, continuing on a new line: 'Pour ce faire il fault' followed by four proposals. The first was to establish a government worthy of being respected, namely, of 'men of quality'. The second was that 'les Princes & Grands' be included in government so that they would feel bound by its decisions. The third recommended transparency in financial dealings so as to intimidate embezzlers into fair dealing. Peiresc concluded by advising that government spending be restricted to only the most pressing matters.[105] In another speech he offered a different justification for caution: 'You see the hate that there is already against the government, you see men who seek out pretexts, and you give them real causes'.[106] In such difficult times, Peiresc declared in a speech that he delivered as the presiding official at an assembly convoked for the election of town consuls at Aix in September 1628, it was necessary 'to put aside not only your passions, jealousies and emulation . . . but also all sorts of interests, affections or preoccupations and all other particular respects and considerations'.[107]

The near-sack of his townhouse during the riots of 1630 led Peiresc to draft a letter defending his actions. It is an extraordinary 'confesson' of a political antiquary despite, or perhaps because of, its formulaic language. He served the public, 'for which alone we have worked almost all our life without ever really wanting to consider our particular interests'. He had directed his studies and works towards that which served the honour of his land 'and the great antiquity and just foundations of its privileges and liberties so legitimately acquired'. He worked to further the glory not only of the country as a whole, but also of its principal cities and places and famous men over the centuries. 'I have been so solicitous of the interests of others, unlike the most part of men of my condition who exert themselves to gain their own bread, as one says, and do their own business than to take any care for the public's when there is nothing there to gain.' It is precisely in these cases, Peiresc continued, 'that we have not spared our labours, nor our little means'. He was sure that 'our inviolable fidelity and our true zeal for the public good would be seen sooner or later and that God would protect our innocence and sincerity'. He could only be reproached for having devoted his efforts 'to serving all the world and particularly men of honour and quality, both within the Kingdom and without, indifferently, without any other design than to do honour to the nation and to our good country'.[108]

And yet, could someone with Peiresc's sophisticated historical sensibility and loyalty to tradition have approved of the slow but thorough asphyxiation of ancient institutions like the *parlements*? It is hard to imagine that he could have been in substantive disagreement with the raucous *parlementaires* of Aix who replied to a royal demand for a special tax on salt in 1628 with their conditional assent, 'as long as it pleases the King to leave them with their fundamental laws, privileges, liberties, forms of estates, and committees, that he could not suffer to see abolished in fact, without edict and any just pretext, against the forms and orders not only of this land, but of the whole kingdom'. Indeed, Peiresc continued, 'I do not want to excuse violence, but yet it is a great heartache to peoples who have so long remained loyal and obeying while all the others threw it off, to then see all their liberties removed and all the order under which they had lived during so many centuries and with the consent of so many great kings'.[109] Similarly, the riot of the *cascaveu* in Aix (called after their symbol, a small round bell, called a 'cascaveoù', attached to a leather strap or white ribbon) that was provoked by the Parisian decision to send in the royal officials known as *élus* to govern in Provence was presented by Peiresc in terms of these constitutional questions: 'a new establishment of *élus* that would breach the privileges and liberties of the province'.[110] Peiresc hoped that the King 'would have some consideration for his people' and repeal 'all these new charges' and so restore 'repose and tranquillity'. He noted that the popular unrest, once sparked off, had quickly turned into a class war.[111] He had himself been in some danger and only the sense of obligation that many, even among the mob, felt towards Peiresc had saved him from violence.[112] It was this experience that provoked the exculpatory letter cited above to his book-binder, factotum and sometime assistant astronomer, who protected his house in Aix from the mob.

CROWN SERVANT

The conflict between the need for clear and incontestable lines of central authority and the historical privileges that sustained ranks, regions, and estates runs right through Peiresc's public life. A *parlementaire* in Aix and a secretary to the Garde des Sceux in Paris, Peiresc's own loyalties were stretched across this fault. For all his regional loyalty, in 1628 Peiresc was commissioned by Louis XIII to draw up a history of French relations with the principality of Orange that would support claims of French sovereignty. This was not the first time that Peiresc put his knowledge of early medieval history to political use and is another illustration of the way in which antiquaries were used as 'scholarly civil servants' and 'practical humanists' in early modern Europe.[113] The particular task given to Peiresc also illustrates why medieval history was so important for state-building strategies long before Louis XIV's practice of *réunions*. It also reminds us of the tragedy of men with Peiresc's dual sense of *patria* as both nation and region, compelled to work for a triumph of the former that could only come at the expense of the latter.

Peiresc was approached by the King in the early summer of 1628 because a long-running feud between the governor of the town of Orange and his sovereign, the Prince of Orange and Nassau, had disintegrated still further and threatened to become entangled in the Huguenot rebellion in the South. Facts of distance and religious differences between a largely Catholic population and a Protestant sovereign made for a potent and unstable cocktail. Yet, what happened in the late 1620s was unusual. At the accession of Prince Maurice in 1618, the Catholic Prince Emmanuel of Portugal was appointed governor of Orange and the Protestant Jean d'Orsmael the seigneur de Valckembourg, as lieutenant. Maurice's brother, Frederick-Henry, rebuilt its château to modern standards of fortification and installed Bernese mercenaries in

1621. Valckembourg's Huguenot sympathies led to the impression that he would be prepared to put the citadel at their disposal. After the death of Maurice in 1625, Valckembourg acted with still greater impunity and indiscretion.[114] By 1627 Jacques Dupuy could write to Peiresc that Grotius, who was an ally of the governor – not surprising since he had been sent to prison by Maurice! – had already transmitted 'the bad news about Orange', a city that was now completely divided.[115]

It was the Huguenot rebellion that drew events to a climax in Orange. In the spring of 1628 the duc de Rohan sought to win over Valckembourg and his fortress. The alarm this raised in Paris led Richelieu to offer the governor 100,000 écus to turn over the château to the King, while leaving Frederick-Henry as titular sovereign and Valckembourg as governor.[116] After accepting the money, Valckembourg had the temerity to write an obnoxious letter to Frederick-Henry complaining about how he had been treated, a copy of which found its way into Peiresc's collection. He complained that for three years he had been made the target of a vicious whispering campaign that left him without money and unable to function.[117] News of this deal infuriated the *stathouder*, who sent two commissioners to Orange to re-establish his authority. Peiresc explained, in a long letter to Dupuy in March 1629, that 'at that very moment emissaries of the Prince of Orange were in the city and are up to I don't know what things'. Peiresc acknowledged that it was impossible to know if the governor remained a 'Huguenot' or had become Catholic, 'but at the least he has not yet made a public profession of the Catholic religion'.[118] The *stathouder*'s agents, however, had the misfortune to arrive during an outbreak of plague. Frederick-Henry then authorized a second, covert mission to topple Valckembourg. His councillor arrived in Orange in June 1630 disguised as a merchant and organized an ambush whose sloppy execution resulted in the governor's accidental murder.[119]

In 1628 when Rohan was negotiating with Valckembourg, it seemed essential to Richelieu to keep the citadel out of Huguenot hands. Richelieu's machinations appear to have prompted an inquiry into the history of French claims that led to Peiresc. Raymond Phelypeux, sieur d'Herbault and Secretaire d'État, and the Bishop of Orange served as the intermediaries. On 11 June 1628 Louis XIII wrote to Peiresc asking him to research 'the rights of our Crown and country of Provence in certain situations that were presented and discussed not long ago in our Council'.[120] In advance of his reply, Peiresc prepared the text of the commission he thought most appropriate. It serves us as an antiquary's ideal conditions of work. 'We command you', Peiresc wrote in the King's voice, 'that you aid in making an exact inspection and research of all the papers, books, registers, and memoirs which you might know of

concerning this subject' and, if necessary, to make extracts from principal state documents. Peiresc specifically had the King authorize his 'Audi-
teurs, Archivaires, ou Gardes' to open the archives for him.[121] The letter
that he sent to the King on 22 June pledged his complete 'diligence and
discretion' and asked for more detailed instructions. In the accompany-
ing letter to Phelypeux, Peiresc suggested that his researches could be
made even more effective if he were granted a commission to explore
the Trésor des Chartes of Provence where he had once seen some useful
material while working on other questions. He expected to be able to
mask the subject of his investigation by also inquiring into the affairs of
Nice or Avignon or Naples where his interest could be passed off as an
expression of his 'seule et particulière curiosité'.[122] Peiresc here demonstrates how the stereotype of the omnivorously curious but impractical
antiquary could actually function as a mask. In an important letter to the
brothers Dupuy in March 1629 Peiresc wrote that he thought the King
should do what he could to secure the situation honourably but without
making light of his strong claim to the sovereignty of Orange. Those
who had encouraged the late Prince Maurice to withhold the homage
due the King of France, he warned, would 'sooner or later' have to
reckon with France.[123]

The manuscript that Peiresc drew up in response to this royal commission is preserved in an autograph draft and a secretary's clean copy
in the file dedicated to the affairs and history of 'Aurenge'.[124] Like the
essay on the origin of *parlements*, *Instructions concernant les droicts du Roy
en sa souverante d'Aurenge, dont la Principaulté est tenue de sa Majesté à
cause de sa comté de Provence* ends with the word 'FIN' in majuscules,
indicating that Peiresc envisioned this as a completed whole. In it,
Peiresc undertook to reconstruct the history of the principality as it
passed from one hand to another through a series of accidents and
long-uncorrected errors. The essential fact of the principality's status as
a vassal of the Count of Provence, who became the King of France as
Charles VIII, was never in doubt in Peiresc's presentation. The narrative
was chronological and incorporated documents in the text whenever
possible. The combination of genealogy and political circumstances –
conflict between France and the Empire in the 1520s and the siege of
Florence in 1530 – had brought the principality into the possession of
the Protestant House of Nassau. The essay concluded, appropriately for
a policy document, with a clear list of proofs of French suzerainty over
Orange.[125]

If there was any single lesson to Peiresc's story, it was that the failure
of the French to know the details of their own sovereign authority over
Orange set in motion, as early as the fourteenth century, a chain of
unforeseeable consequences that had resulted in the rule of a Dutch

grandee over a French town. Errors of fact produced errors of judgement. Ignorance and laziness led to reliance on weak or misleading titles.[126] Peiresc complained that 'His Majesty's officials failed to follow them up' and did not rely upon 'the best and most legitimate titles' but only the corrupt ones.'[127] As recently as 1605, Peiresc wrote, when the Prince of Orange was installed in the château it was 'because one failed, at that time, to be instructed more particularly of the rights that the King had there'.[128]

Peiresc's essay served the task for which it was commanded, setting forth the history of the French Crown's relations with the Prince of Orange. But it was also – and this surely reflects Peiresc's authorship – an object lesson in the usefulness of antiquarian learning for modern politics. Spelman's justification of the utility of antiquarian humanism could, I think, stand also for Peiresc's. 'When States are departed from their original Constitution, and that original by tract of time worn out of Memory; the succeeding Ages viewing what is past by the present, conceive the former to have been like to that they live in; and framing thereupon erroneous Propositions, do likewise make thereon erroneous Inferences and conclusions.'[129] Many complained about the antiquary's narrow, pedantic obsession with the minutiae of archaeological or natural historical research.[130] Both Gassendi, as we saw in Chapter One, and the posthumous editor of Spelman's *Villare Anglicum* (1655) tried to answer this charge by emphasizing the ways in which knowledge of the past affected conduct in the present. Gassendi explained that the study of 'Papers and Coins, whose letters were exceeding small, and half eaten away' was justified 'to the end they may give light to the understanding of good Authors; that the circumstances of Histories may be more perfectly understood; and that the Persons, things and actions, may be more deeply fixed in the mind'.[131] In matters of state, the historical narrative presented by Peiresc showed that one could never be too attentive to details.

Antiquaries were important figures in seventeenth-century political life. They possessed the knowledge and the skills that were essential for running the civil and military bureaucracies of Europe's states. Peiresc's activities as a *parlementaire*, historian of *parlements*, and scholarly civil servant were no different from those of his English colleagues and could easily be compared with the activities of scholars elsewhere in Europe. It was this dimension of Peiresc's persona that was invoked in the dedication to the *parlementaires* of Provence of the partial French translation of Gassendi's *Life* in 1770.[132]

In the previous chapters we examined Peiresc's idea of sociability and its place in a wider European discussion of the norms of civility that

unfolded against the backdrop of changing notions of political community and sovereignty. The life of learning offered a path to excellence
that was independent of political service and obligation. Civil norms
accommodated political philosophy to the harsh realities of a Europe of
kings and oligarchs. But many of those who contributed to this discussion, like Peiresc himself, did participate in politics. It is the weight
of this activity in his moral economy that we need, in conclusion, to
consider.

Gassendi explains that Peiresc believed 'that every man, who by the
condition of his birth, or his own free Election, was destined to some
kind of publick life, ought chiefly to bend his mind to that, which his
Office and Designation required' and only afterward could 'divert to
other studies at his pleasure'. Peiresc's frequent complaints about being
unable to answer correspondence, let alone undertake any scholarship,
because of legal work that lasted from morning into night show that he
lived his beliefs.[133] When he had to cast a vote in the *parlement* Gassendi
wrote that 'he would turn all stones, that he might not do it unpro-
vided'.[134] This is the service ideal bound up in Lipsius' notion of *constantia*. Yet, it does not imply that Peiresc saw in this service much more
than a duty. He never, for example, sought advancement beyond the
office he had inherited. He had before his eyes the example of his master,
du Vair, who when temporarily (as it turned out) stripped of the Seals
in 1616 turned thankfully to his companions, Peiresc and Malherbe and
declared that it was 'the happiest day of his life'. He wanted to cease
talking about politics and make 'a happy retreat' to his country estate of
La Floride between Marseille and Aix, and the habits of civil conversation.[135] Is this a man for whom political life was an essential part of the
pursuit of excellence?

A letter du Vair wrote to de Thou from earlier that year shows that
this ambivalence ran deep. He commiserated with his friend's difficult
situation and, unlike some of his friends, sympathized with de Thou's
desire to retire from politics. But then he also affirmed, with those same
friends, that the public good demanded de Thou's continued service. For
the master of *constantia*, the problem of the philosophical man was to
adapt a clear idea of right and wrong to the constantly changing, ambiguous world of politics. It was the inability to do this that would drive
good men like them from public service.[136] And yet, for the man of the
world the only secure harbour was 'to seek this stoic insensibility' – if it
could ever be attained.[137]

In 1629 two of Peiresc's English friends, Selden and Cotton, were sent
to the Tower for their role in promulgating the Petition of Right. The
exchange of letters on this subject also provides a window into Peiresc's
view of politics and that of his circle. In his letter to Dupuy of 21 July

1629 Peiresc wrote, 'I was very distressed to learn on this trip that poor Selden is a prisoner of state for having spoken too freely in the last assembly of the English Parliament'.[138] From London in August of that year, Peter-Paul Rubens, who had met the two Englishmen through Peiresc's introduction, wrote to Pierre Dupuy, 'I am very sorry that Selden, to whom we owe the publication and the commentary [of *De diis Syris*] has abandoned his studies and immersed himself in the turbulence of politics, which seems to me a profession so alien to his most noble genius and most profound learning, that he must not blame fortune if, in the popular unrest, "provoking the anger of an indignant king", he has been thrown into prison with other parliamentarians'.[139] To Peiresc, Rubens repeated his hope 'that he [Selden] would have kept himself within the boundaries of the *vita contemplativa* without mixing in all these public disorders'.[140] As for himself, Rubens explained to Peiresc in 1634, he had finally 'found peace of mind, having renounced every sort of employment outside of my beloved profession', and abandoned diplomatic service 'in order to recover my liberty'.[141]

Did Peiresc agree with Rubens' judgement that it was a mistake for someone of their temperament to abandon the life of learning and immerse himself in the alien world of politics? When his friend Nicolas Rigault contemplated purchasing an office Peiresc found it 'no less strange' than did the brothers Dupuy. However, he explained, 'if he wants to be of the world I will not reprove his plan' since it brought in a good income for his son. 'But he can say farewell to the Muses if he puts himself to that'.[142] He was keenly aware of the conflict between service and scholarship. Peiresc affirmed to Naudé that there was nothing 'more certain and sweet' than to live with 'as little disturbance to tranquillity as we can find in our condition'.[143] A year later, writing to Cassiano dal Pozzo at the Barberini court, Peiresc declared that 'domestic quiet can prolong life much more than the courtly life with the hardships that accompany it'.[144] Yet, tranquillity – as with Petrarch – was not meant as an escape from the pursuit of excellence but was its prerequisite. Peiresc believed that it was study of the world that could so temper the mind 'as to enjoy the greatest tranquillity possible, and consequently, the greatest good'.[145] This philosophical exercise was what Peiresc's friends recognized in him. Rubens saw him as 'the example of a well-composed soul', and Girolamo Aleandro, invoking Seneca's ideal, called him 'the greatest and most happy man in the world'.[146] How Peiresc and his friends could have believed that study tempered the mind and made a person 'happy' is the question to which, in one way or another, the concluding chapters are devoted.

4

The Theology of a Scholar

Antiquaries and Accommodation

AMIDST PAPERS COMING FROM GUILLAUME DU VAIR, and preserved by Peiresc, was a prayer. 'I propose, my Lord, with your divine help to shun all sin, today and every day; to be rid of the habitual vices, to which I am especially drawn; to direct my actions and mental efforts to your glory and, lastly, to conduct myself in virtuous ways lest not this day, nor my entire life, pass without good works. You, only, do not distance your grace from me.'[1] This is interesting both for its ordinariness – it is the prayer of one who prayed easily – and its provenance – for du Vair's 'theology', related as it was to his philosophy, had a great influence on Peiresc.

It is not, therefore, whether Peiresc was 'religious' that is in question, but what 'religion' meant to him and did for him. The two basic facts of Peiresc's spiritual life are his education by the Jesuits in Avignon as a child and being the absentee *abbé commendataire* of the Benedictine Abbey of Notre Dame de Guîtres, near Bordeaux, as an adult, from 1619.[2] Peiresc worked to rebuild and reform the Abbey in line with the dictates of the Council of Trent and earned Pope Urban VIII's praise for his 'pious efforts'.[3] He once told Gassendi that, during a particularly busy time, he went out little 'other than to the Palace and the Church', and Jean-Jacques Bouchard noted that Peiresc said mass every day in his chamber.[4] His belief seems unexceptional in the secure way that generates few anguished confessions of faith. This comfortableness 'in the world' was the sort of personal piety preached by St François de Sales, whose influence is generally seen as being greatest among the non-erudite.[5] Peiresc's niece, in fact, entered a convent in Aix that took St François as its founder and Valavez suggested that his brother ask Rubens for a portrait of 'feu M. l'éveque de Genève' (he was of course not yet canonized) for the chapel.[6]

Peiresc did not talk much about theology. That is why it is so revealing that he wrote, on receipt of Hugo Grotius' *De veritate religionis Christianae* (On the truth of the Christian religion) in 1627 that 'at that time I had nothing to hand as appropriate and worthy as that piece'.[7] He sent copies of this book to a cardinal in Rome and a Christian convert to Islam in Tunis in the expectation that each would be made better by reading it.[8] This was Grotius' prison book, written in the cell where he had been confined because of his religious convictions and political allegiances – to the Remonstrants and the Grand Pensionary of Holland, Johan van Oldenbarnevelt. Peiresc's embrace of this tract enables us to use it, with appropriate care, as a proxy for his own, unstated, positive theology.

In *De veritate*, Grotius taught a Christianity consisting 'in a holy confidence, whereby we doe wholly yeeld our selves in obedience unto God, and rely on his promises by a steadfast and lively faith, whence arise both hope and true love of God and our neighbor'.[9] Christian dogma was made no more complicated than a belief that God is, is one, perfect, infinite, eternal, omnipotent, omniscient, absolutely good, and the cause of all things.[10] Worship of a God who was 'pure Spirit' was done through '*pureness* of minde and *Spirit*', together with 'such workes as in their own nature without a *precept* are most laudible and honest'.[11] Only in book 2 did Grotius suggest that Christianity best embodied this perfect religion (bk 2, ch. 1) and he did this by 'proving' that the story of Jesus was a true history (chs 2–8). And yet, he also argued that there had been pagans who had anticipated, albeit haphazardly, some of the teachings that Christianity later presented as a coherent whole (bk 4, ch. 12). In *De veritate* Grotius separated apologetics from dogmatics. As he explained in a letter to his friend Vossius, one could not preach doctrines depending on revelation to those who had not received it; in disputation with atheists, pagans, Jews, and Muslims reason alone had to suffice.[12]

Because *De veritate* was so valued in Peiresc's circle, it is worth turning briefly to a short essay written by Grotius in 1611 which has been described as its 'blueprint'.[13] Where *De veritate* focused on relations between Christians and non-Christians, *Meletius* was written as a response to divisions *among* Christians. Whatever the immediate differences, Grotius urged, 'we should be obliged to remember our almost forgotten kinship'.[14] His leading idea was that 'we are citizens of one community' and all differences had to be subordinated to this truth.[15] Meletius, then Patriarch of Alexandria, emphasized above all 'the points of consensus between the Christians'. This common theology, Grotius thought, also 'contained everything that is held to be best in any philosophical school

or among national institutions'.[16] In this one sentence Grotius captured
the central theme of the world in which he travelled: a minimal doctrinal creed facilitated the reconciliation of disputing Christians as well as
the accommodation of non-Christians. Both were made more difficult
by the fact that in Europe 'dogmas are declared to be the most essential
part of the religion, whereas the ethical precepts are disregarded'.[17] The
'remedy' for Europe's problems, and the precondition for accommodating non-European peoples consisted, therefore, 'in limiting the number
of necessary articles of faith to those few that are most self-evident' and
in accepting that if differences did arise, 'even on matters of some importance', the erroneous should not be accused 'with hateful incriminations
for the results of their unintended error'.[18]

The need to distinguish between the essential and the indifferent
put a premium on knowledge of the history of Christianity. Gibbon's
judgement of Grotius reminds us that for a long time his fame rested
on the extraordinary erudition that was required for this kind of work.
'All antiquity was known to Grotius; a knowledge that enabled him to
unfold the Sacred Oracles, to combat ignorance and superstition, to
soften the calamities and mitigate the horrors of war.'[19] Learning was
essential because so many controversies about dogma were themselves
'merely due to words', often because of texts corrupted through their
transmission over the centuries. Reducing the number of articles of faith
had to be coupled with a scholarly effort 'to remove ignorance'.[20] The
prominence of philology followed from this theological preference for
more reason and less dogma. Clean up the texts and many conflicts
would be deprived of the oxygen they needed to thrive. Other contemporaries, such as Ben Jonson, also saw the antiquary as the guardian
of textual integrity and therefore of peace.[21] And some, like Isaac
Casaubon, went still further. He believed that the antiquary, like an
explorer into the past, was capable of rediscovering the ancient, most
authoritative Church in its lost glory. Casaubon was sure enough about
the power of antiquarian research to take the Anglican confession – after
he had satisfied himself as to the antiquity of the rites. He followed the
simple rule enunciated by his friend Jacques-Auguste de Thou in the
preface to his famous history: 'Ce qu'il y a de plus vrai dans la religion,
c'est ce qu'il y a de plus ancien'.[22] This is the domain of *eruditio sacra*: at
the turn of the sixteenth century history, philology, and archaeology were
all mobilized in the service of faith. The Polyglot Bible projects of
Antwerp (1572), Paris, (1628–45), and London (1653–57) were only the
most extraordinary manifestations of this confidence in the happy collaboration of reason and religion.

The purpose of Grotius' minimal credo was to break down the con-
fessional iron curtain that separated European Christians from one

another, or caused them to take up arms against each other.[23] But his doctrinal minimalism also made it possible to see a common ground between Christians and the wider non-Christian world. Neither ancient nor modern pagans differed as human beings from Christians. The possession of reason was man's common inheritance. Study of the world confirmed this simple belief. In his play *Sophompaneas* (1635), Grotius put into the mouth of the Pharaoh Ramses the claim that 'Among men of great diversity' one found different civil laws but also another, that 'is every where, nor is it writ / In Cedar tables, nor in Marble cut; / Nor brasse, but in the heart God hath it put. / Who flies it, flies himselfe: Wild beasts we find, / To love by nature those of their own kind.'[24] Here, the injunction to peace and unity amongst Christians is transformed into the language of natural law and carried to the extreme first suggested in the *Meletius* years earlier: to love those also made in God's image. In the meantime, however, Grotius had written *De iure belli ac pacis* (1625) where in a different conceptual language he had also defended the possibility that a natural, universal law could exist amidst such profound diversity. These, Grotius thought following the Stoics, were really only different expressions of the same common notions.[25] Peiresc reports that Cardinal Francesco Barberini, to whom he had sent a copy of *Sophompaneas*, liked it so much that he would have wanted it performed in Rome, as he had Rospigliosi's sacred opera *S. Alessio*, 'if Mr Grotius' religion did not preclude it'. Peiresc, to his credit, thought it would have made a splendid opera – as did Thomas Mann three centuries later.[26]

The three essential principles of Grotius' theology were the priority of seeking peace, the necessity, therefore, of reducing Christianity to a minimal dogmatic foundation, and the usefulness of scholarship as a means of eliminating the ignorance and consequent misunderstandings that fuelled doctrinally driven conflict. This agenda is what is usually meant by calling Grotius an 'Erasmian'.[27] These principles did, in fact, reflect influential features of Erasmus' thought, though it was Erasmus as a slogan or emblem of eirenicism that Grotius seems especially to have admired.[28] Erasmus' spectacular declaration '*Sancte Socrates ora pro nobis*' was his attestation that Christianity had nothing to fear from pagan thought, but also his vision of a faith accessible to all who possessed reason.[29] Daniel Heinsius, a close friend of Grotius before the Synod of Dort found them on opposing sides and also a student of Scaliger, used Socrates as the vehicle to present an 'Erasmian', mimimal, eirenic creed in which the demands of philosophy and religion converged. 'All is known to the immortal God. Nor can he be deceived by men. The good cannot be separated from the useful. The one good is knowledge, the one evil is ignorance.'[30]

Peiresc shared with the author of *De veritate* an eirenic theology that proposed an ethical Christianity pared down to a few articles of faith more or less accessible to reason which complemented the idea of civil supremacy that united Venetians, Gallicans, Remonstrants, and Anglicans in the first decades of the seventeenth century.[31] In his discussion of Peiresc's religion, Gassendi began by noting his distaste for 'those Logical and Metaphysical niceties, which are no waies profitable, and serve to maintain bawling, and contentious disputes'. Peiresc lamented that so many sharp minds 'should passe over, unknown and unhandled, such things as we see with our eyes, and feel with our fingers' and instead devote themselves to sterile and divisive debate.[32] It was but a short step from sterile metaphysical debates that served the cause of intellectual sectarianism to sterile theological debates that created real schisms, real heretics, and real persecution. In Peiresc's file containing material from Grotius is a heavily underscored document that shows how the decrees of the Synod of Dort contrasted with the 'Veteris Ecclesiae Dogmata', whose content was drawn largely from the early Latin Fathers and Church Councils like the one held at Arles in 314 CE. The contrasts between the ancients declaring as 'anathema' precisely those doctrines that were upheld at Dort by the Dutch Calvinists and at Alèze by the Huguenots could not be sharper. The divergence ranged from justification to soteriology to anthropology: that men were created doomed.[33] For Peiresc shared Grotius' rejection of an overly doctrinal and 'pessimistic' Christianity. 'He was wont to say', wrote Gassendi, 'that he was not without fear, that the Doctors did presume too far, when with such confidence they disputed so many things touching God and matters Divine, besides what the Christian Faith teaches us to believe'. For by claiming these beliefs as articles of faith and then disputing them 'the Majesty of sacred divinity is thereby violated'.[34] Indeed, Peiresc responded appropriately enough to news that reached him of the Roman censure of Grotius' book. 'If he had even once used the term "parable" and also explained why he thought it did not detract from the faith to use the term *fabellae* he would have shut the mouths of those little friars (*frattoni*)'. Sometimes, he concluded, 'it is necessary in things indifferent to accommodate a little to fashion'.[35]

Peiresc would have been fortified in this opinion by his reading of Francis Bacon's essays 'Of Religion' and 'Of Superstition' which he possessed in Italian translations that must have been made from the English (for precisely these essays had been suppressed in the 1619 Florence edition).[36] In the first essay Bacon denounced the use of religion as a source of hatred and violence and the manipulation of reason by the religious 'only as an instrument to forge malice and cruelty'.[37] In the second, he stated his preference for an atheism that left man his 'sense, philosophy, natural piety, laws, reputation, and all that could serve as a guide to virtue' rather than a superstitious religion that 'established an absolute tyranny over the understanding of men'.[38] As staunch a defender of reason as he was, Peiresc remained on the Grotian side of this question: better a doctrinally minimal Christianity that could look like Socinianism to some, than a religion of reason that had made its peace with atheism. Peiresc endorsed Grotius' simple belief in a single, perfect God.[39]

If fundamental principles were put above doubt, all else could be carefully examined. This is reflected in Gassendi's observation that Peiresc 'could better bear that manners should be called in Question and controverted, provided the Statutes of Religion, and Laws of the Country were not meddled with'. Just as Grotius coupled a minimal credo on which all had to agree with a wide range of things indifferent where no coercion was possible, Peiresc here suggests a similar division between a limited number of essential principles which brooked no disagreement and a vast range of issues which demanded no conformity. This distinction is crucial. It enabled Peiresc to work with those of different religions without agreeing with them so long as they did not challenge the civil peace. This attitude might best be characterized by the contemporary English term, 'comprehension' rather than toleration, Erastianism more than Erasmianism.

Diversity was useful because it provided an opportunity to sharpen the capacity to discern between essential and conventional. 'For by this meanes', Gassendi wrote, Peiresc 'conceived an ingenuous man might lay aside that prejudice which makes the vulgar sort of men account the Customs of their own Countrey to be the Law of Nature, and that nothing is well done, which is not setable to their waies and manners'. The distinction between local customs and the universal law of nature was a premise of Grotius' *De iure belli ac pacis*. Travel, like reading, was a means of gaining this knowledge. The result was a person who had trained himself 'to be indiffferently enclined towards all men', like Peiresc, a Catholic comfortable with Protestants, Jews, and Muslims.[40] How many other Europeans of his generation might have observed, as Peiresc did upon considering the miserable condition of Christians living under Ottoman rule, that they 'are accommodated, as Jews are accommodated among us, in those places where they are suffered at all'?[41]

Of course, just as the eirenical, cosmopolitan Grotius intended *De veritate* as a conversion manual, the equally eirenical and cosmopolitan Peiresc tried to persuade his Protestant friends Pacius and Grotius to 'return' to the Catholic fold, and was genuinely scandalized by the conversion to Islam of his correspondent in Tunis, Thomas d'Arcos.[42] It is a startling reflection on Peiresc's theology that he saw Grotius as a Catholic in all but name, while Grotius' co-religionists in the United Provinces accused him of being a Socinian. As for d'Arcos, what seems to have troubled Peiresc most was his lack of commitment to *anything*: 'held for a Turk among the Turks, for a Jew among the Jews, and for a Christian among the Christians' and his being unable to know 'what he is or what he ought to be'.[43]

Peiresc's particular immunity to both Counter-Reformation and Calvinist obscurantism points us towards the load-bearing element in the structure of his world. When sent 'one of those books' with the title *Caelum Christianum* that sought to Christianize the pagan heavens by renaming the planets after the Patriarchs, the zodiac after the Apostles and the constellations after saints, Peiresc 'commended' its piety. But, Gassendi noted, 'he liked not the design of perverting all the knowledge of the Heavenly Bodies' and believed 'that those ancient Figurations of the Stars, though profane, were no hinderance to Christian piety'. As if for confirmation, Peiresc observed that he had seen the figures of the zodiac painted on the roof of a 1,200-year-old church at Vercelli. He only wished – and one would love to know the tone of voice he adopted – that those who made such an effort to engrave new maps of the sky with appropriately Christian names would make the same effort to depict the ceiling of that ancient church.[44]

To Peiresc, these attitudes could only be explained by ignorance. When working to identify the rich trove of luxury objects found in the Treasury of St Denis, many of which had been reset, reinterpreted and reconsecrated by Suger (and are now in the Musée du Louvre) he explained that 'the examination that I am having made of them is not at all to profane them' and was 'without at all derogating from the holy application to which they had been put since the coming of Christianity'.[45] Nor had his earlier identification of the great cameo of the Sainte Chapelle as the apotheosis of Tiberius, rather than the triumph of Joseph, any terrible consequences for Christianity. The monks' obstruction of his agent, Denis Guillemin, Prior of Roumoulles, led Peiresc to observe that ignorance 'is the true mother of all these abundant difficulties'.[46] In a letter to Gabriel de l'Aubespine, the Bishop of Orléans, Peiresc followed Charron in arguing that 'ignorance is always inseparable from arrogance and presumptuousness'. His example was a Jesuit's condemnation as heretical passages in books by his friend Pace that were direct citations from Justinian's Code![47]

Peiresc's Christianity, by contrast, feared little from the exercise of reason. He even valued the divergence of different versions of the sacred text for their 'considerable and useful diversity'.[48] The substantial differences between the Arabic and Samaritan versions of the Pentateuch, for example, led him not to fear the text, but to praise those very discrepancies – unlike the Congregation of the Propaganda Fide which suppressed the Arabic version and simply translated the Latin Vulgate back into Arabic.[49] But, of course, it was precisely the discovery of this diversity that led more insecure – or hard-headed – theologians to attack these polyglot projects as threats to the Christian faith. About them Peiresc could only sigh that 'there could well come a day in a better season' to undertake these sorts of ventures.[50] To his own friends he made clear that the time was now. He several times suggested to P. Gilles de Loches, a Capucin who had travelled widely in Egypt and Ethiopia and had acquired a mastery of Coptic and Ethiopic, that it was more important that he complete his Ethiopic lexicon than preach during Lent.[51] Peiresc went so far as to urge that 'things so noble not remain mired in religious humilities and mortifications with such prejudice to the human race'.[52]

For Peiresc, the condemnation of Galileo was the most glaring example of this explosive concoction of ignorance and insecurity. He simply could not believe that his friends in the Church, specifically Maffeo (Pope Urban VIII) and Cardinal Francesco Barberini, could condemn Galileo on theological grounds. He thought that just as the names of planets and constellations or the pagan identity of ancient gems could be accommodated without damage to faith, so too the truth or falsehood of the Copernican system could have no bearing on the truth or falsity of Christianity.[53] Making Christianity contingent on what at a given moment was believed to be a true scientific theory both belittled Christianity and created an incentive to suppress further inquiry.[54] Making it contingent on a theory actually known to be false was even worse: it would fatally undermine the claim of Christianity to truth. As Father Mersenne put it, 'The Holy Scriptures were not made to teach us philosophy or mathematics'.[55]

This confidence places Peiresc four square in the tradition of scholars like Grotius and Scaliger whose minimal creed made possible a fearless engagement with the wide world of knowledge. They believed, with Erasmus, that Christianity had nothing to fear from erudition, because, by definition, what was true (the Bible) could never be made false.[56] The seventeenth-century philosophy that best reflected this confident, adaptable face of Christianity was neo-Stoicism.

We have, thus far, considered neo-Stoicism as a philosophy of freedom and as a service ethic. But it was also the last in a long line of attempts by philosophically inclined monotheists to justify the study and use of pagan wisdom literature that began with Jewish Hellenists, and then, crucially, by Alexandrian Christians confronting both Jewish and Greek antiquity.[57] Their 'solutions' shaped the conceptual possibilities available to medieval Thomists and Renaissance Neoplatonists. Neo-Stoicism was the eclectic late sixteenth- and early seventeenth-century version of this

expressly accommodating philosophical outlook, 'the last great Renaissance compromise between Christian and pagan inspiration'.[58] Jerome's
expression of the accord between Christianity and Stoicism was amplified
by Lipsius: ' "The teachings of the stoics agree with ours in many things."
Agree? Yes, and what's more, they secretly led to our teaching and piety.'[59]
Lipsius described his own work, in particular *De Constantia*, as 'an attempt
to adapt philosophy to Christian truth'.[60] Julien Eymard d'Angers, in his
study of neo-Stoicism in the first half of the seventeenth century in
France, characterized its larger import as 'an effort to diminish the dis-
tances separating Christianity and Stoicism'.[61]

'Accommodation' is a term generally used to describe the practices of
Christian missionaries in East Asia and the Americas who adapted Christian dogma and ritual to the abilities of native societies in the hope of
more easily winning their faith. But it also captures, in quite precise ways,
the outlook of scholars like Grotius or Peiresc who did not view knowledge as a potential threat to their religion. Indeed, this was the only possible perspective for anyone committed with equal integrity to curiosity
and Christianity. With the stay-at-home philologist as with the missionary, the accommodation of the world to the text was made possible by
the conceptually prior acceptance of the validity of pagan wisdom. This
argument could be pushed one step further: for it is, as I hope to show
in what follows, this prior philosophical accommodation, which in the
late sixteenth and early seventeenth centuries was given expression in
neo-Stoicism, that actually made possible the more famous theological
formulations of the missionaries.[62]

And it was precisely the rational, optimistic view of human nature
underpinning this cosmopolitan openness that was seized upon as the
fatal flaw by the enemies of the Stoics. William Bouwsma has sketched
the tension between the Stoic and Augustinian world-views from the
early Renaissance; their collision in mid-seventeenth-century France was
particularly explosive, perhaps because they had so much in common.
Both were worldly and sceptical, though the Stoics scorned the gifts of
fortune they termed 'secondary' goods, while the Augustinians elaborated
a theory of the selfish, subterranean workings of human psychology.[63]
Neither abandoned reason, though of course the Stoics made more of
the running on this question. That there remained much common
ground is illustrated by the appeal of St François de Sales. For him, the
lesson of *sustine et abstine* – bear up under adversity and be temperate in
good times – that the young Hercules learned at the crossroads appeared
as but the first step in an ascent towards an even more enduring glory.[64]
In the 'Entretien' with M. de Saci, Pascal, by contrast, vividly described
the gulf that yawned between accommodating philosophies like the Sto-

icism of Epictetus and the scepticism of Montaigne, and the repudiation of reason's sovereignty by Augustine.[65]

Fundamentally, as Ernst Cassirer argued in his discussion of 'The Renaissance of Stoicism in Sixteenth- and Seventeenth-Century Ethics' that was a chapter in his book on Descartes (1939), this clash between the 'Augustinian theory of grace' and the 'Stoic ideal of the sovereignty and unconditioned *autarky* of the will' was the expression of fundamentally opposed anthropologies.[66] If the Stoics shared some of the scepticism of the Augustinians, and these some of the worldliness of the Stoics, they were divided, and decisively, by their views of human nature. This is where the balance tipped. Peiresc and Grotius, whatever their sense of the limits of human nature and the need for humility, were basically optimistic about the capacity of individuals, if suitably educated, to govern themselves and pursue excellence. The Augustinians, by contrast, denied this because of their Pauline commitment to the inherent sinfulness of man and, therefore, to the impossibility of pursuing excellence without the gift of grace.[67]

Peiresc stood firmly on the neo-Stoic's side of this divide. His early and lasting apprenticeship to Guillaume du Vair exposed him to these ideas at their source. Du Vair (1556–1621), whom we have encountered already, was a lawyer who became an important supporter of Henri IV and was, for his troubles, rewarded with the post of President of the Parlement of Provence, and later became Keeper of the Seals and Bishop of Lisieux.[68] His importance as an orator, *parlementaire* and colleague of de Thou is widely acknowledged, though as a historical figure he remains insufficiently studied.[69] He was the author of a series of extremely popular texts written in the last two decades of the sixteenth century to aid Frenchmen living through the terrible sieges and bloodbaths of the civil wars. *De la constance* (1594) alone went through fifteen editions before 1642. In the connection he drew between Stoicism and politics du Vair followed Lipsius' model.[70] Like Lipsius, writing at the very same time, du Vair offered consolation and a guarantee of freedom through philosophy, though unlike Lipsius, whose religion was a matter of near-scandal, there was nothing ambiguous or even mildly novel about du Vair's Christianity. It is the utterly uncontroversial character of his synthesis of Stoic and conventional Christian teachings that warrants attention since it is more likely to explain the easy assimilation of these ideas in every European land from Hungary to Scotland.

Du Vair's influence on Peiresc's ideal of comportment and philosophical perspective cannot be underestimated. Some time in the second half of 1620 Peiresc commissioned a portrait of him as a gift. On the frame he had painted the legend: 'Virtue is not represented better by another image' ('Non alia melius pingetur imagine virtus') (plate 11).[71] Du Vair represented to Peiresc the ideal of the excellent man. It was through him that Peiresc was exposed to neo-Stoicism as a theological vehicle capable of accommodating rational inquiry.

Du Vair was quite self-conscious about the nature of his project and its purpose. In the epistle from 'The Author to Monsieur his Father' that prefaced *La Sainte Philosophie* (1584), he explained that 'just as I saw that at Rome the rich temples built by the pagans in honour of their demons had been piously applied to the service of our God, in the same way in this little collection I have taken the trouble to transfer to the usage and instruction of our religion the most beautiful features of the pagan philosophers that I thought could easily be recovered'.[72] In the preface to his second edition of *De constantia* (1585) Lipsius justified the reuse of pagan philosophy for Christian purposes with a similar metaphor of *spolia sacra*.[73] This was, after all, the age in which the *piazze* in front of churches were festooned with ancient obelisks. The ruins of mighty paganism had long evoked a feeling of wonder in many, and for a long time, at the providential triumph of fishermen over philosophers.[74] The Christian supersession of classical paganism, like the spread of the Gospels to the four corners of the earth, proved the truth of the Apostles' message. Neo-Stoicism was the philosophy shaped by this confident triumphalism, whose spirit, during these same decades, also animated sacred archaeology in Rome and the propagation of the faith in East Asia.

The *Sainte Philosophie*, because it is stoical without relying on Stoic teachings, shows how little in the conventional morality needed to be modified to create a Christian Stoicism. It is also Christian without being dogmatic — there is no mention of Christ or saints — showing how a more doctrinally minimal creed easily lent itself to philosophical redescription.[75] The domination of the passions, a traditional Christian theme, had led men to distance themselves from 'cognoissance de soymesme'.[76] Enlightenment was the symbol of God and of improved mental health ('ni rien a Dieu que la lumière').[77] Practice of the virtues of temperance, clemency, patience, and justice was necessary to clean up the murkiness of the soul.[78] Yet, in this darkness the individual had to hope for assistance provided by grace since his own abilities were inadequate to the task.[79] In his papers Peiresc preserved a document entitled 'Oraison de St Augustine' above which he had written in his own hand 'version de Mr du Vair'. Its contents stressed the humility that kept the neo-Stoic earth-bound. 'Verily God, as we are guilty, and as we confess it, and innocently acknowledge it, if you do not pardon us we will perish. And justly.'[80] The believing Christian neo-Stoic's dilemma is here made very clear: while emphasizing reason he could not count on it, and while emphasizing self-mastery, he knew it to be unattainable.

For those who felt that reason was mighty but yet did not have exclusive dominion over man, Seneca gave place to Epictetus. Augustine's account of love and will had traditionally provided the conceptual tools with which an alternative to the philosophers' hyper-rational account of self-control could be fashioned. Christianity offered the wherewithal for a more realistic account of self-government that acknowledged the permanent reality of passions. The Christian could not pretend that passions were extrinsic and to be eradicated because that necessarily impugned the Creator's plan. Virtue, or excellence, had instead to lie in a disposition of the will rather than in eradication of the passions.[81] For this reason, du Vair and others attracted to Stoicism found especially useful Epictetus' distinction between the will, which alone lay somewhat under our control and for which human beings could be held responsible, and all those things which did not and therefore could not. His translation of the *Enchiridion* (1585) began with this rule of conduct.[82] This was a Stoicism that could be read through an Augustinian filter without doing extensive harm to the philosophy. The popularity of this approach is registered in the contemporary appeal of Epictetus: seven different translations of the *Enchiridion* were published in the century after 1550.[83]

Du Vair's translation of Epictetus comes between the publication of his very Christian *Sainte Philosophie* (1584) and the *Philosophie morale des stoiques* (1585). The latter work begins with the declaration of 'a divine and inviolable law . . . that if we will have any good, we must purchase and get it our selves, by our owne labour and industrie'. But to procure this good, man had to live according to nature, and this meant living without 'passions or perturbations of mind'. If 'we can so command our selves and our minds' as to avoid passions and face whatever comes 'we shall be free and happie'. The rule for achieving this end was learned from Epictetus: that what is beyond our power is also beyond our cares; only those things over which we have some control can have some control over us.[84] This was what made Epictetus so useful, and du Vair incorporated chunks of his translation into this new work.[85] Prudence became the most important of the virtues since it instructed man in making this choice, helping him 'to distinguish what is according to Nature, what is not; what we ought to pursue, and what we ought to fly'.[86]

Du Vair's dialogue *De la constance* (1594), like Lipsius' subtitled 'et consolation en calamitez publiques', took place against an even more arresting backdrop: Paris during Henry of Navarre's siege in the summer of 1590. The standard tropes were all invoked: sovereignty of mind, horrors of war, illusions fostered by opinion, fear for the future, and the glory to be won by standing fast against adversity. Poverty and death were to be endured and comfort taken from their inevitability. Physical pain, even the sort of Job-like 'remedilesse agony' which du Vair confessed 'to be the hardest, and most irkesome, of all that may befall us', could still be borne by the excellent man.[87] Also, like Lipsius, du Vair used Stoicism to challenge unthinking patriotism. 'Would we tie the affections of man to so narrow an obiect, as a corner of the earth?' he asked.[88]

Nevertheless, du Vair never wavered in his own devotion to public service nor in his public defence of political action. Unlike Montaigne who, after leaving the office that he was pressured into accepting, had declared that 'the Mayor and Montaigne have always been twain', du Vair spent his whole life in a public service animated by Cicero's famous assertion in *De officiis* that 'we are not born into the world for ourselves alone' but for the good of that whole of which we are but a part.[89] This is the same combination of Stoic cosmopolitanism and strong patriotism that G. H. M. Posthumus Meyjes has found in Grotius and de Thou.[90] In *De la constance*, du Vair asked if it were better to choose a party and vigorously prosecute its cause or retire and preserve one's integrity. Constancy dictated fulfilling the varied responsibilities of office because civilization could be maintained only if individuals did not cease their public-minded labours. 'Sometimes a Castle that holdeth out, affordeth meanes to recover a whole Province: and a wise and discreet Citizen maintaining his credite in his Cittie, may often occasion the common tranquilitie.'[91] He even relied on some casuistry in defusing the challenge to the value of civil life in a letter from St Basil to St Gregory urging contemplation and the flight from bodily matters. Because Basil lived in the world, du Vair commented, and not in some desert monastery, he could not have intended in this passage to defend the monastic rejection of society.

In a letter to a friend who contemplated retiring to a monastery to escape the disorders of the world, du Vair made his feelings plain. 'I prize the solitary life very much, I prize it a great deal, I love it and maybe too much.' But, he continued, one should follow the example of the Church Fathers 'with the same moderation and prudence' that they showed. Solitude was not for everyone. 'The monastic life was introduced neither at a time of troubles [as an escape], nor for those whose prudence and fidelity were necessary for the conduct and government of public affairs.' In stormy times, 'the most skilled pilots' could not abandon both ship and passengers to the fury of chance.[92]

Politics was about duty. As we observed in the previous chapter, though du Vair served the public when asked to do so, he was relieved when asked to step aside. According to the anonymous historian of this event – perhaps Peiresc himself – his generous and elevated discourse, 'so enriched by the most extraordinary maxims of Christian philosophy and infinite testimonies of real interior contentment', encouraged all who heard it. The tranquillity with which du Vair bore both his forced resignation and reappointment showed the signs of one who had not only mastered himself but who attached no intrinsic value to offices beyond fulfilling their demands – exactly as Epictetus counselled.[93]

In fact, du Vair reinterpreted political responsibility, precisely because of its hardships, as a test of individual character, or *constantia*. 'As for the particular injuries that we receive, how can we better show charity and patience?' This was especially true for Christians, who were enjoined to endure in peace and who had for their eternal model one who was crowned 'only after strange works and innumberable labours' performed by soldiers who followed him out of 'patience'.[94]

Du Vair provided an example of moral virtue and a model of the unproblematic accommodation of pagan wisdom as Christian virtue that was so influential in part because it was so banal. If the philosophical form taken by du Vair's brand of accommodation was decisive it was not atypical. In far-off China, even, the Christianity that the famous Jesuit, Matteo Ricci, preached to the Chinese was shaped by neo-Stoicism and its 'Erasmian' minimal credo. Ricci's Chinese writings distil a missionary Christianity from the same sources drawn upon by Grotius for theology and du Vair for philosophy. Here, these complementary halves of contemporary thinking about accommodation – the philosopher who looked backward to pagan antiquity and the missionary who looked out across the vastness of Asia – are presented as clearly as in anything written in Europe for purely domestic consumption. Indeed, it may be because he was not writing for Europeans that Ricci was forced to be, and was free to be, as clear as he was.[95]

The Jesuits offer probably the best-known examples of worldly Christianity. In an extraordinary group, Matteo Ricci has been seen as the most striking example of the early seventeenth-century missionary ambition to accommodate Christianity to the non-Christian world. The relationship between the Jesuits and neo-Stoicism was complex. If some important figures, like Lipsius, were close to the Order, and many, like Peiresc, were educated by it in their youth, many others were not. Ricci's accommodationist theology drew on the language of neo-Stoicism and the prior accommodation of paganism and Christianity that it reflected.[96] In spirit, too, neo-Stoicism would have appealed to a Jesuit missionary. For like other eclectic philosophies – and even Christianity itself – it was imperial in aspiration, able to encompass competing, even seemingly opposing, doctrines. Like Thomism, and Neoplatonism, neo-Stoicism, as the letter from du Vair to his father illustrates, was about controlling an unwieldy past for the Christian present.

In a letter to an Italian friend in 1599, Ricci wrote that 'in everything I accommodated myself to them and, where it was necessary, changed a little the sayings and sentences of our philosophers and a few things taken from our house'.[97] The 'Rites Controversy', the largely Roman dispute about the legitimacy of the Jesuits' practice in East Asia, was also a debate about the legitimacy of a philosophical Christianity that was synthesized from pagan and Christian sources. The greatest enemies of this approach were precisely those who denied the Stoic anthropology upon which accommodationist theologies like Grotius' and Ricci's rested, namely, the Augustine-inspired Jansenists. Their eventual triumph over the Jesuits, punctuated by the Papal Bull and Sorbonnic decrees of 1700, marks the defeat, therefore, of more than a mere method of proselytization.[98]

In three separate works written in Chinese for a Chinese audience, the *Treatise on Friendship*, *Twenty-Five Paragraphs*, and *The True Meaning of the Lord of Heaven*, or *Catechism*, Ricci presented a philosophy of living that was very neo-Stoic and a Christianity that was very Erasmian.[99] Where the one stopped and the other started is not always easy to discern. Had these been written in Europe, for Europeans, they would easily be recognized as belonging to the discussion of civil life and excellence that we explored in Chapters One and Two. The *Treatise on Friendship* (written in 1595, sent to Rome in 1599, and published in Chinese not earlier than 1601), was written at the behest of Chinese friends and drew upon the classical sources found in the Jesuit library in Peking.[100] Chinese adepts, in the preface, described Ricci as having come to China 'to make friends', recasting the Apostolic imperative in early modern language. Yet they were also quick to insist that the friendship described in the book was not the mean exchange of utilities, but rather 'mutual equality, mutual aid, mutual correction, mutual perfection whose foundation could never support a third'.

No friendship, however, could be possible without self-knowledge. Translating Seneca, Ricci asked: 'If you cannot be a friend to yourself, how could you be a friend of others?'[101] Ricci's sharpest dissent was provoked by the possibility that the bond of friendship could be built on interest or utility. He repeatedly likened this to mercantile practice ('un mercante della piazza'), though he admitted that in his own day friendship was on its way to becoming just such a purely commercial relationship.[102] Yet, these same conditions made friendship an even more appealing harbour of constancy.[103] In fact, the ability of a friend to firm up a wavering spirit could help one return to oneself; Ricci's 'tornar a se stesso' was a truly Montaigne-like injunction. The presence and example of a friend could serve 'like a rule, or living law that I have continually before my eyes'.[104]

The *Treatise on Friendship* won fame for Ricci and his mission. In the *Twenty-Five Paragraphs*, written a few years later (*c.*1599–1600), Ricci moved from friendship to constancy and presented the Chinese with a digest of Epictetus' *Enchiridion* in which he focused 'on the mortification of the passions and nobility of virtue'.[105] It is striking that both Ricci and du Vair, at nearly the same time, built Christian philosophies on Epictetus. As Howard Goodman and Anthony Grafton have remarked, 'Ricci was very much an intellectual of his generation when he chose to adapt the *Enchiridion*'.[106] And, like du Vair's *Philosophie morale des stoiques*, Ricci's text is no mere epitome but reflects his own views, adding interpolations that emphasize the difference between those things within ('internal') and without ('external') our control.[107] As in du Vair, happiness is made directly contingent upon taking Epictetus' distinction to heart. 'If a man attempts to obtain only those things which depend properly on him and avoid those things which are properly to be avoided, then he would never be unhappy or miserable.'[108] This was Ricci's comment on the vexed meaning of solitude: a tranquil soul would be happy anywhere, the troubled one unhappy everywhere. 'If the object of desire is outside of you, it can never be satisfied.' Like Sarpi, who proclaimed that 'le cose nostre sono interne', Ricci concluded that all the ancient and modern authors agreed that there was nothing to be gained by seeking outside, and everything by 'remaining at home' (*restar in casa*).[109]

Most striking is an addition that Ricci made in paragraph 16, elaborating on the nature of Epictetus' division between things within and without an individual's control. Where 'the inferior man' is dominated by externals, 'the superior man characteristically holds himself responsible for that which depends on him and constantly says to himself: "They can put me to death, but they cannot harm my spirit"'.[110] Ricci emphasized the importance of freedom of the spirit as the goal of Epictetus' exercise. He elaborated upon Epictetus' assertion that 'peace and tranquillity of the heart' was more valuable than 'the gaining of the whole world' by adding a passage linking the sage's intellectual labour with endurance.[111] He expressed the idea using a military metaphor redolent of Lipsius' historical etymology of *constantia*. 'You must act as if you were attacking with a whole army, and you must put on armor to parry the blows. In this way how can you possibly be afraid of anything?'[112]

If the *Treatise on Friendship* and *Twenty-Five Paragraphs* are largely neo-Stoic essays in self-perfection presented in ways easily assimilable to Confucianism, *The True Meaning of the Lord of Heaven* (1603), or *Catechism* (1603) offers the theology that fits this anthropology.[113] It is a religion reduced to a few points that could be apprehended by reason: exactly as suggested by Erasmus in his *Enchiridion militis Christiani* and Grotius in *De veritate*. In the *History of the Introduction of Christianity to China*, Ricci described the book as 'not dealing with all the mysteries of our faith . . . but only with a few principles, especially those which in some way could be proved with natural reasons and understood by that same natural light'. This was, he thought, the best way to begin the ascent towards the mysteries 'that depend on faith and revealed knowledge'.[114] The articles of faith that he sketched out were very like those suggested by Grotius: God was Creator, omniscient, omnipotent, infinitely good, and perfect.[115] Also like Grotius, Ricci was prepared to condense religion ('the definition of humanity') to a golden rule: 'Love the Lord of Heaven, for He is supreme; and love others as you love yourself for the sake of the Lord of Heaven.' By fulfilling this sole commandment, Ricci wrote, 'everything you do will be perfect'.[116]

The dialogue between a Chinese and Western Scholar that structures the book begins with the leading idea. 'The study of self-cultivation [*Tao*]', the Chinese scholar asserts, 'is a task which all men deem to be of the utmost importance'. Self-cultivation was the mark of the 'superior' man. The term Ricci used carried the connotation of someone whose excellence was not 'an accident of birth' but the result of 'moral stature'.[117] It was only by deciding to do good that this 'superiority' was proven. Because men could take or reject goodness, Ricci wrote, the merit of goodness was increased and became men's own.[118]

Ricci's Christianity, like du Vair's and Peiresc's, rested on a confidence in reason's ability to control the passions. It was 'intellect' that marked man off from animals and allowed him to pursue the origins of things and 'devote himself to the cultivation of the Way'.[119] Of all the great things in the world, Ricci asserted, 'the mind of man is the greatest' and was so far elevated above the things of this world that it could only be fully satisfied in the next.[120] 'The practice of virtue is man's fundamental task', Ricci declared, but this pursuit of self-cultivation was obstructed by 'selfish desires and passions'.[121] Ricci's denunciation of their effect on the mind could have come out of Lipsius or Charron. 'There is no plague in the world more virulent than this. The harm caused by other errors is merely to the body, but the poison of selfish desires penetrates to the very marrow of our minds, causing great harm to our original natures.'[122]

Those guided by their passions risked being led astray. Moreover, it was far easier to follow desire than to fight it. For, while 'the correct path is full of stumbling-blocks' and hard going, the wrong one was 'open and broad'. At the same time, 'the true path resembles the false path, and the false path looks much like the true path, so one must not be mistaken concerning the path that one chooses'.[123] 'Who is contented with his lot', asked the Chinese Scholar sounding like Epictetus, 'and who does not seek for things external to him?'[124] The problem of making the right choice, as noted by so many of his contemporaries, was lack of self-

knowledge. 'Man still fails to understand the truth concerning himself;
how much less, then, can he understand other truths?'[125]

Ricci explicitly linked the 'moral training' necessary for self-
cultivation to learning. To pursue excellence in order 'to acquire a little
knowledge' was pointless, to 'sell knowledge' was base, and to seek
knowledge in order to win fame was 'vanity'. The use of knowledge for
self-cultivation, however, was 'wisdom'. 'Thus', Ricci summed up, 'I would
say that the highest aim of learning is the perfection of oneself' because
this allowed one to unite with God.[126] Only the 'superior man' possessed
the self-knowledge needed for this dispassionate examination. 'He always
tries to reprove himself in detail and with severity' and, though 'others
might call him a hero', he behaved as if 'still deficient in some way'.[127]
He 'constantly cultivates his mind; finds happiness in moral actions; does
not permit himself to suffer anxiety, and is outward-looking'.[128]

But Ricci's view of the relationship between learning about the
world and individual excellence went even deeper, providing one of the
clearest justifications of scholarship as a moral activity produced in
Peiresc's Europe – albeit in its most far-flung outpost. He declared that
'the value of this learning depends entirely on its vigorous implementa-
tion'. He then described as a moral practice what reads rather like a celebration of the life of learning:

> The exposition and discussion of knowledge can help us review what
> has been learnt and cause us to learn something new; it can help us
> gain a thorough understanding of mysteries and resolve doubts. He
> who strives hard and exhorts others to do the same is a person of
> extensive learning and one who is trustworthy. The way of goodness
> is inexhaustible, and therefore any man who learns to do good must
> be prepared to study throughout his life. Every day that he lives must
> be devoted to its study. Any man who says he has reached his goal has
> simply not begun, and anyone who says he no longer wishes to make
> progress in goodness has again reverted to evil.[129]

Yet, as with Peiresc and du Vair, Ricci argued that the human mind
could only reach this goal with God's help and fell back on Augustine,
this time his lament that 'When man does not turn to you, his mind
cannot be at peace and satisfied.'[130] But Ricci specifically referred the
Chinese to the pre-Socratic philosophers. 'In ancient times, in a nation
of the West', the Western Scholar explained, there were two men,
Heraclitus and Democritus. The first laughed at man while the other
wept, 'because they both saw the way he pursued the vain things of this
world'.[131] Also like François de Sales, Ricci argued that human nature
was good, and that if men made the wrong decisions it was because of

the role of passions. 'If a man's nature is free of any ailment it is bound to follow the dictates of reason', the Western Scholar declared. The problem was that 'the feelings and passions are the "feet" of human nature and they are frequently afflicted with selfishness'. The language of 'disease' and 'infection' expresses Ricci's view of the incomplete corruption of man through the Fall. 'Our fundamental nature was originally good' and, however weakened, this capacity to reason 'can be used to recognize one's own sickness, and to effect a recovery'.[132] In the end, Ricci, too, stands on the Stoic side of the divide.

The only experience common to all men was their response to the vicissitudes of physical life. 'They all seek for self-preservation and have no desire to harm themselves.'[133] These were the two pillars upon which Grotius was to rely in erecting his sceptical theory of natural law in the later *De iure belli ac pacis*. And, like Grotius, Ricci expanded this insight into a broader theory of society. 'Humanity', he wrote, 'is the extension of one's own feelings towards others'.[134] The person richest in humanity was therefore 'bound to have an intellect capable of even greater understanding'.[135] This bears an uncanny resemblance to Charron's argument that the universality of the sage was the prerequisite for his great virtue. But how could local loyalties be stretched into cosmopolitan ones? Ricci claimed that though 'the inferior man' loved only his own, 'superior men of the utmost humanity can extend their love to distant places so that it embraces all nations in the world and reaches everywhere'.[136] Cosmopolitanism was part of a deeper commitment to human beings as the reason for the world's existence.[137] The 'superiority' of the cosmopolitan was founded on self-knowledge: recognizing one's own fallibility made it possible to love, not criticize or fear, others.[138]

Self-perfection and anthropocentrism made possible the cosmopolitanism that underlay both neo-Stoicism and the accommodationist arguments that Ricci based upon it. If, as Clement of Alexandria proposed, the truth of the Lord of Heaven was already in the hearts of men, then Gentiles living righteously could be saved. 'There are a few people in the world', Ricci wrote, 'who, though good now, always behaved morally in the past, and who, though following the truth now, never flouted it in the past'. Pagans could act morally because the truth – or divine spark, in Alexandrian terms – had been scattered throughout mankind from the beginning of time even though only revealed at a later date. 'The truth I am speaking of', Ricci concluded, 'is the truth which the Lord of Heaven has engraved on men's minds, and which He ordered sages and worthies to carve on tablets of stone and to record in books'.[139]

In fact, the historical account of Confucianism that Ricci offered in his history emphasized its Christian-like belief in divine reward and punishment and the immortality of the soul. He represents it as the model of an 'Erasmian' church, possessing neither temples, priests, ministers, solemn rites, commandments, nor coercive force.[140] Nor did the Confucians escape from idolatry only to lapse into atheism (the standard explanation of accommodationists for the widespread existence of idolatry in a world of people capable of natural monotheism); even their adoration of ancestors was free from idols and superstition.[141] The wholly Erasmian goal of this religion was 'peace, tranquillity of the kingdom and good government'. And Ricci declared that all this 'conforms to the light of nature and the truth of Catholicism'.[142]

Ricci's 'Erasmian' – though perhaps 'Grotian' better captures its spirit – brand of Christian Stoicism perfectly suited his Chinese audience. Not only was it a rational theology, like Confucianism, but it served the needs of state-building, also like Confucianism, which Ricci described as 'an academy, instituted for the good government of the republic'. Confucians could be made Christians, 'since in its essentials [Confucianism] contains nothing against the essence of the Catholic Faith, nor', he added even more daringly, 'does the Catholic faith obstruct it at all, since it greatly assists the peace and quiet of the republic'.[143] Ricci believed that blurring the line between theology and philosophy could work to the advantage of a proselytizing Christianity; European critics of his gambit saw in this the triumph of history over revelation. For if the sacred truth could be described philosophically by Christians, and could be comprehended by those lacking grace but possessing reason, then there was nothing any longer to differentiate religion from a philosophical school.

Cassirer noted that the first half of seventeenth century was dominated by two conflicting anthropologies. We have been focusing on one of them, the Stoic perspective embraced by Peiresc. The works of Grotius, du Vair, and Ricci help round out the picture of Peiresc's theology presented in Gassendi's biography and found in Peiresc's own papers. Their minimal, if not wholly rational, credo provided firm footing for those bravely setting forth to study the world. *Historia, archaeologia,* and *philologia sacra* were names given to scholarly inquiries that were typical early seventeenth-century theological manifestations of this anthropology. The role of reason lay at the core of the division sketched out by Cassirer between seventeenth-century Stoic and Augustinian anthropologies.

We can see this at work already in Ricci's own time, back in Europe, in an exchange of letters between two otherwise like-minded scholars, Isaac Casaubon, the Huguenot who fled Paris for London, and Paolo Sarpi, the atheist 'Theologian-Consultant' of the Most Serene Republic. Replying to Casaubon's anguished query about whether he should adopt Anglicanism because it was closest to the ritual of the ancient Church, Sarpi observed tartly that on earth there was no perfect Church, only more or less corrupted ones ('hic optima est illa quae minimis

corruptelis'). Moreover, because of the rhetorical language of the Church
Fathers it was extremely difficult to figure out what they had actually
meant. Even more fundamentally, Sarpi thought all this scholarly attention to the external form of the Church misguided. 'Because we are pre-
occupied with the ornaments of a house why should everything else be
left to the flames?'[144] Two months later, Sarpi returned to the impossibility of a perfect Church in a world of imperfect men. 'We are foolish',
he wrote, 'because we are human'. And then, like Donne, Charron, and
Montaigne, Sarpi insisted that the true sage ought to mind his own business. 'No wise man ought to bother to correct public ills. It should be
enough to you if you can correct me.'[145]

Sarpi couldn't bear Casaubon's enthusiasm. But the Augustinian coun-
terattack, when it came, targeted not only the scholar's commitment to
reason but also the related project of accommodation. This is part of what
lay behind the 'Rites Controversy' and the Roman debate about missionary practice in Asia. Because antiquaries played such an important
role in the study of 'Ecclesiasticall Antiquities' the Augustinian challenge
marks a crucial turning point in the social standing of the antiquary in
a wider Christian society. In the end, however, it was not the learned
writers who triggered the decisive reaction. Indeed, serious studies of
pagan religion multiplied over the course of the seventeenth century.
It was only after the learned arguments were seized upon by 'free
thinking' polemicists hostile to Christianity that the battle was joined.

François La Mothe le Vayer (1583–1672) was a noted sceptic and intellectual troublemaker (though also tutor for a while to the young Louis
XIV) and he cynically exploited Ricci's implied claim that righteous
pagans could be saved. *La Vertu des payens* (1641) was a polemic against
Christianity as a revealed religion masked, just barely, as a serious scholarly defence of the most accommodating of accommodationist positions.
Julien Eymard d'Angers has shown where and how le Vayer actually fabricated his references.[146] His motives, however, are not our concern here.
For our purposes, the book is important because it presents the most
extreme argument in favour of accommodation produced in the first half
of the seventeenth century.[147] Le Vayer seized upon the Christian sources
who defended the claim that the Fall had left man only partially corrupted because it left open the possibility that men could be saved
without grace. He repeated, as Ricci's, the claim 'that many of the vertuous Chinese were saved by observing the simple Law of Nature'.[148]
Non-Christians were those who ignored this 'light of reason natural to
all men' and were thus led to vice. In this formulation Christianity is
identified with the use of natural reason.

La Mothe le Vayer repeated Augustine's assertion that 'all those who
taught the greatness and goodness of the one creator God of all things,

whether they were Scythians, Indians, Persians, Egyptians, or whatever other Nation, ought to be preferred to others, having approached closest to the light of Christian Faith'. With this, le Vayer introduced a bold claim for the salvation of Confucius, marking a significant moment in the history of cosmopolitanism. Drawing on Ricci yet again, le Vayer observed that the Chinese nation was the one guided most consistently by the light of reason and closest to that true religion whose origin Clement of Alexandria long ago, and Ricci more recently, had discerned in the reason shared by all men. Unlike the Greeks, Romans, and Egyptians, the Chinese 'had recognized since time immemorial only one God, whom they named the King of Heaven'. Le Vayer styled Confucius the Chinese Socrates. Both had rejected the useful sciences in order to study human customs and so brought philosophy down from the sky.[149]

Only knowledge of the Gospels separated Le Vayer's virtuous pagans from virtuous Christians. But at this extreme, revealed religion lost its importance. *La Vertu des payens* pushed the fundamental optimism of Stoic anthropology to its conceptual limit and drew down the powerful response of Antoine Arnauld, Abbot of Port-Royal and the leader of French Jansenism. *La Nécessité de la foi en Jésus Christ pour être sauvé* (1641) was written as a reply to le Vayer though it was not published until 1701. It is a full-scale attack on accommodation as a threat to Christianity with le Vayer's arguments held up as an example of where cosmopolitanism inevitably led.[150]

Arnauld's central claim was that belief in one, good, Creator god was by itself insufficient for attaining salvation. This required an explicit affirmation of Jesus Christ, something not found among any of the supposedly virtuous pagans nor in the creed of the accommodationists.[151] All faith needed to be based on authority while pagan religion was instead based on reason. There were other contrasts too: Christianity was obscure and supernatural where paganism was clear and natural. In short, it resembled philosophy rather than theology – too much like du Vair, Grotius, and Epictetus, and not enough like the Gospels. This philosophical knowledge of God 'by the sole light of reason' was what le Vayer and others called faith in order 'to accommodate' a pagan audience.[152] The emphasis on the rationality of Christianity and the universality of reason was the necessary foundation of an accommodationist religion and it was this that Arnauld condemned as the vanity of philosophers.[153]

Saving the pagans on any other terms described a religion that was not Christianity. Accommodation was an insidious approach since it protested its loyalty while slowly diluting the content of Christianity. Implicit faith, which was all that could be offered up on the pagan's behalf, was not the same as explicit belief in the Crucifixion. Monotheism was not identical with Christianity and a belief in God's general providence alone did not a Christian make. Nor, finally, was the light of reason sufficient for salvation because the corruption of human nature had shrouded the soul in deep shadow.[154] Without Incarnation and Crucifixion, the teachings Arnauld called the 'fondement de la Théologie de Saint Paul', the righteous pagan would always misunderstand human nature. For they and their modern admirers, the neo-Stoics, set too much store by reason. Their philosophy rested on an anthropological fallacy: human beings were simply *not* rational creatures capable of self-mastery.[155] For Arnauld, the most 'constant maxims' of the neo-Stoics were nothing other than 'lessons in pride for teaching men to depend on nothing but themselves and to worship only their own reason', which they called virtue.[156] The vision of man held up by Lipsius and other later theorists of *constantia in publicis malis* presented a new kind of idolatry.[157] Making man into God was what the Stoics proposed and what no true Christian could ever accommodate.[158] All the convoluted efforts of Peiresc and du Vair trying to remain true to both St Augustine and Epictetus were, from Arnauld's perspective, just feeble self-deceptions.

If the elimination of dogma was unacceptable, so was the ostensible purpose of this manoeuvre: the seeking of peace as a religious rather than political injunction. Arnauld viewed this Grotian–Erasmian ideal as 'weakening our belief and diminishing the articles of our faith'. Equally to be condemned were those others who insisted that there needed to be only one article of faith, belief in Jesus Christ, 'and that all else is indifferent so long as it does not trouble the government'. Broad *adiaphora* was dangerous, according to Arnauld, because it favoured state over conscience and allowed the ruler to widen or narrow that freedom in the name of public tranquillity, whether justified or not.[159] This was, it will be recalled, precisely the political theology subscribed to by Peiresc. A third group did not even require this and were satisfied with belief in one god within the law of nature provided, again, that it did not violate the laws of state. This was the practice of Socrates, the Athenian idolator who chose not to spurn the state religion despite his disbelief and it could be extended to the inhabitants 'of a pagan in China, a Mahommetan in Turkey, a Lutheran in Saxony, a Protestant in England, a Calvinist in Geneva, and a Catholic in Rome' who might also worship without belief. 'This', Arnauld added tartly, 'is what one calls an accommodation full of wisdom and prudence'.[160]

Underpinning the intellectual programme of Jansenists like Arnauld was an insistence on reason's limits. In the case of Arnauld, this took the shape of a rejection of rational soteriology. But in Guez de Balzac's *Socrate chrestien*, it became a frontal assault on the very practice of 'Ecclesiastical Antiquities'. Balzac, whom we have already encountered in Chapter Two, bid fair to be the Peiresc of the Parisian chattering classes. Always in search of *succès de scandale*, his literary works and *salon* style made him a symbol of the taste for modern conversation that swept Paris around 1630. But after finding himself on the losing end of an attempt to curry favour with Richelieu, Balzac turned to a more contemplative life. Begun in the 1630s near the start of this 'exile', though published posthumously in 1652, the *Socrate chrestien* tackles the rational anthropology of the neo-Stoics and antiquaries head-on. It sets forth a redefined relationship between scholarship and a religion of Folly that is nearly a mirror image of the accommodationists' compound of neo-Stoicism, erudition, and eirenicism.[161]

Like Erasmus in the *Ciceronianus*, Balzac was concerned with the question of what a modern Christianity should look like.[162] He thought it had to go beyond the rational and limited scepticism of the neo-Stoics. This meant renouncing reason and the human aspiration to self-perfection altogether in favour of a hope for salvation granted in spite of irremediable unworthiness. In the first discourse Balzac staked out a view of Christianity that closely resembled the concluding section of Erasmus' *Praise of Folly*. Not only did Christ destroy idolatry, he had 'confounded human *Sagesse*, taken away speech from the philosophers'.[163] The Folly of the Cross was the single most important piece of knowledge that Christians needed to have.[164]

So, while Balzac, like du Vair, saw in the ruins of the baths of Diocletian since converted to a church the symbol of an unlikely triumph, it did not lead him to endorse *historia sacra*.[165] On the contrary, the supplanting of a pagan by a Christian Rome was a cause for awe, but not archaeology. Sacred philology was a particular target. 'What audacity', Socrate wrote, for a citizen of this lower world, a mere earthling ('Habitant de la Terre'), 'to mix himself up in the superior matters and affairs of Heaven.'[166] 'The Word of God will always be difficult, always obscure' even after 'thousands of Expositions, mountains of Commentaries and Legions of Commentators'. The meaning of the Bible exhausted and would continue to exhaust all its possible interpreters, including the most learned. 'It is certain', Socrate observed, 'that to succeed in such difficult reading one must not bring purely human eyes and an ordinary spirit, much less the eyes of a Grammarian and the spirit of a sophist'. The philological drive for detail and certainty was founded on a false, even presumptuous, faith in human reason and its capacity to make sense of the world.[167] If even 'Scaliger himself put his foot wrong' on occasion, what could be hoped of the demi-savants and scholars of the second rank who lived amidst the stultification of the provinces, far 'from the library of M. de Thou and the conversation of *Messieurs* Dupuy'?[168]

Gassendi's Peiresc acknowledged the sceptical force of the stoics and the Augustinians. He 'hated' the 'vices of Impiety, Cruelty, Malice, Perfidiousness, and the rest'. But, continued Gassendi, 'distinguishing humane nature from the pravity thereof, and taking the same into serious consideration' his reaction was one of pity, not anger or despair. He lamented 'that through weakness and blindness, men could not continue in the way of virtue'. If only men could understand how little was needed to live – literally, if they had perspective ('perspectum haberent') – 'they would abandon all deceit and fraud, by which superfluous things are sought'. Self-knowledge could produce a world in which 'Humanity, Honesty, Moderation' would not be such rare commodities.[169] Peiresc the admirer of Grotius could not suppress an anthropological optimism, however hedged, abstract, and utopian.

Peiresc's use of the language of vision and blindness to characterize human nature highlights the prevalence of what Anthony Levi has described as Neoplatonic imagery in the clash between the Stoics and Augustinians, each of whom interpreted the metaphor in accordance with their wider views. Susan James has identified this as one of the common tropes in seventeenth-century discussions of the relationship between passion and error.[170] The opening page of Lipsius' philosophical dialogue *De constantia* has him explaining that Langius, his wise interlocuter, drove away clouds of vulgar opinions and showed him the path to light. The civil wars in the Netherlands easily lent themselves to description as tempestuous.[171] The *Opinio* that deceived men into choosing the wrong path was described by Charron as 'shadow and appearance, but vain and false . . . mother of all ills and confusion; from her come all passions and troubles'.[172]

Du Vair, for his part, also took blindness and (storm) clouds as symbols of the dangers lurking in an unphilosophical life. In *La Sainte Philosophie* he wrote that attaining the most perfect happiness was impossible so long as 'we are enveloped in the shadows of the world'.[173] In his *Meditations sur Iob*, du Vair argued that from this story one could learn patience, the foundation of all the virtues. The conditions of life were precisely those of drifting in a wide, wide sea.

> Since the life of man is nothing but a floating sea of miseries, where the afflictions hit harder each in turn than the waves stirred up by storm and where the calms, if sometimes they are found there, are for the most part nothing but the warnings of a storm to come, with what could those who must make this voyage better equip themselves than with this divine patience and equanimity that makes a secure anchor for the most agitated spirits and the most tormented souls?[174]

Ricci, in *The True Meaning of the Lord of Heaven* lamented the human condition in these very same terms: 'Alas! Men appear like persons in a vast ocean who see their ship buffeted by wind and wave and about to break up and sink. Their minds are troubled as they drift to the very corners of the ocean.' But those who possessed an 'Interior Equilibrium', as Ricci entitled one of the moralizing songs that he translated into Chinese for the Emperor in 1601, would be able to bear equally with success and failure ('sustine et abstine'), endure strong winds and pounding waves, and remain, always, immobile ('eppure non si muove').[175]

But the problem was that it was difficult to see the correct course, let alone steer it, in the midst of a storm. *Stoa Triumphans*, ascribed to Virgilio Malvezzi, makes this point clearly. It described the perils of adversity as a life shipwrecked in a storm. Bound to the surges and billows of the waves, the only response was to roll with them. In making this point the author drew on another set of metaphors that evoked the wisdom of the sage: 'A wise man beares his head above the clouds (Sen. Ep. 59) [Seneca, *Epistulae morales*]: tempests cannot reach him, he is not shaken with winds nor shattered with thunder: Princes and states may well be Lords of our bodies, but cannot of our souls (Sen. Benef. 3) [Seneca, *De beneficiis*].'[176] Rising above the clouds meant also rising above the frame of reference provided by our creatureliness. 'He that is immerst (both soule and body) in this puntilio or narrow point, such as the Globe of Earth is, doth live alwaies in the center of this point'. It was the 'higher speculations' of the stoics that offered a path to freedom. Were the earth, by contrast, to be reduced to 'a point of the Universe' then man and all his concerns would be put in proper perspective.[177] The value of fishing, in Izaak Walton's presentation, was that it induced this perspective without requiring the stoic's strength of mind. It was, therefore, a way to the same end that was accessible to more people. 'But we'll take no care when the weather proves fair, nor will we vex now, though it rain; we'll banish all sorrow and sing till tomorrow, and Angle and Angle again' (plate 12).[178]

The most precise use of the metaphor of storms and clouds for the state of the mind was, like so many of these works, written in prison. In one of the *Familiar Letters to his Lady of Delight* that Sir Henry Marten wrote from the Tower of London, where he, like John Eliot, would die, he offered remarkable testimony to the role of *constantia* in the education of the wise man. 'The Skill is not in being weather-wise', Marten wrote,

but weather-proof. In one thing, the storms I mean, are contrary to those the clouds pour upon us: for in that case it is best to keep all our clothes about us, and houses over our heads; in my case, to throw off all we can, and snugg like a snaile within our own selves, that is, our mindes, which no body but we can touch.[179]

This strength of mind was the light of reason. 'Reason', Matteo Ricci wrote, 'stands in relation to a man as the sun to the world, shedding its light everywhere. To abandon principles affirmed by the intellect and to comply with the opinions of others, is like shutting out the light of the sun and searching for an object with a lantern.'[180]

It was this vision of enlightenment that the Augustinian critics of the rational freedom of the Stoics renounced. They thought human beings constitutionally unable to liberate themselves by themselves from their fallen condition. Jean-François Senault, the Oratorian and Augustinian, whose important *De l'Usage des passions* (1640) made one of the most acute attacks on the possibility of rational self-control, presented an alternative meteorology of the soul.[181] He described the passions as motions in the sensitive appetite that 'raiseth tempests as winds do waves, and the Soul would be at quiet in her interiour part, were she not moved by this power'. Like all those inspired by Pauline theology, he denied that it was possible for reason to cure a mind naturally dominated by passion. The philosophers offered only false wisdom and delusive enlightenment. 'Blindess', he wrote, 'is to be preferred before their false lights'.[182]

To Senault and the Augustinians, the neo-Stoics' interpretation of storm and sun was completely backward. Because they had misunderstood human nature none of their arguments, or remedies, could be admitted. 'They consider only the appearances of things; they stop at accidents, their weakness cannot penetrate into substances; they are like the Sun, and as they take all their light from him, they endeavour to imitate him in their actions.' Insofar as light and sun were emblematic of the merely sensory world they led away from the true 'cognizance of divine things to furnish us with the like of what is humane'. The only way to reach any true understanding of life in the world was through the mind's eye with its faithful vision. Reason itself had to be subdued, according to Senault, and the senses ignored. If the commands of religion 'take from us our liberty, she preserves our honour, she frees our understanding from the tyranny of our senses, she submits it to the legitimate Empire of the supreme Intelligence, which she illustrates unto us by her light; she takes us from earth, that she may raise us up to Heaven'.[183]

For Senault, as for Jansenists like Arnauld, Pascal, and Nicole, the fundamental problem with the Stoic argument was its mistaken anthropology, that it 'promiseth to change men into Angels, to raise them above mortal condition, and to put storms and thunder under their feet' when everyday experience showed, rather, that they swirled about man's head.[184] With reason unable to exercise any control over the passions, 'the waves rise up even unto Heaven; that part of man which ought always to be at quiet' – the mind, of course – 'is engaged in the storm, and had need of others help to appease the troubles she is agitated withal'.[185] And yet, even Senault had to admit that if there was nothing more difficult to achieve there was also no achievement more honourable for a man than to overcome his passions.[186]

Peiresc seems to have been confident that reason could make order in human affairs, though he was well aware of its limitations. 'We do those shadows tread', his contemporary John Donne observed, 'And to brave clearnesse all things are reduc'd'. 'Brave clearnesse' described the modern stoic's sense of sight. Nicolas Poussin's moving painting of 'huge Orion, that doth tempests still portend' (1658) (plate 13) captures, in the single image of a giant blinded by a storm cloud seeking enlightenment, both sides of the debate about human nature that raged in Paris in the years immediately after Peiresc's death.[187]

5

HISTORY AS PHILOSOPHY

Time and the Antiquarian

WHEN ERASMUS SAW IN HERCULES an emblem for the humanist's labours he must have been thinking about the hours upon hours spent reading and writing in darkness and in light, in heat and in cold, in sickness and in health. In the seventeenth century, the popularity among aristocratic patrons of the arts of visual representations of the story of Hercules choosing at the crossroads beween virtue and pleasure – Annibale Carracci's version in the Farnese Palace (1595) became 'canonical', according to Panofksy – reflects the recognition that strength of mind, more than that of body, was necessary for living well in the world. The freedom of the one able, like Hercules, to master himself was also seen as especially important for the historian. Or so thought Jacques-Auguste de Thou, one of the early influences on the young Peiresc and famous across Europe for his *History*.

In letters to friends that were published along with his text, de Thou defended his impartial judgement of affairs and of men in terms of 'la liberté qui convient à l'Histoire'. Yet, in a century 'so corrupted by passions and flattery' his own obedience to 'the law of history', of telling the whole truth, had made him a marked man, even in his own country.[1] Confronted with the political fall-out at the court of the Regent, Marie de' Medici, for his notoriety in papal Rome, de Thou retreated to the countryside. He recounted his activities in a contemporary letter. 'I passed the time', he wrote, 'in exercises of piety [*pietatis studiis*] that restored tranquillity to my soul'. After beseeching divine assistance, de Thou reconsidered the decisions he had taken with especial concern to avoid two accusations: of having been moved too much by his own sense of hurt and, at the other extreme, of having acted in a way unworthy of his past.

He then jotted down all his thoughts on the matter, in no particular order, and sent them as the body of the letter, as if writing to an impartial judge.[2] The echoes are of Ignatius' description of the mechanics of choice, with the Jesuits' director of souls transformed into the absent friend.

It was this same stoicizing philosophy of self-mastery and constancy – as a younger man de Thou had written a poem entitled 'Iobus sive de Constantia' (1587) – that coloured de Thou's correspondence with two other antiquaries, themselves friends of the younger Peiresc, Isaac Casaubon and William Camden. Casaubon, from his safe refuge in Jacobean London, reminded de Thou 'that such is the fate of human things that they often turn out otherwise than we had expected'. Nowhere was this more true than in courtly politics. But why complain, and why be surprised? 'We are born into the world but to see these disorders, that renew themselves without cease and which can never be remedied'. What remained was 'to bear with an even temperament what by the nature of human things cannot be changed'.[3] Camden, writing a few years later, observed that the same malevolent herbs growing in de Thou's garden would soon be found in his own. 'One must have patience'. Though they lived in a century that was an 'enemy of truth and moderation', good conscience had nothing to fear. 'However it might be, we march on our route always with a steady step and oppose the attempts of calumny with the shield of patience'.[4] De Thou's reply was worthy of Camden's sentiments. 'We navigate, both of us, the same sea. We are in an equal danger; we have to fight against the same winds and the same tempests. We are threatened by the same reefs.' But there was no reason to fear. 'Do we not find in our philosophy sufficient relief for sustaining and for repulsing the efforts of our enemies as well as the powerful motives of constancy and courage? This is what I expressed once before in my poem about Job'. 'The time has finally come', de Thou concluded, 'for the one and the other of us to put our maxims of philosophy to work'.[5]

What was the relationship between their philosophy and their work as historians? This is another way of asking Walter Benjamin's question when he insisted that it was 'absolutely indispensable' to establish 'the philosophical basis' of baroque philology – in short, to understand *why* they did what they did. And at the end of a long career spent thinking about antiquaries Arnaldo Momigliano also confessed that the antiquary remained 'deeply mysterious in his ultimate aims'.[6] Perhaps, then, we need to pay more attention to the reasons why men like Peiresc did what they did. He often justified his researches, however arcane they might appear to us, in terms of their contribution to the public good. But what kind of public and what sort of good was served by knowing about Gnostic gems or pre-Columbian clothing?

Gassendi's explanation put the emphasis on a 'Baconian' advancement of learning. Peiresc, he wrote, was driven by the powerful belief that 'the least invention, or observation of any man' ought to be preserved, 'being alwayes in hopes, that either himself, or some other would be advantaged thereby'.[7] It was for this very reason that he was so careful to make sure that objects were documented, texts published and that what remained in manuscript be kept in public libraries, where it was more likely to remain accessible, than in private ones.[8] There was, however, a still worse fate: John Aubrey wrote of his terror at ancient manuscripts being 'put under Pies' or used 'to wrap herrings'.[9] This slow but steady collecting of information defined the course of knowledge's progress. In an influential article, Krzysztof Pomian identified this practice of 'accumulation' as the hallmark of antiquarian scholarship and cited as examples Bacon and Peiresc. He contrasted this approach with humanist historiography that aimed at moral instruction.[10]

But there is more to Bacon's motivation, and Peiresc's as well, than increasing information.[11] For in *The Advancement of Learning* Bacon also emphasized learning as training for the mind. His 'local' objective was to defend antiquaries from the allegation – still current enough in Matthew Arnold's day to be rehearsed in the opening pages of *Culture and Anarchy*, and in our own to be the subject of Richard Hofstadter's *Anti-Intellectualism in American Life* – that there was such a thing as 'excessive' learning, and that knowledge could make one unfit for positions of social responsibility. The force of his rebuttal helps us understand just how an antiquary could have been a hero to an age revelling in the creative force of intellectual labour.

> For if by a secret operation it make men perplexed and irresolute, on the other side by plain precept it teacheth them when and upon what ground to resolve; yea, and how to carry things in suspense without prejudice till they resolve. If it make men positive and regular, it teacheth them what things are in their nature demonstrative, and what are conjectural; and as well the use of distinctions and exceptions, as the latitude of principles and rules. If it mislead by disproportion or dissimilitude of examples, it teacheth men the force of circumstances, the errors of comparisons, and all the cautions of application; so that in all these it doth rectify more effectually than it can pervert.[12]

For his part, Peiresc, in an extraordinarily intimate letter of 1636 to his Roman agent Claude Menestrier, spoke of a 'charge de conscience' that lay upon the scholar not to 'abandon' objects to those 'men of quality' who did not know what to do with them. Peiresc was not simply reiterating the distinction he drew – and we examined in Chapter One – between a working collection and an ornamental one. He told Menestrier how, in 1625, when Aleandro visited him in the retinue of Cardinal Barberini, he had brought as a gift – knowing too well Peiresc's obsession with ancient metrology – a series of bronze weights. Peiresc remonstrated with Aleandro for depriving his patron of this object. 'But he rebuked me furiously', Peiresc recalled, 'and reproached me that I not render myself guilty in the eyes of posterity of having deprived her of the fruits that could be extracted from these fine pieces. That, moreover, it would be worth almost as much to toss these into the sea as to give them to men of this sort.'

Behind this little story lies a passionate sense of how knowledge could 'serve the public'. 'Conscience' is the key word. Peiresc felt an obligation to keep alive all that had survived the 'shipwreck of antiquity' as if it were a living thing. By selling objects into collections where they would remain unstudied and unpublished, Peiresc warned Menestrier, 'you might have, some day, a very remorseful conscience for having contributed by your care and your efforts to the loss of a monument of Antiquity worthy of memory, when you could succeed at saving the life it had been granted – so unhoped for – up until now'. Peiresc contrasted this with 'my patience and my study' that had brought so many things to light that would otherwise have remained unknown.[13] Similarly, unless absolutely necessary he never insisted on the shipment of unique objects, but devoted great pains to instructing the appropriate intermediaries in the making of casts and drawings, lest some monument that had survived hundreds if not thousands of years 'perish completely, whether in the hands of workers or on the road'.[14]

Yet, even Peiresc's own precious treasury very nearly fell victim to this fate. After his death in 1637 his possessions passed into the hands of his brother Valavez, for many years his collaborator. But after the death of Valavez in 1645 the papers and objects were inherited by his son and Peiresc's nephew, a worthless rake who saw in these only a possible source of revenue – or of kindling – nearly bringing true the worst fears of Peiresc's friends. This fate 'is so ordered by the eternal providence of God,' François Henry wrote in a letter published in later editions of Gassendi's *Life*, 'that all men may remember, in the midst of their most eager Collections of Books (who are apt with too much confidence to brood over their learned Treasures) that such things as are collected in time, will likewise after certain revolutions, passe away with time'.[15] That anything survived at all was due to the efforts of the grandson of Peiresc's half-sister (from his father's remarriage), Thomassin de Mazaugues. A lover of learning who fashioned himself the 'Imitator of the Culture of Peiresc' ('Cultus Peireskii Aemulus') he rescued the manuscripts and catalogued them. Thomassin's coat of arms bore the device *Tempus edax rerum* (plate 14).

'No period', Erwin Panofsky wrote, 'has been so obsessed with the depth and width, the horror and the sublimity, of the concept of time as the Baroque'.[16] The desire to check the progress of 'time which consumes metals and marbles', of 'eating age', animated Peiresc and his friends.[17] It was time, Gassendi wrote in the dedication of his *Life*, that had reduced the ancient, legendary Maecenas to but a name, and he 'feared, lest the same may happen to this our *Mecaenas*'. He described time's work as darkness inexorably descending over the works and days of man: 'For the Fame and Memory of things, resembles the evening Twi-light, or shutting in of the day, which being at first exceeding clear, does by little and little, in such sort vanish away, as to be swallowed up in darkness; and therefore History is needful, as a Torch, to bring the same to light.'[18] Peiresc, he wrote, had tried to do just this, he had 'endeavoured to give light to the darknesse of History, from the Testimony of Instruments and Authentick Acts and Records' ('ex ipsa fide instrumentorum actorumque authenticorum adferre lucem studuerit').[19]

Time was the true nemesis of all those who studied the past. In a boast that almost immediately became legendary, Cyriac of Ancona explained of the antiquary's art that it was able to overcome 'the ruins of time' ('temporis labe') and the 'carelessness of men' ('Hominumque incuria') and 'awaken from the land of the dead not only the lost famous titles of men' but also 'to recall the names of towns from the underworld into light'. Impressed with these superhuman powers, he exclaimed, in a lost echo of Cicero, 'O mighty and divine strength of my art'.[20] Bringing the dry bones of the past back to life became one of the most powerful professional descriptions of the antiquary, and is a potent metaphor for the Renaissance as a whole. The activity also touched something very personal in those engaged in it. Francis Bacon spoke of 'reverence', John Donne 'joy', William Dugdale 'delight', and Gassendi a 'satisfaction' and 'pleasure' in discovering what the ancients thought that more than recompensed them for their toils.[21] Like Cyriac, these men experienced the remoteness of the past as a challenge to the possibility of self-knowledge and its overcoming – they believed it possible – as a triumph of the living over the very idea of mortality. Lorenzo Pignoria borrowed from Peiresc an Indonesian idol (plate 15) which he thought might represent 'Time, the best revealer of all things hidden' and he illustrated it on the last pages of his path-breaking 1615 study of the gods of America and Asia – surely a worthy match for the *Plus Ultra* that Bacon famously proclaimed on the title page of his *Great Instauration* (1620).[22]

But the confrontation with time that the antiquary lived in his daily study of its sadly broken remains was also the most effective schooling possible in being philosophical about life. This was also the central purpose of neo-Stoicism, the lifestyle that aspired to the status of philosophy and was so prominent during Peiresc's lifetime outside of the universities – or at least philosophy faculties – among the aristocrats and scholars who filled minor and major offices in the estates and bureaucracies of Europe's governments. A mind able to distinguish between fleeting appearances and enduring truths, things within one's control and those without, and between precepts derived from reason and urges fed by passion was more capable of attaining tranquillity amidst disorder and inner freedom under conditions of external constraint – features painfully familiar to those living through decades of civil and religious wars. The learned ability to worry about only those things worth worrying about was a strategy for reducing exposure to risk – what early moderns called 'fortune'. This training was especially valuable for those in government service since it enabled them to survive under regimes whose rulers could act as arbitrarily as nature.

It is a striking fact that this philosophy found its warmest reception in the same audience that was also deeply engaged with antiquarian study of the past. If, as Lipsius' 'Ego e Philologia Philosophiam feci' suggests, antiquarianism was responsible for neo-Stoicism, the reverse is to some extent also true. 'The Age of the Antiquaries', to use Momigliano's phrase, was also the age in which neo-Stoicism flourished because history was felt to provide a certain kind of consolation to men who were so desperately seeking it. If 'applied Stoicism' was all about putting things in perspective, who could comprehend this better than the antiquary who spent his days poring over the broken remains of ancient glory? Who better knew that time was the destroyer of all things?[23]

This theme is brilliantly represented in a painting that dates from near the beginning of the antiquarian movement that swept Rome in the sixteenth century. Dominated by the legend from Ovid's *Metamorphoses* (XV. 234) 'Time devourer of things, and you envious age, destroy all' ('Tempus edax rerum tuque invidiosa vetustas omnia destruitis'), the Frisian artist Hermannus Posthumus' canvas of 1536 has been described as 'the most extraordinary painting of Roman ruins ever made in the Renaissance' (plate 16).[24] It is both an acknowledgement of the inexorable grinding triumph of time and a call for the documentation and preservation of the ancient city's fast-disappearing remains. The little figures probing the vast ruins are Cyriac's heirs, artist-antiquaries like Posthumus and his friends Maarten van Heemskerck and Lambert Sustris who struggled to make order in this half-submerged wreckage of antiquity. The fantastic landscape only accentuates the role of archaeology in the pursuit of the past.[25]

By the time Joachim du Bellay arrived in Rome, in June 1553, some of the protection of ruins advocated by Posthumus had already begun. But the contrast between the blasted remains and the modern city growing up all around them was still shocking. In *Les Antiquitéz de Rome* (1558), a work that articulates many of the same themes as du Bellay's more famous manifesto of the French Renaissance, the *Deffence et illustration de la langue françoyse* (1549), he offered the tourist's lament: 'thou stranger, which for Rome in Rome here seekest, / And nought of Rome in Rome perceiv'st at all'. He, too, blamed ravenous time. For Rome had become 'the pray of time, which all things doth devowre'. The 'sacred ruines' and monuments stood witness to its much greater power. 'And though your frames do for a time make warre / Gainst time, yet time in time shall ruinate / Your workes and names, and your last reliques marre'.[26] 'O world's inconstancy', exclaimed the poet.[27] Yet so great was her fame that even 'though time doth Commonwealths devowre, / Yet no time' could ever wipe the city from memory.[28] If Rome still lived 'In spight of time' (no. 5) it was due to her poets, not her masons. In the contest between worn stone and well-hewn words the poet saw his chance for glory.

The familiar Elizabethan English is that of Edmund Spenser, whose translation of the *Antiquitez* as the *The Ruines of Rome* appeared in his *Complaints* (1591). Du Bellay's Rome evoked the inconstancy of all things human that Spenser returned to in the *Two Cantos of Mutabilitie* which, 'under the legend of Constancie', probed the popular belief that 'MUTABILITY in them doth play/ Her cruell sports, to many mens decay'.[29] In *The Ruines of Time*, also published in the *Complaints*, Spenser focused more closely on the tense relationship between 'time the destroyer' and 'scholarship the preserver'.

Not Rome, but the ruins of Romano-British Verulamium, occasioned the poem. The ancient remains of the city had been discovered in the Middle Ages and carted off to build the Cathedral of St Albans.[30] The spirit of the ruined city, weeping by the wayside, bemoaned the 'vaine worlds glorie, and unstedfast state / Of all that lives, on face of sinfull earth'.[31] The inconstancy of the world is blended with the traditional images of *vanitas*, the 'bubble glas of breath' and life that 'Doth as a vapour vanish, and decaie'.[32] The catalogue of great men and great peoples that have graced, and then departed, the world's stage leads up to Rome and the fate of ancient Britain after the fall of the Roman Empire.

'But me no man bewaileth', laments the spirit of the city. 'They are all gone', both the inhabitants of Verulamium and any 'that mentioneth my name / To be remembered of posteritie'.[33] Against time's all-conquering march stood one man, '*Cambden* the nourice of antiquitie / And lanterne unto late succeeding age'. Despite 'fortunes injurie, / And times decay, and envies cruell tort', he had succeeded in resuscitating the memory of the ancient city. In celebration of *Britannia* (1586), Spenser prophesied, '*Cambden*, though time all moniments obscure, / yet thy just labours shall endure'.[34] To du Bellay's elevation of the poet as guardian of immortality, which Spenser echoes later in the poem ('But such as neither of themselves can sing, / Nor yet are sung of others for reward, / Die in obscure oblivion', ll.344–6), is added the antiquary.

Camden's *Britannia*, undertaken at the suggestion of his Dutch friend, the geographer Abraham Ortelius, was a landmark of antiquarian scholarship. The description of his method offered a model to contemporaries.

> I have travailed over all England, I have conferred with most skillful observers in each country, I have studiously read over our owne countrie writers, old and new, all Greeke and Latine authors which have once made mention of Britain. I have had conference with learned men in other parts of Christendome: I have beene diligent in the Records of this Realme. I have looked into most libraries, Registers, and memorials of Churches, Cities, and Corporations, I have poored upon many an old Rowle, and Evidence: and produced their testimonie (as beyond all exception) when the cause required, in their very owne words (although barbarous they be) that the honor of veritie might in no wise be impeached.

By means of this approach Camden thought it possible to 'rake out, and free from darknesse such places as . . . TIME hath overcast with mist and darknesse by extinguishing, altering, and corrupting their old true names'. He excused the errors that might have been made 'For who is so skilfull that strugling with TIME in the foggie dark sea of Antiquity may not run upon rocks'.[35]

When encouraging others to publish their research on Anglo-Saxon, Camden noted that without publication 'it is to be feared that devouring Time in few yeeres will utterly swallow it, without hope of recoverie'.[36] In the same vein, another pioneering student of Anglo-Saxon, Richard Verstegan, also declared that '*Time* overwears what erst his silence wrought, / And also seeks Remembrance to deface'. It was the drive to overcome this fate that led men to 'make a Mirror of his Hower-glasse'. 'This deep desire', Verstegan continues, 'hath lastly moved me, / On Pilgrimage *Times* traces to ensue, / The Reliques of his ruines for to see'.[37]

Francis Bacon's definition of antiquarianism as a contest against time is far the most eloquent. He classified 'antiquities' as one of the three forms of history and described it as 'history defaced, or remnants of history which have casually escaped the shipwreck of time'. The account of the antiquary's practice that follows makes a pair with Camden's.

> *Antiquities*, or remnants of histories, are (as was said) like the spars of a shipwreck: when, though the memory of things be decayed and

almost lost, yet acute and industrious persons, by a certain persever-
ance and scrupulous diligence, contrive out of genealogies, annals,
titles, monuments, coins, proper names, and styles, etymologies of
words, proverbs, traditions, archives, and instruments as well public as
private, fragments of histories scattered about in books not historical,
– contrive, I say, from all these things or some of them, to recover
somewhat from the deluge of time; a work laborious indeed, but
agreeable to men, and joined with a kind of reverence; and well
worthy to supersede the fabulous accounts of the origins of nations;
and to be substituted for fictions of that kind.[38]

But what made this work 'agreeable' and what inspired 'reverence'?
The greatest dignity of learning, Bacon thought, was that it addressed a
fundamental human desire for 'immortality, or continuance'. This also
explained the rearing of families, cultivation of land, and the building of
cities. Because 'the monuments of wit and learning are more durable
than the monuments of power or those of hands' they could serve this
ambition. Antiquities brought men into contact with this deep human
truth. The words of Homer had outlasted countless palaces, and historians' accounts of the lives of ancient heroes survived the statues that had
long since turned to dust. The 'images of men's wits and knowledge',
Bacon wrote, 'remain in books, exempted from the wrong of time and
capable of perpetual renovation'. He declared that humane 'letters' were
like ships which 'pass through the vast seas of time, and make ages so
distant to participate of the wisdom, illuminations, and inventions, the
one of the other'.[39] To the poet for whom ruins were muse, Bacon added
the antiquary, like those tiny figures in Posthumus' painting whose 'per-
severance' and 'diligent' collecting, observing, and comparing of time's
flotsam and jetsam offered future generations the promise of contact with
their most distant past.

The personal dimension of the encounter with the past is rarely more
fully described in a scholarly genre that tends to avoid the first person.
We do not, for example, possess any extended reflection by Peiresc on
why he did what he did. It is for this reason that the work of the
Silesian poet and antiquary Martin Opitz is so valuable. Opitz
(1597–1639), a Protestant from Breslau, is famous now as the founder of
modern German poetry with his *Buch von der deutschen Poeterei* and
Deutsche Poemata (both 1624).[40] But like Grotius, Opitz was known in
his own time as a poet *and* as an antiquary. He studied with Janus
Gruter, and was a friend of Matthias Bernegger, Lipsius' disciple, Galileo's
translator, and Peiresc's man in Strasbourg. Opitz also translated into
German two of the works that Peiresc praised most highly, Grotius' *De
veritate* and John Barclay's *Argenis*, and it was Grotius who introduced

him into the Cabinet Dupuy during a brief stay in Paris in 1630. Though
Peiresc was then incommunicado because of the quarantine restrictions
imposed on a plague-ridden Provence, it is hard to imagine that Opitz
did not hear about him from Pierre and Jacques Dupuy, and we know
for certain that Grotius mentioned his name in a letter to Opitz of
1631.[41] Some of his 'inscriptions de Transylvanie' eventually found their
way into Peiresc's hands, having first travelled from Opitz to Bernegger
to Grotius, and these may be the ones now preserved in the Bibliothèque
Nationale in Paris.[42] Opitz' philosophical and philological formation was
similar to that of Peiresc and his friends. His reflections on the moral
economy of antiquarianism gave content to his art and can stand as
something of a surrogate for Peiresc's silences.

Travel integrated Opitz into the Republic of Letters. He could have
become acquainted with neo-Stoicism in Heidelberg, where he studied,
and surely must have in Leiden where he met G. J. Vossius and fell under
the influence of Daniel Heinsius. After leaving Leiden in 1621 Opitz
journeyed to wind-swept and libraryless Jutland where he composed his
Trostgedichte in Widerwertigkeit des Krieges [A Poem of Consolation in the
Adversity of War] (published 1633), described as one of the earliest and
most important receptions of neo-Stoicism in German literature.[43] The
familiar theme of attaining inner freedom won through rational self-
control in spite of a hostile world is set against the backdrop of a Europe
torn by war. A discarded subtitle was 'Uber die Beständigkeit' [On Con-
stancy], while the finished copy, which proclaimed *in Widerwertigkeit des
Krieges*, echoed Lipsius' *De constantia seu consolatio in publicis malis* as well
as du Vair's *De la constance in calamitez publiques* but with the backdrop
now of the Thirty Years War rather than the Revolt of the Netherlands
or the French Wars of Religion.[44]

The same year he wrote this poem Opitz journeyed to Transylvania,
to the court of the Protestant Hungarian Prince Bethlen Gabor in
Weißenburg (Alba Iulia, Gyulafehérvar) where he had been invited to
teach. There, Opitz wrote *Zlatna oder von der Ruhe des Gemüthes* (1622),
subtitled after Seneca in the appended panegyrical Latin poetry 'De
tranquillitate animi'.[45] In this poem, neo-Stoicism is not demanded by
calamitous current events, but by the equally jarring impact of the individual's encounter with the remains of the past. With Opitz, as with
Peiresc, we have a neo-Stoic who was an antiquary. But his calling as a
poet turned his sentiments about the past into his subject matter, putting
the complex appeal of the material past into words.

Zlatna, a small town near Weißenburg, was the residence of Heinrich
Lissabon, whose wandering Sephardi family managed its gold mine and
who became Opitz' companion and escape from the routine of a barbarous provincial court.[46] What is unusual about this poem is not its

typical reflections on the vanity of the world, nor its equally typical favourable description of country life as opposed to courtly, but its use of serious antiquarianism to frame an argument about the best life. The inscriptions left by Trajan's colonists and the names that still spoke from the stones, Scauriones, Syros, Frontones, Flamonios, Seneccciones, Marcus Ulpius, had, in part, defied the destructive power of time – and, like a good pupil of Gruter, Opitz carefully copied down the inscriptions, printed them in the notes to the poem and sent them on to his teacher for inclusion in a later edition of his *Inscriptiones antiquae totius orbi Romani* (first published in 1602).[47] Walking daily amidst the gravestones led Opitz to imagine his own urn full of funereal ashes.[48] The first version of Poussin's *Et in Arcadia Ego* (1630) might record a similar confrontation with Roman antiquity. Panofsky argued that it was less moralizing a *memento mori* than Guercino's earlier painting of the same title and also less classicizing than Poussin's later treatment (*c.*1636). Rather, the painting marked the immediacy of just such an encounter with the remains of the ancient world (plate 17).[49]

From the antiquary's passionate desire to reconstruct the world of ancient Rome Opitz passed on, almost imperceptibly, to the polymath's fascination with everything about the world at large. 'We leave aside not the origin of all things, from where, from who and how all things began, why the earth stands, the sky is smooth, and clouds give fire, all are known to us'.[50] With this we are far indeed from the disapproval of his contemporary, John Donne, who in the *Second Anniversary* posed a similar set of questions in order to caricature the polyhistor as a hunter of idle curiosities. Opitz had greater confidence in reason and in 'Die edle Wissenschaft' that was not only an ornament in good times and a source of strength in bad, but showed the way to endure with constancy in times of darkest necessity.[51] This link between intellectual and moral excellence was rarely so clearly drawn.

Opitz explicitly linked the scholar's, and particularly the antiquary's, knowledge of the world with the Stoic's ideal of living well in it. 'Those who reckon rightly about the course of the world learn to live according to nature and not build from the appearance of vain things that are only made and broken by time.'[52] Drawing on a familiar range of metaphors, Opitz argued that those who did not live according to reason were doomed to wander as if blind, while those who possessed it would be able to face even death with equanimity.[53] To achieve this heroism Opitz turned to learning in one of the clearest contemporary articulations of the relationship between study of the past and moral excellence. 'Thus I wished likewise to do, and my creative forces sought all the time with labour', and what others passed over because of its difficulty 'I conquered through diligence'. The object of Opitz' labour was, precisely, an antiquarian project. 'The overthrow of states, the customs of the ancient peoples, their food, their clothing, how variously they struggled, where this and that happened, indeed, all times, from the beginning of the world, I will make completely known to me'.[54]

In Transylvania, Opitz the poet-antiquary discovered what Opitz the poet-philosopher had discovered in Jutland: that time destroyed all but that not all losses were complete. Peiresc's master, du Vair, observed, paraphrasing St Augustine's discussion in *Confessions* (bk 11), that 'we live in time but do not really know what time is'.[55] Like Opitz, Peiresc applied this truth to his study of the past. The history of languages, for example, one of his favourite subjects in the last decade of his life, was shaped by this dynamic of change over time. 'The corruption of languages', Peiresc wrote to P. Gilles de Loches, 'is subject to changes and deteriorations or distancing from their beginning'.[56] Perusal of old glossaries showed how 'changes, and sometimes confusion according to the diversity of lands, nations and centuries, turned the most ancient meaning of many words to another sense'.[57] Many things false 'according to the rules and uses' of one time were perfectly correct in another. The interpretation of the past had to be governed by time and all that did not conform to 'the diverse uses according to the diversity of the centuries' could not be admitted as true.[58]

Only by being able to recognize the mechanics of change could the historian establish a chronology and separate the desired material from the accretions that interested less. This was why Gassendi was upset that Rabbi Salomon Azubi from Carpentras, who translated astronomical tables for him, had altered the first page of his astronomical tables 'to relate them to our times, rather than leave them as the author had written in relation to his times'.[59] Similarly, in a letter to the jeweller Alvares in Paris, his contact with other Portuguese in India, Peiresc explained that when asking for drawings of ancient objects ornamented in more recent times he wanted the modern adornments left off because 'these settings are not helpful, even obstruct me more than they help, since I am only looking for what the ancients could have made there, and not what the moderns have added to them, which does nothing but make more costly to me what could be ancient and deprive me of the means to buy it'.[60]

For Peiresc it was change, whether in a language or a ritual or an image, that was the key to historical explanation, for it made possible the notional stratigraphy that guided the scholar's handling of evidence. That it was an antiquary recognizing that change was the 'normal condition' of the world might seem odd, since the common view has it that political historians, following ancient models like Thucydides or Tacitus, built narratives around events and were therefore guided by chronology, while antiquarians, following Herodotus, instead produced static accounts in which theme rather than chronology served as the basic measurement.

Awareness of change was the first step to explaining what, when, where, how and, most importantly, why things changed. Of course, long before Peiresc antiquaries had used the remains of the ancient world in order to understand it. Even before the northerner Hermannus Posthumus had sounded the humanist's trumpet with his declaration that 'the ruins of Rome themselves teach us what it was like' ('Roma quanta fuit ipsa ruina docet'), Raphael had explained to Pope Leo X that his knowledge of antiquities reflected the time he had spent studying them 'minutely', measuring them 'with diligence', reading the best authors 'continuously' and then comparing 'the works with their writings'.[61] In his utterly conventional claim that the excellence of the built landscape inspired its inhabitants to excellence, Raphael contrasted the great style of the ancient city with the utterly crude ('così goffa') workmanship of medieval Roman architecture.[62]

But Peiresc was truly unusual in recognizing that the *goffa* – according to Ingrid Rowland the ancestor of the modern 'goofy' – could be a valuable resource for the scholar even if it failed to do justice to the ideal of antiquity.[63] Of course, he was as open to the beautiful as the next person. He valued the contribution of artists to his studies, and knew enough to pay attention to the greats: he kept a list of paintings he had seen at Fontainebleau, bought engravings of works by Michelangelo, kept 'the music' ('la musique') from Rinuncini's *L'Euridice* (1600), and knew enough about opera to explain to Mersenne how it worked and to contrast it with French sung drama.[64] But what stands out in his practice is the way he was able to distinguish between the aesthetic and the documentary functions of art and to value the latter as much as the former, when appropriate.

Near the beginning of his epistolary relationship with Rubens – Peiresc's most revealing letters often came at the beginning of a correspondence when he tried to state his interests in the clearest terms – he felt obliged to explain why he was so fascinated by material of poor quality whereas Rubens, and most everyone else, sought after the obviously beautiful. Sometimes, Peiresc mused, one had to content oneself with the crude when the fine could not be had, just as sailors made do with dried biscuit on the high seas. Any effort to make sense of what had suvived the shipwreck of time, Peiresc argued, could not afford to discard evidence for aesthetic reasons. 'I experienced, in days gone by', Peiresc continued, 'almost the same fastidiousness concerning many things of crude workmanship' ('goffa maestria'). But just as the absence of wine in Flanders had forced him to consume beer, which he then preferred to even the best wines, so too an early exposure to works of poor workmanship had developed his taste for such objects.[65] Moreover, while works of surpassing beauty had always their protectors, these poor little objects ran the risk of being ignored. Yet it was only these, Peiresc argued, with 'which one could fill in and restore the many gaps in ancient history in the most obscure and barbarous centuries'.[66]

The broken past was worth as much to Peiresc as 'precious stones' because he knew what to look for.[67] From the historian's point of view, the ugly or the mistaken could be just as helpful for better understanding the past and, therefore, the self. He explained to Pierre and Jacques Dupuy in December 1636, near the end of his life, 'that one could even draw from the scholar's errors, and from the most consequential of them, the same benefit and pleasure that we have when we consider how small was that portion of the inhabited world known to previous generations, and then to see the progress from century to century'. The history of error was also a record of progress. 'I find everywhere some little thing from which I can glean and profit, regardless of it not being of the highest taste.'[68] Peiresc described this ability to find the tasty morsels in an otherwise insipid stew, to seek out things of value wherever they could be found, not only as a methodological first principle, but as evidence that he had 'made progress in the contemplative life'.[69]

Running through Peiresc's letters is the relationship between studying the history of learning, false starts, blind alleys and all, and living a decent life. To Tommaso Campanella, who soon after his arrival in Paris had managed to squander all the goodwill that Peiresc had expended on his behalf, he explained that 'sometimes opinions that seem ridiculous to others such as, for example, those of Christians to Muslims or, on the contrary, those of Muslims to Christians', could, for a sympathetic interpreter, 'pass as the most grave mysteries and of greatest importance'.[70] Similarly, those who believed theories since proven untrue, such as the Antipodes, or more recently – and here Peiresc was putting a fine point on things in a letter of 1636 to a Barberini retainer – the geocentric cosmos, 'would have to, sooner or later, accustom themselves to tolerate it, whatever repugnance they find there'.[71] Peiresc reminded Campanella, in that remarkable letter of July 1635, that if one examined the teachings of the ancient Greek philosophical schools with 'human charity' one found some things of value while the rest could be explained 'in terms of the ignorance of their times'.[72] Campanella was not, therefore, to describe Epicurus' philosophy – the subject of Gassendi's labour – as 'ridiculous' merely because it seemed 'so strange'.[73]

Peiresc did not hesitate to apply the lessons of his learning to the living of his life. 'I am of the humour', he wrote, 'that I do not much enjoy the efforts of those who wait upon the confutation of the opinions of others' since 'the brevity of human life does not allow these things without grave necessity'. It seemed to him 'much more noble' to help someone make the best of his own arguments – literally, 'to establish their foundations' – and only to refute what absolutely could not be passed over. Peiresc's closing peroration urged Campanella to seek out what was best in each person, not worst, 'leaving to the painter the praise that might be appropriate for his art, and to the singer that of his music and to the architect that of his buildings, and so forth'.[74] Because 'the weakness of human genius is too great to be able to penetrate every secret of nature in one try', and because 'the brevity of human life does not allow that one person alone is sufficient, it is necessary to adopt the observations of a good number of others from past centuries and future ones to clarify that which fits better'. This was why, he concluded, a little interpretative – and interpersonal – charity was necessary in the scholarly world, something Campanella had not needed to think much about in the deep, dark dungeons of the Inquisition.[75]

Peiresc urged this same, essentially moral, outlook on the persecutors as well as the persecuted. He pleaded with Marin Mersenne to 'abstain from scolding someone for ignorance nor even for a big mistake without some urgent necessity'. Much better to say that one could not approve of an argument than to denounce those others who did approve. He thought that Mersenne's works 'would be worth double' if instead of criticizing others he offered constructive arguments of his own.[76] Mersenne seemed persuaded and even took the extraordinary step of submitting the pages of a new work (the *Harmonie universelle*) to Peiresc's judgement as they rolled off the presses. Any harsh criticisms of astrologers and the like that remained, he promised, 'will be the last that will leave my hands'.[77] However, a year later Peiresc found himself again urging Mersenne 'to search for words more sweet and less acidic than those that sometimes come first to the mouth', saying that 'it is good to review a second time what one writes too precipitously'.[78] When Mersenne had the temerity to attack one of Peiresc's friends in a letter to him, he was exasperated. 'For the honour of God, abstain from this at least in the letters that you write to me!' What especially troubled him was Mersenne's tendency to criticize others 'without having decisive information' since there were always things that we ourselves did not know. This was why, 'I have often told you, it is better to enjoy the rose and leave aside the thorns, and praise what is praiseworthy in someone without taking pleasure in biting them'.[79]

In his plea for relaxation of the sentence against Galileo, Peiresc reminded Cardinal Francesco Barberini that the early Church had taken the 'long view' and 'like a good mother, did not cease to show great veneration for the other religious ideas and indications of the piety and divine zeal' of men like Tertullian and Origen who had erred whether 'by innocence or otherwise'. The Church had even castigated those who dared to lump their errors with those of real heretics. 'Given the human condition [*infermità*], that it can fall into some kind of sin', Peiresc concluded that this 'fragility is not always unworthy of excuse or pardon'. Posterity would, therefore, find it strange that the current Church was unable to excuse or pardon an old man who had already retracted an opinion that was, in any event, not absolutely prohibited. 'How could so many inventions, amongst the most noble that were discovered in many centuries, not merit indulgence for an obscure joke' ('scherzo problematico')?[80] A year later, writing to Holstenius in the Barberini household, Peiresc returned to this theme. Just as it was 'a species of participation in divine actions' to do good to another, 'it is not less worthy to pardon those who because of infirmity or blindness forget their duty towards us'.[81] These words are a good example of Peiresc acting 'full of kindly feeling, courtesy and consideration'.[82]

Like Thomas Fuller's portrait of the 'True Church Antiquary' – and Fuller was once suggested as the English translator of Gassendi's *Vita* – Peiresc counselled others, and even the greatest in the land, to live by a simple rule deduced from learning. 'Not forcing others to his own opinion, but leaving them to their own liberty; not filling up all with his own conjectures, to leave no room for other men; nor tramples he on their credits, if in them he finds slips and mistakes. For here our souls have but one eye; (the apostle saith, 'We know but in part).'[83]

In that letter to Dupuy of December 1636 on the value of ugly things or disproven arguments, Peiresc again had recourse, as in the letter to Campanella of the previous year, to the example of the diversity of ancient Greek philosophical schools. He explained that he enjoyed studying the different maxims of those 'who take such diverse routes in order to arrive at the knowledge of nature and use such diverse arguments for supporting their conceptions and conjunctures'. Nowhere in the correspondence that I have seen does Peiresc come closer to mentioning Michel de Montaigne than in this evocation of the first of the *Essais*, 'Par divers moyens on arrive a pareille fin'. Nevertheless, along with Lipsius, du Vair, and Charron, the spirit of Montaigne looms over Peiresc.[84]

In his own deliciously idiosyncratic fashion, Montaigne had contemplated the philosophical value of antiquarian learning. In the essay 'On Coaches', discussion of the Old and New worlds is bridged by a passage explaining that the inadequacy of a single individual's point of view showed 'how puny and stunted is the knowledge of the most inquisitive men. A hundred times more is lost for us than what comes to our knowledge, not only of individual events . . . but of the circumstances of great polities and nations'. The 'pitiful' state of human learning threatened to give 'us a very false idea of everything'. The only remedy was to try and master all fields of knowledge for without this breadth of inquiry, spanning the entire known world, there could be 'no foundation for our scientific laws'. It is this further claim that seems to underpin the antiquary's – quixotic, surely, for Montaigne – ambition to grasp not single events, but the past in whole cloth. Yet the very 'multiplication and succession of forms' that offered the only possibility of more secure knowledge also brought even the most diligent inquirer up against the *ne plus ultra*. Solon's words, recorded by Cicero and quoted by Montaigne just prior to this passage, suggest a link between the practice of the antiquary and its foundation in a stoicizing teaching to 'be philosophical' about life.

> If we were vouchsafed a sight of the infinite extent of time and space stretching away in every direction, and if our minds were allowed to wander over it far and wide, ranging about and hastening along without ever glimpsing a boundary where it could halt: from such an immensity we would grasp what almighty power lies behind those innumerable forms.[85]

Discovery of the 'Almighty Power' was a goal of theologians and historians animated by a commitment to the reality of a providential, sacred history. The more one knew and understood, the more clearly visible was the finger of God. But Montaigne's passage also suggested that such a lifetime dedicated to learning could also give the sage a Socratic sense of his own limitations.

As with Montaigne's Solon, so Peiresc's pursuit of limitless knowledge brought him a keener sense of his place in the wider scheme of things. Gassendi explicitly declared that his study of antiquity 'comprehends principally Universal History, which he had so printed in his mind and memory, that a man would have thought he had lived in all places and times'. Peiresc 'held it evermore as a Maxime' that history was useful not merely as illustration – the example given is law – 'but to the ordering of a mans life, and the possessing of his mind' ('vitae animoque eximia quadam atque liberali delectatione afficiendo'). History was better than philosophy not only because it taught by example rather than by words, but because, Gassendi continued, it 'makes in some sort, that we ought not to think much of our short life, making the same [person] partaker of things and times which are past' ('participem rerum temporumque praeteritorum').[86] Peiresc's universal knowledge made him more philosophical; it led him 'to elevate his mind above the vulgar condition'. Gassendi went on to explain what this entailed:

to be indifferently inclined towards all men, and to become like
Socrates, a Citizen, not of one Country only, but of the whole World
[*universi totitus civem*]; to admire nothing in humane affaires, and in
a word, to have his mind so tempered, as to enjoy the greatest tranquillity possible, and consequently, the greatest good.[87]

Gassendi's description, likening Peiresc to Socrates, himself a model of
the wise man in the works of Montaigne and Sarpi, closely follows the
outlines of Charron's picture of the sage. He is the

citizen of the world; like Socrates, he embraces with affection the
whole human species. He embraces all humanity in his sentiments,
travels everywhere as if at home, views like a sun, with equal, constant
and indifferent regard, as if from a high watchtower, all the changes,
diversities and vicissitudes of things, without himself changing and
always holding himself the same to himself.[88]

In Gassendi's portrait of Peiresc as the wise man we find our answer
to the question of why he studied the past. If time eventually scythed
all, parents, friends, and nations alike, leaving men alone and uncertain,
learning offered the consolation of understanding. This is what Gassendi
referred to when he wrote that Peiresc 'could hardly well endure to see
an ingenuous man, who was a stranger in his own world'.[89]

A few years after the appearance of Gassendi's *Life of Peiresc*, Daniello
Bartoli showed that this deeply personal statement had echoes in the
wider world. His *Learned Man Defended and Reformed* (1645) took up the
idea that learning was the true homeland of the wise because with it
one could be at home anywhere. Knowledge, in other words, made one
a 'citizen of the world'.[90] Neither exile nor prison could deprive the
scholar of his real homeland.[91] 'To know the world', Bartoli wrote in a
memorable phrase, 'is to possess it'.[92]

The greatest of heroes were, therefore, those who expanded the
bounds of knowledge. 'Oh, how many,' Bartoli exclaimed, 'seeking things
not before found; have found things not before sought!'[93] Bartoli's argument was one long paraphrase from Seneca's *Epistulae Morales* (no. 33).
'Who then will prescribe bounds, and limits to the free flight of the
ingenious, confining them within the straights of the things already
found; as if there could not be any new Discoveries? If this Law had
been known to Antiquity, we should at this day have known nothing'.[94]
Bartoli took the side of Erasmus who mocked the slavish Ciceronian as
an ass.[95] He made explicit the link that we have been elaborating
between knowledge-as-citizenship, and the scholar as an exemplar of
moral heroism. They were like the greatest of explorers, he wrote,

who in Learning essay to make the first way to the discovery of new places; (which is nothing inferiour to the sailing of un-navigable Oceans;) it is necessary, that amongst the annoyances, and toils of the long Voyage, of an un-practised study; amongst the familiar, and frequent conspiracies of desperation; he conquer himself a thousand times: attending, as those Glorious Heroes, Conquerours of the Golden Fleece; more to the glory of the end, than to the trouble of the means.[96]

If the 1640s marked the high point of this antiquarian ideal of learning and virtue, it was during this same decade that its foundations also began, quite visibly, to give way.[97] While all across Europe ancient constitutions collapsed into civil war, the tense equilibrium between Stoic and Augustinian anthropologies that we examined in the previous chapter was irrevocably shattered. Amidst the general upheaval, whose consequences were immediate and inescapable, the impact of this latter shift was slower to hit and more subtle, if ultimately just as powerful. The balance between free inquiry and belief, between commitment to books and to observation of the world, to history and to mathematics, was maintained by a confidence in the very possibility of their being held together and it was just this that was sapped, slowly but surely.

This subtle shift is already visible in Thomas Browne's *Hydriotaphia. Urne Burriall, or a Discourse of the Sepulchrall Urnes Lately Found in Norfolk* (1658), an apt pendant to Opitz' *Zlatna* from the other end of Europe. He saw the urns as 'sad and sepulchral Pitchers . . . the ruines of forgotten times'. The presence of antiquities, he wrote in the dedication, just as Opitz wrote in his, 'raiseth your thoughts unto old things, and consideration of times before you'. Like the 'Todtentopff' that Opitz saw amidst the Roman gravestones and imagined being filled with his own ashes, Browne saw the urns as 'artificial *mementos*, or coffins by our bedside, to minde us of our graves'.[98] Just as Opitz described inscriptions that had withstood time, weather, and fire, Browne noted that 'Time which antiquates Antiquities, and hath an art to make dust of all things, hath yet spared these *minor* Monuments'. Yet these ashes which, unlike Opitz' stones, gave no indication of their formerly living contents, survived only 'as Emblemes of mortall vanities; Antidotes against pride, vainglory, and madding vices'.[99]

But Browne does not belong to the generation of Peiresc, either in body or in spirit. For he was sure that the antiquary's most conscientious effort would fail because 'there is no antidote against the *Opium* of time'. Parents were buried in the memories of their children and children now alive in that of those yet unborn. 'To be read by bare Inscriptions like many in *Gruter*' – referring to the masterwork of Opitz' teacher

– 'to hope for Eternity by Ænigmaticall Epithetes or first letters of our names [as in inscriptions], to be studied by Antiquaries, who we were, and have new Names given us like many of the Mummies, are cold consolations unto the Students of perpetuity'.[100] Though the words are (almost) the words of Cyriac, the sentiment is worlds away from his boasted divine art of recalling to life the lost names of the dead from the night of oblivion.

By the second half of the seventeenth century Europe had acquired new culture heroes. The New Science had begun to canonize its saints, and by the eighteenth century polite society worshipped at their altars. Peiresc became a dimly remembered figure. Samuel Sorbière, writing to Thomas Hobbes in 1663, complained that a certain Marquis de Sourdis was but a 'pseudo-Peireskius', lacking 'qualities such as friendliness, polished conversation, favour towards all, munificence or a desire to be helpful, generous expenditure, and other virtues which make men such as Peiresc equal to kings'.[101] A close friend of Gassendi, Hobbes was sure to have caught the reference to Peiresc. By the end of the century an English antiquary and colleague of John Aubrey, Martin Lister, making the rounds of Parisian cabinets, described Peiresc simply as 'Maecenas'.[102] Pierre Bayle fixed his identity for posterity as a facilitator of others' learning by calling him the 'Procureur Général' of the Republic of Letters.

In Provence, memories were sharper. It was Charles Plumier (1646–1704), a Marseillais and Botanist Royal, who secured Peiresc's fame amongst the botanists by naming the oldest of the succulents after Peiresc, subtly echoing Peiresc's own fascination with ancient things and the connections between them.[103] Indeed, it was as a representative of Provence's once glorious provincial culture that Peiresc was, occasionally, remembered in the eighteenth century.[104]

Among antiquaries, not surprisingly, memories lingered longest. Gronovius, in his study of ancient coins, lamented the loss of Peiresc's collection in passionate and eloquent terms.[105] The learned Benedictine, Bernard de Montfaucon, who was able to draw heavily on Peiresc's manuscripts and objects for his *Antiquitée expliquée* (1719–21) praised him as one 'who hath collected more Monuments on almost every part of Antiquity than any man I know', and the abbé Du Bos included Peiresc amongst the illustrious antiquaries who interpreted the great cameo of the Sainte Chapelle.[106] Laurence Sterne's *Tristram Shandy* (1759), with its innumerable and interminable learned digressions, unexplained juxtapositions of odd facts, and repeated inclusion of documents with little or no comment, a monument to the antiquarian style that William Robertson and Edward Gibbon were about to make obsolete, fittingly includes Peiresc in its commemoration.[107] Uncle Toby retold, with some embellishment, Gassendi's account of how 'the learned *Peireskius*' walked

500 miles on foot to see Stevinus' (1548–1620) famous flying chariot with his own eyes, earning praise as an 'indefatigable labourer' out of 'love for the sciences'. Dr Slop's disparaging 'the more fool *Peireskius*' elicited from Walter Shandy a classic defence of the antiquary: 'Why is *Peireskius*, or any man else, to be abused for an appetite for that, or any other morsel of sound knowledge?'[108]

The very occasional late eighteenth-century *éloge* of Peiresc went no further than Gassendi's narrative but now viewed its subject through the lens of enlightenment. Because we are so much more familiar with this later language of individual excellence, these presentations not only make the 'Peireskean virtues' more accessible to us, but they show us just how the seventeenth century's virtues were adapted to suit eighteenth-century taste. One writer, for instance, concluded a survey of Peiresc's life with a Rousseauesque tirade against the misuse of wealth – contrasted of course with Peiresc's sobriety – that had led eighteenth-cenury Frenchmen to 'torment nature, build in order to destroy and destroy in order to build' and to exchange the accumulated wealth of years for the pleasures of a few months.[109] Another, an Oratorian and Professor of Rhetoric at Marseille, looked backward and discerned the line leading from Montaigne to Peiresc to the *lumières*. 'Peyresc', he observed, 'principally searched for the history of man in that of peoples. He found him everywhere the same; the same vices and the same virtues, the same inclinations form everywhere the basis of his character'. The traveller arriving in France would 'easily recognize' the same human beings despite the variety of our 'usages', 'modes', and 'habits'. 'So Peiresc', the author continued, echoing the antiquary's connection between travel through space and time, 'comparing centuries and peoples did not find, so to speak, any difference amongst them other than of manners'.[110]

This is a portrait of the antiquary as *philosophe*. Peiresc's historical knowledge enabled him to see over time 'errors replaced or fortified by new errors', but also 'some truths that float up, are seized upon by accident, are exposed for a long time to the insults of ignorance and developed with difficulty'.[111] Indeed, as we have seen, Peiresc took just this pleasure in studying the errors and misunderstandings of previous generations. Edward Gibbon described this kind of historical empathy as the sign of a 'philosophical knowledge of antiquity'.[112] His younger contemporary, the Commissioner for Antiquities in Rome, Ennio Quirino Visconti, described the learning of the antiquaries (he called it 'archeological science') as 'the fruit of a judicious reading of the classics, of a diligent comparison of monuments, of a sure taste for the fine arts, a deep knowledge of the customs, laws, religion, and the character of the ancient peoples, a knowledge which is not distinct from philosophy'.[113]

Gibbon's model antiquary was Anne-Claude-Philippe de Tubières-Grimoard de Pestel de Levis, Comte de Caylus (1692–1765) – like Montfaucon another beneficiary of Peiresc's labours and, according to Marc Fumaroli, Peiresc's spiritual heir. He, too, tried to convey to readers the personal motivations that drove such awesome, and also off-putting, labours. In the *préfaces* to his seven-volume *Recueil des antiquitées égyptiennes, etrusques, grecques, romanes* (1756–62) he offered an emotional account of the pleasures of discovery.[114] In the preface to volume five he explained that the antiquary worked with 'the simple particuliars', with 'some atoms in the immensity of the void'. He knew of a handful of names that had survived oblivion, 'or who obtained two or three lines of an inscription, of which one often cannot even make out the sense; or, if it is possible to read it, one generally learns that a certain man had lived'.[115] If it so happened that a historian had mentioned the person's name, all the better. 'This is the essential point,' Caylus wrote, 'and the principal object of these reflections' because it showed off the greatest advantage of antiquarian scholarship: the ability to make the word flesh. Even a tiny fragment of information like this showed 'to the antiquary the millions of men immured in the abyss of time, which will carry him off in turn in its whirlwind'. If even rulers could slip into oblivion, how vain were the efforts of all those who commissioned extravagant monuments to preserve their fame. 'The reflection on oneself that these examples trigger is perhaps the most effective means to destroy Egoism, that great enemy of man and the most troubling defect in society'.[116] The most encyclopaedic knowledge, as Montaigne and Peiresc affirmed, only brought man up short against his natural limitations – and this was its great value. These reflections, Caylus thought, would enlighten ('éclairer') the inquirer.[117]

And yet, during these same years, under the same banner of enlightenment, in the columns of the *Encyclopédie*, the antiquary's scholarship was condemned to the harshest of all modern fates: being old-fashioned. Caylus served Diderot as a model of 'anticomanie' that could be castigated as 'baggage de l'esprit'. Diderot, like the seventeenth-century Englishmen Earle and Mermion, condemned the lust for things old.[118] But there was more to Diderot's attack. At stake in the *philosophes*' assault on Caylus – and no indictment more powerful than Jean Baptiste Chardin's *Le Singe antiquaire* (1743) (plate 18) had been levelled in the preceding century – as Jean Seznec and Krzysztof Pomian have shown, was a repudiation of the social role of antiquities and the implicit claim that knowledge was a prerequisite for cultural authority.[119] To Caylus' insistence on careful study of broken fragments Diderot and his friends opposed the 'divine, but blind impulsion' and 'the demon that works within'.[120] Their commitment to the natural, signalled in their praise of natural history

collections, represented at one and the same time a radical democratiza-
tion of the grounds of aesthetic judgement and a dramatic rejection of
the value of history for living well.

This was what John Keats meant when he wrote that 'what the imagination seizes as Beauty must be truth – whether it existed before or
not', or, most famously, that all one needed to know was that 'Beauty is
truth, truth beauty'.[121] In Chapter One we noted that for Peiresc and
Gassendi, but also for acute later observers, like Piranesi and Nietzsche,
there existed a complex relationship between the antiquarian reconstruction of the past and the work of imagination. They argued that the
act of historical scholarship was impossible without imagination and
memory. Not so for Keats. 'Memory', he declared, which was also
identified by Kant as the specific virtue of the polyhistors, 'should not
be called Knowledge'. Keats instead suggested in almost Whitman-like
prose that the creative vision did not much depend on the kind of
knowledge that books provided. 'Now it appears to me that almost any
Man may like the Spider spin from his own inwards his own airy Citadel
– the points of leaves and twigs on which the Spider begins the work
are few and she fills the Air with a beautiful circuiting: man should be
content with as few points to tip with the fine Web of his Soul and
weave a tapestry empyrean'.[122]

Just as the antiquarian ideal had been supported by neo-Stoicism, Keats
completed his rejection of history as guide to life by repudiating one of
the ideas most tightly bound up with this amalgam of antiquarianism
and neo-Stoicism. Montaigne, Querenghi, and also de Sales had counselled retreat to an 'arrière-boutique', 'anticamera', or 'solitude locale et
réele' in order to preserve a sense of perspective and, therefore, freedom,
in the midst of life's turbulence. Keats denied that these existed because
human beings were incapable of the rational self-disciplining that was
necessary to distinguish between, as Epictetus put it, what was truly ours
and what was external to us. 'What a happy thing it would be', Keats
began,

> if we could settle our thoughts, make our minds up on any matter in
> five Minutes and remain content – that is to build a sort of mental
> Cottage of feelings quiet and pleasant – to have a sort of Philosoph-
> ical Back Garden, and cheerful holiday-keeping front one – but Alas!
> this never can be: for as the material Cottager knows there are such
> places as France and Italy and the Andes and the Burning Mountains
> – so the spiritual Cottager has knowledge of the terra semi incognita
> of things earthly; and cannot for his Life, keep in the check rein . . .[123]

And yet, even Keats' praise of imagination could not utterly slip the
clutches of history. He urged his brother to 'recollect that no man can

live but in one society at a time – his enjoyment in the different states
of human society must depend upon the Powers of his Mind – that is
you can imagine a roman triumph, or an olympic game as well as I
can'.[124] But could someone without any knowledge of Rome, or of tri-
umphs, 'imagine a *roman* triumph' as well as someone who had? Diderot
or Keats might have wished for a liberation of taste but could they have
believed that human creativity was *ex nihilo*? Indeed, Keats' claim that
imagination was necessary because one could live only one life is the
classic defence of history as *magistra vitae* – once we substitute 'study' for
'imagination'.

But if history was to remain necessary, what kind of knowledge of the
past could be had? Discussing the deaths of the ancient gods Keats' contemporary G. W. F. Hegel, put this problem at the centre of his concerns.
'The statues', he explained, 'are now only stones from which the living
soul has flown, just as the hymns are words from which belief has gone.
The tables of the gods provide no spiritual food and drink, and in his
games and festivals man no longer recovers the joyful consciousness of
his unity with the divine.' The gulf separating the ancient world from
the modern is expressed in a different religious sensibility that makes it
impossible to understand the spirit that animated the creations of this
earlier period. 'They have become what they are for us now', Hegel continued, 'beautiful fruit already picked from the tree, which a friendly Fate
has offered us, as a girl might set the fruit before us'. In these circumstances, the remains of antiquity 'cannot give us the actual life in which
they existed, not the tree that bore them, not the earth and the elements
which constituted their substance, not the climate which gave them their
peculiar character, nor the cycle of the changing seasons that governed
the process of their growth'. In other words, that knowledge which was
absolutely necessary for a proper understanding of the past was precisely
what was denied those who sought it. 'So Fate does not restore their
world to us along with the works of antique Art, it gives not the spring
and summer of the ethical life in which they blossomed and ripened,
but only the veiled recollection of that actual world.'[125]

For Hegel, time's passage barred access to the past as lived, and left
posterity only a form emptied of meaning. Antiquarian scholarship was
constrained to stop at the surface of things and could only hope to
reconstruct that form. No longer a direct experience – Hegel writes of
'an act of divine worship' – historical reconstruction was 'an external
activity – the wiping off of some drops of rain or specks of dust from
these fruits, so to speak – one which erects an intricate scaffolding of
the dead elements of their outward existence – the language, the historical circumstances, etc. in place of the inner elements of the ethical
life which environed, created, and inspired them.' The antiquaries' best

efforts could never grasp the real beliefs animating a past culture, the
moeurs et esprit sought after by Caylus as by Diderot and Gibbon.
The inaccessibility of the past meant that scholarly reconstruction
produced a reality that existed only in the mind of the inquirer: we
'enter into their very life but only to possess an idea of them in our
imagination'.[126]

The recognition that there was a never-to-be closed abyss separating
the past – all pasts – from the present, and that neither the might of the
imagination nor the utterly natural human desire to reverse the course
of time could ever succeed, is the painful subject of Keats' 'Ode on a
Grecian Urn'. His poem straddles this abyss. Like the funeral urns that
prompted Opitz and Browne to their musings, Keats contemplated the
'still unravish'd bride of quietness', the 'foster-child of silence and slow
time', and felt the immensity of the distance separating him from it.

> What leaf-fring'd legend haunts about thy shape
> Of deities or mortals, or of both,
> In Tempe or the dales of Arcady?
> What men or gods are these? What maidens loth?
> What mad pursuit? What struggle to escape?
> What pipes and timbrels? What wild ecstasy? . . .
> Who are these coming to the sacrifice? . . .
> What little town . . . is emptied of this folk, this pious morn?

Keats thought that none of these questions, all of which, were of
course, the very questions that fill the pages of the Peiresc archive and
drove a scholarly life that was celebrated across Europe, could ever be
satisfactorily answered.[127] We are left only with words to describe what
once was lived. Keats' contemporary Byron, in Rome as in a 'desert
where we steer / Stumbling o'er recollections', declared of the antiquaries' attempts to answer these questions: 'we but feel our way to
err'.[128] This was, indeed, the lasting triumph of 'old age', the mellower
cousin of Ovid's and Posthumus' *invidiosa vetustas*. For the present, and
all the presents yet to unfold, Keats suggested that beauty alone and not
history, with its insatiable lust for lost detail, could reach across the darkened centuries.

CONCLUSION

PEIRESC DIED ON 24 JUNE 1637. In the last letter that Grotius wrote to him, sent from Paris on 22 May, he concluded a survey of news from the Netherlands by praising a book 'partly physics and partly mathematics' by a 'Cartesius Gallus', but said that he was unable to acquire a copy. This was the *Discourse on the Method*, which would be published on 8 June but a copy of which had been passed from Constantin Huygens to Mersenne in Paris on 5 January. The name of Descartes is otherwise absent from Peiresc's correspondence.[1]

It would be tempting, and certainly convenient, to see the publication of the *Discourse* and the death of Peiresc, occurring within such a short span of time, as marking an important shift in the shape of learning. For Descartes' famous rejection of history as the foundation of truth would seem to have deprived men like Peiresc of the philosophical justification for their work, and indeed, for their particular conception of virtue. But it would be just as easy to see a decisive break in the debate between Balzac and Goulu in 1628 in which Descartes took the side of the former and Dupuy and Peiresc of the latter, or in the misunderstanding between Mersenne and Peiresc over the interpretation of symbols in 1634, or in the sharp disagreement over possible anthropologies between La Mothe le Vayer and Arnauld in 1641.

One could also argue, with no small justification, for the survival of the relationship between learning and virtue that Peiresc embodied and for the absence of anything so radical as a break. If Descartes seemed to put paid to the value of history, the 'provisional morality' that he sketched out in the *Discourse* reflects an emphasis on the same virtues that Gassendi had presented through his celebration of Peiresc:

conversation, constancy, and friendship, all to be attained through study of the world and the self. Over the course of the next century, this ideal – albeit with its philosophical content increasingly diluted – was disseminated across Europe through the academies, *salons*, clubs, and magazines that educated the Continent's literate public in the art of living well. Nor did this 'modern conversation' ever displace the fascination with antiquity: the Rothschild dynasty, so often seen as archetypally 'modern', began with Meyer Amschel, a dealer in coins, medals, and antiquities in the Judengasse in Frankfurt – part of the 'service economy' of an antiquarian culture. Whether in the city or the provinces, knowing one's way around the past remained a mark of civility, as Laurence Sterne made clear in *Tristram Shandy*. And, put into the mouth of 'the man of culture' in Matthew Arnold's *Culture and Anarchy*, the same arguments used to justify antiquarian learning in the seventeenth century were recycled to defend general education at the end of the nineteenth.

That the practice of the antiquary also survived in that of the unloved local historian, connoisseur, or antiques dealer, is generally considered as unimportant as they are. But the preservation of the antiquary's vision of society in that of the Enlightenment philosophical historian – that is something else entirely. The revolutionary redefinition of the city as the manners and customs of its inhabitants rather than its form of government, as Guazzo suggested, had redirected the attention of those seeking an understanding of civil life towards the structures of everyday existence: law, religion, economics, social order. The pre-eminence of political history reflected the primacy of politics; the transformation hinted at by Guazzo shifted the value towards understanding *moeurs* and *esprit*. This was the terrain of the antiquaries, who devoted themselves to studying just these aspects of ancient civilizations. For Arnaldo Momigliano the importance of Gibbon lay in his adoption of antiquarian methods to answer philosophical questions about the rise and fall of empires. William Robertson's *History* of Charles V's Europe began with a preface that could have been written by a Peiresc with its set-piece disquisitions on 'Interior Government, Laws and Manners' and 'The Political Constitution of the Principal States in Europe at the Commencement of the Sixteenth Century' – except that its style was pleasing and its proofs all relegated to the back of the book, where they could do the polite reader little harm. Adam Smith's history of Europe in book 3 of *The Wealth of Nations* features law, agriculture, commerce, and religion as the engines of political change. Momigliano was surely correct to see in the success of philosophical history the ironic triumph of the antiquary since remaking the practice of history in the antiquary's image but in the philosopher's language actually doomed the seemingly un-philosophical antiquary to oblivion.

These Enlightenment narrative histories perpetuated as an approach to modern society one that had been developed by antiquaries for studying the ancient world. This antiquarian style exercised just as powerful an influence on political thinking beyond the circle of luminaries like Gibbon, Robertson, Smith, and Adam Ferguson. A typical figure is Thomas Pownall, British governor of colonial Massachusetts in the early 1760s, and the author of treatises that explained imperial sovereignty and colonial obligation in terms of the development of society. After returning to England, Pownall published a series of articles trying to explain Celtic and pre-Columbian artifacts in their social context in the journal of the Society of Antiquaries. Like his more famous contemporaries, he was fascinated by the development of man from the earliest to latest stages and 'the varied efforts that he makes, to supply the encreased extended demands of his advancing civilization'. He turned the antiquary's typical fascination with objects like ancient vases from Central America to the needs of the historian of civilization. 'Do not these vestigia of things existing point out that there have been which have again fallen back to savageness and oblivion, advances in the state of man to arts and civilization of which no history can have the least traces?'[2]

The persistence of the antiquarian in European culture is real. And yet the passage from Peiresc to Descartes, while it may have only mnemonic value, nevertheless points towards something definite: never again would an antiquary represent, and be represented as, the ideal of individual excellence. The era spanned by Gassendi's biographies of Brahe and Peiresc had come to an end. The retrospective construction of a high road to the New Science, which Peiresc did not travel, created its own new heroes, the philosopher and scientist. Similarly, the flourishing of a vernacular 'pop culture' of the sort that saw in Guez de Balzac one of its first idols and Mme Rambouillet's *salon* its first 'scene', left no place for the antiquary. His focus on the past, and not the prettiest remains of it either, counted as a definite drawback once being fashionable mattered. To some, love of antiquity even seemed to hint at a kind of treason, or at least untrustworthiness: 'to have a relish for ancient coins', one observer wrote, 'it is necessary to have a contempt of the modern'.[3] As an easily identifiable 'Ancient', however sophisticated his questions and methods, the antiquary was one of the big losers in the quarrel that spilled across the Channel from France to England at the end of the seventeenth century. If Voltaire's prayer, 'God preserve me from devoting 300 pages to the story of Gassendi!', did not exist we might have had to invent it, so perfectly does it capture this change of style and substance.[4] Since so much of the antiquary's cultural prominence reflected the appeal of neo-Stoicism, the destructive attack on self-mastery and constancy launched by Pierre Nicole in France and Bernard Mandeville in England sapped an essential justification for the antiquarian immersion in the past. Moreover, within the learned world the accumulation of information and technical improvements led to the rise of discrete disciplines and the cult of the expert. The polymath became endangered – and deeply misunderstood – as his habitat was slowly enclosed. The defensiveness of the cornered *érudit* only fuelled the charges of pedantry that rang out loud and clear from the Baltic to the Bay of Biscay, and especially along the Seine. Prodigious book learning seemed either foolish – Shadwell's *Virtuoso* learned to swim lying on a table because interested only in 'the speculative part of swimming' – or hilariously pretentious – Lessing called his *Junge Gelehrter* an 'überstudierter Pickelhering' – or monstrous – none greater than Goethe's Faustus whom we first meet 'hemmed in by books' and 'mouldering bones of beasts and men' – or merely scholastic – George Eliot's Casaubon, that 'bat of erudition' purveying 'small explanations about as important as the surplus stock of false antiquities kept in a vendor's back chamber'. All of these figures are made in the antiquary's image, and reflect in rather precise ways (that are too complex to chart here) the changing face of the man of learning. The combination of these complicated narratives, the triumph of the ideology of the New Science, of the moderns, of an Augustinian anthropology, of vernacular popular culture, and of intellectual specialization, displaced antiquarianism from a position of cultural prestige and made it harder and harder to conceive of this kind of historical study as a philosophical exercise. It requires of us, now, a great effort of imagination to understand how, in 1640, an astronomer and an antiquary could have been held up as examples of the new thinking.

Rediscovering Peiresc's Europe can help us make sense of all this, and also the complex 'pre-histories' – an anachronistic way of thinking, to be sure, that can only be indulged in conclusions to books – of two themes central to post-Enlightenment politics and culture. First, recovering Peiresc's celebrity shows us how a cultural ideal came to inform a purely political category. He was famous for his learned sociability and specific virtues like constancy, conversation, and friendship: attributes that made and then maintained the civil communities that proliferated in the sixteenth and seventeenth centuries. The crisis of legitimate political authority that we associate with the early modern civil wars and political doctrines based on necessity would only be resolved at the end of the eighteenth century by the development of new notions of sovereignty based on representative consent. With this, the ancient ideal of the citizen ruling and being ruled in turn gave way to the modern figure of the represented citizen, otherwise an oxymoron by ancient lights. This shift

made untenable the classical claim that a political education characterized by participation in government was the precondition for individual
excellence. Instead, those civil, or Peireskean, virtues, whose arena
was originally the academy and Republic of Letters and later the *salon*,
coffee-house, and club, were adapted as the content of this new kind
of citizenship appropriate to a new kind of state. But in repackaging
an early seventeenth-century aristocratic, learned ideal for a literate and
polite eighteenth-century mixed-gender society, a perplexing question
emerged. Could a vision of excellence that rested on an aristocratic
notion of rational self-control be extended from a select group of the
like-minded to a heterogeneous national audience without becoming
incoherent? The answer was equivocal: admitting that political society
was a commerce of unequals united only by self-interest while remaining unwilling to give up on a notion of excellence, however diluted. The
ambivalence in this redefinition of the modern citizen – already visible
at the beginning of the eighteenth century in the debate between
Shaftesbury and Mandeville – is still with us.

Second, the antiquary as a cultural ideal points towards the relationship, not between politics and moral excellence, but between learning
and moral excellence. For the high profile of the antiquary in early
modern Europe reflects a widespread belief, now so distant that it needs
to be excavated, that historical education was a philosophical exercise.
This explains the affinity between neo-Stoicism and antiquarianism. But
it also reminds us that any opposition between history and the antiquarian is even more slippery. For acknowledging the moral value of
studying the crude, broken, fragments of the past is to acknowledge that
historia is still *magistra vitae* – precisely the justification of historical study
offered by the antiquaries' supposed rivals, the humanist historians who
wrote of kings and battles in their polished Latin. If, by the late eighteenth century, the antiquary was no longer a figure of the European
avant-garde, the idea that learning's justification was in shaping the soul
for living well had actually gained in persuasiveness – though changing
its appearance and its language. This is the redefinition of individual
excellence in terms of culture embodied in the German aristocratic ideal
of *Bildung* and, with the tension alluded to in the previous paragraph, in
its nineteenth-century American democratic heir, the liberal arts college.
Momigliano suggested that the antiquary's love of learning was his most
substantial contribution 'to the "ethics" of the historian'.[5] But not just
to the historian. For three and a half centuries after Peiresc voiced his
fear that the criminalization of Galileo's scholarship could be 'to the disadvantage of the liberal arts' we remain, more or less, still convinced of
their necessity for the individual and society.[6]

Like Gassendi, I have tried to write an intellectual history of the first decades of the seventeenth century by evoking the life of a single, extraordinary mind. And like Emerson, who wrote that 'looking where others look, and conversing with the same things, we catch the charm which lured them', I have tried to catch that charm and make it speak.[7]

NOTES

INTRODUCTION

1 Umberto Eco, *The Island of the Day Before*, tr. William Weaver (New York, 1995), p. 153. Exactly preserving posterity's verdict, Eco refers to the gentleman's friend as 'Canon of Digne', a clear reference to Peiresc's dear friend Pierre Gassendi who actually was the Canon of Digne. Peiresc's identity must be divined.

2 Pierre Gassendi, *The Mirrour of True Nobility and Gentility*, tr. W. Rand (London, 1657), bk 6, p. 236. This book, first published in 1641 as *Viri illustris Nicolai Claudii Fabricii de Peiresc senatoris aquisextiensis vita*, remains the best account of the life. Pierre Humbert, *Un Amateur: Peiresc 1580–1637* (Paris, 1933) and Georges Cahen-Salvador, *Un Grand Humaniste: Peiresc 1580–1637* (Paris, 1951) are surpassed by Henri Leclerq, *'Peiresc'*, *Dictionnaire d'archéologie chrétien et de liturgie*, ed. F. Cabrol, 15 vols (Paris, 1939), XIV, pp. 1–39. Still worth reading is Raymond Lebègue, 'État present des études Peiresciennes', *Revue Archéologique* 40 (1952) pp. 55–63.

3 Peiresc to Francesco Barberini, 31 January 1635, *Le opere di Galileo Galilei. Edizione nazionale* (Florence, 1966 [1890]), XVI, p. 202.

4 It is located on the lunar limb at 46.5°S and 67.6°E. See Mary A. Blagg and K. Müller, *Named Lunar Formations* (London, 1935), p. 183.

5 Walther Haage, *Kakteen von A bis Z* (Leipzig, Radebul, 1982), p. 588 details the con-troversy that subsequently arose because of the misspelling. I thank Ralph Lerner for bringing this to my attention. For the olives, see BN MS N.a.f. 5169, fol. 18ᵛ and for Peiresc's gift of 'deux bouteilles de malvoisie' to his former law professor on 8 January 1624, fol. 6ᵛ. His interest in exotic foods extended much further: in other letters Peiresc offered his opinion on the taste of sorbet brought from Cairo (Peiresc to Bignon, 15 March 1637, *Lettres de Peiresc*, ed. Philippe Tamizey de Larroque, 7 vols, Paris, 1888–98, VII, p. 640) and strawberries from Quebec (Peiresc to Valavez, 21 May 1626, ibid., VI, p. 530).

6 In the article 'Peiresc' Bayle wrote: 'Je dirai seulement que jamais homme ne rendit plus de services à la République des Lettres que celui-ci. Il en étoit pour ainsi dire le Procureur Général: il encourageoit les Auteurs, il leur four-nissoit des lumières & des matériaux, il emploit ses revenus à faire acheter, ou à copier les mon-umens les plus rares, & les plus utiles. Son com-merce de Lettres embrassoit toutes les parties du monde: les Expériences Philosophiques, les raretez de la Nature, les productions de l'Art, l'Antiquariat, l'Histoire, les Langues, étoient également l'object de ses soins, & de sa curiosité. Vous trouverez le détail de toutes ces choses dans sa Vie, composée élégamment & savamment par Pierre Gassendi. Il ne sera pas inutile de remarquer que cet homme si célébre par toute l'Europe, & dont la mort fut pleurée part tant de Poëtes & en tant de Langues, & mit en deuil pompeusement les Humoristes de

Rome, étoit inconnu à plusieurs François, hommes de mérite & d'érudition.' Pierre Bayle, *Dictionaire historique et critique*, 4 vols (Amsterdam and Leiden, 1730, 4th edn), III, p. 638.

7 Or he survived as a symbol of ruin-drenched melancholy, as in the poetry of Marcel Proust's friend and correspondent Robert de Montesquiou: 'L'auteur curieux, au nom rare: Peiresc' (*Perles rouges*, sonnet XVII) and in their letters (*Correspondance de Marcel Proust. 1910 et 1911*, ed. Philip Kolb, 21 vols, Paris, 1970, X, p. 116). I thank Michael Maar for bringing this to my attention.

8 Jules Michelet, *Journal*, ed. P. Viallaneix, 4 vols (Paris, 1959), I, p. 562.

9 Arnaldo Momigliano, *The Classical Foundations of Modern Historiography*, (Berkeley and Los Angles, 1990) p. 54; Trevor-Roper, 'The Baroque Century', *The Age of Expansion. Europe and the World 1559–1660*, ed. Trevor-Roper (London, 1969), p. 34; Marc Fumaroli, *Nicolas-Claude Fabri de Peiresc. Prince de la République des Lettres. IVᵉ Centenaire de la naissance de Gassendi: Conférence organisée par l'Association Pro-Peyresq dans la Maison d'Erasme à Anderlecht le mercredi 3 juin 1993.* (Brussels, 1993), pp. 1–34; and Alain Schnapp, *La Conquête du passé. Aux origines de l'archéologie* (Paris, 1993), p. 134.

10 The absence of 'The Antiquary' from the characteristic types included in a volume entitled *Baroque Personae* (ed. Rosario Villari, Chicago, 1995) is an indication of widely held current perceptions.

11 See John D. Lyons, *Exemplum: The Rhetoric of Example in Early Modern France and Italy* (Princeton, 1989); Timothy Hampton, *Writing from History. The Rhetoric of Exemplarity in Renaissance Literature* (Ithaca, 1989); Thomas M. Greene, *The Light in Troy. Imitation and Discovery in Renaissance Poetry* (New Haven and London, 1982). In recognition of the importance of this theme, a series of articles on 'the crisis of exemplarity' was published in the *Journal of the History of Ideas*, 59 (1998).

12 F[rançois] H[enry] to Pierre Borilly, 31 December 1654, printed in Gassendi, *Mirrour*, p. 292.

13 A fascinating example of the way in which printing worked to obscure manuscript remains, like those of Peiresc, is found in a work by Pierre Dupuy, Peiresc's friend, that also remains in manuscript. It is a cento-like collection of political ideas, similar to Lipsius' *Politica*, in which the 'argument' is made through the presentation of authorities and their judgements. In the chapter on weights and measures, for which Peiresc's expertise would probably

have made him a source, there is no mention of him, only an elusive reference to the custom of selling bread by weight in Rome and Jerusalem, 'ainsy que i'ay appris d'un autheur escrit à la main'. Even if this does not refer to Peiresc it illustrates how the author of an unpublished work was not even entitled to be named. Pierre Dupuy, 'Opuscules politiques recueillis des estats, royaumes, republiques et Empires du Monde. De leurs loix, coustumes et Forme de gouverner. Enrichis d'exemples memorabiles tirez des histoires anciennes et modernes', Paris, BN, MS Dupuy 603, p. 430.

14 Friedrich Nietzsche, 'Encyclopädie der klassischen Philologie', para. 2 'Die französische Philologie', *Nietzsche Werke. Vorlesungsaufzeichnungen*, ed. Fritz Bornmann and Mario Carpitella (Berlin and New York, 1993), p. 356; Wilhelm Dilthey, 'Die Funktion der Anthropologie in der Kultur des 16. und 17. Jahrhunderts', *Sitzungsberichte der königlich Preussischen Akademie der Wissenschaften* (1904), pp. 2–33 (reprinted in his *Gesammelte Schriften*, Leipzig and Berlin, 1921, pp. 416–52). For an attempt to put Dilthey's argument into a broader perspective see now Larry Frohman, 'Neo-Stoicism and the Transition to Modernity in Wilhelm Dilthey's Philosophy of History', *Journal of the History of Ideas*, 56 (1995), pp. 263–87.

15 The remarks of the Professor of Medieval History in the University of Cambridge, printed at the head of a very antiquarian-looking volume published over forty years ago, remain as true today as they were when first offered: 'The very word [antiquary] suggests contrasts with modern historical scholarship. At the present day we have reached such a pass that the word "antiquary" is not always held in high esteem, while "antiquarianism" is almost a term of abuse. We have our historians, ancient, medieval, and modern, our linguists, our pre-historical archaeologists, genealogists, numismatists, heralds, each showing a tendency to squat in one field and defend his exclusive right to cultivate it by being rude to visitors from elsewhere. We are all, or nearly all, specialists'. C. R. Cheney, 'Introduction: The Dugdale Tercentenary', *English Historical Scholarship in the Sixteenth and Seventeenth Centuries. A Record of the Papers Delivered at a Conference arranged by the Dugdale Society to Commemorate the Tercentenary of the Publication of Dugdale's 'Antiquities of Warwickshire'*, ed. Levi Fox (Oxford, 1956), p. 4.

16 See P. J. J. van Thiel, 'La Collection de portraits réunie par Peiresc à propos d'un portrait de Jean Barclay conservé à Amsterdam', *Gazette des Beaux-Arts*, 65 (1965), pp. 341–54;

David Jaffé, 'The First Owner of the Canberra Rubens, Nicholas-Claude Fabri de Peiresc (1580–1637) and his Picture Collection', *Australian Journal of Art*, 5 (1985), pp. 23–45. Rubens' pupil Anthony Van Dyck stayed *chez* Peiresc during the summer of 1625 and painted his portrait as a going-away present; this now lost painting was engraved by Vorsterman.

17   BN MS N.a.f. 5169 shows that of approximately 1,066 bundles of mail – each of which could contain many individual letters – almost exactly the same number were addressed to Parisian (382) as to Provençal destinations (384). It should be noted, however, that the overall volume of the Paris post was heavier. Where local couriers often carried letters destined for lone recipients this was rarely the case for Paris. One hundred and sixty-six bundles were directed to Rome, most via Avignon and 117 to the rest of France, though many of these went through Paris. The decisive fact seems to have been the location of Peiresc's brother Valavez; after his return to Provence in 1626 the balance between Paris and Provence shifted dramatically. From then, Peiresc sent only 190 bundles to Paris and 295 to other points in Provence. Also, as Peiresc's interest in the Near East increased the balance of volume between Paris and Provence shifted to reflect his dependence on merchants from Marseille and Toulon. (For purposes of calculation I have included Levant-bound post under Provence since it was carried by local merchants. There were 17 bundles whose destinations I could not determine.)

18   Peiresc to Cardinal Bichi, 29 October 1630, *Lettres de Peiresc*, VII, p. 619. Peiresc's service to the Barberini began with his efforts to publish the sacred poems of Maffeo Barberini in France and translate a reliquary of the Magdalene to the Barberini chapel in S. Andrea delle Valle. Victor Saxer, 'Lettres de Peiresc au cardinal Maffeo Barberini, alias Urbain VIII sur le détachement et l'expédition de reliques de sainte Marie-Madeleine à Saint-Maximin (1618–1624)', *Provence Historique*, 31 (1981), pp. 12–27.

19   Peiresc's relations with other members of the Cabinet Dupuy need to be examined on an individual basis. He came to have close ties to Gabriel Naudé after taking an initial dislike to him, and also François Luillier. But there is no indication that much of a relationship existed with the other member of Pintard's famous 'tetrade', François La Mothe le Vayer; in March 1630 Gassendi seems to have sent Peiresc a copy of his *Dialogues faits à l'imitation des anciens* and

in November 1633 – the outbreak of plague in Provence and the subsequent quarantine had disrupted communication – Peiresc explained that '[je] ne cognoys rien en toutes ces grandes élevations d'esprit' (Peiresc to Gassendi, 10 November 1633, *Lettres de Peiresc*, IV, p. 384). The classic study of this circle remains René Pintard, *Le Libertinage érudit dans la première moitié du XVIIᵉ siècle* (Geneva, 1983 [1943]).

20   See Claude Saumaise to Peiresc, 15 October 1635, *Peiresc. Lettres à Claude Saumaise et à son entourage*, ed. Agnès Bresson (Florence, 1992), p. 388. For this see *Olai Wormii et ad eum Doctorum Virorum Epistolae*, 2 vols (Copenhagen, 1751), I, pp. 70, 559; II, p. 1033. Their paths almost crossed several times: although born eight years after Peiresc, Worm passed through Padua and Naples several years before him and spent a year in Montpellier (1609–10) several years after him. If we compared the distribution of Peiresc's correspondents with those of Théophile Renaudot in the first volume of his *Recueil des gazettes. Nouvelles, relations & autres choses mémorables de toute l'année 1632* (Paris, 1633) we find a great deal of overlap – Paris, London, Rome, and Constantinople – but also divergence, with Renaudot's Europe reflecting an emphasis on political and military, rather than intellectual, news in years of international war: Brussels, Madrid, Naples, Danzig, Leipzig, Vienna, Nürnberg, Mayence, Augsburg, Cologne, Metz, Maastricht, and The Hague.

21   It was, for example, through this connection that he must have obtained the services of a Turk and a Maronite as translators (see Peiresc to Dupuy, 5 June 1635, *Lettres de Peiresc*, III, p. 325; 7 October 1635, ibid., p. 385). In a fascinating illustration of Peiresc's role as *metteur-en-scène*, he once sought to connect Portuguese merchants in Goa through their Parisian contact with an Aixois who had just taken up residence near Aden, in Yemen (Peiresc to Alvares, 8 February 1635, ibid., VII, p. 34, n. 1).

22   This occasionally raised eyebrows. The Imperial Librarian in Vienna had an Italian servant explain to Peiresc, in Italian, that he was 'not expert in the French language' and would therefore prefer future letters to be written in Latin. Peiresc then proceeded to write in Italian (Ehringer to Peiresc, 25 September 1633, BN MS Dupuy 705, fol. 49ʳ).

23   For comment on the difference between medieval study of the ancient world and Renaissance antiquarianism, see Arnaldo Momigliano, 'Ancient History and the Antiquarian', *Contributo alla storia degli studi classici*

(Rome, 1955), p. 73; Roberto Weiss. *The Renaissance Discovery of Classical Antiquity* (London, 1969), chs 1 and 2; Eric Cochrane, *Historians and Historiography in the Italian Renaissance* (Chicago, 1981), ch. 15; Stuart Piggott, 'Antiquarian Thought in the Sixteenth and Seventeenth Centuries', *English Historical Scholarship in the Sixteenth and Seventeenth Centuries*, ed. Fox, p. 98.

24 While Momigliano's interest in this broad theme spans the nine volumes of his *Contributi*, the classic discussions are 'Ancient History and the Antiquarian'; idem, 'L'eredità della filologica antica e il metodo storico', *Secondo contributo alla storia degli studi classici* (Rome, 1960), pp. 463–80; and idem, 'The Rise of Antiquarian Research', *Classical Foundations of Modern Historiography*, ch. 3. For recent evaluations of Momigliano's argument see *Ancient History and the Antiquarian: Essays in Memory of Arnaldo Momigliano*, ed. M. H. Crawford and C. R. Ligota (London, 1995); Mark Salber Phillips, 'Reconsiderations on History and Antiquarianism: Arnaldo Momigliano and the Historiography of Eighteenth-Century Britain', *Journal of the History of Ideas*, 57 (1996), pp. 297–316.

25 Anthony Grafton, *Defenders of the Text: The Traditions of Scholarship in an Age of Science 1450–1800* (Cambridge, Mass., 1991) and idem, *Joseph Scaliger. A Study in the History of Classical Scholarship*, 2 vols (Oxford, 1983, 1993); Stuart Piggott, *Ruins in a Landscape. Essays in Antiquarianism* (Edinburgh, 1976); Schnapp, *La Conquête du passé*; Krzysztof Pomian, *Collectionneurs, amateurs et curieux. Paris, Venise: XVIᵉ–XVIIᵉ siècles* (Paris, 1987); Paula Findlen, *Possessing Nature. Museums, Collecting, and Scientific Culture in Early Modern Italy* (Berkeley, 1994); Michael Hunter, *John Aubrey and the Realm of Learning* (London, 1975) and idem, *Science and the Shape of Orthodoxy: Intellectual Change in Late Seventeenth-Century Britain* (Woodbridge, 1995); Bruno Neveu, *Erudition et religion aux XVIIᵉ et XVIIIᵉ siècles* (Paris, 1994); Simon Ditchfield, *Liturgy, Sanctity and History in Tridentine Italy: Pietro Maria Campi and the Preservation of the Particular* (Cambridge, 1996); Ingrid Rowland, *The Culture of the High Renaissance: Ancients and Moderns in Sixteenth-Century Rome* (Cambridge, 1998); David Freedberg, *The Eye of the Lynx: Galileo, his Friends and the Beginnings of Modern Natural History* (Chicago, forthcoming); Francis Haskell, *History and its Images. Art and the Interpretations of the Past* (New Haven and London, 1993); *Documentary Culture. Florence and Rome from Grand-Duke Ferdinand I to Pope Alexander VII*, ed. E.

Cropper, G. Perini, and F. Solinas (Bologna, 1992); and *Cassiano dal Pozzo. Atti del seminario internazionale di studi. Napoli, 18–19 dicembre 1987*, ed. Francesco Solinas (Rome, 1987).

26 Edmund Spenser, *The Faerie Queene* (1590), proem to bk 2, ii, ll. 3–6. For the close relationship between discovery and the practice of antiquarian scholarship in this period see Corrado Vivanti, 'Alle origini dell'idea di civiltà. Le scoperte geografiche e gli scritti di Henri de la Popelinière', *Rivista Storica Italiana*, 74 (1962), pp. 225–49; J. H. Elliott, *The Old World and the New 1492–1650* (Cambridge, 1992 [1970]); Anthony Grafton, *New Worlds, Ancient Texts. The Power of Tradition and the Shock of Discovery* (Cambridge, Mass., 1992); Joan-Pau Rubiés, 'Instructions for Travellers: Teaching the Eye to See', *History & Anthropology*, 9 (1996), pp. 139–90.

27 For example, Brian Walton's state-of-the art scholarship in his *Prolegomena* to the London Polyglot Bible was reprinted in Cambridge in 1827, while John Selden's *De diis Syris* (1617) was used by Friedrich Creuzer in his *Symbolik und Mythologie der alten Völker* (1819–23) which was, in turn, heavily cited by Walter Benjamin in his *Ursprung des deutschen Trauerspiels* (Berlin, 1928).

28 William Jacob, 'To the much admired Antiquary, William Somner, the great restorer of the Saxon tongue' (1659) quoted in Graham Parry, *The Trophies of Time. English Antiquarians of the Seventeenth Century* (Oxford, 1995), p. 1; Sir Henry Spelman's essay 'Of the Ancient Government of England', *Reliquiae Spelmannianae* (London, 1723), p. 49. A third seventeenth-century Englishman, John Selden, likened the antiquary to the explorer of the heavens, comparing a new edition of a commentary on the Jerusalem Talmud to the achievement of Galileo. Selden to Francis Tayler, 25 June 1646, printed in *Memoires of the Life and Writings of the Right Rev. Brian Walton*, ed. Henry John Todd, 2 vols (London, 1821), I, p. 41n.

29 Grafton, *Scaliger*, II, p. 242.

30 'Il faut avouer que vous dominez sur tous les autres hommes du monde, en cette recherche de l'antiquité, d'autant que vous avez joint la pratique avec la theorie. La plupart de nos Sçavans n'ayant exercé que l'une des parties, s'étant contenté de sçavoir ce que les livres leur en pouvoient apprendre, que n'est rien au prix de ce que les choses memes nous enseignent, lors que nous venons à mettre sous notre vue, les tenir & manier dans nos mains'. Claude Saumaise to Peiresc, quoted in Baudelot de Dairval, *De l'Utilité des voyages, et l'avantage que*

la recherche des antiquitez procure aux sçavans, 2 vols (Paris, 1686), I, pp. 285–6.

31   Thomas Smith, in his biography of Camden quoted in Piggott, *Ruins in a Landscape*, p. 35.

32   For this world see the essays Gaetano Cozzi collected in *Paolo Sarpi. Tra Venezia e l'Europa* (Turin, 1979); Enrico de Mas, *Sovranità politica e unità christiana nel seicento anglo-veneto* (Ravenna, 1975); idem, *L'attesa del secolo aureo (1603–1625). Saggio di storia delle idee del secolo XVII* (Florence, 1982); Corrado Vivanti, *Lotta politica e pace religiosa in Francia tra cinque e seicento* (Turin, 1963); Hugh Trevor-Roper, *Renaissance Essays* (London and Chicago, 1985); idem, *Catholics, Anglicans and Puritans* (London, 1987); idem, *From Counter-Reformation to Glorious Revolution* (Chicago, 1992); Debora Kuller Shuger, *Habits of Thought in the English Renaissance. Religion, Politics, and the Dominant Culture* (Berkeley, 1990); Jean Jehasse, *La Renaissance de la critique. L'essor de l'humanisme érudit de 1560 à 1614* (St Etienne, 1976); Marc Fumaroli, *L'Âge de l'eloquence: rhétorique et 'res literaria' de la Renaissance au seuil de l'époque classique* (Geneva, 1980), III; R. J. W. Evans, *The Wechel Presses: Humanism and Calvinism in Central Europe, 1572–1627* (Oxford, 1975). The quote is from Evans, 'Rantzau and Welser: Aspects of Later German Humanism', *History of European Ideas*, 5 (1984), pp. 157–72, at p. 166.

33   For the connections between Lipsius and Guazzo, see Emilio Bonfatti, *La 'Civil Conversazione' in Germania. Letteratura del comportamento da Stefano Guazzo a Adolph Knigge 1574–1788* (Udine, 1979), ch. 2; idem, 'Magistratura e tragedia. Il *De Constantia* di Justus Lipsius e il servo fedele di Grillparzer', *Intersezioni*, 3 (1983), p. 266. For Lipsius and Montaigne, see Richard Tuck, *Philosophy and Government 1572–1651* (Cambridge, 1993), pp. 45–64. Montaigne's *Essais* were translated into Italian (*Discorsi morali, politici et naturali*) in 1590 and English (*Essays, or Morall, Politike and Millitarie Discourses*) in 1603. There was no contemporary Spanish translation; the age of Philip II, who had banned foreign travel for study, was not a propitious one for a book like Montaigne's. Similarly, no German translation was undertaken until 1793–99 (*Gedenken und Meinungen über allerley Gegenstände*, 7 vols). Was there something about the political climate in the German-speaking lands before the age of Schiller that made Lipsius more accessible and appealing than Montaigne?

34   On ideas of friendship in early modern Europe see Ulrich Langer, *Perfect Friendship:*

Studies in Literature and Moral Philosophy from Boccaccio to Corneille (Geneva, 1994).

35   For this see the work of Françoise Waquet, 'Qu'est-ce que la République des Lettres? Essai de sémantique historique', *Bibliothèque de l'Ecole des Chartes*, 147 (1989), pp. 473–502; idem, *Le Modèle français et l'Italie savante: conscience de soi et perception de l'autre dans la République des Lettres (1660–1750)* (Rome, 1989); idem and Hans Bots, *La République des Lettres* (Paris, 1997); Anne Goldgar, *Impolite Learning: Conduct and Community in the Republic of Letters, 1680–1750* (New Haven and London, 1995).

36   Nannerl Keohane, *Philosophy and the State in France from the Renaissance to the Enlightenment* (Princeton, 1980), ch. 4; A. M. Battista, *Politica e morale nella Francia dell'età moderna* [collected essays], ed. Anna Maria Lazzarino del Grosso (Genoa, 1998); R. J. W. Evans, *Rudolf II and his World: A Study in Intellectual History 1576–1612* (Oxford, 1984 [1973]), pp. 95–6; idem, *The Wechel Presses*; the two volumes of essays entitled *Europäische Sozietätsbewegung und demokratische Tradition*, ed. Klaus Garber and Heinz Wissman (Tübingen, 1996); and this author's review article 'Citizenship and Culture in Early Modern Europe', *Journal of the History of Ideas*, 57 (1996), 725–42.

37   For example, Reinhard Koselleck, *Critique and Crisis. Enlightenment and the Pathogenesis of Modern Society* (Cambridge, Mass., 1988 [1959]); Jürgen Habermas, *The Structural Transformation of the Public Sphere* (Cambridge, Mass., 1991 [1962]); J. G. A. Pocock, *The Machiavellian Moment* (Princeton, 1975); François Furet, *Interpreting the French Revolution* (Cambridge, 1981 [1978]); Franco Venturi, *The End of the Old Regime* (Princeton, 1989–91 [1979–84]). For the medieval antecedents of many of these ideas see Jean Leclercq, *Otia Monastica. Études sur le vocabulaire de la contemplation au moyen âge* (Rome, 1963); Brian Patrick McGuire, *Friendship & Community: the Monastic Experience, 350–1250* (Kalamazoo, 1988); Dilwyn Knox, '*Disciplina*: The Monastic and Clerical Origins of European Civility', *Renaissance Society and Culture. Essays in Honor of Eugene F. Rice, Jr.* (New York, 1991), pp. 107–36; idem, 'Erasmus' *De Civilitate* and the Religious Origins of Civility in Protestant Europe', *Archiv für Reformationsgeschichte*, 86 (1995), pp. 7–55.

38   See Donald R. Kelley, *The Foundations of Modern Historical Scholarship: Language, Law and History in the French Renaissance* (New York, 1970), chs 8–10; R. B. Wernham, 'The Public Records in the Sixteenth and Seventeenth

Centuries', *English Historical Scholarship in the Sixteenth and Seventeenth Centuries*, pp. 24–5.

39 Anthony Grafton, 'The World of the Polyhistors: Humanism and Encyclopedism', *Central European History*, 18 (1985), pp. 31–47; Wilhelm Kühlmann, *Gelehrtenrepublik und Fürstenstaat. Entwicklung und Kritik des deutschen Späthumanismus in der Literatur des Barockzeitalters* (Tübingen, 1982), pt 1 'Der Gelehrte in der Gesellschaft'; R. J. W. Evans, 'Learned Societies in Germany in the Seventeenth Century', *European Studies Review*, 7 (1977), pp. 129–51; idem, 'German Universities after the Thirty Years War', *History of Universities*, 1 (1981), pp. 169–90; Conrad Wiedemann, 'Polyhistors Glück und Ende von Daniel Georg Morhof zum Jungen Lessing', *Festschrift Gottfried Weber*, ed. Heinz Otto Burger and Klaus von See (Bad Homburg, Berlin and Zürich, 1967), pp. 215–35.

40 Sabine MacCormack, *Religion in the Andes. Vision and Imagination in Early Colonial Peru* (Princeton, 1991), p. 186.

41 The single most influential modern interpretation of neo-Stoicism has been that of Gerhard Oestreich, presented in English in *Neostoicism and the Early Modern State*, ed. Brigitta Oestreich and H. G. Koenigsberger, tr. David McLintlock (Cambridge, 1982). I intend to discuss elsewhere the context in which his ideas were developed, the Wehrpolitischen Institut of the University of Berlin *c.*1938. For other important recent work see Mark Morford, *Stoics and Neostoics: Rubens and the Circle of Lipsius* (Princeton, 1991); Tuck, *Philosophy and Government, 1572–1651*; Günter Abel, *Stoizismus und frühe Neuzeit. Zur Entstehungsgeschichte modernen Denkens im Felde von Ethik und Politik* (Berlin, 1978); Anthony Levi, *French Moralists: The Theory of the Passions, 1585 to 1649* (Oxford, 1965); Julien Eymard d'Angers, *Recherches sur le stoicisme aux XVI et XVII siècles*, ed. L. Antoine (Hildesheim and New York, 1976); Geoffrey Miles, *Shakespeare and the Constant Romans* (Oxford, 1996); Gilles D. Monserrat, *Light from the Porch: Stoicism and English Renaissance Literature* (Paris, 1984). The contributions of Léontine Zanta, *La Renaissance du stoicisme au XVI° siècle* (Paris, 1913); Dilthey, 'Die Funktion der Anthropologie in der Kultur des 16. und 17. Jahrhunderts'; and Morris Croll, 'Juste Lipse et le Mouvement anticicéronien à la fin du XVI° et au début du XVII° siècle' (1914), *Style, Rhetoric and Rhythm. Essays by Morris W. Croll*, ed. J. Max Patrick, et al. (Princeton, 1966), pp. 7–45, remain of fundamental importance.

42 In the preface Lipsius acknowledged that 'in the same way in which, in our *Constantia* we

formed citizens for enduring and obeying, here [we formed] those who rule for governing' (quoted in Abel, *Stoizismus*, p. 79). In 1594, in Tours, the *Politica* and *Constantia* were in fact published in a single, handy pocket-book. For this see Oestreich, *Neostoicism and the Early Modern State*, p. 14 and Giampiero Stabile, 'La sagezza: fondazione antropologia e codice di disciplinamento in Pierre Charron', *Sagezza e prudenza. Studi per al ricostruzione di un' antropologia in prima età moderna*, ed. Vittorio Dini and Giampiero Stabile (Naples, 1983), pp. 150–1. For the eclecticism of Lipsius' sources, see Jacqueline Lagrée, *Juste Lipse. La restauration du stoicisme* (Paris, 1994), p. 29.

43 Neo-Stoicism seems to have become especially popular recently with students of seventeenth-century English literature: Adriana McCrea, *Constant Minds. Political Virtue and the Lipsian Paradigm in England 1584–1650* (Toronto, 1997); Reid Barbour, *English Epicures and Stoics. Ancient Legacies in Early Stuart Culture* (Amherst, Mass., 1998); and Andrew Shifflet, *Stoicism, Politics and Literature in the Age of Milton. War and Peace Reconsidered* (Cambridge, 1998).

44 See Anna Maria Battista, *Alle origini del pensiero politico libertino. Montaigne e Charron* (Milan, 1966); Jonathan Dewald, *Aristocratic Experience and the Origins of Modern Culture. France, 1570–1715* (Berkeley, Los Angeles, and Oxford, 1993); David G. Halsted, *Poetry and Politics in the Silesian Baroque. Neo-Stoicism in the Work of Christophorus Colerus and his Circle* (Wiesbaden, 1996); Hugh Trevor-Roper, 'The Great Tew Circle', *Catholics, Anglicans and Puritans. Seventeenth-Century Essays* (London, 1987), pp. 166–230; James Amelang, *Honored Citizens of Barcelona: Patrician Culture and Class Relations, 1490–1714* (Princeton, 1986); Jonathan Brown, *Images and Ideas in Seventeenth-Century Spanish Painting* (Princeton, 1978), ch. 1; Evans, 'Learned Societies in Germany in the Seventeenth Century'; idem, *The Making of the Habsburg Monarchy 1550–1700. An Interpretation* (Oxford, 1979); and Iain Fenlon and Peter N. Miller, *The Song of the Soul: Understanding 'Poppea'* (London, 1992), chs 3–6.

45 For this see Jill Kraye, 'Conceptions of Moral Philosophy', *The Cambridge History of Seventeenth-Century Philosophy*, ed. Daniel Garber and Michael Ayers, 2 vols (Cambridge, 1997), II, p. 1286.

46 Pierre Hadot, *Exercises spirituels et philosophie antique* (Paris, 1981), esp. pp. 27–37; on the meaning of Roman Stoicism see Hannah Arendt, *The Life of the Mind. Two: Willing* (New York, 1978), p. 74.

47 Evans, *Rudolf II and his World*, pp. 92–6. See now an attempt to follow up this suggestion: Jan Papy, 'Lipsius and Marcus Welser: the Antiquarian's Life as *Via Media*', *The World of Justus Lipsius: A Contribution towards his Intellectual Biography*, ed. Marc Laureys, *Bulletin de l'Institut Historique Belge de Rome*, 68 (1998), pp. 173–90.

48 Momigliano himself hinted at the deeper connection between antiquarianism and philosophy: 'Antiquarians were traditionally close to the philosophers because their systematic approach to institutions and beliefs allowed a critical evaluation of the principles underlying a system of law or religion'. Momigliano, *Classical Foundations of Modern Historiography*, p. 78.

49 In this approach I am very much indebted to Evans's life of Emperor Rudolf II. He argued that Rudolf 'provides the key to a wider perspective. Nowhere do we see more clearly the various strands which made up the intellectual fabric of the years before 1600 than in Prague.' I would say the same for Peiresc, but replace 1600 with 1640 and Prague with Paris and Provence. Evans, *Rudolf II and his World*, p. 292.

50 'Es lag in der Natur der Sache, daß die Untersuchung sich streckenweise in das Gebiet rein literaturgeschichtlicher, ja selbst rein textkritischer Erörterungen begeben mußte: keine Einzelwissenschaft kann Antworten auf alle Fragen bereithalten, die eine Schwesterdisziplin aus ihrer ganz anderen Problemstellung heraus an sie zu richten hat; und wenn ein Ikonograph sich vor bestimmte Textprobleme geführt sieht, wird er nicht immer erwarten dürfen, gerade diese – vom Standpunkte des Philologen oder Literaturhistorikers oft gar nicht sichtbaren – Probleme bereits in vollem Umfang gelöst zu finden, sondern er wird, so gut es geht, sich selber weiterhelfen mußen.' Erwin Panofsky, *Hercules am Scheidewege und andere antike Bildstoffe in der neueren Kunst* (Berlin, 1930), pp. vii–viii.

I   PEIRESC: FREE MIND AND FRIEND

1 There is also an eighteenth-century German re-edition of the Latin text, published in Quedlinburg in 1706, with complete front and end-matter. See Lynn Sumida Joy, *Gassendi the Atomist: Advocate of History in an Age of Science* (Cambridge, 1987), ch. 3 for an important account of the biography and its place in Gassendi's intellectual development.

2 See the typology of *Lives* by Thomas F. Mayer and D. R. Woolf in their Introduction to *The Rhetorics of Life-Writing in Early Modern Europe. Forms of Biography from Cassandra Fedele to Louis XIV* (Ann Arbor, 1995), pp. 13–16. For the older genre of *hommes illustres*, see T. C. Price Zimmerman, 'Paolo Giovio and the Rhetoric of Individuality', *The Rhetorics of Life Writing*, pp. 39–62; Carlo Dionisotti, 'La galleria degli uomini illustri', *Lettere italiane*, 33 (1981), pp. 482–92 (I thank Tom Cerbu for bringing this article to my attention); Martina Hansmann, *Andrea del Castagnos Zyklus der 'Uomini Famosi' und 'Donne Famose': Geschichtsverständnis und Tugendideal im florentinischen Frühhumanismus* (Münster, 1993), ch. 2; Patricia Eichel-Lojkine, 'Les Vies d'hommes illustres', *Nouvelle Revue du Seizième Siècle*, 12 (1994), pp. 63–77. I thank Raïa Zaimova for this reference.

3 E. R. Curtius, *Latin Literature and the European Middle Ages* (London, 1953 [1948]), p. 167. For recent discussions of exemplarity see John D. Lyons, *Exemplum: The Rhetoric of Example in Early Modern France and Italy* (Princeton, 1989), and Timothy Hampton, *Writing from History: The Rhetoric of Exemplarity in Renaissance Literature* (Ithaca, 1989).

4 Josef Ijsewijn, 'Die humanistische Biographie', *Biographie und Autobiographie in der Renaissance*, ed. August Buck (Wiesbaden, 1983), pp. 1–19, pp. 5, 7.

5 Seneca, *Epistulae morales*, tr. Richard Gummere, 3 vols (Cambridge, Mass., 1979 [1917]), I, XLII.I, p. 279. Gassendi wrote of the debt future generations would have to Peiresc, 'with imitation of who some peradventure, will be so far possessed, as to endeavor to raise themselves, as Phoenixes out of his ashes, not without some benefit to mankind' (Gassendi, *Mirrour*, sig. A1ʳ). In the *Polyhistor* (Lübeck, 1714 [1688]), Daniel Morhof described Sarpi's spirit as possessed of a 'excellentissimum ingenium, quod per omnes scientias, artes & linguas se diffunderat. Prompus erat consilio, animo semper praesens, extrema vita pericula summa generositate contemnens, &, ut breviter dicam, sui temporis Phoenix' (bk 1, ch. 19, para. 23, p. 221).

6 Francis Bacon, 'De dignitate & augmentis scientiarum', *The Works of Francis Bacon*, ed. and tr. James Spedding, Robert Leslie Ellis, and Douglas Denon Heath, 7 vols (London, 1857–59), IV, bk 2, ch. 7, p. 305. Quotations from Bacon's *Advancement of Learning* will be taken from this English translation of Bacon's own Latin expanded version of 1623 – the one that Peiresc read. The swans refer to Ariosto, *Orlando Furioso*, cantos 34 and 35.

7 By contrast, Wilhelm Kühlmann's 'case study' of Matthias Bernegger reflects the emphasis of his book on the politico-military ('Lipsian' in Oestreich's influential characterization) utility of antiquarian philology (*Gelehrtenrepublik und Fürstentstaat. Entwicklung und Kritik des deutschen Späthumanismus in der Literatur des Barockzeitalters*, Tübingen, 1982, pt 1, ch. 3: 'Paradigmenwechsel: Matthias Bernegger (1582–1640) als Vertreter der politisch-historischen Philologie des Frühbarock').

8 Gassendi, *Mirrour*, sig. (a)^v. At the end of the preface to his biography of Tycho Brahe Gassendi again returned to the comparison of learned men with generals, explaining that he presented Brahe's astronomical achievements in detail in the same way that a biographer of a general could not ignore the military engagements in which his subject's excellence was displayed. *Opera Omnia*, 6 vols (Leiden, 1658), IV, pp. 384–5.

9 Gassendi, *Mirrour*, sig. (a)^v. Gassendi's commonplace presents casually what Pierre Charron offered as evidence for his insistence on the priority of private life: 'Ce qui se fait en public est une farce, une feinte; en privé et en secret c'est la verité; et qui voudroit bien juger de quelqu'un, il le faudroit voir à son à tous les jours, en son ordinaire et naturel, le reste est tout contrefait'. *De la Sagesse* (Paris, 1986 [1601]), bk 1, ch. 53, p. 341. Charron, in turn, reflects Montaigne's preference for biography because of its focus on human motivation ('Of Books', *The Complete Essays*, tr. and ed. M. A. Screech (Harmondsworth, 1993 [1991]), p. 467).

10 Chapelain to Balzac, 15 January 1640, *Lettres de Jean Chapelain*, ed. Tamizey de Larroque, 2 vols (Paris, 1880–83), I, p. 556.

11 Chapelain to Balzac, 20 January 1640, ibid., p. 558.

12 'Le siècle à venir participera à cette utilité et bénira ce beau travail mais le fruit principal qu'il en tirera sera de ce que sans doute un si glorieux exemple proposé à tous les temps ne laissera pas la vertu de ce grand personnage sans imitateurs, et sera comme la semence des nouveaux Mécenes des Lettres et des futurs promoteurs des Sciences, en quoy l'on peut dire que vous ferés plus que Mr de Peyresc mesme qui n'a peu exciter à cette entreprise que ceux qui l'ont veu ou qui vivoient de son temps, au lieu qu'en luy prolongeant la vie par le soin que vous avés pris de l'escrire, vous pourrés vous dire l'autheur de toutes les bonnes inspirations qui viendront aux hommes puissans de favoriser les Muses à son

exemple.' Chapelain to Gassendi, 5 February 1640, ibid., p. 561.

13 Chapelain to Balzac, 20 January 1640, ibid., p. 558.

14 Chapelain to Balzac, 12 February 1640, ibid., p. 569.

15 For example, Bernard de Montfaucon, *Antiquity Explained and Represented in Sculptures*, tr. David Humphreys, 2 vols (London, 1721–22), I, sigs b^v–b2^r.

16 For insightful treatments of the close link between *Lives* and antiquarianism, see Arnaldo Momigliano, *The Classical Foundations of Modern Historiography* (Berkeley and Los Angeles, 1990), p. 155; idem, *Development of Greek Biography* (Cambridge, Mass., 1971), p. 13; Marc Fumaroli, 'From *Lives* to Biography: The Twilight of Parnassus', *Diogenes* (1987), pp. 1–27.

17 'Quam ob causam ego Vitas Virorum doctorum & illustrium, qui vel ad literas vel ad Rempublicam adhibentur, non superficiaria aliqua & jejuna opera, sed quam plenissime, describi velim, ut vel ipsa *micrologia* in his mihi placeat. Nam vel ex minimis rerum circumstantiis aliqua, quae in usum tuum erunt, capies.' Morhof, *Polyhistor*, bk 1, ch. 19, 'De Vitarum Scriptoribus', para. 2, p. 215. This argument memained foundational: compare Morhof with James Boswell's 'Introductory' to his *Life of Samuel Johnson*, intro. Claude Rawson (New York, 1992), pp. 12–15.

18 'Ex illis arcana quaedam colligi possunt, quae non scientiam tantum, sed & prudentiam hominis literati, augent. Ut enim in Vita Civili, ita quoque in vita hominis literati, prudentia quaedam opus est in omni negotio' (ch. 19, para. 1, p. 215). William Bates, in his dedication to the Duke of Bedford of his *Vitae selectorum aliquot virorum qui doctrina, dignitate aut pietate inclaruere* (London, 1681) also emphasized the value of exemplary teaching while rejecting its traditional subject matter: not 'rebus magnificis, bellorum stragibus, caeterisque ejusmodi inanem quandam voluptatem' (sig. [A2]). Interestingly, Peiresc's is not among the thirty-two *Lives* it reprints. I thank Marc Fumaroli for this reference.

19 'Ego certe eam ob causam magni facio vitam Peirescii a Gassendus scriptam, quod in omnes partes excurrat & se diffundat, quam noster ille forte in eo *micrologion* damnaverit' (*Polyhistor*, ch. 19, para. 5, p. 216). 'Noster ille' refers to Roland Maresius, whose contrasting opinions are presented through lengthy quotations from his *Epistolarum Philologicarum Libri Duo* (Paris, 1655).

20   Morhof, *Polyhistor*, ch. 19 p. 239. Samuel
Hartlib, promoter of the translation of
Gassendi's *Vita* into English, also linked it to
these other *Lives*: 'Vincentius Pinellus was
Genuensis was just such another as Peireskius,
so that his vita[,] Peiresk and Pietro Pauli are
the chiefest vitae. Pinelli vita is much out of
print and therefore should be reprinted by M^r
Vlack' (*Ephemerides* 1656, Hartlib Papers,
Sheffield University Library, 29/5/68B). 'Pietro
Pauli' is likely to be a conflation of Sarpi's real
first name and the pseudonymous anagram used
for the *History of the Council of Trent* (Pietro
Soave Polano); 'Vlack' was the publisher in The
Hague (A. Vlacq) who had reprinted Gassendi's
Vita.

21   'Je n'ay que faire de vous dire quel héros
est ce Mr de Peyresc . . . Quelque jour vous
verrés sa vie escritte par un homme de grand
sense et trouverés qu'en son genre c'est un
Fra Paolo et une lumière de ce siècle'
(Chapelain to Balzac, 12 April 1637, *Lettres de
Jean Chapelain*, I, p. 150). As for Micanzio's *Life*,
we know manuscript copies were circulating in
Paris in the 1630s: Peiresc asked the Dupuy
brothers to have the *Life* copied out for him in
a letter of 27 November 1632 (*Lettres de Peiresc*,
II, p. 378), repeated the request on 6 February
1633 (II, p. 434), and acknowledged receipt in a
letter of 11 July 1633 (II, p. 562). A copy –
perhaps *the* copy – is found in BN MS Dupuy
307. On the pre-publication circulation of
Micanzio's *Vita* see Enrico de Mas, *L'attesa del
secolo aureo 1603–1625* (Florence, 1982), pp.
260–2.

22   Paolo Gualdo, *Vita . . . Pinelli . . . in qua
studiosis bonarum artum proponitur typus viri
probi et eruditi* (Augsburg, 1607), p. 108. Marc
Fumaroli has written about the influence of
Gualdo's *Life* on Gassendi: '*Nicolas-Claude Fabri
de Peiresc. Prince de la République des Lettres*', *IVe
Centenaire de la naissance de Gassendi. Conference
organisée par l'Association Pro-Peyresq dans la
maison d'Erasme à Anderlecht le mercredi 3 juin 1992*
(Brussels, 1993), pp. 22–6; idem, 'Venise et la
République des Lettres au XVIe siècle', *Crisi e
rinnovamenti nell'autunno del rinascimento a
Venezia*, ed. Vittore Branca and Carlo Ossola
(Florence, 1991), p. 348.

23   'Il quale si mirabilmente riesce in rapp-
resentare al vivo, I meriti, et virtu heroiche, et
altre rare qualita et perfettioni di se grand
huomo, quanto era il Sr G.V.° in eccitare I
lettori all'ammiratione et imitatione di esse: in
muovergli à compassione delle aversità che vi
sono descritte, et ad un estremo dolore di tanta
perdita che ci ha fatta la republica litteraria,

havendo ella il tutto felicissimamente conse-
guito, et spieghato nel piu puro, piu scielto, et
piu grave stile che habbia l'arte'. Peiresc to
Paulo Gualdo, 25 September 1609, BNM, MS
Ital. x 68 (= 6401), fol. 54^r; printed with minor
changes in *Lettere d'uomini illustri che fiorirono
nel principio decimosettimo* (Venice, 1744), p.
229.

24   Gassendi, *Mirrour*, year 1601, p. 46. The
Vita . . . Pinelli focused on Pinelli's scholarly
persona (for example: scholarly generosity, pp.
30ff.; friendship, p. 47, reading and organization
of information, p. 25; Paduan circle, p. 71) and
could have best served Gassendi as a model for
bk 6. What it lacks is the *res gestae* that is bks
1–5 of the *Vita*.

25   Gassendi, 'Epistle Dedicatory', *Mirrour*,
sig. (a)2^r. The view of antiquities – and by
extension annalistic biography – as an imperfect
form of historical writing ('history defaced,
or remnants of history which have casually
escaped the shipwreck of time') was presented
by Bacon in 'De augmentis scientiarum', bk II,
ch. 6.

26   Gassendi, *Mirrour*, year 1637, p. 157. One
reader recognized in this Gassendi's main
theme: 'What was the habit of his body,
what the manners of his minde, and what his
Studies, have bin so punctually set down by
Gassendus . . .' (François Henry to Pierre
Borilly, 31 December 1654, printed in *Mirrour*,
p. 292).

27   See for reading practices ibid., (bk 6, p.
199), note-taking (p. 191), filing (pp. 192 and
197), letter-writing (p. 193), book-buying,
binding, copying (pp. 194–6), and use of secre-
taries (p. 198).

28   'La partie qui m'y touche principalement est celle où vous parlés de la forme de son
corps, de sa façon de vivre, de ses moeurs et de
ses estudes, et je suis trompé si ce n'est celle qui
sera la plus utile et la plus estimée.' Chapelain
to Gassendi, 5 February 1640, *Lettres de Jean
Chapelain*, I, p. 561.

29   The subtitle of the second Latin edition
(1651) was: 'In which – besides the admirable
and very exquisite actions of that man – the
concealed treasures of historical and antiquarian
matter are revealed, the secrets of very abstruse
sciences are unlocked, and especially those of
each art and nature are told'. ('In qua praeter
Admiranda Exquisitissima Viri Gesta Historicae
& Antiquariae Rei latentes Thesauri aperiuntur,
abstrusiores Matheseos Arcana reserantur, nec
non Artis & Naturae singulae ennarantur').
Gassendi also used biography to frame his most
important philosophical contribution, the

attempt to revive interest in Epicurus (*De vita et moribus Epicuri*, 1647).

30 A comparison of the two *Lives* is revealing. That of Peiresc offers not only a more nuanced portrait of the protagonist and a much richer picture of the world in which he lived, but also shows the author's hand much more clearly. It was meant as a history of the age and as a guide to future intellectual and social practice. The *Life* of Brahe, on the other hand, was perforce written long after the subject's death, relied on printed sources only and was very much a history of astronomy.

31 The particular copy I refer to is in the Special Collections Department of the University of Chicago Library, shelf-mark QB35.G25.

32 Gassendi, *Mirrour*, year 1612, p. 154. For Peiresc the astronomer, see Seymour L. Chapin, 'An Early Bureau of Longitude: Peiresc in Provence', *Navigation. Journal of the Institute of Navigation*, 4 (1954), pp. 59–66; idem, 'The Astronomical Activities of Nicolas Claude Fabri de Peiresc', *Isis*, 48 (1957), pp. 13–29; Jean Bernhardt, 'Les Activités scientifiques de Nicolas-Claude Fabri de Peiresc (1580–1637)', *Nouvelles de la République des Lettres*, 1 (1981), pp. 165–84. Paris, BN F. fr 9531 fol. 194.

33 Peiresc to Thomas d'Arcos, 30 May 1636, *Lettres de Peiresc*, VII, p. 178: 'estant bien certain que deux ou trois observations bien exactes sont pour faire changer une bonne partie des vieux fondements de l'astronomie, et consequemment de la géographie'.

34 For Orion, see Carp. Bibl. Inguimb., MS 1803, fol. 189ʳ; for the moon, David Jaffé, 'Mellan and Peiresc', *Print Quarterly*, 7 (1990), pp. 168–75.

35 For an overview of this 'project', see Gassendi, *Mirrour*, year 1600, p. 146; year 1612, p. 156; year 1628, p. 26; year 1635, p. 132; for the map see Peiresc to Dupuy, 4 March 1628, *Lettres de Peiresc*, I, p. 549; 12 August 1636, III, p. 542; Peiresc to Holstenius, 2 July 1636, ibid., V, p. 445. Peiresc's memoir on an invention 'pour régler la mesure des Longitudes de Geographie' is in BN F. fr. 9531, fol. 116ʳ.

36 For an example, see Pierre Humbert, 'Un Manuscrit inédit de Gassendi', *Revue des Questions Scientifiques*, 53 (1934), pp. 5–11.

37 'Il y a plus de peine et de difficulté aux observations celestes, mais beaucoup moins pourtant que vous n'en imaginez, car j'en ay fait faire en divers lieux à des simples Jardiniers, à des simples Libraires, Relieurs, à des Massons et autres artisans moins susceptibles, ce sembloit, de telles commissions qui n'ont pas laissé de reussir trez bien et de servir fort utilement.' Peiresc to

Thomas d'Arcos, 30 May 1636, *Lettres de Peiresc*, VII, p. 180.

38 Peiresc described astronomical observation as 'capables de produire de si beaux et utiles moyens d'ayder le public, que de toute l'antiquité profane il ne reste rien de plus digne ou plus memorable aujourd'huy que ce peu d'observations celestes qu'ont autres fois mises par escript Hipparque et quelques autres, qui nous ont donné des eschelles pour monter, s'il se peut dire, dans les cieux.' Peiresc to Cesaire de Rosgoff, 6 May 1636, *Correspondance de Peiresc avec plusieurs missionaires et religieux de l'ordre des Capucins 1631–1637* (Paris, 1891) , p. 233.

39 Gassendi, *Mirrour*, bk 6, p. 207. Guez de Balzac echoed Bacon's definition of antiquities, 'history defaced, or some remnants of history that have casually escaped the shipwreck of time', by describing Peiresc as 'une piece du naufrage de l'Antiquité' (Balzac to Luillier, 15 August 1640, quoted in *Gallia Orientalis* ed. Paul Colomies (Paris, 1665), p. 179).

40 See Peiresc's letters to the brothers Dupuy of 28 April 1624, 4 January 1627, 29 January 1627, early February 1627, 10 February 1627, 17 July 1627 (all in *Lettres de Peiresc*, I).

41 Peiresc to Dupuy, 9 January 1635, ibid., III, p. 253; Peiresc to Valavez, 17 February 1625, ibid., VI, p. 109; Peiresc to Dupuy, 28 April 1624, ibid., I, p. 32 (the texts are in Carp. Bibl. Inguimb. MS 1789 fols 44–6); Peiresc to Scipione Cobelluzzi, 14 May 1624, BN MS N.a.f. 5172, fol. 17ʳ. As soon as he heard that what he called the *Traicté du progrez des sciences* was being translated into Latin he commented that 'ce sera un bien curieuse piece' (Peiresc to Dupuy, 25 January 1624, *Lettres de Peiresc*, I, p. 21).

42 Their intent is made especially clear if we look at the phrases that they consistently rendered as 'advancement of learning'; in no case had Gassendi explicitly echoed Bacon's language: 'non destitit tamen interea pluribus curis distineri' (*Mirrour*, year 1610, p. 147); 'statim in bonarum literarum gratiam peregit' (ibid., year 1616, p. 172); 'non destitit fovere literarum curam' (ibid., year 1635, p. 135); 'quaesito nempe bonis seu viris, seu artibus emolumento curam' (ibid., bk 6 p. 172).

43 Bacon, *Advancement of Learning, Works*, III, bk 1, p. 292.

44 Montaigne, 'On Educating Children', *Essays*, p. 176.

45 Peiresc to P. Célestin de Sainte-Lidivine, 29 April 1633, *Lettres de Peiresc*, VII, p. 856.

46 'Tanto è grande l'amore ch'iò porto a la cognitione della vera Philosophia naturale che si

può scorgere nell'istesso libro della natura più tosto che in qualsi voglia altro, non ch'io voglio sminuir la stima che meritan que' grand huomini che n'hanno scritto.' Peiresc to Cassiano dal Pozzo, 30 May 1635, Peiresc, *Lettres à Cassiano dal Pozzo (1626–1637)*, ed. Jean-François Lhote and Danielle Joyal (Clermont-Ferrand, 1989), p. 192.

47 Eugenio Garin, 'La nuova scienza e il simbolo del *libro*', *La cultura filosofica del rinascimento italiano* (Florence, 1979), pp. 451–65; Thomas M. Headley, *Tommaso Campanella and the Transformation of the World* (Princeton, 1997), pp. 94 and 164.

48 'Car c'est le vray libvre de philosophie comme nous reiteroit à toutz momentz le bon homme Campanella, de qui je n'ay pas eu de nouvelles . . .' Peiresc to Bourdelot, 28 February 1635, *Lettres de Peiresc*, VII, p. 724.

49 '. . . dont il semble que le monde veuille estre en perpetuelle ignorance, pour ne pas se donner le soing d'en rechercher les causes, ou du moins les plus veritables effects, dans l'experience et dans le libvre des libvres, qui est celuy de la nature mesme, où il se trouve bien d'autres choses que tout ce qui se void dans les libvres plus ordinaires.' Peiresc to P. Césaire de Rosgoff 6 May 1636, *Correspondance de Peiresc avec Capucins*, p. 232.

50 See Cecilia Rizza, *Peiresc e l'Italia* (Turin, 1965), p. 233 on his reaction to Fortunio Liceti's *De Lumine*. Peiresc also used that same word, 'mortification' to condemn the failure to make instrument-aided observations and instead to prefer 'croire les mathématiciens en ce qu'il se disent de la longitude, latitude, grandeur des estoiles, et autres notices nécessaires' (Letter to P. Anastasio, December 1636, quoted in Georges Cahen-Salvador *Un Grand Humaniste: Peiresc 1580–1637* (Paris, 1951), pp. 234–5).

51 *Mirrour*, bk 6, p. 207. Gassendi's account of Peiresc's eclipse observations (*Mirrour*, year 1600, p. 146; year 1612, p. 156; year 1628, p. 26; year 1635, p. 132) and production of astronomical tables (year 1610, p. 145) provide examples of observation and comparison deployed in astronomical research.

52 Compare the questions addressed to Thomas d'Arcos about an excavation (17 September 1630, *Lettres de Peiresc*, VII, p. 89) and about animals from sub-Saharan Africa (3 August 1634, ibid., p. 135).

53 Worm asked him to send around a young man to survey monuments in the vicinity and supplied him with a list of questions for the surveyor. 'He should take note of (1) the site, what county and parish it is in, (2) the orientation, eastwards, westwards, and so on, (3) the dimensions of the monument, its length, breadth, and thickness, (4) he should make a drawing showing the external appearance and structure of the monument, (5) he should add the interpretation he decides on, (6) local stories about the monument, even if fanciful, (7) noteworthy events in the vicinity, together with any other particulars that may be material to our investigations'. Quoted in Ole Klindt-Jensen, *A History of Scandinavian Archaeology* (London, 1975), p. 20.

54 Gassendi, *Mirrour*, year 1605, p. 97.

55 For a sample, see Tamizey de Larroque (ed.), *Notes inédités de Peiresc sur quelques points d'histoire naturelle* (Digne, 1896). No references are provided, however. Drawings are scattered throughout Peiresc's manuscripts but are collected in BN Est. Rés. Aa 53–4.

56 See Jaffé, 'Mellan and Peiresc'; Ch. Ruelens, 'Le Peintre Adrien de Vries', *Bulletin-Rubens*, 1 (1882), pp. 72–98, 171–95; Hippolyte Guillibert, *Portraits de Peiresc et du Vair par Finsonius* (Paris, 1909); E. M. Müntz, 'Lettre de recommandation de Peiresc au peintre *Lagouz*', *Nouvelles Archives de l'Art Français*, 4 (1876), pp. 250–1; Antoine Schnapper, *Le Géant, la licorne, la tulipe. Collections françaises au XVIIᵉ siècle* (Paris, 1988), p. 178.

57 For instructions on copying inscriptions see Peiresc's letters to d'Arcos, 17 July 1632, *Lettres de Peiresc*, VII, p. 104 and P. Célestin de Sainte-Lidivine, 29 April 1633, ibid., p. 864. For making casts of objects without damaging them see those to d'Arcos, 3 August 1634, ibid., pp. 134–5 and Guillemin, 21 March 1633, ibid., v, p. 138. This same first-hand knowledge also gave Peiresc an understanding of how forgers worked (to d'Arcos, 10 May 1631, ibid., VII, p. 94; to Menestrier, 31 March 1627, ibid., v, p. 514). For this theme see Anthony Grafton, *Forgers and Critics. Creativity and Duplicity in Western Scholarship* (Cambridge, Mass., 1990).

58 Gassendi, *Mirrour*, year 1599, p. 20.

59 John Evelyn, *Acetaria. A Discourse of Sallets*, ed. Tom Jaine (Totnes, Devon, 1996), p. 33; referring to *Mirrour*, year 1630, p. 45.

60 Gassendi, *Mirrour*, year 1623, p. 216.

61 Peiresc to P. Célestin de Sainte-Lidivine, 29 April 1633, *Lettres de Peiresc*, VII, p. 856.

62 Writing to Aycard in Toulon, Peiresc explained that if he had shared his father's and uncle's apprehensions he would never have undertaken to travel 'd'où j'ay tiré mes plus grands et principaulx advantages' (Peiresc to Aycard, 5 June 1633, ibid., p. 303).

63 Gassendi, *Mirrour*, bk 6, pp. 207–8.

64 Bacon, *Advancement of Learning*, *Works*, III, bk 1, p. 285.

65 Gassendi, *Mirrour*, bk 6, p. 209.

66 Ibid., year 1613, p. 159.

67 Ibid., bk 6, p. 212.

68 'Mais toutes mes estudes ont eu un object trop different du vostre . . .', Peiresc to Mersenne 18 April 1634, *Correspondance du P. Marin Mersenne religieux minime*, ed. Mme Paul Tannery, Cornélis De Waard and René Pintard, 17 vols (Paris, 1939–88), IV, p. 176. Henceforth *Mersenne Correspondance*.

69 Peiresc to Mersenne, 16 July 1634, ibid., p. 246.

70 Mersenne to Peiresc, 24 August 1634, ibid., p. 330.

71 Peiresc to Mersenne, 19 December 1634, ibid., pp. 415–16.

72 'J'ay trouvé, dis-je, des occasions d'admirer grandement la punctualité des Anciens bien plus grande que ne croyent ceux qui courrent la poste, comme on dict, et qui n'y veullent pas regarder de si prez.' Peiresc to Mersenne, 5 May 1635, ibid., v, p. 169.

73 'Vous me pardonnerez, s'il vous plaist, Monsieur, si je vous importune par de si excessives ponctualitez que les miennes, mais c'est mon naturel que je ne sçaurois despouiller.' Peiresc to Menestrier, 24 March 1633, *Lettres de Peiresc*, v, p. 623.

74 Gassendi explained that he provided such a detailed account of Peiresc's repetition of Galileo's observations 'to intimate, how vehemently Peireskius endeavoured, that this new invention might be speedily perfected' (*Mirrour*, year 1610, p. 145). For a modern consideration of Peiresc's observations see Chapin, 'The Astronomical Activities of Nicolas-Claude Fabri de Peiresc', p. 17.

75 Gassendi, *Mirrour*, year 1632, p. 76.

76 Ibid., year 1609, pp. 134–7. Discussion of eclipse observations, like that of 1630, tends to include measurements (year 1630, p. 42), while inquiries in non-numerate disciplines, such as natural history or antiquities, were described in exacting detail. See the accounts of Peiresc's study of the anatomy of a giant tortoise (year 1609, p. 118), chameleons (year 1637, p. 151), prevailing winds of Provence (year 1621, p. 211–13) and marine fossils embedded in local mountains (year 1630, p. 51). By way of contrast, Hunter notes that though a keen observer Aubrey was not concerned 'with testing and quantifying phenomena, with rigorous proof and with exact weighing and mea-

suring' (Michael Hunter, *John Aubrey and the Realm of Learning* (London, 1975), p. 24).

77 Gassendi, *Mirrour*, year 1599, p. 21; year 1601, p. 38; year 1602, pp. 67 and 73.

78 Ibid., year 1636, pp. 140–1. See Peiresc to Dupuy [18 March 1636], *Lettres de Peiresc*, III, p. 455; 24 June 1636, ibid., p. 510; Peiresc to Holstenius, 7 May 1637, ibid., v, p. 478 – with discussion of the formal attestation!

79 'J'ay veu des choses, si incroyables sans les voir, que je suis quasi aussy disposé à me laisser surprendre que tout aultre à bonne foy'; 'Ce furent cez considerations qui me firent demeurer en suspens à cet advis, et quand il seroit absolument faulx et controuvé, j'ay esté aultres foys si heureux que fondant des experiances sur des faux advis, je n'ay pas laissé d'y rencontrer des merveilles aultant et plus inesperées que celles dont on m'avoit faict feste. C'est pourquoy je tasche de ne rien negliger jusques à tant que l'experiance nous ouvre la voye à la pure verité . . .' (Peiresc to Dupuy, 7 April 1636, ibid., III, p. 465–6). Krzystof Pomian (*Collectionneurs, amateurs et curieux. Paris–Venise: XVI–XVIII* siècle, Paris, 1987, p. 80) places the regime of curiosity between theology and science; in these terms Peiresc seems to stand somewhere between curiosity and science.

80 For Peiresc's participation, see BN MS Dupuy 673, fols 149–69, 'Procès verbal de l'ordre tenu depuis le 23ᵉ Febvrier jusqu'au 24ᵉ Avril 1611', fol. 162ᵛ. Peiresc's file 'Des energumeres, Sorcelleries' is in Carp. Bibl. Inguimb., MS 1779. A general account of the episode, including a discussion of du Vair's position, can be found in Robert Mandrou, *Magistrats et sorciers en France au XVIIᵉ siècle* (Paris, 1980), pp. 198–209. I thank Jean-Marie Apostolides for calling my attention to the *procès Gauffridy*.

81 Peiresc to Dupuy, 27 November 1632, *Lettres de Peiresc*, II, p. 379.

82 Peiresc to Mersenne, 3 July 1635, *Mersenne Correspondance*, v, p. 278.

83 Gassendi, *Mirrour*, year 1611, pp. 149–50.

84 Lorraine Daston and Katharine Park, *Wonders and the Order of Nature 1150–1750* (New York, 1998), pp. 228–30.

85 Gassendi, *Mirrour*, 1580, p. 9. An instance in which the common people attributed the appearance of certain scars to devil worship led Peiresc 'afterwards to doubt whether in the whole businesse there were not some secret imposture, or dotage ('stupor animi')' (year 1611, p. 149).

86 For the echo of Bacon, see *Advancement of Learning*, *Works*, III, bk 1, pp. 288–9.

87 Gassendi, *Mirrour*, 1609, p. 139.

88 Ibid., bk 6, p. 218.

89 Ibid., 1610, p. 142.

90 For the comet see ibid., year 1618, p. 187, and for the visions, year 1621, p. 205. In 1624 Peiresc finally arranged for a coral fishing expedition in the course of which he saw that when cut open, the coral oozed a sticky substance and 'therefore conjectured, how Coral might come to grow upon the Scull forementioned' (ibid., year 1624, p. 7).

91 A legend of St Jean the Evangelist found in an old manuscript he had acquired was 'la plus ridicule qui se pourroit jamais imaginer, car elle luy faict faire la pierre philosophale et convertir des houssines en or, et puis rechanger l'or en houssines et mille autres badineries encore plus niaises.' Peiresc to Dupuy, 11 August 1627, *Lettres de Peiresc*, i, p. 327.

92 For a more detailed discussion of 'comparison' see Miller, 'The Antiquary's Art of Comparison: Peiresc and *Abraxas*', *Zu Begriff und Problem der Philologie (ca. 1580 bis ca. 1730)*, ed. Ralph Häfner (Max Niemeyer Verlag, forthcoming).

93 Gassendi, *Mirrour*, year 1608, pp. 123–4. For another version of this story, see Peiresc to Malherbe, 15 July 1609, *Lettres à Malherbe*, ed. Raymond Lebègue (Paris, 1976), pp. 26–7.

94 Gassendi, *Mirrour*, year 1613, pp. 161–3. For an account of this episode, see Krzysztof Pomian, 'Le Cartésianisme, les érudits et l'histoire', *Histoire. Religion. Philosophie* (Warsaw, 1966), p. 201, n. 82; and, though without connecting it to Peiresc, Schnapper, *Le Géant, la licorne, la tulipe*, p. 101.

95 Gassendi, *Mirrour*, year 1631, p. 60; Peiresc to Dupuy of 26 December 1631 (*Lettres de Peiresc*, ii, p. 293). Peiresc was unwilling 'to deny in any way' the possibility of giants even as he remained sure that large bones had to come from large animals, such as whales or elephants (Peiresc to dal Pozzo, 4 October 1635, *Lettres a Cassiano dal Pozzo*, p. 207). Peiresc asked Holstenius, on the off-chance that he would soon visit Sicily again, to examine any fossil remains that he might see, especially of giants, and describe what they looked like *in situ* before being handled by men (7 May 1637, *Lettres de Peiresc*, v, p. 477). The reason for this wariness is made clear in a letter to d'Arcos where Peiresc describes how merchants could satisfy the craze for marvels by passing off other material as authentic (10 May 1631, ibid., vii, p. 94).

96 'Pour estre bon juge de l'antique ou du moderne, il fault avoir veu et manié aussy bien de l'un que de l'autre. Mais il y a des gens si desgoustez que le sucre mesme les importune, aymants mieux quelque tranche de jambon bien sallé pour les faire boire avec plus d'alteration que de se contenter d'estancher leur soif. J'ay veu estant à Rome vendre au marché de Campo di Fiore et de Piazza Navona telle quantité de medailles antiques aussy bien que de cez modernes que l'on pend aux chappelletz que les unes n'y sont pas moins communes que les aultres, et ne s'ensuit pas que les unes soient aussy modernes que les autres.' Peiresc to Mersenne, 23 July 1635, *Mersenne Correspondance*, v, p. 332.

97 Pierre Borilly to François Henry of 31 December 1654, quoting from Kircher's *Obeliscus Pamphilius* (Rome, 1650), sig. a4^r, in Gassendi, *Mirrour*, p. 287.

98 '. . . j'espere de faire bien mieux valloir que ne font d'autres, qui ne recouvrent des livres que pour les enfermer dans des cachots impenetrables, où ils tombent d'une sort de tenebres en d'autres plus obscures'. Peiresc to Cassien de Nantes, 10 August 1635, *Correspondance de Peiresc avec Capucins*, pp. 165–6.

99 Peiresc to Menestrier, 20 October 1633, *Lettres de Peiresc*, v, p. 659.

100 Naudé to Gassendi, 17 August 1637, in *Mirrour*, p. 275.

101 Peiresc to Menestrier, 25 August 1631, *Lettres de Peiresc*, v, p. 590.

102 Peacham, *The Compleat Gentleman* (London, 1634), pp. 111–12. The book's subtitle is instructive: 'Fashioning him absolute in the most necessary and commendable qualities, concerning minde or body, that may be required in a noble gentleman'.

103 'Je distingue fort encore une fois ce genre d'hommes qui se disent curieux, & que j'appelle oiseaux de proye ou de colifichetiers, de noms qui leurs conviennent mieux, d'avec ceux que l'amour des sciences, le droit d'y faire des decouvertes par leur capacité, ou le desir de profiter aux gens de lettres a fait rechercher avec passion ce que nous apellons veritablement des antiques. Voilà les seuls antiquaires de qui j'entens parler'. Charles César Baudelot de Dairval, *De l'Utilité des voyages, et l'avantage que la recherche des antiquitez procure aux sçavans*, 2 vols (Paris, 1686), i, p. 345.

104 Referring to antiquaries La Bruyère wrote: 'D'autres ont la clef des sciences, où ils n'entrent jamais; ils passent leur vie à déchiffrer les langues orientales et les langues du nord, celles des deux Indes, celles des deux poles, et celle qui se parle dans la lune; les idiomes les

plus inutiles avec les caractères les plus bizarres et les plus magiques sont précisément ce qui réveille leur passion et qui excite leur travail.' In a striking formulation that would be reprised by Nietzsche two centuries later, he continued: 'Ces gens lisent toutes les histoires et ignorent l'histoire, ils parcourent tous les livres, et ne profitent d'aucun'. *Les Caractères ou les moeurs de ce siècle*, in *Oeuvres complètes*, ed. Julien Benda (Paris, 1951), pp. 388–9.

105 '. . . ce qui est rare, unique, pour ce qu'on a et ce que les autres n'ont point', ibid., p. 386. This echoes Peiresc's words, see n. 116.

106 The classic treatment is Charles Mitchell, 'Archaeology and Romance in Renaissance Italy', *Italian Renaissance Studies*, ed. E. F. Jacob (London, 1960), pp. 455–83; for Piranesi see now Norbert Wolf, *Giovanni Battista Piranesi: der römische Circus. Die Arena als Weltsymbol* (Frankfurt am Main, 1997).

107 Casaubon, *Treatise of Use and Customs* (1638), quoted by John Aubrey, *Monumenta Britannica*, ed. John Fowles (Knock-ne-cre, Milbrook Port, Dorset, 1982), pt III, pp. 666–7.

108 Peacham, *The Compleat Gentleman*, p. 105.

109 Gassendi, *Mirrour*, year 1600, p. 30. Just this sort of learned fantasy was ridiculed by Robert Burton: 'Your supercilious criticks, grammatical triflers, notemakers, curious antiquaries, find out all the ruines of wit, *ineptiarum delicias*, amongst the rubbish of old writers; and what they take they spoil, all fools with them that cannot find fault; they correct others, & are hot in a cold cause, puzzle themselves to find out how many streets in Rome, houses, gates, towres . . . what clothes the Senator did wear in Rome, what shoes, how they sat, where they went to the close stool'. *The Anatomy of Melancholy* (New York, 1927), pp. 95–6.

110 'Et pense bien que feu Monsieur le President son père, qui avoit tant prins de peine pour aller grimper sur les Pyrenées, ne luy auroit pas facilement pardonné l'obmission de cette recherche, pour en pouvoir parler comme tesmoing occulaire, attendu la grande difficulté qu'il y a bien souvent de s'imaginer les choses telles qu'elles sont, et de les croire si admirablement comme elles sont, sans les avoir veues sur les lieux memes'. Peiresc to Dupuy, 15 December 1629, *Lettres de Peiresc*, II, p. 207. This passage of de Thou's history was copied out by Peiresc, see Carp. Bibl. Inguimb, MS 1821 fols 204–5. De Thou's older contemporary, Montaigne, took a similar view of the role of imagination ('On Vanity', *Essays*, p. 1128).

111 Friedrich Nietzsche, *On the Advantage and Disadvantage of History for Life*, tr. Peter Preuss (Indianapolis, 1980), section 3, p. 18.

112 Gassendi, *Mirrour*, year 1600, pp. 30 and 32. Aubrey sketched 'by Imagination' Old Sarum and ancient Wessex, replete with hill-forts, barrows, roads, and dykes so as to reconstruct 'the total ancient environment' (these last are Hunter's words, *John Aubrey*, p. 174).

113 The words are of Henry Poullain, quoted in Schnapper, *Le Géant, la licorne, la tulipe*, p. 138.

114 [John Earle], *Micro-cosmographie: Or, a Piece of the World Discovered: in Essayes, and Characters* (London, 1629), pp. 33–6.

115 Mermion, *The Antiquary* (London, 1641), sig. C^r. A few decades later, abstruse natural philosophy had replaced the arcana of the past as the butt of satire, and the *Antiquary* was substituted on stage by the *Virtuoso*. Veteranno's 'heir', Sir Nicholas Gimcrack, explained that he had learned to swim lying on a table because 'I content myself with the speculative part of swimming: I care not for the practice. I seldom bring anything to use; 'tis not my way. Knowledge is my ultimate end'. Thomas Shadwell, *The Virtuoso*, ed. Marjorie Hope Nicholson and David Stuart Rhodes (Lincoln, NB, 1966), II.i, p. 47.

116 Gassendi, *Mirrour*, bk 6, p. 204. Peiresc's friend John Selden evoked this balance in the dedication of his *History of Tythes* to their mutual friend Robert Cotton: 'For as on the one side it cannot be doubted that the too studious affectation of base and sterile antiquity (wch is nothing else but to be exceeding busie about nothing) may soon descend to Dotage: so on the other the neglect or only vulgar regard of the fruitfull and precious part of it wch gives necessarie light to posteritie in matters of state, law, Historie and the understanding of good aucthors is but preserving that kind of ignorant infancie which our short lives alone allow us before the many ages of former experience.' Quoted in Kevin Sharpe, *Sir Robert Cotton 1586–1631: History and Politics in Early Modern England* (Oxford, 1979), p. 39.

117 'La vanité est la plus essentielle et propre qualité de l'humaine nature', Charron, *De la sagesse*, bk 1, ch. 36, p. 229.

118 Charron, *De la sagesse*, bk 1, ch. 36, p. 234. 'Finalement la Couronne et la perfection de la vanité de l'homme se montre en ce qu'il cherche, se plaist, et me sa felicité en des biens vains et frivoles, sans lesquels il peut bien et commodément vivre: et ne se soucie pas, comme il faut, des vrays et essentiels.'

119 Charron, *Petit Traicté de sagesse* in *De la Sagesse*, p. 860.

120 Ibid., ch. 3, p. 852; bk 2, ch. 8, p. 497; Montaigne, 'Du Pedantisme', *Essais* in *Oeuvres complètes*, ed. Albert Thibadaut and Maurice Rat (Paris, 1962), I, ch. 25, p. 135. Note that Montaigne exempted Adrian Turnèbe, whom he described as 'le plus grand homme [des lettres] qui fut il y a mil ans', from this critique because his learning did not interfere with his judgement: it was the dehumanizing aspect of book learning that Montaigne and later Charron attacked. Bacon acknowledged that scholars discredited themselves in three principal ways, by 'vain imaginations, vain altercations, and vain affectations', but thought that nevertheless learning could escape the charge of vanity so long as it did not lead men to forget their mortality, make them unhappy or encourage them to believe that the mysteries of God could be grasped through nature alone (Bacon, *Advancement of Learning, Works*, III, bk 1, pp. 282 and 291). Eugene Rice has described this as a decisive transformation of the idea of wisdom into something 'purely human and a perfection of the natural man, naturally derived from the dictates of the autonomous human reason, experience, contemporary ideals and practice, and the Greek and Roman moralists'. Eugene F. Rice Jr., *The Renaissance Idea of Wisdom* (Cambridge, Mass., 1958), p. 177 and, more generally, ch. 7 'Pierre Charron and the Triumph of Wisdom as a Moral Virtue'.

121 For the meaning of curiosity, see Pomian's essays, collected in *Collectionneurs, amateurs et curieux. Paris, Venise: XVIᵉ–XVIIᵉ siècle* (Paris, 1587); André Labhardt, 'Curiositas: notes sur l'histoire d'un mot et d'une notion', *Museum Helveticum*, 17 (1960), pp. 206–24; Daston and Park, *Wonders and the Order of Nature*, esp. pp. 305–16.

122 Describing to Peiresc an old man he met in a village near the canyon of Verdon, in Provence, Gassendi noted the agility of the eighty-year-old in the mountains, but concluded that 'ce n'est pas là ce qui le rend recommandable: c'est l'extreme curiosité qu'il a d'apprendre toutes choses et de les mettre par escript.' Gassendi to Peiresc, 25 May 1635, *Lettres de Peiresc*, IV, p. 497.

123 Samuel Pufendorf, *Les Devoirs de l'homme et du citoyen*, tr. Jean Barbeyrac, 2 vols (London, 1741 [1673]), para. 9, p. 150.

124 Voltaire, *The Philosophy of History* (London, 1766), p. 1.

125 In a letter to their mutual friend, Giovanni Battista Doni, Mersenne wrote that

Peiresc was judged by 'nous tout le premier homme du monde en matiere de lettres et qui merite plus de statues qu'il n'y en a dans Rome, quoqu'il soit si esloigné de cez vanitez que nous le regardons comme un miroir et un exemplaire de debonnaireté et de vertu chrestienne'. 2 February 1635, *Mersenne Correspondance*, V, p. 41.

126 Fulgenzio Micanzio, *Vita del Padre Paolo* in Paulo Scarpi, *Istoria del Concilio Tridentino*, ed. Corrado Vivanti, 2 vols (Turin, 1974), II, pp. 1288 and 1372.

127 Ibid., pp. 1396–7: 'al coltivare l'animo sua, il maggior bene di questa vita, et all'umilità'.

128 Ibid., p. 1323.

129 Paolo Sarpi, *Pensieri, naturali, metafisici e matematici*, ed. Luisa Cozzi and Libero Sosio (Milan and Naples, 1996), pp. 617–18: 'Sopra il tutto fuggi quel rigore che si chiama virtù, ma è vizio pestifero quella rettitudine catoniana'.

130 'Non credere che la vocazione tua sia il negozio, ma l'ozio, qual procurerai quanto potrai, e pensa che la più illustre delle azzioni tue è il vivere.' Ibid., p. 667.

131 Montaigne, 'On Experience', in *Essays*, III.13, p. 1266.

132 Sarpi, *Pensieri*, p. 625.

133 Ibid., p. 628. The story is found in Seneca, *De Tranquillitate Animi*, XVII.3–6.

134 Sarpi, *Pensieri*, p. 617.

135 Sarpi, *Pensieri*, p. 621. A series of references to the sayings of Epictetus – used extensively by Guillaume du Vair and Matteo Ricci (see Chapter Four) – support this focus on what is truly one's own. See also Charron, *De la Sagesse*, bk 2, ch. 2, p. 412.

136 Gassendi, *Mirrour*, bk 6, p. 187. For more description see Maren-Sofie Røstvig, *The Happy Man. Studies in the Metamorphoses of a Classical Ideal. Volume I: 1600–1700*, 2 vols (Oslo, 1962 [1954]), I, chs 1–2; Hugh Trevor-Roper, 'The Great Tew Circle' in *Catholics, Anglicans and Puritans* (London, 1987), pp. 166–230; and Marc Fumaroli, *Héros et orateurs. Rhétorique et dramaturgie cornéliennes* (Geneva, 1990).

137 For the immense popularity of *De Beneficiis* in early modern Europe see Marvin Becker, *The Emergence of Civil Society in the Eighteenth Century* (Bloomington, 1994), p. 18.

138 Micanzio to Cavendish, 10 September 1621, *Lettere a William Cavendish (1615–1628)*, ed. Roberto Ferrini, intro. Enrico de Mas (Rome, 1987), p. 140. For this correspondence see Vittorio Gabrieli, 'Bacone, la riforma e Roma nella versione Hobbesiana d'un carteggio di

Fulgenzio Micanzio', *English Miscellany*, 8 (1957), pp. 195–249.

139 Gassendi, *Mirrour*, bk 6, p. 211.

140 'Specimen animi bene compositi et vera philosophia imbuti', Rubens to Peiresc, early August 1630, *Correspondance de Rubens et documents epistolaires concernant sa vie et ses oeuvres*, ed. Charles Ruelens and Max Rooses, 6 vols (Antwerp, 1887–1909), v, p. 312 [henceforth *Rubens Correspondance*] quoted by Jean-Jacques Bouchard, 'Prayse of Peireskius', in Gassendi, *Mirrour*, p. 255.

141 Peiresc to Mersenne, 10 November 1635, *Mersenne Correspondance*, v, p. 464.

142 Gassendi, *Mirrour*, bk 6, p. 168.

143 'Au reste bien que les incommodités et les maladies qui vous affligent me soient extrèmement sensibles, je tire néantmoins une grand consolation de la force avec laquelle j'observe que vous les supportés. Je m'en fay une leçon d'importance pour l'avenir, si je dois en estre attaqué, et estime en vous dans cette rencontre la modération que je trouve à dire en la plus part des hommes qui sont esclaves de leurs désirs, qui ne méditent jamais que sur le plaisir et qui voudroient n'estre hommes que par cette partie' (Chapelain to Peiresc, 5 October 1633, *Lettres de Jean Chapelain*, I, p. 50). Micanzio also presented Sarpi as one who ruled his passions. 'He moderated his natural emotions, but I do not believe that he ever extinguished them. Rare were the men who have been able to command themselves' and it would be difficult to find anyone who was 'more patron and who more commanded his affections than him' (*Vita*, p. 1287; also p. 1380).

144 Gassendi, *Mirrour*, bk 6, p. 177.

145 Gassendi, *Mirrour*, bk 6, p. 169. Shadwell's risible *Virtuoso*, Gimcrack, by contrast was 'A sot that has spent two thousand pounds in microscops [*sic*] to find out the nature of eels in vinegar, mites in a cheese, and the blue of plums which he has subtly found out to be living creatures' (*The Virtuoso*, I.i, p. 22).

146 'Enfin le temps et les maximes que j'avois practiquees parmy mes maladies douleureuses et aultres adversitez ont prevalu et m'ont remis en assiete.' Peiresc to Mersenne, 10 November 1635, *Mersenne Correspondance*, v, p. 464.

147 Gassendi, *Mirrour*, bk 6, pp. 162–3.

148 We know that Peiresc possessed Cornaro's popular *Della vita sobria* (Peiresc to Bonnaire, 20 May 1624, *Lettres de Peiresc*, VII, p. 685) and referred to him as 'scrittore della sanità' in a letter to Aleandro (Vat. MS Barb.-Lat. 6504,

fol. 232). It is impossible to assess its importance for Peiresc's practices except to note the continuity between this sixteenth-century representation of 'continence and that of Peiresc: 'Fu bene mia spezial intentzione far conoscere in questo modo il valore e la virtù d'un gentil'uomo, nato in città libera, la costanza nel difendersi dalle sirene de i sentimenti, la pazienza nel'astenersi da i cibi dilettevoli al gusto, la toleranza in non saziarsi dei buoni, e finalmente la vittoria ripportata dalla costui sobrietà contra le delizie, le quali l'invitavano e tiravano a servirle e loro ubbidire' (Dedicatory letter of Bernardin Tomitano, in Luigi Cornaro, *Dela vita sobria*, ed. Arnaldo di Benedetto (Milan, 1993), pp. 26–7).

149 BN MS Lat. 8958 fol. 312: 'Felix nimium prior aetas / Contenta fidelibus arvis / Nec inerti perdita luxu, / Facili quae sera solebat / Ieiunia solvere glande' and 'Utinam modo nostra redirent / In mores tempora priscos!' Boethius, *De consolatione philosophia*, tr. H. F. Stewart et al. (Cambridge, Mass., and London, 1978), II.v, pp. 206–9.

150 Hence Peiresc's ability to cede to his worthless nephew both the 'most beautiful apartment' in the family house and his father's study with whatever books the nephew desired, in order to buy domestic peace – unsuccessfully, as it turned out (Peiresc to Dupuy, 2 September 1636, *Lettres de Peiresc*, III, pp. 554–5).

151 Gassendi to Peiresc, 16 November 1635, ibid., IV, p. 567.

152 Peiresc to Dupuy, 18 August 1629, ibid., II, p. 161.

153 'Cependant, au lieu de meilleure matiere, je vous envoie coppie d'un des registres de Seneque de la traduction de Malerbe [*sic*], qui n'a pas nuy à ma consolation en nostre petite solitude, principalement dans la contemplation des revolutions presentes' (Peiresc to Dupuy, 13 September 1631, ibid., p. 285). Malherbe translated the first ninety of Seneca's letters to Lucilius (published 1632) and the first two books of *De beneficiis* (published 1632).

154 In a letter 'recommending' Peiresc to de Thou, du Vair wrote, 'Vous trouverez qu'il n'a point perdu le temps depuis qu'il a eu l'honneur de vous voir et s'estre rendu digne d'estre animé et estimé de vous autant qu'homme de son age et de sa profession. Sa compagnie véritablement douce est la principale consolation que j'aye icy'. Du Vair to de Thou, 15 April 1602, *Lettres inédites de Guillaume du Vair*, ed. Philippe Tamizey de Larroque (Paris, 1873), p. 22.

155 Peiresc to Dupuy, 16 January 1635, *Lettres de Peiresc*, III, p. 257; 'Mais il faut se contenter de jouyr des biens que Dieu nous donne aultant et si longuement qu'il luy plaist les nous laisser, aussy bien que des enfants et des parents et amys et le loüer de ceux qu'il nous laisse, lesquels il nous pouvoit avoir ostez aussy bien que les autres' (Peiresc to Dupuy, 28 December 1623, ibid., I, p. 14).

156 The loss of several leaves of a valuable ancient papyrus book led Peiresc to explain to Jacques Dupuy that 'puis qu'il se fault consoler de la perte des personnes, il fault bien le faire aussy pour la perte des aultres choses moings cheres et moings precieuses' (Peiresc to Dupuy, 24 April 1635, *Lettres de Peiresc*, III, p. 295). The loss of the even more valuable Marmor Parium to Lord Arundel must have been painful but was represented by Peiresc as immaterial since the *Marmora Arundelliana*, published by Arundel's expert, and Peiresc's friend, John Selden, gave to the learned world the same benefit that he had envisioned (Gassendi, *Mirrour*, year 1628, pp. 33–4).

157 '... car vostre santé et commodité me sont beaucoup plus cheres que toutes cez petites curiositez'. Peiresc to Guillemin, 16 January 1633, *Lettres de Peiresc*, V, p. 96.

158 These are found in Carp. Bibl. Inguimb., MS 1815 fols 398–54 in the midst of other speeches and documents referring to du Vair's activities.

159 Gassendi, *Mirrour*, bk 6, p. 168.

160 Ibid., p. 169.

161 'Mais parce que notre nature est beaucoup plus sensible a l'aigreur des adversitez que à la douleur des prosperitez nous sommes bien plustost abbatus des unes que relevez des autres, & pourtant devons nous employer nos plus puissants efforts pour n'y estre point surpris, & nous armer contre tous ses assauts d'une assuree Constance, bouclier impenetrable, Royne & Maistresse de toutes les vertus, & si fort estimee parmy tous nos anciens'. 'Consolation à Monsieur de Richelieu sur la mort de Madame de Richelieu sa femme 1618', Carp. Bibl. Inguimb., MS 1789, fol. 143^r.

162 'La patience est le vray port de toutes nos miseres, & le seul antidote pour repousser nos maux'. Ibid., fol. 143^v.

163 To Pierre Dupuy, on the occasion of the death of his mother, Peiresc said little because they were 'men of such resolve' and had 'no need of such weak consolations' as he could provide (Peiresc to Dupuy, 23 May 1631, *Lettres de Peiresc*, II, p. 272). Peter-Paul Rubens, on the other hand, receiving a similar letter from Pierre

Dupuy, objected. 'You are very prudent in commending me to Time, and I hope this will do for me what Reason ought to do. For I have no pretensions about ever attaining a stoic equanimity; I do not believe that human feelings so closely in accord with their object are unbecoming to man's nature, or that one can be equally indifferent to all things in this world'. Rubens to Dupuy, 15 July 1626, *The Letters of Peter Paul Rubens*, tr. and ed. Ruth Saunders Magurn (Evanston, Ill., 1991 [1955]), p. 136.

164 'Il est bon besoing d'avoir estudié comme vous avez faict en la bonne philosophie, pour estre preparé à la constance et patience telle qu'il fault avoir dans les obstacles qui se rencontrent aux affaires les plus favorables. Nous avions vaincu des difficultez nompareilles' – referring to preparations for an expedition he had organized to the Levant that was cancelled because of an outbreak of the plague and imposition of a quarantine on Provence. Peiresc to Holstenius, 6 August 1629, *Lettres de Peiresc*, V, p. 338.

165 '... d'examiner toutes choses, considerer à part et puis comparer ensemble toutes les loix et coutumes de l'univers que luy viennent en conoissance, et les juger ... de bonne foy et sans passion, au niveau de la verité, de la raison et nature universelle' (Charron, *De la sagesse*, bk 2, ch. 8, p. 500). Susan James has suggested the persistence of this idea through the seventeenth century. For Malebranche, the New Science, with its insistence on close observation and exact documentation, also served as a philosophical practice since working on the small banished the hubris that came from thinking too much about the huge (*Passion and Action. The Emotions in Seventeenth-Century Philosophy*, Oxford, 1997, p. 176).

166 Gassendi even drew on the language of neo-Stoicism to explain Peiresc's achievements as an astronomer (*Mirrour*, year 1612, p. 154). Micanzio painted Sarpi's moral portrait in the same subdued hues. He was the possessor of an 'eroica pazienza' (*Vita*, p. 1313) and 'un'ugualità e costanza maravigliosa' (ibid., p. 1371). The summit of his virtue was a 'cuor intrepido et una costanza nella rettitudine invariable' (ibid., p. 1398).

167 Erasmus, *Adages*, tr. and annotated R. A. B. Mynors in *Collected Works of Erasmus*, XXXIV (Toronto, 1992), pp. 170–1.

168 Quoted in G. J. Toomer, *Eastern Wisdom and Learning. The Study of Arabic in Seventeenth-Century England* (Oxford, 1996), pp. 72–3.

169 Jean-Jacques Bouchard, 'Prayse of Peireskius', Gassendi, *Mirrour*, p. 246.

170 Ibid., bk 6, p. 190.

171 Ibid., year 1595, p. 13.

172 Charles Perrault, *Les Hommes illustres qui on paru en France pendant ce siècle* (Paris, 1697), p. 45.

173 Again, the comparison with Gassendi's *Life* of Brahe is telling: he too is praised for beneficence but Gassendi succeeds in enumerating his acts in five points and one quick paragraph (*Opera Omnia*, 6 vols (Leiden, 1658), IV, p. 466). Pierre Charron provides a series of rules for beneficence, *De la sagesse*, bk 3, ch. 11, p. 661. For a parallel treatment of these very same issues – the reciprocal relationship between friendship, gratitude, and beneficence in humanist literature and seventeenth-century practice – see Antonio M. Hespanha, 'La economia de la gracia', in *La Gracia del derecho. Economia de la cultura en la Edad Moderna*, tr. Ana Cañellas Haurie (Madrid, 1993), pp. 151–76 and, more fully, from the standpoint of a legal historian, see Bartolomé Clavero, *Antidora: anthropologia católica de la economia moderna* (Paris, 1996). I thank Tamar Herzog for suggesting I read these.

174 Gassendi, *Mirrour*, sig. [A8]v.

175 Ibid., sig. (a)v.

176 Gassendi, *Mirrour*, bk 6, p. 169.

177 Jean-Jacques Bouchard, 'Prayse of Peireskius', Gassendi, *Mirrour*, p. 246.

178 Pierre Bayle, *Dictionaire Historique et Critique*, 4 vols (Amsterdam and Leiden, 1730), III, p. 638. For Peiresc as a patron is Lisa Sarasohn, 'Nicolas-Claude Fabri de Peiresc and the Patronage of the New Science in the Seventeenth Century', *Isis*, 84 (1993), pp. 70–90. I thank Paula Findlen for bringing this to my attention.

179 Gassendi, *Mirrour*, bk 6, pp. 169–72.

180 Gassendi, *Mirrour*, year 1634, p. 112.

181 Peiresc to Dupuy, 31 October 1634, *Lettres de Peiresc*, III, p. 197.

182 Peiresc to Dupuy [October 1636], ibid., p. 589.

183 Gassendi, *Mirrour*, bk 6, p. 170.

184 See Seneca, *De beneficiis*, in *Moral Essays*, tr. John W. Brasore (Cambridge, Mass., 1989 [1935]), IV.xviii.1–2, p. 241.

185 Gassendi, *Mirrour*, bk 6, p. 173.

186 Seneca, *De beneficiis*, II.xviii.5. Charron offers a taxonomy of friendship in *De la Sagesse* (bk 3, ch. 7, pp. 638–42).

187 Gassendi, *Mirrour*, bk 6, pp. 174–5; Seneca, *De Beneficiis*, V.xi.5.

188 Seneca, *De tranquillitate animi*, in *Moral Essays*, tr. John W. Brasore (Cambridge, Mass., 1979 [1932]), VII.3.

189 Cicero, *De amicitia* XVII.62–3, p. 173 and XVIII.65, p. 175.

190 Mersenne to Gassendi, 17 November 1635, *Mersenne Correspondance*, V, p. 485.

191 '. . . et binae quoque mihi causae. aut quia in manibus semper iste: aut quia CONSTANTIA, quae caeterarum virtutum sanguis et robur est, est anima amicitiae'. This copy of the 1591 Leiden edition is in BN Est. Rés. R.2526, quoted in Abel, *Stoizismus und frühe Neuzeit zur Entstehungsgeschichte modernen Denkens im Felde von Ethik u. Politik* (Berlin, 1978), p. 280.

192 Describing the learned Vienna of the 1580s Robert Evans wrote that 'Platonic protestations of friendship and introductions for travellers give the authentic flavour of a sort of educated freemasonry stretching from London to the Ottoman frontier' and that the residue of this world is preserved in the letters and album books of the period. R. J. W. Evans, *The Making of the Habsburg Monarchy 1550–1700. An Interpretation* (Oxford, 1991 [1979]), pp. 24 and 30.

193 See Seneca *Epistulae morales*, tr. Richard Gummere, 3 vols (Cambridge, Mass., 1970 [1917]) IX.8, p. 47.

194 Ibid., VII.8, p. 35.

195 Gassendi, *Mirrour*, year 1596, p. 15.

196 Ibid., year 1635, p. 134.

197 'Et parce que je n'accuse pas volontiers mes amys, j'y cherche touts les plus honnestes pretextes d'excuses que me peult fournir ma foible imagination.' Peiresc to Jacques Dupuy, 4 March 1636, *Lettres de Peiresc*, III, p. 449.

198 '. . . car je n'entends nullement de perdre son amitié, estant resolu d'aymer mes amys avec toutes leurs humeurs, comme je ne vouldrois pas perdre l'usage des roses pour les espines qui y sont meslées'. Peiresc to Dupuy, 4 August 1628, ibid., I, p. 657. In an undated letter to Holstenius of 1637 Peiresc attributed the expression that 'il faut cueillir la rose et laisser l'espine' to Italians (ibid., V, p. 486).

199 '. . . car comme j'ay souvent des gousts extraordinaires, et que je suis bien aise que mes amys me les souffrent, je pense estre obligé d'en faire de mesme envers ceux qui ont d'autres gousts que les miens, et c'est comme cela qu'en recherchant pour l'amour de mes amys des choses que je sçavois estre de leur goust et qui n'estoient nullement du mien, je m'y suis laissé neantmoings prendre quelques foys sans y penser, comme à la moustarde, et m'y suis enfin trouvé affriandé voulusse je ou non, dont je ne me suis pas tant repenty.' Peiresc to Dupuy, 4 May 1629, ibid., II, pp. 89–90.

200 'Mais estants touts hommes, il fault nous compatir les uns les aultres'. Peiresc to Dupuy, 10 June 1636, ibid., III, p. 505. In another

letter he returned to this theme: 'Nous sommes toutes hommes, et difficilement pouvons nous esviter de broncher bien souvent' (Peiresc to Dupuy, 23 September 1636, ibid., p. 571).

201 Gassendi, *Mirrour*, bk 6, pp. 216–17. Peiresc's awareness of the intensity of scholarly envy led him to ask Dupuy to keep some information secret 'à cause de la jalousie des aultres curieux' (Peiresc to Dupuy, 1 May 1634, *Lettres de Peiresc*, III, p. 95), and asked that a gift of cats for Cardinal de' Bagni not be presented in public 'et, si besoing est, de nuict pour esviter toutes jalousies' (Peiresc to d'Arene, [1637], ibid., VII, p. 196).

202 Peiresc to Dupuy, 17 October 1634, *Lettres de Peiresc*, III, p. 187; Peiresc to Dupuy, 25 August 1628, ibid., I, pp. 704–5; Peiresc to Camden, 14 January 1620, ibid., VII, p. 807.

203 '. . . l'assiduité de l'estude rendant ce monde là plus austere et plus saulvage qu'il ne fauldroit certainement'. Peiresc to Bouchard, 30 August 1635, ibid., IV, p. 143.

204 '. . . je prends un plaisir extreme de voir cesser toutes matieres de malentendu entre gents qui peuvent touts contribuer quelque chose au service du public, quoyque les uns de puissent faire office que de pionniers lorsque les aultres font office de bons soldats et de cappitaines, estant besoing d'avoir des uns et des aultres pour la necessité de la société humaine'. Peiresc to Holstenius, 31 July 1636, ibid., V, p. 452.

205 See Anne Goldgar, *Impolite Learning: Conduct and Community in the Republic of Letters, 1680–1750* (New Haven and London, 1995).

206 Stefano Guazzo, *The Civile Conversatione of M. Steeven Guazzo*, intro. Sir Edward Sullivan, 2 vols (London and New York, 1925 [rpt of 1581 edn]), p. 168.

207 The purpose of this fascinating list becomes clearer when one recalls that the *Polyhistor* was the textbook for Morhof's course of lectures which were designed to provide young men with the tools needed for an academic existence (Morhof, *Polyhistor*, ch. 15, 'De Conversatione Erudita', pp. 167–79).

208 Conversation did not require presence; from the time of Erasmus onwards correspondence was seen as uniting absent friends in a more fixed, but no less intimate form of communication. Peiresc was one of the century's great letter-writers and Gassendi presents his system of writing letters as yet another set of rules for others to follow (*Mirrour*, bk 6, pp. 216–17). For communication in the Republic of Letters, see Giuseppe Olmi, '"Molti Amici in varij luoghi": studio della natura e rapporti epistolari nel secolo XVI', *Nuncius. Annali di Storia*

di Scienze, 6 (1991), pp. 3–31; Paul Dibon, 'Communication in the Respublica Literaria of the Seventeenth Century', *Res Publica Litterarum*, 1 (1978), pp. 43–55; *Commercium Litterarium. Forms of Communication in the Republic of Letters 1600–1750*, ed. Hans Bots and Françoise Waquet (Amsterdam and Maarsen, 1994).

209 'Mais il est malaisé de bien exprimer ses conceptions par la seule escritture; il y fault la veue et communication de preseance'. Peiresc to Holstenius, 29 January 1629, *Lettres de Peiresc*, V, p. 303. Exactly the same idea, in the same context, was expressed by the sixteenth-century Florentine antiquary Vincenzo Borghini in the same words: 'Le dispute così lunghe et tanto sottili hanno bisogno della presentia et della voce viva, et non si possono, né forse debbono, rimettere a una lettera familiare' (Borghini, *Lettera intorno a' manoscritti antichi*, ed. Gino Belloni, Rome, 1995, pp. 10–11).

210 Gassendi, *Mirrour*, bk 6, p. 164.

211 Ibid., p. 176. The notes he kept on conversations seem to follow directly from the practice of his mentor Pinelli who would retire into his private study after his guests left and jot down observations and comments so as not to forget them (*Vita Pinelli* quoted in Morhof, *Polyhistor*, p. 181). The other great seventeenth-century biographer of a scholar, Micanzio, also praised Sarpi's conversation skills, writing that he possessed 'una desterità maravigliosa, alla socratica' (*Vita*, p. 1307).

212 Seneca, *De beneficiis*. II.xvi.1.

213 Gassendi, *Mirrour*, bk 6, p. 177.

214 Ibid., p. 168.

215 Ibid., pp. 176–7.

216 Jacques Ferrier, 'Peiresc et les dames', *L'Été Peiresc. Fioretti II. nouveaux mélanges*, ed. Jacques Ferrier (Avignon, 1988), pp. 161–82.

217 Peiresc to Barclay, 15 October 1620, *Lettres de Peiresc*, VII, p. 432; the letters to Mademoiselle de Barclay are in the same volume, pp. 493–507; 'Je regrette bien la perte du pauvre M^r le President Aymar, pour l'amour principalement de Madame la Presidante sa femme, qui meritoit plus de bonheur que cela' (Peiresc to Borilly, 21 January 1631, ibid., IV, p. 13).

218 Gassendi, *Mirrour*, year 1604, p. 82.

219 Ferrier, 'Peiresc et les dames', p. 165; Peiresc to Guillemin, 2 May 1633, *Lettres de Peiresc*, V, p. 153.

220 Peiresc to Dupuy, 21 August 1635, *Lettres de Peiresc*, III, p. 363.

221 Micanzio's account of the barely failed papal attempt to assassinate Sarpi enabled him to emphasize the 'typical piety and constancy' with which he bore pain (*Vita*, p. 1354). Sarpi

showed the same constancy on his deathbed (p. 1381) about which Micanzio commented 'that the way of dying is the sincere argument of the life and lifts all of the masks' (p. 1404). Sarpi's death was presented entirely as a demonstration of: his 'fortitude of soul' (p. 1407); 'constancy' (p. 1408); 'a constancy of soul' and revealed an 'inestimable tranquillity' (p. 1409).

222   '. . . puis, disoit-il, que nous approchons du terme qu'il la fault quitter du tout, et pour ce faut il penser à bien mourir qui est la closture de la comedie. Ce sont ses propres parolles qui respondent bien à touts ses escriptz' (Peiresc to Barclay, 18 August 1621, Lettres de Peiresc, VII, p. 486). In the same letter he described du Vair as having 'faict une si saincte mort et si glorieuse . . . qu il n'eust sçeu desirer de faire une plus digne et plus honorable mort' (p. 485). In an earlier letter to Barclay reporting the death of de Thou, Peiresc described him as having 'fist une fort belle mort et fort digne de la vie qu'il avoit tenue' (p. 363).

223   The expression is Seneca's – in Monteverdi and Busenello, L'incoronazione di Poppea, II. I. Elie Diodati invoked these same popular attributes when conveying the news of Peiresc's death to Galileo and urging him to bear the tidings with 'your usual constancy in moderating sadness' and with the hope that 'reason will triumph in you over the exccess of emotions' (Diodati to Galileo, 7 July 1637, Le Opere di Galileo Galillei, ed. Antonio Favaro, 20 vols (Florence, 1966 [1890]), XVII, p. 130).

224   John Eliot, The Monarchie of Man, ed. Alexander B. Grosart, 2 vols (n.p., 1872), II, p. 151. For Cotton's gift, Sharpe, Sir Robert Cotton 1586–1631, p. 106.

225   Eliot, Monarchie of Man, p. 156.

226   Ibid., p. 160; Seneca, Epistulae morales, XXIV.13.

227   For the 'Invisible College' see Charles Webster, 'New Light on the Invisible College: The Social Relations of English Science in the mid-Seventeenth Century', Transactions of the Royal Historical Society, 5th ser. 24 (1974), pp. 19–42. Recent work on Hartlib makes no mention of the relationship between Peiresc and Hartlib that is mediated by this translation project (see Samuel Hartlib and Universal Reformation: Studies in Intellectual Communication, ed. Mark Greengrass, Michael Leslie, and Timothy Raylor (Cambridge, 1994), though Charles Webster did (The Great Instauration. Science, Medicine and Reform 1626–1660, London, 1975, p. 306). For the Hartlib circle and antiquarianism see Stan A. E. Mendyk, 'Speculum Britanniae'. Regional Study, Antiquarianism, and Science in

Britain to 1700 (Toronto, 1989), ch. 7; and for the broader intellectual context, Richard W. F. Kroll, The Material Word. Literate Culture in the Restoration and Early Eighteenth Century (Baltimore, 1991), ch. 3.

228   Rand explained that Benjamin Worsley first drew his attention to Gassendi's biography in 1646 and Samuel Hartlib actually gave him the book to read (William Rand, 'Epistle Dedicatory', Mirrour, sig. A3ʳ). A letter of 1651 from Thomas Smith to Hartlib sheds a more revealing light on the pre-publication history. Apparently, Hartlib had first approached him with the translation project. Smith explains: 'But ad rem I intended to have made an attempt upon Peirescius as soon as I came hither [to Cambridge]'. A series of obligations had held him back. Moreover, one of his colleagues 'told me & others are of his mind that he thinkes it will not sell though it be never so well translated as long as the Latin Original which is reprinting may be had at any easy rate. Yesterday I told the Master of Iesus College of your desires,' Smith continued, '& he said that no man whom he knew was fit to do it but Mr Fuller, who wrote the Holy War, And that his name would carry it of [sic] best' (Smith to Hartlib 3 September 1651, Hartlib Papers, Sheffield University Library, 15/6/25A). In The Holy State, and the Profane State (1642) Fuller sketched the character of 'the true church antiquary'.

229   Rand, 'Epistle Dedicatory', sig. A4ʳ. In the entry of his diary for 5 March 1657 Evelyn records, 'Dr. Rand a learned Physitian dedicated to me his version of Gassendus's Vita Peireskij' (The Diary of John Evelyn, ed. E. S. de Beer (Oxford, 1959), p. 377). Abraham Cowley's dedication to Evelyn of 'The Garden' makes plain the difference between the model of excellence represented by Peiresc, which mingled the active and contemplative, and the one that equated contemplation alone with the 'best' life (see Røstvig, The Happy Man, pp. 35 and 218–20).

230   Michael Hunter, 'John Evelyn in the 1650s: a Virtuoso in Quest of a Role', Science and the Shape of Orthodoxy: Intellectual Change in Late Seventeenth-Century Britain (Woodbridge, 1995), pp. 67–98, at pp. 68 and 74.

231   Gassendi, Mirrour, Rand's 'Dedication', sig. A5ʳ.

232   For this wider debate see the classic works of Ruth Kelso, The Doctrine of the English Gentleman in the Sixteenth Century, University of Illinois Studies in Language and Literature 14 (Urbana, 1928); W. L. Ustick, 'Changing Ideals of Aristocratic Character and Conduct in Seventeenth-Century England', Modern

Philology, 30 (1932), pp. 147–66; George C. Brauer, Jr., *The Education of a Gentleman: Theories of Gentlemanly Education in England, 1660–1775* (New York, 1959). *The Compleat Gentleman* was a popular title and used for books published in London in 1678 and 1728; it was also the English title for the translation of Baltasar Gracián's *Discreto* (1730 [1646]). Aubrey was himself the (unpublished) author of an *Idea of Education of Young Gentlemen* which contained a practical curriculum to educate young nobles for careers as 'Lawyers, Ambassadors, Commanders by Land or Sea, Architects, Sollicitors, Chymists, Surveyors, &c.' (quoted in Hunter, *John Aubrey*, p. 54).

233   Rand, 'Dedication', *Mirrour*, sig. A4ʳ–A5ʳ.

234   One of the printed poems in praise of the book put the choice this way: 'Away with sports of charge and noice, / Sweeter are cheap and silent toyes. / Such as *Actaeons* game pursue, / Their fate oft makes the Tale seem true. / The sick or sullen *Hawk* to day / Flyes not; tomorrow, quite away'. Tho. Weaver, 'To my dear Friend, Mr Iz. Walton, in praise of Angling, which we both love', *The Compleat Angler*, in *The Compleat Walton*, ed. Geoffrey Keynes (London, 1929), p. 11.

235   Walton, 'The Anglers Song', ibid., p. 69.

236   This same trajectory, shown in the choice of Evelyn as dedicatee by both Rand and Cowley, is also traced by Walton's friend Charles Cotton who translated du Vair's *Morall Philosophy of the Stoicks* (1664) and then continued *The Compleat Angler* (1676) with praise of retirement and solitude (see Røstvig, *The Happy Man*, I, pp. 265–6). These are examples of the 'hovering' between Stoic and epicurean emphases to which Røstvig so deftly refers at pp. 43–4. Note that Walton also wrote the preface to the English translation of Gracián's *El Héroe* (1652), a Stoic's survival manual for living at court.

237   Rand, 'Epistle Dedicatory', *Mirrour*, sig. [A6ʳ].

238   *Diary and Correspondence of John Evelyn*, ed. William Bray, 4 vols (London, 1650), III, p. 225.

2   CONSTANCY, CONVERSATION, AND FRIENDSHIP

1   Dante, *Convivio*, ed. Piero Cudini (Milan, 1980), pt. IV, III; pp. 221–8. For Dante's role in the long-term presentation of this question see Klaus Garber, 'Sozietät und Geistes-Adel: Von Dante zum Jakobiner-Club. Der frühneuzeitliche Diskurs *de vera nobilitate* und seine institutionelle Ausformung in der gelehrten Akademie', *Europäische Sozietätsbewegung und demokratische Tradition. Die europäischen Akademien der frühen Neuzeit zwischen Frührenaissance und Spätaufklärung*, ed. Klaus Garber and Heinz Wismann, 2 vols (Tübingen, 1996), pp. 7–9.

2   See Claudio Donati, *L'idea di nobiltà in Italia. Secoli XIV–XVIII* (Roma and Bari, 1988), p. 9; the tracts on true nobility edited and translated by Albert Rabil, Jr. in *Knowledge, Goodness and Power: The Debate over Nobility among Quattrocento Italian Humanists* (Binghamton, 1991); Francesco Tateo, 'La disputa della nobiltà', in idem, *Tradizione e realtà nell'umanesimo italiano* (Bari, 1967), pp. 355–421; George McGill Vogt, 'Gleanings for the History of a Sentiment: *Generositas virtus, non sanguis*', *Journal of English and German Philology*, 24 (1925), pp. 101–24; Charity Cannon Willard, 'The Concept of True Nobility at the Burgundian Court', *Studies in the Renaissance*, 14 (1967), pp. 33–48; Ruth Kelso, *The Doctrine of the English Gentleman in the Sixteenth Century* (Gloucester, Mass., 1964 [1929]) has a very useful 'bibliographical list of treatises on the gentleman and related subjects published in Europe to 1625'. *Virtus vera nobilitas* was adopted as the motto of Trinity College, Cambridge, some time between 1690 and 1770. I thank Jonathan Smith for information about dating.

3   See Davis Bitton, *The French Nobility in Crisis 1560–1640* (Stanford, 1969), esp. ch. 5, 'The Relevance of Virtue'; Ellery Schalk, *From Valor to Pedigree. Ideas of Nobility in France in the Sixteenth and Seventeenth Centuries* (Princeton, 1986), esp. ch. 8 'Education, the Academies, and the Emergence of the New Image of the Cultured Noble-Aristocrat'; more from the perspective of social history see Mark Motely, *Becoming a French Aristocrat. The Education of the Court Nobility 1580–1715* (Princeton, 1990); and George Huppert's classic *Les Bourgeois Gentilshommes* (Chicago, 1977). Montaigne's criticism of both sides in the French debate illuminates it from within: James J. Supple, *Arms versus Letters: The Military and Literary Ideals in the 'Essais' of Montaigne* (Oxford, 1984). For a general overview E. R. Curtius still repays rereading, *European Literature and the Latin Middle Ages* (London, 1953 [1948]), ch. 9, esp. sections 6–7 and more recently Wilhelm Kühlmann, *Gelehrtenrepublik und Fürstenstaat. Entwicklung und Kritik des deutschen Späthumanismus in der Literatur des Barockzeitalters* (Tübingen, 1982), pp. 351–63.

4   This is a well-trodden path, most recently by Marvin B. Becker, *Civility and Society in Western Europe, 1300–1600* (Bloomington, 1988);

Roger Chartier, 'Distinction et divulgation: la civilité et ses livres', *Lectures et lecteurs dans la France d'ancien régime* (Paris, 1987); and Carlo Ossola, *Dal 'cortegiano' all' 'uomo di mondo'* (Turin, 1987).

5 Luigi Pizzolato, *L'idea di amicizia nel mondo classico e cristiano* (Turin, 1993), p. 6. For the substantial ancient literature on friendship see the bibliography in David Konstan, *Friendship in the Classical World* (Cambridge, 1997), and for the Middle Ages, Brian Patrick McGuire, *Friendship and Community: The Monastic Experience 350–1250* (Kalamazoo, 1988). An emphasis on intimate friendship of the sort that is discussed in this chapter does not at all preclude the simultaneous existence, and even preponderance of, for example, friendship based on utility. Nor does it exclude the possibility of a sexual dimension; if Alan Bray ('Homosexuality and the Signs of Male Friendship in Elizabethan England', *History Workshop*, 29 (1990), pp. 1–19) cautioned against collapsing the categories of male friendship and homosexuality, Alan Stewart recently suggested that the identification of the two is not anachronistic (*Close Readers: Humanism and Sodomy in Early Modern Europe*, Princeton, 1997, p. xvi). Rather than asserting that there is a single kind of friendship and a single use, I am here focusing on one particular vision of it and tracing its relation to other virtues over time (see Konstan, *Friendship*, pp. 1–23 for a similar presentation). For a survey of the sociology of friendship in early modern Europe see Guy Fitch Little, 'Friendship and Patronage in Renaissance Europe', *Patronage, Art, and Society in Renaissance Italy*, ed. F. W. Kent and Patricia Simons (Oxford, 1982), pp. 47–62; and for seventeenth-century France, Sharon Kettering, *Patrons, Clients and Brokers in Seventeenth-Century France* (Oxford, 1986).

6 Seneca, *Epistulae morales*, tr. Richard Gummere (Cambridge, Mass., 1970 [1917]), LXXXI, 12–14, II, p. 227, XLVIII, 2–4, I, p. 315. See also Pizzolato, *L'idea diamicizia*, p. 7. It was for this reason that Cicero claimed 'that friendship cannot exist except among good men'. *De Amicitia*, tr. William A. Falconer, (Cambridge, Mass., 1979 [1923]), V.18, p. 127.

7 'A friend loves', Seneca wrote; 'a lover is not necessarily a friend' (Seneca, *Epistulae morales*, XXXV). Aristotle broke with Plato when he stressed that friends were joined by the faculty of reason (Horst Hutter, *Politics as Friendship: the Origins of Classical Notions of Politics in the Theory and Practice of Friendship*, Waterloo, Ont, 1978, p. 92).

8 Seneca, *Epistulae morales*, VII.8, p. 35.

9 'For friendship is nothing else than an accord in all things, human and divine, conjoined with mutual good will and affection, and I am inclined to think that, with the exception of wisdom, no better thing has been given to man by the immortal gods' (*De Amicitia*, VI.21, p. 131). Ibid., XVII.62–3, p. 173: 'We ought therefore, to choose men who are firm, steadfast and constant, a class of which there is a great dearth; and at the same time it is very hard to come to a decision without a trial, while such trial can only be made in actual friendship' (see also XVIII.65, p. 175; Seneca, *De Beneficiis*, tr. John W. Basore (Cambridge, Mass., 1989 [1917]) II.XVIII.5).

10 Seneca, *Epistulae morales*, IX.11, I, 49: 'Ista, quam tu describis, negotiatio est, non amicitia, quae ad commodum accedit, quae quid consecutura sit spectat'. See also LXXVIII.4, II, 183.

11 John Michael Parrish, 'A New Source for More's *Utopia*', *The Historical Journal*, 40 (1997), pp. 493–8.

12 Francis Petrarch, *The Life of Solitude*, ed. and tr. Jacob Zeitlin (Urbana, Ill., 1924), bk 1, ch. 3, p. 127.

13 Petrarch, *The Life of Solitude*, bk 1, ch. 1, p. 108. The conjunction of *otium* and *libertas* is a sure step away from the classical prejudice that saw them as entirely antithetical. For this I rely on Brian Vickers, 'Leisure and Idleness in the Renaissance: the Ambivalence of Otium', *Renaissance Studies*, 4 (1990), pp. 1–37 and 107–54. The citation is from Seneca, *Epistulae morales* LXXXII 3–4.

14 'Now what I maintain is not that solitude develops such a mind but that it is conducive to preserving and strengthening it' (Petrarch *The Life of Solitude*, bk 1, ch. 1, p. 126).

15 Petrach, *The Life of Solitude*, bk 1, ch. 1, p. 108.

16 Ibid., pp. 162–4; the reference is to Cicero, *De officiis*, 1.44, though Petrarch maintains that Cicero's condemnation of solitude referred 'only of the extreme and inhuman kind of solitude'.

17 'I never persuaded those for whom I said solitude was advantageous that in their desire for solitude they should despise the laws of friendship. I bade them fly from the crowds and not from friends.' (*The Life of Solitude*, bk 1, ch. 5, p. 162). Although book 2 is devoted precisely to praising the hermit's life I prefer to follow Petrarch's own rejoinder to critics who read him as a spokesperson for unsociability (*The Life of Solitude*, bk 2, p. 309).

18 *The Life of Solitude*, bk 1, ch. 5, pp. 164–5.

19 Ibid., bk 2, ch. 14, pp. 306–7.

20   Mathieu Palmier, *La Vie civile*, tr. Claude des Rosiers, revised and corrected by Claude Gruget (Paris, 1557), sig. Aii^r. Mario Richter argues that the translation of della Casa's *Galateo* in 1562 marked the introduction of Italian ideas of civility to France and does not mention this earlier work (Mario Richter, *Giovanni della Casa in Francia nel secolo XVI*, Rome, 1966, p. 55).

21   Hans Baron, *The Crisis of the Early Italian Renaissance* (Princeton, 1966 [1955]), pp. 106, 330. For a general reassessment of Baron's claims see James Hankins, 'The "Baron Thesis" after Forty Years and Some Recent Studies of Leonardo Bruni', *Journal of the History of Ideas*, 56 (1995), pp. 309–37.

22   'Il vivere bene è il sommo grado dell'opere humane, ne puo alchuno ben vivere, se non raffrena le passioni dell'animo suo, laqual cosa malagevolmente puo fare chi vive sanza amaestramenti dapprovati auctori'. Matteo Palmieri, *Libro della vita civile* (n.p. [Florence], n.d. [1529 or 1530]), fol. 10^v.

23   Ibid., fol. 11^v.

24   'Tosto si conosceva il primo segno dell'animo bene composto essere stare fermo & seco medesimo non deviando da i primi ingegni, considerare, e trivolgere i termini fondamenti li di qualunque scientia o arte & a quelli con ogni decto & facto corrispondere, sappiendo che ogn'altria via vaga & instabile, & sanza fructo'. Ibid., fol. 20$^{r–v}$.

25   Ibid., fol. 21^v.

26   Though Palmieri is not one of the examples he discusses. Erwin Panofsky, *Hercules am Scheidewege. Und andere antike Bildstoffe in der neuren Kunst* (Leipzig and Berlin, 1930). There is now a new edition (Berlin, 1997) with a long article reviewing the book's *fortuna* by Dieter Wuttke.

27   Palmieri, *Della vita civile*, fol. 22^v.

28   Ibid., fols 29^r, 33^r. 'Sia adunque la principale fortezza, se medesimo vincere, conosca chi noi siamo, & a che nati, che ordine habbino le cose del mondo, & quanto brievemente trapassino, iudichi che cosa è honesta, & bene, & in quelle sommamente saffatichi, fugga tutti i non ragionevoli appetiti, impari la corta buffa da beni sottoposti alla fortuna, & quegli con franco animo sprezi. Molte cose sono da molti stimate excellenti, & grandi, le quali con ragione spregiare è proprio dell'animo forte, & in stesso constante'. Just as Cato of Utica's strength of mind could serve an unlawful end, suicide, the trained reason displayed in self-knowledge could also indulge one's vanity, as happened sometimes with scholars.

29   For Cato, see *Della vita civile*, fols 33^v–34^r. See the author's 'Stoics who sing: Lessons in citizenship from early Modern Lucca', *Historical Journal* (2001).

30   The work's modern editor, Amedeo Quondam, descibes it as a 'filosofia della virtù' ('La virtù dipinta. Noterelle (e divagazioni) guazziane intorno a Classicismo e "Instituto" in Antico regime', *Stefano Guazzo e la Civil Conversazione*, ed. Giorgio Patrizi (Rome, 1990), pp. 288–9).

31   On Italian academies of the late sixteenth and seventeenth centuries, see Luigi Benzoni, 'L'Accademia: appunti e spunti per un profilo', *Ateneo Veneto*, n.s. 26 (1988), pp. 37–58; idem, *Gli affanni della cultura. Intelletuali e potere nell'Italia della controriforma e barocca* (Milan, 1978); *Università, accademie e società scientifiche in Italia e in Germania dal cinquecento al settecento*, ed. Laetitia Boehm and Ezio Raimondi (Bologna, 1981).

32   Giorgio Patrizi's explanation that calling the *Civil Conversatione* a 'libro europeo' means 'poter ricostruire la complessa tram di rapporti ideologici e culturali in cui l'opera si muove, fungendo da elemento di catalizzazione e agglutinazione per numerosi e complessi temi morali, estetici, linguistici' is what I hope to show. 'La *Civil Conversatione* libro europeo', *Stefano Guazzo e la Civile Conversazione*, ed. Patrizi, p. 10.

33   Luigi Benzoni ('L'Accademia: appunti e spunti per un profilo', p. 48) and Emilio Bonfatti ('Vir aulicus, vir eruditus', *Res Publica Litteraria. Die Institutionen der Gelehrsamkeit in der frühen Neuzeit*, ed. Sebastian Neumeister and Conrad Wiedemann, 2 vols, Wiesbaden, 1987, I, p. 181) emphasize the role of the academy as that intermediate space. Patrizi's description of the project of civil conversation could serve as well for the *respublica litteraria*: 'questa idea – la "civil conversatione" – è in realtà un progetto e diviene presto un'ideologia è un mito intelletuale' (Giorgio Patrizi, 'Una retorica del molteplice: forme di vita e forme del sapere nella "civil conversatione"', *Stefano Guazzo e la Civil Conversazione*, p. 52). Marc Fumaroli has stressed that the early modern Republic of Letters differed from both ancient and medieval antecedents and served after the Council of Trent 'as the last common homeland of Christians divided into rival churches and rival nations' ('Venise et la Republique des Lettres au XVIe siècle', *Crisi e rinnovamenti nell'autunno del rinascimento a Venezia*, ed. Vittore Branca and Carlo Ossola (Florence, 1991), p. 353).

34   Chappuys also translated Castiglione's *Courtier* and parts of the *Decameron* and the

romantic best-seller *Amadis of Gaul*. For biographical information see Jean-Pierre Niceron, *Mémoires pour servir à l'histoire des hommes illustres dans la République des Lettres*, 43 vols (Paris, 1738), XXXIX, pp. 90–114; G. Boccazzi, 'I traduttori francesi di Stefano Guazzo. I: Gabriel Chappuys', *Bulletin du Centre d'Études Franco-italien*, 3 (1978), pp. 43–56; Louis Berthé de Besaucèle, *J. B. Giraldi 1504–1573. Étude sur l'évolution des théories littéraires on Italie au XVI siècle. Suivie d'une notice sur G. Chappuys, traducteur Français de Giraldi* (Paris, 1920). The other contemporary French translation, by 'F. Belleforest', had described Guazzo's book as dealing with 'la conversation civile & des moyens que faut que le Gentilhomme tienne pour se composter sagement en toute compagnie'. *La Civile Conversation*, tr. F. Belleforest (Paris, 1582), p. 3. The dedicatory letter is dated August 1579, one month after Chappuys'.

35   'I'ay pensé que cette belle sentence avoit besoing d'interpretation & de quelque moderation, pource que Seneque n'entend pas qu'il nous faille entierement distraire des compagnies, pour suivre la solitude & vivre seuls, en maniere d'hermites, mais nous advise de regarder avec quels personnages nous devons converser & frequenter, nous admonnestant de fuir tant qu'il nous sera possible la multitude. . . .' Guazzo, *La Civile Conversation*, tr. Gabriel Chappuys (Lyon, 1579), sig. 2ᵛ.

36   'ces choses, dit il [Seneca] se font mutuellement & les hommes qui enseignent & remonstret, aprennent beaucoup'. Ibid., sig. 3ʳ.

37   The second book covered conversations with those one met outside the home, the third with conversation within the household and the fourth, not translated into English until the 1586 edition, presented a 'sample' conversation at the academy in Casale.

38   Except where otherwise indicated I quote from the marvellous Elizabethan translation, *The Civile Conversation of M. Steeven Guazzo* intro. Sir Edward Sullivan, 2 vols (London and New York, 1925 [rpt of 1581 edn]), p. 17. All references will be to volume 1. On this translation see John Lievesay, *Stefano Guazzo and the English Renaissance* (Chapel Hill, N.C., 1961), ch. 2.

39   Guazzo, *The Civile Conversation*, p. 18.

40   Guazzo, *The Civile Conversation*, pp. 27 and 35. Ossola also argues that civil conversation is to be understood as the antithesis of a narrow interpretation of Petrarchan solitude (*Stefano Guazzo e la civile conversazione*, p. 131).

41   These themes are addressed by Giorgio Patrizi, 'Una retorica del molteplice', pp. 52–3;

Emilio Speciale, 'Discorso del gentiluomo', ibid., pp. 28, 33 and 40; Bonfatti, 'Vir aulicus, vir eruditus', I, pp. 179–82. The use of Guazzo as a guide to modern politics – proof of this identification of civil society with politics – is clearest in Germany. See Patrizi, '*Civil Conversatione* libro europeo', p. 13 and, more generally, Bonfatti, *La 'Civil Conversatione' in Germania. Letteratura del comportamento da Stefano Guazzo a Adolph Knigge 1574–1788* (Udine, 1979), ch. 2, and Richard Auernheimer, *Gemeinschaft und Gespräch. Stefano Guazzos Begriff der 'Conversatione Civile'* (Munich, 1973).

42   Guazzo, *The Civile Conversation*, p. 168. Compare this with Castiglione's declaration that 'io scriva qual sia al parer mio la forma di cortegiania più conveniente a gentilomo che viva in corte de'principi, per la quale egli possa e sappia perfettamente loro servir in ogni cosa ragionevole, acquistandone da essi grazi e dagli altri laude; in somma, di che sorte debba esser colui, che meriti chiamarsi perfetto cortegiano tanto che cosa alcuna non gli manchi' (*Il libro del cortegiano*, in *Opere di Baldassare Castiglione, Giovanni della Casa, Benevenuto Cellini*, ed. Carlo Cordié, Milan and Naples, 1960). For the contrast between courtier and the citizen, see Lievesay, *Stefano Guazzo and the English Renaissance*, pp. 44–46 and Daniel Jelavitch, 'Rival Arts of Conduct in Elizabethan England: Guazzo's *Civile Conversation* and Castiglione's *Courtier*', *Yearbook of Italian Studies*, I (1971), pp. 178–97.

43   Pierre Charron, *De la Sagesse*, (Paris, 1986 [1601]), bk 1, ch. 54, p. 343.

44   'La conversazione come risposta costruttiva alla malinconia, nelle parole di Annibale, obbliga l'individuo ad una prova di sé nel mondo, a "riuscire con honore"' (Patrizi, 'Una retorica del molteplice', p. 51). Trevor-Roper described the melancholy studied by Burton as not 'depression of the spiritual but a kind of pervasive social inertia, an incapacity for deliberate self-improvement and rational activity' ('Robert Burton and *The Anatomy of Melancholy*', in *Renaissance Essays*, Chicago and London, 1985, p. 257).

45   Guazzo, *The Civile Conversation*, p. 26.

46   Ibid., p. 30.

47   Ibid., p. 31. Just 'as all things upon the earth are made for the use of man, so man is created for the use of man, to the intent that following nature as their guide and Mistress, they have to succour one another, to communicate together common profites, in giving and receiving, uniting and binding themselves together by Artes, Occupations and Faculties' ibid., p. 35.

48 Ibid., p. 43.

49 Ibid., p. 56.

50 Ibid. 'l vivere civilmente non dipende dalla Città, ma dalle qualità dell'animo. Così intendo la conversatione civile, non per rispetto solo della Città, ma in consideratione de' costumi, et delle maniere, che la rendono civile' Stefano Guazzo, *La civil conversazione*, ed. Armedeo Quondam, 2 vols (Ferrara, 1993), I, p. 40.

51 Guazzo, *The Civile Conversation*, p. 110.

52 Ibid., p. 224.

53 Ibid., p. 167.

54 The most detailed early modern discussion of the political implications of friendship and conversation is found in Venice; see Gaetano Cozzi, 'Una vicenda della Venezia barocca: Marco Trevisano e la sua "eroica amicizia"', *Bollettino dell'Istituto di Storia della Società e dello Stato Veneziano*, 3 (1960), pp. 61–154 and the author's 'Friendship and Conversation in Seventeenth-Century Venice', *The Journal of Modern History* (2001).

55 Guazzo, *The Civile Conversation*, pp. 7–8.

56 Ibid., p. 9. Patrizi has sketched the line that runs from Guazzo to Faret's *L'Honnête Homme* (1633) ('*Civil Conversatione* libro europeo', p. 16).

57 Though, as Donati interestingly points out, after 34 editions between 1574 and 1631 no further ones were produced (Donati, *L'idea di nobiltà*, p. 153). Neither the editors nor the contributors to the gigantic (two volumes and 1,800 pages of text) *Europäische Sozietätsbewegung und demoktratische Tradition* seem to have noticed the importance of this book since it is mentioned precisely three times. Guazzo is unmentioned in Becker, *Civility and Society in Western Europe, 1300–1600* and is allowed only four pages (pp. 136–9) in Ossola, *Dal 'cortegiano' all' 'uomo di mondo'*. The influence of Guazzo's model on the visual arts has recently also been suggested: Ricardo de Mambro Santos, *La Civile Conversazione pittorica: reflessione estetica e produzione artistica nel tratto di Karel van Mander* (Rome, 1998).

58 Bonfatti, *La 'Civil Conversazione' in Germania*, pp. 75–81.

59 '... unde tanquam ex instructissimo aliquo penu, divina illa Moralis Philosophiae praecepta, cujuslibet hominum statui & conditioni convenientia, possis deprimere'. Guazzo, *De civilis conversatione* (Amberg, 1598), sig. 4^r.

60 Bonfatti, *La 'Civil Conversazione' in Germania*, pp. 96–7. Salmuth also translated into Latin and commented upon another text that sought to adapt ancient wisdom in the service

of the modern age, Guido Panciroli's *Raccolta di alcune cose piu segnalate, che ebbero gli antichi e di alcune altre trovate da' moderni* (Hamburg, 1599–1602, 2nd edn 1607–8). I thank Anthony Grafton for this reference.

61 '... sed utrumque Philosophiae genus miscuerit, contemplandi & agendi; atque insuper tertium etiam discernendi verum a false adhibuerit, ratiocinandi arte non circa proprium subjectum versante, sed aliarum duntaxat administra & interprete'. Guazzo, *De Civili Conversatione* (Strasbourg, 1614), sig. *2^v. See Bonfatti, *La 'Civil Conversazione' in Germania*, p. 95.

62 'Id quod Stephanus Guazzus in praesenti hoc tractatu De Conversationi Civili, quem Moralis Philosophiae medullam non inepte dixeris...' *De civili conversatione*, 1614 edn, sig. *4^r.

63 Bonfatti offers a good account of the parallels and differences between *De constantia* and *La civile conversazione* (*La 'Civil conversazione' in Germania*, pp. 97–104). For the relationship between neo-Stoicism and the political uses of sociability see Gerhard Oestreich, *Neostoicism and the Early Modern State* tr. McLintock (Cambridge, 1982). I am not discussing the next Latin edition, of Elias Reusner (1606), which reused Salmuth's translation but transformed the text from a dialogue into a series of *Dissertationes Politicae*, fundamentally altering its tone and bearing witness to the contemporary dominance of Lipsian-style cultural politics (see Bonfatti, *La 'Civile Conversazione'*, p. 116).

64 'Ex quo libri hujus quodammodo apparet utilitas: dum in eo id potissimum agitur, quomodo homo solitarius, quem Heraclitus aut Deum esse dicebat, aut belvam, curato animi morbo, ad vitae societatem revocari, & in ea laudabiliter versari possit' (*De civili conversatione*, 1614 edn, sig. *4^v). That communities once founded took a political shape is made clear in the 1673 edition in which the dialogue was transformed into political dissertations 'in vita communi utilissimarum' (*De civili conversatione dissertationes politicae*, tr. Elia Reusner, Leipzig, 1673 [1606], sig. A2^r).

65 This edition has the Italian and French texts on facing pages, displaying concretely the way in which the literature on civility was an attempt to Italianize French society.

66 Ludovico Bryskett, *A Discourse of Civill Life: containing the Ethike part of Morall Philosophie. Fit for the Instructing of a Gentleman in the Course of a Vertuous Life* (London, 1606), sig. A4^v; also p. 27. The work was written in 1582–84.

67   G. B. Giraldi, *Dialogues philosophiques et tres-utiles Italiens-Francois, touchant la vie civile. Contenans la nourriture du premier âge: l'instruction de la Ieunesse & de l'homme propre à se gouverner soy mesme,* tr. Gabriel Chappuis (Paris, 1583), fol. 60ᵛ–61ʳ. Bryskett, *Discourse,* p. 61.

68   Ibid., fols 366ᵛ–377ʳ: 'Essendo adunque la Felicità civile, ultimo & perfetto fine delle attioni virtuose, vi è necessaria l'amicitia à conseguirla perfettamente, perche la conversatione, senza amore, non è ne puo essere grata' ('Comme donc la Felicité humaine soit la derniere & parfaite fin des vertueuses actions, l'amitié est necessaire pour l'obtenir parfaitement, car la conversation, sans amour, n'est & ne peut estre agreable'); '& perso si legge che il levare l'amicitia dal mondo non sarebbe di minor danno alla humana generatione, che se vi si levasse la luce del Sole' ('& pourtant lit on, qu'oster l'amitié du monde, ne seroit pas moins dommageable à l'humaine generation, que si l'on ostoit la lumiere du Soleil') ibid., fol. 366 [365]ᵛ.

69   Ibid., fol. 378ᵛ.

70   Ibid., fol. 366 [365]ᵛ.

71   'Ora, in qual modo sia da usare questo lume naturale di virtù per farsi umanamente perfetti e capaci di maggiore e più vero lume . . .' (Paolo Paruta, *Della perfezzione della vita politica,* in *Storici, politici e moralisti del seicento. Tomo II. Storici e politici veneti del cinquecento e del seicento* ed. Gino Benzoni and Tiziano Zanato, Milan and Naples, 1982, p. 506). For an account of the work that illuminates its contemporary resonances see Gaetano Cozzi, 'La società veneziana del rinascimento in un'opera di Paolo Paruta: "Della perfettione della vita politica"', *Deputazione di Storia Patria per le Venezie. Atti dell'Assemblea del 29 Giugno 1961* (Verice, 1961), pp. 13–47; for how Paruta's work was seen by some later political writers see Innocenzo Cervelli, 'Giudizi seicenteschi dell'opera di Paolo Paruta', *Annali dell'Istituto Italiano per gli Studi Storici,* I (1967–68), pp. 237–308 and, more speculatively, Tibor Klaniczay, 'Die politische Philosophie des Manierismus: Paruta und Lipsius', *Das Ende der Renaissance. Europäische Kultur um 1600,* ed. August Buck and Tibor Klaniczay (Wiesbaden, 1987), pp. 23–35.

72   See William J. Bouwsma, *Venice and the Defense of Republican Liberty. Renaissance Values in the Age of Counter Reformation* (Berkeley and Los Angeles, 1968), ch. 5.

73   The translation, *Perfection de la vie politique* (Paris, 1582), by François Gilbert de la Brosse simply states that it presents the claims on behalf of the active and contemplative lives

and emphasizes the importance of serving the public good (sig. eʳ). Yet, in Paruta's late *Soliloquio,* he called 'happy' the one least attached to this world, able to preserve his tranquillity by fleeing fortune's storms. 'I thought Riches, Honors, and all worldy Greatness', Paruta confessed, 'to be the garnishings wherewith men, and chiefly such as are nobly born, ought to adorn themselves; I called the lives of such as lived better, and more retired from the world, meer madness' (*Political Discourses,* tr. Henry Earl of Monmouth, London, 1657, p. 198).

74   Paruta's modern editors compare his views to Guazzo's, *Della perfezzione della vita politica,* pp. 497–9.

75   Ibid., p. 511.

76   Ibid., p. 639.

77   Ibid., p. 513.

78   Ibid., pp. 523–4.

79   'Cotesta laude – soggiunse monsignor di Ceneda – si compera a troppo gran prezzo, cioè con la servitù di se stesso, la quale è compagna perpetua della vita civile.' Ibid., p. 515.

80   'Ci ritroviamo d'avere col travaglio cambiato il riposo, et il vero dominio di noi stessi con l'obligo di dover vivere a voglia altrui. Tale è la condizione dell'uomo civile'. Ibid.

81   The classic presentation of these positions is William J. Bouwsma, 'Two Faces of Renaissance Humanism: Stoicism and Augustinianism in Renaissance Thought', reprinted in idem, *A Usable Past: Essays in European Cultural History* (Berkeley, 1990), pp. 19–73.

82   'Non sarà dunque la vita civile per sé eligible, né tale che in lei debba spendervi l'opera e 'l tempo l'uomo savio, che sempre intende alle cose più perfette et a ciò che ha rispetto di fine, non che ad altro fine conduce.' Paruta, *Della perfezzione della vita politica,* p. 518.

83   'Assai chiaro mi pare che niuno cosa altrettanto sia contraria alla felicità, quanto esser si vede il maneggio della republica, a cui non può entrare alcuno che non venga schiavo e sottopore tutto il corso di sua vita alla fortuna' (ibid., p. 519). 'Onde si comprende quanto poca convenevolezza ella abbia con l'uomo savio, il quale, vivendo secondo le leggi della natura, contento del poco, facilmente sodisfa insieme a' bisogni et a' desiderii, per accostarsi quanto più alla sufficienza di se stesso, in cui è riposta la nostra vera beatitudine' (ibid., p. 518). Such a man could live under a tyrant and still maintain his liberty by virtue of this ability to cast off attachments to external goods the way sailors tossed a ship's goods overboard in a storm (p. 610).

84 'Conversatio est hominum societas, & grata confabulatio qua mediante invicem animi recreantur' (Ripa, *Iconologia*, Padua, 1625, II, p. 133). Aristotle: 'Non debet homo sana mentis ubicunque conversari'. Seneca: 'Cum illis conversari debes, qui te meliorem facturi sint', both quoted in Ripa, *Iconologia*, II, p. 133.

85 'O herba maravigliosa, e di rara virtù! e che vogliam noi credere ch'ella sia, se non la conoscenza di se medesimo, la quale come ricordo sacrosanto, come divino Oracolo soleva già scriversi sovra le porte de' templi?' (Aleandro, 'Del modo, che tener devono i Saggi, e Letterati Cortigiani per non essere dalla Core (quasi da novella Circe) in sembianze di brutti animali trasformati'. *Saggi accademici dati in Roma nel Accademia del Sereniss. Principe Cardinal di Savoia da diversi nobilissimi ingegni raccolti e publicati*, ed. Agostino Mascardi (Venice, 1630), p. 3.

86 'Questa è la via da far godere in mezzo de gli altri tumulti un tranquillo riposo, da far stare con l'animo pieno di gioia, e co'l volto ridente, mentre si scorge fra gl'incantesimi della Corte altri scioccamente dolersi per una ripulsa havuta: altri spinger addietro il compagno, e farsi scala dell'altrui ruina: altri macerarsi per la falita altrui: altri detestar la vita oziosa, nella quale vien lasciato: altri spander con prodiga mano le proprie facoltà per comperar vento: altri applicarsi à sì faticosa servitù, che resister non vi possa la fiacchezza della sua complessione; e correndo ciascuno dietro l'aura d'una vana felicità, esser'architetto à se medesimo di perpetua infelicità.' Aleandro, 'Del modo', pp. 3–4.

87 'Comprende l'huom saggio l'occolta forza dell'ambizione, la quale internandosi nell'annella de'desideri, quasi penetrativa calamità, fà, che l'uno tiri l'altro, e ne forma una longa catena. Stà egli libero da cotal catena, perche non si lascia domare da gl'insani appetiti, dandogli vigore il conoscimento è di se stesso, e delle cose, ch'abbagliar sogliono le deboli vedute.' Ibid., p. 4.

88 'Ma dall'altro canto, se un'huomo veramente scienziato, e pieno di meriti, e che sà ponderar se stesso con la bilancia dell'Orafo, si trova senza que'difetti, I quali dall'acquisto degli honori potrebbero distornarlo . . .' Ibid., p. 8.

89 'Grande è colui, diceva Seneca, il quale sà adoperar I vasi di terra, come se fosson d'argento; ma quegli non è minore che fà quel conto de vasi d'argento, come se di terra fossero. Stà l'huom prode nella Corte ugualmente preparato alla condizione privata, ed'à quella de gli alti honori, se pur delibera Iddio di dargliene.' Ibid., p. 10.

90 'E in questa guisa, mentre frà le instabilità di quà giù sarà le nostra dimora, verremo à godere una soave tranquillità frà le perturbazioni, un bel sereno frà le nuovole, un sicuro posta frà le tempeste . . . E s'altri honori non ci verra fatto di conseguire, ci contenteremo di questo; d'haver in noi stessi l'imagine del nostro facitore, che per testimonianza de S. Ambrogio, è l'maggior' honore, che all'huomo possa venire, e ci accorgeremo, che'l sommo delle Signorie, e de gl'Imperi è'l saper reggere, e governare se medesimo.' Ibid., p. 12.

91 For Peiresc and Mascardi, see Cecilia Rizza, *Peiresc e l'Italia* (Turin, 1965), p. 167.

92 'L'hora della nostra vita quanto sia interna, è sfuggevole, e corta: se una parte ce ne toglie la patria, una i parenti, una gli amici, che cosa ne rimane in man nostra da dispensare agli studi?' Agostino Mascardi, 'Che gli eserciti di lettere sono in Corte non pur dicevoli, ma necessarii', *Prose volgari* (Venice, 1630), p. 7.

93 'E' Signori una Accademia come una ben guernita armeria; in essa trova ciascuno armi al suo stato dicevoli, e per difendersi da' colpi dell'avversa fortuna, e per combatter contro la ribellion de gli affetti.' Ibid., p. 10.

94 'L'Academia parimente è un certo mezzo, per la quale trapassando i Giovani più nobili, usciti da più basse scuole in tempo, che più servono I capricii, e gli anni si fan degni di salire alla suprema sfera del politico governo. E ciò in qual modo? Certo non in altro, che in purgar nell'Academia le passioni loro da ogni vitio in guisa, che già fatti giusti verso se medesimi in haver sommesso alla ragion Regina il talento servo, come che rubello, possan' ne maneggi publici esser giusti verso gli altri, come conviensi.' *Tacito abburatto discorsi politici et morali* (Naples, 1671 [1643]), pp. 11–12; these discourses were delivered before the Academia degl'Addormentati.

95 Brignole Sale, ibid., pp. 9–10.

96 The simple answer was reputation since even the tyrant's immortality was in the hands of those who wrote his story. 'Le parole d'un Oratore sono tuoni all'animo del tiranno; le acutezze de' poeti sono lancie, che lo trafiggono: la gravità degli storici è peso, che l'opprime, e stò per dire, che l'inciostro, con cui si scrive, è sangue, che dalle vene di lui con violenza distilla.' Mascardi, 'Sopra un testo del Quinto libro della Politica d'Aristotele', *Prose volgari*, pp. 93–4.

97 'Hora questo triumvirato è tanto da tiranni temuto, che chiudono le accademie, accioche dal grembo loro gravido di sapienza, non escano in luce que due nobilissimi parti

gemelli, Generosità & Amicitia . . . L'amicitia si
concepisce, nasce, e s'avanze nelle accademie,
che tanto è à dire, la vita civile riceve la sua perfettione dalle accademie.' Ibid., p. 94.

98 Ibid., p. 96.

99 'É Signori l'Accademia un divitioso
mercato di virtù, dove l'uno permuta con l'altro
le merci dell'intelletto; e si come chi da tutti
riceve, da tutti diventa più ricco, non altrimente,
chi da ciascuna impara, ciascuna avanza nelle
scienze, dice Plutarco.' Ibid., p. 97.

100 For Querenghi see Emilia Veronese
Ceseracciu, 'La biblioteca di Flavio Querenghi,
professore di filosofia morale (1624–47) nello
studio di Padova', Quaderni per la Storia dell'U-
niversità di Padova, 9–10 (1976–77), pp. 185–
213; Lucciano Stecca, 'Montaigne e Flavio
Querenghi', Montaigne e l'Italia (Geneva, 1991),
pp. 83–101. I thank Warren Boutcher for bringing these to my attention.

101 The dedication to the Duke of Parma
is followed by a preface to the reader and then
a series of letters, nearly all from the Duke of
Urbino, praising an essay that had first been
circulated in manuscript, then printed anony-
mously, and was now placed at the head of the
collection, the 'Alchimia delle passioni dell'animo'. The essays followed, and were themselves
followed by other letters defining the intellectual achievement that they represented. The
book concludes with letters from Querenghi
commenting on his own purposes in the
Discorsi.

102 Querenghi, 'Alchimia', Discorsi morali
politici e naturali (Padua, 1644), pp. 1–2.

103 'Tuttavia hor, ch'io sono molto avanti
ne gli anni, gli amici mi fanno mutar parere,
perche vedendomi essi malvolontiere partire
senza, che resti qualche memoria di me,
laudano, che si stampi (oltre il mio libro latino,
venuto d'Olanda ultimamente) anco questa
particella di varii Discorsi volgari, che mi trovo;
perche io non facia come i pesci, che non las-
ciano impresso nell'acqua alcun vestigio dopo di
loro. E se i letterati non havranno bisogno de'
miei Discorsi, havranno desiderio almeno i miei
cari amici d'un mio ritratto del naturale in
questa mia vicina patenza. A questi che mi
amano, io scrivo . . . Noi contentiamci d'haver
molti compagni.' Ibid., sig. a2ʳ.

104 Michel de Montaigne, 'To the Reader',
The Complete Essays, ed. and tr. M. A. Screech
(Harmondsworth, 1993 [1991]), p. lix. 'Au
Lecteur', Essais, in Oeuvres complètes, ed. A.
Thibaudet and M. Rat (Paris, 1962), p. 9: 'à la
commodité particulière de mes parens et amis:
à ce que m'ayant perdu (ce qu'ils ont à faire

bien tost) ils y puissent retrouver aucuns traits
de mes conditions et humeurs, et que par ce
moyen ils nourissent plus entière et plus vifve
la connoissance qu'ils ont eu de moy'.

105 'Montagna: era tinto di lettere, ma non
profonde; haveva quella sua maniera di scrivere,
ma naturale: era finalmente più soldato che let-
terato. Ma V.S. che porta eruditione et lettere
dal centro di tutte le scienze, che aiuta e lima
la natura coll'arte, supera di gran lungo' (Letter
from 'H.D.' [Enrico Davila] to Querenghi, Discorsi, p. 347). Davila added that he had had occasion, recently, to put Querenghi's philosophy
into action and had found it much more useful
than that of the sceptics and the Stoics, each
with their differently unnatural points of departure (ibid.).

106 Guillaume Sohier to Querenghi, ibid.,
p. 348.

107 'ne possono accommodare il pensiero à
far degli huomini mercantia, come si fà delle
pecore, che non ad altro fine si tengono in Casa,
che per cavarne la lana' (Querenghi, 'La vera
maniera di far beneficio', ibid., p. 27).

108 Thus, in a letter to a Monsignor
Barisoni printed in the frontmatter of the Discorsi, Querenghi writes that he is sending his
writings for approval and to satisfy the obligations of the 'amore hereditario passato da' nostri
Zii in noi'. Moreover, of such 'vera Amicitia'
there was said to be nothing 'in questo Secolo,
che s'accosti alle Antiche, certo è questa, che mi
viene lasciata dal Zio' (b4ʳ). In response, Barisoni
affirmed that 'l'amicizia e la fede anche fra di
noi dovessero durare eterne' (C1ʳ). He wrote
that the Discorsi, and their author, were full of
prudence and learning and, what was 'so rare in
our century', 'una sincera, e ferma amicizia'
(c2ᵛ).

109 'Vi lascio queste poche memorie; e
per sodisfare alle vostre dimande, e perche se ci
divide la sorte, non siate però affatto privo
della conversatione, e consiglio del vostre
fedelissimo amico. Potrete, sebene è disuguale il
cambio, conversare in mia vece con questi
miei scritti, e consigliarvi talhora con essi, & in
questo modo sarà minore il danno, che vi è
per arrecare la mia lontanaza, e men grave il
dispiacere, che sete anche voi per sentire, mentre
io vi starò lontano.' Querenghi, Discorsi, p.
362.

110 Ibid.

111 'Ma anche l'huomo è naturalmente
mutabile; onde che bisogno hà egli d'aspettar le
mosse, se è mobile per se stesso, ne si vede
costante in altro, che nel mutar proposito.'
Querenghi, 'Alchimia', pp. 7–8.

112 Ibid., p. 3. 'Dovresti dalla tua anti-camera, non più, come prima, frequentata, imparare le svariate vicende della vita, e mutar il gusto del seguito, in quello della solitudine, perche esser felice non puoi, mentre mutando gli huomini di giorno in giorno parere, resti tù solo ne' tuoi desideri costante'. Montaigne wrote: 'Il faut avoir femmes, enfans, biens, et sur tout de la santé, qui peut; mais non pas s'y attacher en manière que nostre heur en despende. Il se faut reserver une arrière bou-tique toute nostre, toute franche, en laquelle nous establissons nostre vraye liberté et princi-pale retraicte et solitude' ('De la Solitude', *Essais*, I.39, p. 235).

113 'Eri deluso dalla falsa imagine delle cose, & hor, che l'esperienza t'hà fatto certo del-l'inganno, ti lamenti? Non facesti perdita alcuna, perche fin dal principio le cose eran quali son hora; ma tù non te n'accorgervi . . . L'imparare sempre porge diletto. Il disingannarsi una volta non è senza utilità' (Querenghi, 'Alchimia', *Dis-corsi*, pp. 3 and 6). On *desengaño* see Otis H. Green, 'Desengaño', *The Literary Mind of Medieval and Renaissance Spain* (Lexington, Kentucky, 1970), pp. 141–70. I thank Timothy J. Reiss for bringing this to my attention.

114 'Non seppe quel gran difensore della Religione nostra provar in miglior modo la falsità delli Dei de' Gentili, che co'l mostrar la loro origine, e le loro sepolture; nè io ti saprei meglio persaudere, che questi i tuoi Idoli non sono quelli, che tu credi, se non co'l metterti avanti la loro aspra, e misera vita.' Querenghi 'Alchimia', *Discorsi*, pp. 8–9.

115 Ibid., p. 7.

116 'La Natura è il Cocchiere: Vuol fare à suo modo: chi è montato, non pensi, e non speri di smontare; è di dovere fermarsi su'l piano di questa vita. Dica pure, *Io vengo*.' 'Disprezzo della Morte', *Discorsi*, p. 10.

117 'Et io che posso aspettare? egli sapien-tissimo s'accommodava volontariamente alla necessità della natura.' 'Utilità del precedente discorso', *Discorsi*, p. 15.

118 'Se s'hà ambitione d'esser Signore, perche non si comanda à gli affetti, che sono vassalli potenti, e ribelli?' 'Contra l'adulatione', *Discorsi*, p. 57.

119 'Così io non intendo d'estirpar dalla radice gli affeti, che questa sarebbe una Stoica crudeltà. La ragione, che la parte divine tien di nostra natura, e'n cima siede; di che sarebbe Regina, se le mancassero i sudditi? gli affetti sono i guierieri della ragione' ('Contra l'adula-tione', *Discorsi*, pp. 57–8). It is also true of Agostino Mascardi: 'Io per me credo, che non

sia fra la dottrina Stoica, & Accademica divario alcuno, se bene l'una, e l'altra s'intendono; perche lo Stoico, pur che la ragione non rimanga da gli affetti oppressata, e la loro vio-lenza non provi, altro non cerca; l'Accademico moderando le passioni le fa vassalle, e tributarie dalla ragione' ('Come si permettano ad huomini prodi le lagrime, e le doglienze senza danno della Virtu', Mascardi, *Prose volgari*, p. 45). It is worth observing that Mascardi, like du Vair, drew on Augustine, that is to say on a Christ-ian, theory of the passions – the pagans were, aside from the late Stoics, more apt to see the passions exterminated than controlled.

120 'Nuova Medicina, nella quale non curantur contraria contrariis, sed similia sim-ilibus. Over conversione morale cavata dalla nat-urale degli Elementi' (Querenghi, *Discorsi*, p. 66). Albert Hirshman, *The Passions and the Interests* (Princeton, 1978) remains the standard account of this argument.

121 'Intendo dunque per vita di Villa quella, che s'usa hoggi di frà noi mista d'attione, e con-templatione, non lontana in tutto, e per tutto dal commercio, e da i commodi civili.' 'Si cerca dunque, se la Vita della Villa sia migliore della vita Cittadinesca', Querenghi, *Discorsi*, p. 114.

122 Querenghi, 'Utilità del precedente dis-corso', ibid. p. 17. 'Hò cercato di formare un compendio di i compendi stessi, & con due soli precetti facili, & brevi mi sono affaticato, d'istruir l'huomo nel commercio & nella conversatione civile'. Pierre Charron in *De la Sagesse* made a twofold distinction, between the 'ordinary commerce with the world', like travel, business, and random encounters and 'special' conversation with a select, private, and familiar audience (*De la sagesse*, bk 2, ch. 9, p. 503).

123 Carlo Ossola observes that Francesco Alunno, *Della fabrica del mondo* (1574) gave the derivation of 'conversare' from the Latin 'con-versari, consuetudine uti' (*Dal 'cortegiano' all' 'uomo di mondo'*, p. 132. In seventeenth-century French usage, 'conversation' was synonymous with 'company' or group (Elise Goodman, *Rubens: the Garden of Love as 'Conversatie à la mode'*, Amsterdam and Philadelphia, 1992, p. 87, n. 29).

124 For an example of how the scholarly civil servant Gabriel Harvey read his Guazzo, see the copy in the British Library, shelf-mark c.60.a.1. He used the analytical index as a guide to commonplaces such as 'aforismi del mondo', 'aforismi civili'. The latter included 'Qual si più utile la solitudine o la conversatione', 'Qual conversatione più diletta', 'Quali habbiano maggior forza la lingua o gli occhi'. There is

heavy underlining in the sections discussing solitude.

125   In a letter to Ralegh of 1589, quoted in Stephen Greenblatt, *Renaissance Self-Fashioning from More to Shakespeare* (Chicago, 1980), p. 169; Spenser, *Faerie Queene*, bk 6, canto 1, stanza i.

126   [John Earle], *Micro-cosmographie: Or, a Piece of the World Discovered, in Essays and Characters* (London, 1669 [1629]), p. 36.

127   Goodman, *Rubens: the Garden of Love*, p. 8. For an overview of this conflict, see Marc Fumaroli, 'La Conversation', *Les Lieux de mémoire III Les France 2. Traditions*, ed. Pierre Nora (Paris, 1992), pp. 679–743; idem, 'La République des Lettres (III). Conversation et sociétés de conversation à Paris au XVIᵉ siècle', *Rhétorique et société en Europe XVIᵉ–XVIIᵉ siècles, Annuaire de la Collège de France* (1989–90), pp. 461–77; Barbara Krajewska, *Mythes et découvertes: le salon littéraire de Madame de Rambouillet dans les lettres des contemporains* (Paris and Seattle, 1990); Elizabeth C. Goldsmith, *'Exclusive Conversations': The Art of Interaction in Seventeenth-Century France* (Philadelphia, 1988); and George Huppert's classic, *Les Bourgeois Gentilshommes*. For a complex philosophical study of women in contemporary French thought see Ian Maclean, *Woman Triumphant. Feminism in French Literature 1610–1652* (Oxford, 1977), ch. 5: 'Feminist Thought and Society: *Honnêteté* and the *Salons*'.

128   Marc Fumaroli, *L'Age de l'éloquence: rhétorique et 'res literaria' de la Renaissance au seuil de l'époque classique* (Geneva, 1980), pp. 545–6, esp. notes 286–9. For further discussion see Jean Jehasse, *Guez de Balzac et le génie romain 1597–1654* (Paris, 1972), pp. 109–37. The only monograph on the subject remains Émile Roy, *De Joan. Lud. Guezio Balzacio contra Dom. Joan. Gulonium disputante* (Paris, 1898). Goulu's earlier translations of Epictetus had been prized by St François de Sales.

129   The statement by Père Camus referred to how Balzac's *Lettres* were intended to be read, quoted in Jehasse, *Guez de Balzac*, p. 117.

130   It included Seneca's *Letters*, Charron's *De la sagesse*, Montaigne's *Essais*, La Mothe le Vayer's *Dialogues*, Cicero's *De Officiis*, the letters of Pliny, Horace, Juvenal, and Marcus Aurelius (*Naudeana et Patiniana*, Amsterdam, 1703, pp. 65–6).

131   Reinhard Krüger, 'Der *honnête homme* als Akademiker. Nicolas Farets *Projet de l'Académie* (1634) und seinen Voraussetzungen', *Europäische Sozietätsbewegung und demokratische Tradition*, I, pp. 349 and 379–84; [Nicolas Faret], *Projet de l'Académie, pour servir de préface à ses status*, ed. Jean Rousselet (Saint-Étienne, 1983), p. 48. Peiresc thought it modelled on the Florentine Academia della Crusca and with the same, limited intention of polishing the French language (Peiresc to Dupuy, 9 April 1634, *Lettres de Peiresc*, III, pp. 75 and 264).

132   For the references to Belgentier, see, for example, *Lettres de Peiresc*, II, pp. 254 and 257.

133   '. . . la consolation que nous apportoient en cet exil les lettres de noz amys, et surtout les vostres, sans lesquelles nous ne sçaurions rien qui vaille des choses du monde, et encores moings des livres, nom plus que si nous estions dans les sables de Libye, de ce qu'au contraire bien que nous soyons comme au milieu d'un desert, bien esloigner de tout commerce et communication, voz lettres arrivants nous transportent en un moment jusques au milieu de vostre academie, voire du cabinet du Louvre, qui n'est pas une petite felicité pour ceux qui ayment mieux estre dans une grande tranquilité d'esprit plus tost loing que prez de la Court, et qui ont neantmoings assez de curiosité pour en apprendre volontiers des nouvelles si certaines comme sont celles qui viennent de vostre main'. Peiresc to Dupuy, 17 January 1630, ibid., p. 230.

134   Peiresc to Dupuy, 8 November 1626, ibid., I, p. 80: 'Car vous nous faictes approcher le theatre de la Cour, comme si les actes qui s'y jouent se faisoiént en veue de noz fenestres, et qui plus est vous nous y faictes voir par forme d'intermeses tout ce qui se passe de plus digne dans l'Angleterre, dans les Pais Bas, dans l'Allemagne et quasi dans toute l'Europe, sans que nous bougions de nostre cabinet . . .'

135   'Vous pouvant asseurer que c'estoient les regrets du pauvre feu Mᵍʳ le garde des sceaux Du Vair, tant qu'il demeura en cette charge, de ce qu'il se trouvoit engaigé à l'un des personages de la Tragedie, et qu'il avoit perdu toute la liberté et commodité de la vie qu'il savouroit si doucement en ce païs, d'où il n'estoit que simple spectateur du train de la Cour, comme d'une comedie beaucoup plus agreable à voir de loing, que quand on s'y voit embarrassé dedans.' Peiresc to Bouchard, 14 July 1632, ibid., IV, p. 74.

136   Peiresc to Bouchard, 28 June 1634, ibid., p. 112. Some of his advice could have been drawn from a manuscript text that he entitled 'Forfantarie Corteggiane' whose 84 commonplace rules he dutifully underscored (Carp. Bibl. Inguimb., MS 1802, fols 602–12).

137   Maurice Magendie, *La Politesse mondaine et les théories de l'honnêteté, en France au*

XVIIe siècle, de 1600 à 1660 (Geneva, 1970 [1925]), p. 55, 4 July 1633; p. 421, 21 April 1628 and 22 July 1636 – all to Pierre and Jacques Dupuy.

138 Ibid., p. 458, Peiresc to Guillemin, 6 September 1624; p. 35, Peiresc to Dupuy 29 September 1627; p. 417, Peiresc to Guillemin, 28 March 1633. Jacques Ferrier provides another long list of gifts of imported luxury goods as well as local specialities including food, drink, perfumes, and clothes that Peiresc sent to female acquaintances, relatives, and spouses of friends ('Peiresc et les dames', *L'Été Peiresc. Fioretti II. nouveaux mélanges*, ed. Jacques Ferrier (Avignon, 1988), pp. 176–7).

139 'Encores faut il quelques foys aux choses indifferantes s'accommoder un peu à la mode, et ne pas porter des longs chappeaux poinctus quand l'usage est receu d'en porter de bien bas et de ronds comme on faict à cette heure.' Peiresc to Dupuy, 29 September 1627, *Lettres de Peiresc*, I, p. 389.

140 See Peiresc's letters to Barclay, such as 13 February 1619, 4 May 1621, and 11 June 1621 (ibid., VII, pp. 384, 457, and 469).

141 See Peiresc to Dupuy, ibid., II, pp. 338 and 603; Peiresc to Dupuy, 2 June 1628 quoted in Raymond Lebègue, *Les Correspondants de Peiresc dans l'ancien Pays-Bas* (Brussels, 1943), p. 41 referring to Rubens. For Faret, see Peiresc to Dupuy, *Lettres de Peiresc*, I, p. 279, and to Mademoiselle de Barclay, 6 April 1622, ibid., VII, p. 504, where Faret is described as a 'bien honneste homme'.

142 Peiresc to Dupuy, 18 April 1633, *Lettres de Peiresc*, II, p. 498.

143 'Combien que je vous diray que ce n'est pas pour faire le renchery que je vous ay mandé combien je deviens indifferant aux nouvelles du monde, ma passion predominante ayant tousjours esté pour les nouvelles des livres, et des aultres curiositez tant de la nature que des antiquitez.' Peiresc to Dupuy, 9 May 1633, ibid., p. 517.

144 '. . . il n'y aura pas bien grande perte pour nous, et qui ne mérite d'estre preferée à la tyrannie qu'il nous eust voulu imposer de luy escrire, dont je trouve qu'il ne se ne rend gueres digne, voulant vendre trop cherement des coquilles dont il r'avalle luy mesmes le prix en les profanant et divulgant comme il faict, avec ses adresses à des gents de peu'. Peiresc to Dupuy, 15 January 1634, ibid., III, p. 15.

145 Dupuy to Peiresc, 12 April 1627, ibid., I, p. 842.

146 Peiresc to Dupuy, 16 May 1627, ibid., p. 229.

147 Peiresc to Dupuy, 31 March 1627, ibid., p. 179; 14 July 1628, I, p. 669. Nearly ten years later Peiresc was still complaining about Balzac's rhetoric, 'cez viandes creuses' (11 March 1636, ibid., III, p. 452.

148 Peiresc to Guillemin, 6 September 1624, ibid., v, p. 30. Descartes, interestingly, took the side of Balzac. See 'Clarissimo Viro Domino★★★. Censura quarumdam Epistolarum Domini Balzacij', *Oeuvres de Descartes. Correspondance*, ed. Charles Adam and Paul Tannery (Paris, 1987), I, pp. 5–13.

149 'Ie ne savois point le merite extraordinaire de ce M^r le Conseiller de ★★★ [Peiresc] & vous estes le premier qui me l'avez mis à si haut prix . . . un homme extremement curieux, grand amateur de Relations & de Nouvelles, grand chercheur de Medailles & de Manuscrits, grand faiseur de Cognoissances aux Pais estrangers, grand Admirateur de tous les Docteurs de l'Academie de Leyden, &c. Il me semble que tout cela ne fait pas un grand personnage . . . il y a de la difference entre les vertus heroiques, & les vertus des particuliers: entre la gloire & la bonne reputation; & par consequent entre M^r le President de Thou, & M^r le Conseiller de ★★★ [Peiresc]'. Balzac to Chapelain, 1 May 1637, quoted in *Gallia Orientalis*, ed. Paul Colomies (Paris, 1665), p. 180.

150 'Monsieur de la Rouchefoucault n'avoit jamais ouy parler de vostre Mr de Peiresc, & que force autres personnes qui ne sont ny barbares ny ignorantes ne le cognoissent non plus que luy', quoted ibid., p. 180.

151 'Il ne m'a point semblé estrange que M. De L[a] R[ochefoucauld] n'ait jamais ouy parler de Mr de Peyresc. L'estude de ce seigneur n'avoit rien de commun avec celle du défunt qui estoit un vray et solide sçavant et qui regardoit les lectures de M^r de La R[ochefoucauld] comme des amusemens plustost que comme des occupations utiles et dignes d'un homme sérieux . . . Ainsy pour n'avoir pas esté connu de luy, Mr de Peyresc ne laisse pas d'éstre un héros en son genre, et j'espère que sa vie descritte par Mr Gassendi vous en laissera persuadé'. Chapelain to Balzac, 28 August 1639, *Lettres de Chapelain*, ed. Tamizey de Larroque, 2 vols (Paris, 1880–83), I, p. 489.

152 Krüger, 'Der *honnête homme* als Akademiker', *Europäische Sozietätsbewegung*, p. 355; Renate Baader, 'Akademie und Salon – oder: Der Unsterbliche und die zehnte Muse. Das Widerspiel der Geschlechter und Stände zwischen Renaissance und Absolutismus', *Europäische Sozietätsbewegung*, pp. 437–66; Wilhelm Kühlmann, *Gelehrtenrepublik*

und Fürstenstaat pp. 316–18; and the six essays on the theme of 'Die gelehrte Frau im 17. Jahrhundert' in *Res Publica Litteraria. Die Institutionen der Gelehrsamkeit in der frühen Neuzeit*, ed. Sebastian Neumeister and Conrad Widemann, 2 vols (Wiesbaden, 1987), II, pp. 549–640.

153 Quoted in Jehasse, *Guez de Balzac*, p. 132.

154 Joseph Addison, the *Spectator*, 119, in Richard Steele and Joseph Addison, *Selections from the Tatler and the Spectator*, ed. Angus Ross (Harmondsworth, 1988), p. 210.

155 'The key lay in the *salons*, coffee-houses and taverns of modern cities. Here men and women met each other as friends and equals and were able to enjoy the sense of ease that good conversation could bring.' Nicholas Phillipson, 'The Scottish Enlightenment', *The Enlightenment in National Context*, ed. Roy Porter and Mikuláš Teich (Cambridge, 1981), pp. 26–7.

156 'May we not esteem as happiness that self-employment which arises from a consistency of life and manners, a harmony of affections, a freedom from the reproach of shame or guilt, and a consciousness of worth and merit with all mankind, our society, country, and friends – all which is founded in virtue only? A mind subordinate to reason, a temper humanised and fitted to all natural affections, an exercise of friendship uninterrupted, a thorough candour, benignity, and good nature, with constant security, tranquillity, equanimity (if I may use such philosophical terms), are not these ever and at all seasons good?' (Shaftesbury, *The Moralists*, in *Characteristicks of Men, Manners, Opinions, Times*, ed. John M. Robertson, 2 vols (Indianapolis, 1964), III, pp. 148–9; also p. 252). For this subject see Esther Tiffany, 'Shaftesbury as Stoic', *PMLA*, 38 (1923), pp. 642–84 and with a greater emphasis on the place of sociability in neo-Stoicism Lawrence E. Klein, *Shaftesbury and the Culture of Politeness: Moral Discourse and Cultural Politics in Early Eighteenth-century England* (Cambridge, 1994).

157 See Kühlmann, *Gelehrtenrepublik und Fürstenstaat*, pt. II, ch. 4, section 1.

158 Eric Auerbach, *Das französische Publikum des 17. Jahrhunderts* (Munich, 1933), pp. 32 and 43; Jürgen Habermas, *The Structural Transformation of the Public Sphere* (Cambridge, Mass., 1991 [1962]). Gerhard Hess examined the tension that the spread of aristocratic culture produced in the generation of Peiresc (*Pierre Gassend. Der französische Späthumanismus und das Problem von Wissen und Glauben*, Jena and

Leipzig, 1939, pp. 6, 9, 12 and 16). But note Hess' suspicious, and certainly gratuitous, recruitment of La Mothe le Vayer as a spokesman for the superiority of German to Hebrew (p. 28) and the egregious opening sentence of his edition of La Bruyère's *Les Charactères ou les moeurs de ce siècle* (Leipzig, 1940) that implicitly compares the age of Louis XIV to Hitler's *Reich* (p. vii).

159 Cesare Ripa, *Iconologia*, ed. Cesare Orlandi (Perugia, 1765), II, p. 67.

160 Addison, the *Spectator*, no. 119, in *Selections from the Tatler and the Spectator*, p. 277. '. . . ma nel riflettere alle giuste ragioni, per le quali fu stabilito, ed a' beni, che da esso sono derivati, e derivare dovrebbono, mi trovo costretto a non fermare su di ciò il mio parere'. Orlandi, 'Conversazione moderna', pp. 64 and 66.

161 '. . . il primo loro oggetto, che fu l'ammansare gli Uomini dati tutti alle stragi, l'ingentilire le zotiche persone, il togliere dagl'infami notturni raggiri i scapestrati giovani' (ibid., p. 65). Timon was the typical representative of the position associated with Hobbes and Jansenists like Nicole, that humans were unsociable creatures and that any social life that did exist was the product of that very unsociability. See, for example, the extensive presentation in Simone Luzzatto, *Socrate overo dell'humano sapere* (Venice, 1651), pp. 277–309.

3 THE ANCIENT CONSTITUTION AND THE ANTIQUARIAN

1 Edmund Spenser, *The Faerie Queene*, bk 2, canto IX, stanzas xlvii–lx.

2 Momigliano's essay appeared in the *Journal of the Warburg and Courtauld Institutes* in 1950 and was republished in his first *Contributo alla storia degli studi classici* (1955). It is to this volume, though not to this essay by name, that Pocock refers his readers (p. 7). The pages noted by Pocock were those in which Momigliano dealt with seventeenth- and eighteenth-century discussions of method and evidence.

3 In his long (100-page) postscript to the second edition of the *Ancient Constitution* (Cambridge, 1986) Pocock did not offer any reconsideration of this foundational claim or defend it against critics because no one seems to have paid it any attention. The works of Donald R. Kelley (*Foundations of Modern Historical Scholarship: Language, Law and History in the French Renaissance*, New York, 1970, esp. chs 8–9) and Julian Franklin (*Jean Bodin and the Sixteenth-Century Revolution in the Methodology of Law and*

Politics, New York, 1963) focused more on the relationship between legal antiquarianism and historical method rather than that between antiquarianism and early modern political thought more generally.

4 Kevin Sharpe, *Sir Robert Cotton 1586–1631: History and Politics in Early Modern England* (Oxford, 1979); Colin G. C. Tite, *The Manuscript Library of Sir Robert Cotton. The Panizzi Lectures 1993* (London, 1994).

5 For Cotton, see Harold Love, *Scribal Culture in Seventeenth-Century England* (Oxford, 1993), pp. 85–7; Colin G. C. Tite, *Impeachment and Parliamentary Judicature in Early Stuart England* (London, 1974), pp. 24–53; W. R. Gair, 'The Politics of Scholarship: a Dramatic Comment on the Autocracy of Charles I', *The Elizabethan Theatre III. Papers Given at the Third International Conference on Elizabethan Theatre held at the University of Waterloo, Ontario, in July 1970,* ed. David Galloway (Waterloo, 1973), pp. 100–18; on politics in the Dupuy circle see Jérôme Delatour, 'Les frères Dupuy (1582–1656)', thèse, Paris, École des Chartes (1996); *Philippe Fortin de la Hoguette. Lettres aux Frères Dupuy et à leur Entourage (1623–1662),* ed. Giuliano Ferretti, 2 vols (Florence, 1997).

6 See G. Oestreich, 'Die antike Literatur als Vorbild der praktischen Wissenschaften im 16. und 17. Jahrhundert', *Classical Influences on European Culture. AD 1500–1700,* ed. R. R. Bolgar (Cambridge, 1976), pp. 315–24; and the essays in *Geist und Gestalt des frühmodernen Staates* (Berlin, 1969), especially 'Der römische Stoizismus und die oranische Heeresreform', pp. 11–34; 'Zur Heeresverfassung der deutschen Territorien von 1500 bis 1800', pp. 290–310; 'Graf Johanns VII. Verteidingungsbuch für Nassau-Dillenburg 1595', pp. 311–55.

7 Gassendi, *Mirrour,* year 1633, p. 93. In a letter to Naudé of 1635 thanking him for sending studies of Roman military practice, he observed that Saumaise was now preparing a similar study for the Prince of Orange that would show 'que toutes les modernes qui en ont traicté ont faict de grandes equivoques et qu'ilz n'ont nullement entendu la vraye forme de camper des Romains, et de ranger leurs armées en bataille' (Peiresc to Naudé, 28 June 1635, *Lettres à Naude (1629–1637),* ed. Phillip Wolfe, Paris, Seattle and Tübingen, 1983, p. 50).

8 See Wilhelm Kühlmann, *Gelehrtenrepublik und Fürstenstaat. Entwicklung und Kritik des deutschen Späthumanismus in der Literatur des Barockzeitalters* (Tübingen, 1982), ch. 2; idem, 'Geschichte als Gegenwart: Formen der politis-

chen Reflexion in deutschen "Tacitismus" des 17. Jahrhunderts', *Res Publica Litteraria. Die Institutionen der Gelehrsamkeit in den frühen Neuzeit,* ed. Sebastian Neumeister and Conrad Wiedermann, 2 vols (Weisbaden, 1987), I, pp. 325–48.

9 BN MS Dupuy 603, 'Opuscules politiques recueillis des estats, royaumes, republiques et Empires du Monde. De leurs loix, coustumes et Formes de gouverner. Enrichis d'exemples memorabiles tirez des histoires anciennes et moderness', pp. 414–30. Peiresc's manuscript is BN F. fr. 9533.

10 Gassendi, *Mirrour,* year 1609, pp. 131–3; year 1624, pp. 17–18. See, for comparison, Cotton's policy paper, 'A Speech . . . at the Councell Table: being called thither to deliver his Opinion touching the Alteration of Coyne' in *Cottoni Posthuma. Divers Choice Pieces of That Renowned Antiquary Sir Robert Cotton* [ed. James Howell] (London, 1651).

11 It is to him, and to the general (Moncke) who facilitated King Charles II's restoration, that the English translation of the Jesuit Daniello Bartoli's celebration of the scholar (*L'uomo di lettere difeso e emendato,* 1646) was dedicated in 1660.

12 Peiresc to Dupuy, 2 March 1629, *Lettres de Peiresc,* II, p. 36: 'J'en ay recueilly quelques unes de cez pais de deça que je bailleray volontiers, mais je vouldrois bien, en aydant à la despance, si besoing est, les faire imprimer en cahier à part, comme on a faict celles d'Espagne, pour voir tout d'une veue le rapport des unes aux aultres et servir principalement à la cognoissance des origines de nostre pais.'

13 Richard Verstegan's *Restitution of Decayed Intelligence in Antiquities Concerning the Most Noble and Renowned 'English' Nation* (1605), the pioneering work on Anglo-Saxon, repeatedly invokes the 'English Nation' as its subject in the dedication of the work to James I. See Graham Parry, *The Trophies of Time. English Antiquarians of the Seventeenth Century* (Oxford, 1995); Kurt Johannesson, *The Renaissance of the Goths in Sixteenth-Century Sweden. Johannes and Olaus Magnus as Politicians and Historians* (Berkeley, Los Angeles and Oxford, 1991 [1982]); Oscar Almgren, 'Om tillkomsten av 1630 års antikvarie-institution', *Riksantikvarieämbetets 300-årsjubileum* (Stockholm, 1931), pp. 28–47 (German summary at p. 47); Jakob Benediktsson, 'Introduction', *Ole Worm's Correspondence with Icelanders* (Copenhagen, 1948); Nathan Edelman, *Attitudes in Seventeenth-Century France towards the Middle Ages* (New York, 1946), ch. 2,

'The Attraction of Medieval Studies'; Kelley, *Foundations of Modern Historical Scholarship*, ch. 10, 'The Rise of Medievalism: Etienne Pasquier Searches for a National Past'; Marc Fumaroli, 'Aux Origines de la connaissance historique du moyen âge: humanisme, réforme et gallicanisme au XVIe siècle', *XVIIe Siècle*, 115 (1977), pp. 5–29.

14 Alexis Tocqueville, *The Old Regime and the French Revolution* tr. Stuart Gilbert (Garden City, N.Y., 1955), part I, ch. 4.

15 Quoted in Sharpe, *Sir Robert Cotton 1586–1631*, p. 23.

16 References are scattered through the correspondence: see, for example, Peiresc to Dupuy, 22 January 1627, *Lettres de Peiresc*, I, p. 129; 24 February 1627, ibid., p. 140; 31 March 1628, ibid., p. 578; 2 June 1628, ibid., p. 624; 20 September 1632, II, p. 348 (where he jealously eyed the complete collection in the possession of the Bishop of Marseille); 3 January 1633, ibid., p. 403.

17 Files preserved in Carpentras, Bibliothèque Inguimbertine, explicitly devoted to news and history of foreign lands, include: MSS 1772, 1773 England, 1773 Scotland, 1813 Germany, Scandinavia and Poland, 1807 the Low Countries and the Empire, 1806 Spain and Aragon, 1821 Austria, 1822 Switzerland and the Valtelline and 1798, 1802 Italy. Other materials are organized thematically, with registers on royal ceremonies (1794) and marriages and funerals (1795) that draw on material from several European countries, though most heavily from England and France. See also Peiresc to Dupuy, 16 May 1627, *Lettres de Peiresc*, I, p. 220; Peiresc to Barclay [October 1620], ibid., VII, p. 433.

18 The two examples are from BN MS Dupuy 660 fols 98 and 183. On Tacitism see Arnaldo Momigliano, *The Classical Foundations of Modern Historiography* (Berkeley and Los Angeles, 1990), ch. 5, 'Tactius and the Tacitist Tradition', and for a survey of the literature Peter Burke, 'Tacitism, Scepticism, and Reason of State', *The Cambridge History of Political Thought 1450–1700*, ed. J. H. Burns (Cambridge, 1991), pp. 479–98. Gibbon saw Tacitus as the bridge between traditional political history and antiquarianism. He therefore called Tacitus 'the only writer I know that comes up to my ideal of such a philosophical historian' (*Essay on Literature*, London, 1764, p. 107). Several of Peiresc's antiquarian friends wrote discourses on Tacitus; for example, Girolamo Aleandro, 'De Taciti Interpretatione praefationes duae',Vat. MS Barb.-Lat. 2006, fols 13–44. Even Momigliano

seems to have arrived at antiquarianism via Lipsius and Tacitism (Riccardo di Donato, 'Materiali per una bibliografia intelletuale di Arnaldo Momigliano', *Athenaeum. Studi di Letteratura e Storia dell'Antichità*, 83, 1995, pp. 241–4).

19 Petrus Cunaeus joined the two, thanking his friend Borelius for making available to him his main source, Maimonides' *Mishneh Torah*, which 'ex Oriente eorum voluminum comportavit, quae nunquam aut raro vidit noster orbis'. Cunaeus, *De Republica Hebraeorum libri III* (Leiden, 1632, 2nd edn), sig.[*8^r].

20 For Cunaeus see Aaron L. Katchen, *Christian Hebraists and Dutch Rabbis. Seventeenth Century Apologetics and the Study of Maimonides' 'Mishneh Torah'* (Cambridge, Mass., 1984), pp. 37–54; and the introduction of Lea Campos Boralevi to her new edition of *De Republica Ebraeorum* (Florence, 1996). I thank Béla Kapossy for bringing this to my attention. Grotius' knowledge of rabbinic literature, by contrast, was scanty (see Edwin Rabbie, 'Hugo Grotius and Judaism', *Hugo Grotius Theologian. Essays in Honour of G. H. M. Posthumus Meyjes*, ed. Henk J. M. Nellen and Edwin Rabbie Leiden, 1994, p. 103).

21 '. . . le plaisir que j'ay eu de voir les belles observations de cest autheur ne me l'a pas lasché de la main que je ne l'aye achevé de lisre; je serois bien ayse d'apprendre de vous s'il est encores vivant, de quel age et en quel employ, car j'estime que cest homme mérite bien qu'on en face cas' (Peiresc to Dupuy, 3 January 1633, *Lettres de Peiresc*, II, p. 403). For the Elzevir series see Vittorio Conti, '*Consociatio Civitatum*. L'idea di repubblica nelle *Respublicae* Elzeviriane', *Repubblica e virtù. Pensiero politico e monarchia cattolica fra XVI e XVII secolo*, ed. Chiara Continisio and Cesare Mozzarelli (Rome, 1995), pp. 207–26.

22 For Peiresc and *De diis Syris* see his letters to Camden of 1 September 1617, *Lettres de Peiresc*, VII, p. 762 and to Selden, 29 January 1618, Carp. Bibl. Inguimb., MS 1809 f. 165^r; for his reaction to *De successionibus*, see Peiresc to Dupuy, 19 September 1633, *Lettres de Peiresc*, III, p. 602.

23 Most of Peiresc's Hebrew materials are found in the first third of BN MS Lat. 9340. See also the letters to Ehingerus on weights and measures, 3 January and 5 September 1633, printed in *Amoenitates literariae, quibus variae observationes, scripta item quaedam anecdota & rariora Opuscula Exhibentur*, ed. Johann George Schellhom (Frankfurt and Leipzig, 1730 [1727]), III, pp. 261–74 and the material in The Hague,

Museo Meermanno-Westreenianum MSS 10.C.30 and 10.C.31.

24 It was on this trip that Peiresc saw Aleandro for the first time in twenty-three years and made the acquaintance of Cassiano dal Pozzo and Giovanni Battista Doni. After the dinner Peiresc gave at his home in honour of the Cardinal and his entourage they visited his study and Peiresc presented the Cardinal with the famous 'Barberini Ivory' now in the Louvre. To the account given by Gassendi (*Mirrour*, year 1625, pp. 8–9) and Peiresc in his letters to Valavez of 20 April (*Lettres de Peiresc*, VI, pp. 145–9) and 24 November 1625 (ibid., pp. 297–302) should be added the narrative of the visit that seems to have been prepared by Peiresc himself (Carp. Bibl. Inguimb., MS 1797, fols 278–94). On the visit more generally see Cecilia Rizza, *Peiresc e l'Italia* (Turin, 1965), pp. 32–4.

25 Gassendi, *Mirrour*, year 1627, p. 20. For discussion of the institution and functioning of the 'ordinaire', see Peiresc's letters to Dupuy [February 1627], *Lettres de Peiresc*, I, p. 134; 5 June 1627, ibid., p. 260; 26 February 1628, ibid., pp. 540–1; 8 December 1627, ibid., p. 428; 9 December 1627, ibid., p. 439.

26 Gassendi, *Mirrour*, year 1627, p. 20.

27 BN MS N.a.f. 5169, fol. 8ʳ.

28 In a letter to the Bishop of Orléans, Peiresc thanked him for urging upon Louis XIII and Richelieu greater attention to the re-establishment of maritime commerce. 'Vous obligeriez grandement ceste province si vous pouviez disposer les puissances souveraines à ceste entreprinse, laquelle est l'un des plus assurez moyens de l'agrandissement des Estatz.' 11 August 1627, *Lettres de Peiresc*, VII, pp. 250–1.

29 'Sur l'entretenement des Galleres et l'Intelligence en Cour de Rome', Carp. Bibl. Inguimb., MS 1789, fols 34–41 and 'Sur l'alliance avec le Turc', Carp. Bibl. Inguimb., MS 1777 fols 7–8. For information about de Brèves, a fascinating character, see Gérard Duverdier, 'Du Livre religieux a l'orientalisme. Gibra'il as-Sayuni et François Savary de Breves', *Le Livre et le Liban* (n.p., n.d.), pp. 159–72; idem, 'Les Charactères de Savary de Brèves et la présence française au Levant au XVIIᵉ siècle', *L'Art du livre à l'Imprimerie nationale* (Paris, 1973), pp. 69–87 and this author's 'Making the Paris Polyglot Bible: Humanism and Orientalism in the Early Seventeenth Century', *Gelehrtenkultur im Zeitalter des Konfessionalismus*, ed. A. Grafton and H. Jaumann (Wolfenbüttler Forschungen, forthcoming).

30 Carp. Bibl. Inguimb., MS 1775 unpaginated; printed in Peiresc, *Abrégé de l'histoire de Provence et autres texts inédits*, ed. Jacques Ferrier and Michel Feuillas (Avignon, 1982), pp. 288–316.

31 Gassendi, *Mirrour*, bk 6, p. 182.

32 Ibid., pp. 182–3.

33 Carp. Bibl. Inguimb., MS 1864.

34 Peiresc sought out records of maritime law and commerce from Toulouse (Peiresc to Guillaume de Catel, 23 March 1614, *Lettres de Peiresc*, VII, p. 844), Barcelona (Carp. Bibl. Inguimb., MS 1775 fols 3–5; Peiresc to Dupuy, 2 August 1627, *Lettres de Peiresc*, I, p. 316), the Crown of Aragon (Peiresc to Gassendi, 5 August 1634, ibid., IV, p. 527), and Montpellier (Peiresc to Dupuy, 16 May 1627, ibid., I, p. 230). For Peiresc's interest in Genoa and the 'privileged position' of its history in Peiresc's library see Rizza, *Peiresc e l'Italia*, pp. 151–5. We know, for instance, that Peiresc put the Genoese political thinker Andrea Spinola on a list of important Italians he thought should be visited by the wise traveller (ibid., p. 26), but there are, in fact, few surviving traces of what seem like a large number of personal ties to the city. Prominent among the books he desired to have from Genoa on a list prepared in 1628 was a copy of the *Leges Novae Reipublicae Genuensis*, the new constitution of 1576 that was designed to settle the social problem, as well as genealogies of the prominent families, the *vecchi*. The catalogue of the manuscript *relazioni* in the library of the Genoese Alessandro Sauli in 1634, like Peiresc's own, shows a European, rather than purely local, outlook (Carp. Bibl. Inguimb., MS 1769 fols 278–89). For Peiresc's use of Barberini as a research assistant, see Peiresc to Valavez, 10 May 1626, *Lettres de Peiresc*, VI, p. 511.

35 Du Vair to de Thou, 29 April 1603, *Lettres inédites de Guillaume du Vair*, ed. Philippe Tamizey de Larroque (Paris, 1873), p. 23. Peiresc's prospectus is Carp. Bibl. Inguimb., MS 1864, fol. 211ʳ: 'Si m.d.V. [Monsieur du Vair] se mettoit à descrire les troubles de Provence, il pouroit faire. Comme s'il parloit au feu roy Henry IIII. en suite d'un commandement a luy faict de luy donner une relation veritable des principaux mouvements qui ont esté dans sa Province durant les troubles. Il pourroit bien ourdir une histoire de ce qui s'est passé, et excuser par ce moyen son travail, en oeuvre non du tout digne d'un homme de son merite que ne semble devoir entreprendre que des choses grandes, et excedants les limites d'une si petite Province, combienque les merveilleux evenements qu'il y a eu sont bien remarquables à la

posterité. aultantq[ue] sçauroit estre ceux d'une republiq Grecq anciennement. & à comparer à tout le reste de la France ensemble.'

36 Carp. Bibl. Inguimb., MS 1791, untitled, fols 297–300.

37 Peiresc to R. P. Dom Adam Chaffaut, 18 October 1613, Lettres de Peiresc, VII, p. 874: 'Mais ce qui est plus ancien que de l'an 1200, ne peult faillir d'estre grandement utile, pour la cognoissance de l'histoire de cez siècles là, qui estoient si barbares, et si engourdis en la simplicté, et surtout ce qui est puis l'an 900 jusques en l'an 1100'.

38 See Peiresc to Holstenius, 6 August 1629, ibid., V, p. 345; Peiresc to Dupuy, 28 April 1629, ibid., II, p. 84.

39 'Il est passé des siecles de grande simplicité, pendant lesquels on se laissoit persuader un peu trop facilement toutes choses possibles sans aultre preuve que des simples conjectures de ce qui pouvoit avoir esté, sans en rechercher des preuves concluantes, en mesme temps que l'on forgeoit des romans pour les histoires profanes qui estoient mieux receus et quasi plustost creus que les vrayes histoires, tesmoings ceux de Charlemaigne, de Turpin, de Rolland, Ollivier, Ogier at aultres que l'on a eu tant de peine à descreditter, encores qu'on eust de quoy les convaincre par tant de veritables histoires du temps bien authentiques.' Peiresc to Gassendi, 13 November 1633, ibid., IV, p. 383.

40 For background, see Salvatore S. Nigro, 'The Secretary', Baroque Personae, ed. Rosario Villari (Chicago, 1995), pp. 82–99.

41 Some evidence for this is found in Du Vair to Peiresc, 24 July 1610, BN MS F. fr. 9544, fol. 129; Du Vair to de Thou, 12 December 1612, BN MS Dupuy 802, fol. 38; Carp. Bibl. Inguimb., MS 1815 fols 412ff.; and the 'Cahier, contenant les tres humbles Remonstrances que la noblesse de Provence presente au Roy, tenant ses Estats generaux, convoquez par son commandement, en sa ville de Paris, l'annee Mil six cens Quatorse', BN MS N.a.f. 5174, fols 81–100.

42 For du Vair, see BN MS Dupuy 661, for the Queen Mother, Carp. Bibl. Inguimb., MS 1826, fols 135–50 and for the entry, fols 253–9. Many additional examples could be given.

43 See for example, Peiresc to Dupuy, 31 March 1628, Lettres de Peiresc, I, p. 579; Peiresc to du Vair, 17 August 1619, BN MS N.a.f. 5172, fol. 71.

44 Peiresc to Menestrier, 3 June 1627, Lettres de Peiresc, V, p. 527; 4 May 1628, ibid., pp.

539–40; 26 November 1628, ibid., pp. 554–5; 25 January 1629, ibid., pp. 556–7.

45 Peiresc to Dupuy, 1 May 1635, ibid., III, p. 304.

46 Peiresc to Barclay, 8 May 1621, ibid., VII, p. 463.

47 'Mais je vous conseillerois bien de les concevoir en termes si reservez et si ajustez qu'il y ayt moyen d'entendre une bonne partie de voz intentions, sans que le sense litteral y soit si preciz' (Peiresc to Gassendi, 5 January 1634, ibid., IV, p. 410). The reaction of his Roman friends to the condemnation of Galileo left him 'astonished' – they wrote nothing at all about it (Peiresc to Dupuy, 4 July 1633, ibid., II, p. 556).

48 '. . . que dans la tyrannie des ministres de Geneve, qui ne laissent guieres plus de liberté que l'Inquisition d'Espagne, quoy qu'en sens contraire'. Peiresc to Dupuy, 20 March 1635, ibid., III, p. 284.

49 For reliable guides to this landscape see the essays Gaetano Cozzi collected in Paolo Sarpi tra Venezia e l'Europa (Turin, 1979); Enrico de Mas, Sovranità politica e unità christiana nel seicento anglo-veneto (Ravenna, 1975); idem, L'attesa del secolo aureo (1603–1625). Saggio di storia delle idee del secolo XVII (Florence, 1982); Hugh Trevor-Roper, Renaissance Essays (London and Chicago, 1985); idem, Catholics, Anglicans and Puritans (London, 1987); idem, From Counter-Reformation to Glorious Revolution (Chicago, 1992); R. J. W. Evans, Rudolf II and his World (Oxford, 1984, [1973]); Marc Fumaroli, L'Âge de l'éloquence: rhétorique et 'res literaria' de la Renaissance au seuil de l'époque classique (Geneva, 1980), pt III; and Jean Jehasse, La Renaissance de la critique. L'essor de l'humanisme érudit de 1560 à 1614 (St Etienne, 1976).

50 Manlio D. Busnelli, 'Les Relations de Fra Paolo Sarpi et du Président J.-A. de Thou d'après leur correspondance inédite', Annales de l'Université de Grenoble, new ser. 3 (1926), pp. 173–200; Gaetano Cozzi, 'Paolo Sarpi tra il cattolico Philippe Canaye de Fresnes et il Calvinista Isaac Casaubon', Bollettino dell'Istituto di Storia della Società et dello Stato Veneziano, I (1959), pp. 27–154; Lettere di Sarpi ai Protestanti, ed. M. D. Busnelli, 2 vols (Bari, 1931); P. Sarpi, Lettere ai Gallicani, ed. B. Ulianich (Wiesbaden, 1961). For the best treatments of Sarpi 'in context' see Cozzi, Paolo Sarpi tra Venezia e l'Europa and David Wootton, Paolo Sarpi. Between Renaissance and Enlightenment (Cambridge, 1983).

51 Gassendi, Mirrour, year 1600, p. 24.

52 'Del resto se per cagioni di libri ò d'altro V.S. mi giudicasse mai degno di servirla in queste bande, come la preggo di fare, io l'assicuro, che da gli effetti le farò vedere, con che riverenza io conservo la memoria de' suoi favori, et conservò tutto'l tempo della mia vita talmente che mi scorderò piu tosto di me stesso.' Peiresc to Sarpi, 20 July 1602, BN MS N.a.f. 5172, fol. 97, quoted in Rizza, *Peiresc e l'Italia*, p. 168.

53 Chapelain to Balzac, 12 April 1637, *Lettres de Jean Chapelain*, ed. Philippe Tamizey de Larroque, 2 vols (Paris, 1880–83), I, p. 150.

54 '. . . une trez belle piece, et laquelle estoit capable d'un grand effect, et d'avoir un grand cours' (Peiresc to Camden, 15 July 1619, *Lettres de Peiresc*, VII, p. 801). To Aleandro, a much more sensitive audience, Peiresc observed warily that 'Vi si veggono certi particolari minutissimi, così delli voti et suffragij delli Prelati del Concilio, come delli molti brocardi che potevano esser andati in volta all'hora, che se fossero veri, (si come non è da credere) sminuirebbero grande-mente l'authorità, et il credito delle risolutioni sanctissime che vi furono prese' (Peiresc to Ale-andro, 3 July 1619, *Correspondance de Peiresc & Aleandro 1616–1620*, ed. Jean-François Lhote and Danielle Joyal, 2 vols, Clermont-Ferrand, 1995, II, pp. 95–6). In his reply of 29 July Aleandro made nothing of the volume, saying that many were writing the history of the Council and that he thought it suspicious that the author was unknown and that no place of publication was given (ibid., p. 107). When, however, Peiresc sent him Sarpi's *Historia particolare delle cose passage tra il Sommo Pontefice Paolo V et la Serenissima Repub-lica di Venetia* in 1624, Aleandro exploded, saying its author 'era nero ministro del Diavolo che si dice esser padre delle menzogna, se ben egli veramente non credeva ne nel Diavolo ne in Dio' (quoted in Rizza, *Peiresc e l'Italia*, p. 174).

55 See for example, Peiresc to Dupuy, 29 January 1625, *Lettres de Peiresc*, I, p. 55; 3 Feb-ruary 1629, ibid., II, p. 19; 6 February 1633, ibid., p. 434.

56 Peiresc to Dupuy, 4 February 1624, ibid., I, p. 28.

57 Carp. Bibl. Inguimb., MS 1769, fol. 732. Rizza, who published the text, agreed with Cozzi's opinion that it was probably a product of the post-Sarpian circle of Domenico Molino (Rizza, *Peiresc e l'Italia*, pp. 178–9 and discussed p. 181, Gaetano Cozzi, 'Una vicenda della veneziana barocca: Marco Trevisan e la sua eroica amicizia', *Bollettino dell'Istituto di Storia della Società e dello Stato*, II (1960), pp. 101–2, n. 55). Yet the presence of the same complete text

in BN MS Dupuy 111, fols 93–4 in a volume entitled 'Lettere de R. P. Maestro Paulo da Venetia dell' ordine de' Servi' and signed 'Pierre Dupuy 1630', containing autograph letters from Sarpi as well as copies, written between 1608 and 1617, would seem to call this disattribution into doubt.

58 On Sarpi's fideism and its political con-sequences see Gaetano Cozzi, 'Paolo Sarpi tra il cattolico Philippe Canaye de Fresnes e il calvin-ista Isaac Casaubon', *Paolo Sarpi tra Venezia e l'Eu-ropa*, pp. 126–33 and especially the extraordinary letters to Casaubon of 22 June and 17 August 1610 (translated in *Paolo Sarpi Opere*, ed. G. and L. Cozzi, Turin, 1969, pp. 287–90). Also Wootton, *Paolo Sarpi. Between Renaissance and Enlighten-ment*; Vittorio Frajese, *Sarpi Scettico. Stato e chiesa a venezia tra cinque e seicento* (Bologna, 1994).

59 A copy is BN MS Dupuy 352.

60 See Paul F. Grendler, 'Pierre Charron: Precursor to Hobbes', *Review of Politics*, 25 (1963), pp. 212–24, at p. 221; Vittorio Frajese, 'Sarpi interprete del *De la Sagesse* di Pierre Charron: I *Pensieri sulla Religione*', *Studi Veneziani*, n.s. 20 (1990), pp. 59–85; Richard Tuck, *Philosopy and Government 1572–1651* (Cambridge, 1993), pp. 187–9 and 346–8; idem, *Hobbes* (Oxford, 1989), pp. 76–91; Jean-Robert Armogathe, 'Bellarmin, Sarpi et Hobbes: l'inter-prétation politique des écritures', *L'interpre-tazione nei secoli XVI e XVII*, ed. G. Canziani and Y. C. Zarka (Naples, 1993); A. M. Battista, *Alle origini del pensiero politico libertino. Montaigne e Charron* (Milan, 1966), pp. 191–216 and 278–80.

61 Grotius, *Of the Authority of the Highest Powers about Sacred Things. Or, the Right of the State in the Church. Wherein are Contained Many Judicious Discourses, Pertinent to our Times, and of Speciall Use for the Order and Peace of all Christ-ian Churches* (London, 1651). For discussion, see Giole Solari, 'Il *Jus circa sacra* nell'età di Ugone Grotio', *Studi storici di filosofia del diritto* (Turin, 1949), pp. 25–71.

62 Gassendi, *Mirrour*, bk 6, p. 210.

63 Enrico de Mas has written that 'In uomini come Bacone, Grozio, Andrews, Wotton, Casaubon, Sarpi, nei quali l'umanesimo politico si fondava con un Cristianesimo ragionevole (ma non interamente razionalizzato), la fede religiosa era anche una dottrina della tolleranza, perché andava molto oltre i confini della propria Chiesa e della giurisdizione del sovrano, fino ad assumere dimensioni ecumeniche e universali; la sintesi di religione e politica dipendeva da un delicato equilibrio interiore, che era altresì il loro equilibrio personale di uomini di sapere e

d'azione, dove teoria e prassi giungevano all'unità, senza venature superstitioze e senza decadimenti intelletuali' (*L'attesa del secolo aureo (1603–1625)*, p. 105). For more on this see this author, 'Statecraft and Culture in Early Modern Europe', *The Historical Journal*, 38 (1995), pp. 161–73.

64 Gassendi, *Mirrour*, bk 6, p. 210. The clear implication is that 'necessity knows no law'. Robert Cotton's *Twenty Four Arguments* in favour of executing or imprisoning Jesuit missionaries captured in England also, typically, reflects this position: 'for albeit that here in England, it is well knowne to all true and loyall subjects, that for matter of Roman doctrine, no mans life is directly called into question but that their disobedience in reason of state is the motive of their persecution' (*Cottoni Posthuma*, pp. 128–9).

65 Gassendi, *Mirrour*, bk 6, p. 210. For Grotius, according to Posthumus Meyjes, 'Salutary is what serves the community. Not one moment does it occur to Grotius that the church has been entrusted with a unique secret or that she represents a system of values that transcends rational and moral categories' (G. H. M. Posthumus Meyjes, 'Hugo Grotius as an Irenicist', *The World of Hugo Grotius*, Amsterdam and Maarssen, 1984, p. 53). For the parallel role of the Torah in Sarpi's political thought see Sarpi, *Pensieri, naturali, metafisici e matematici*, ed. Luisa Cozzi and Liberio Sosio (Milan and Naples, 1996), nos 403, 405, 407, 413, 414, and 423. The intellectual origins of Grotius' theory of natural law are discussed in Fiorella de Michaelis, *Le origini storiche e culturali del pensiero di Ugo Grozio* (Florence, 1967) and Tuck, *Philosophy and Government 1572–1651*.

66 See Michael Roberts, *Gustavus Adolphus: A History of Sweden*, 2 vols (London, 1958), II, pp. 422–3. For relevant passages see *De iure belli ac pacis* (Paris, 1625), bk 3, ch. 6, para. 2, ch. 8, para. 1; bk 4, ch. 9, para. 14, and especially bk 2, ch. 1, para. 10 and bk 3, ch. 1, para. 2.

67 Peiresc to Barclay, 4 May 1621, *Lettres de Peiresc*, VII, pp. 457 and 461.

68 Peiresc to D'Andilly, 7 September 1622, ibid., pp. 42–3. In an earlier letter to the same, Peiresc had recommended Grotius as 'le plus recommandable de tout ce siecle pour ses bonnes lettres' (10 July 1622, ibid., p. 41).

69 His first letter to Peiresc began: 'Ex literis, Vir Reverende, quas am Amplissimo Viro D. Viquio accepisti, intelligo quantum et Regi, et ipsi, et aliis, qui eiusdem sunt ordinis, debeam' (Grotius to Peiresc, 9 June 1621, no. 651, *Briefwisseling van Hugo Grotius*, ed P. C. Molhuysen et al., 15 vols, The Hague, 1936, II, p. 9). The death of

du Vair elicited from Grotius a poem of condolence addressed to Peiresc ('Ad Virum Amplissimum Nicolaum Peiresium Senatorem Super Morte Viri Summi Wilelmi Veri', BN MS Dupuy 583, fol. 70; printed as a broadside (n.p., 1621) and partially translated in *Mirrour*, year 1621, p. 203).

70 'I am not idle but I proceed in my work, de Jure Gentium, which if it prove such as may gain the good will of the Readers, Posterity will be obliged to thank you, who have stirred me up unto this work, both by your assistance and exhortation.' Grotius to Peiresc, 11 January 1624, no. 869, *Briefwisseling*, II, p. 327, quoted in Gassendi, *Mirrour*, year 1624, p. 3.

71 'You, whom a good part of all France has chosen with the most important judgements, I seek that you render judgement about this book – but remember that it was written in exile. If I would, in addition to this, demand that you continue to like me, I would do wrong to your goodness and constancy' ('Tu, quem summis iudiciis suis tantae Gallia[e] portio praefecit, etiam de hoc libro iudices rogo: sedita ut in exsiliio scriptum memineris. Si ad hoc postulem at amare me pergas bonitati et constantia tua iniuriam feccero'). The letter is dated by Peiresc on the flyleaf 'Ides Mai 1625 una cum libro de Jure belli ac Pacis'. The volume is in the collection of the Académie des Sciences, Agriculture, Arts et Belles-Lettres d'Aix, Musée Archéologique et Bibliographique Paul Arbaud; I wish to thank the *conservateur*, M. Morel, for making it available to me. In a letter to Valavez of 10 July 1625, Peiresc mentions the difficulty he was having in acquiring the proper leather for the binding (*Lettres de Peiresc*, VI, p. 220).

72 Grotius, *De iure belli ac pacis*, bk 2, ch. 20, para. 49, p. 455: 'nihil enim est in disciplina Christiana quod humanitate societate noceat, imo nihil quod non profit'. Peiresc: 'ipsam hic per se considero, non quatenus ei aliquid insyncerum admiscetur'. Peiresc reported to the Dupuy, with obvious pleasure, that Cardinal Barberini had interceded with the Holy Office to prevent the book's being censored (27 April 1627, *Lettres de Peiresc*, I, p. 245).

73 Grotius to Peiresc, 18 April 1622, no. 745, *Briefwisseling*, II, pp. 204–5. A summary account of Grotius' view of the prehistory of Greek and Latin is found in BN MS Dupuy 661, fol. 256.

74 Grotius to Peiresc 13 January 1628, no. 1212, *Briefwisseling*, III, p. 222; Peiresc to Grotius 10 March 1628, no. 1239, ibid., p. 263. Peiresc observes that Grotius' annotations would be received with great interest by 'nos meilleurs

amys et entre autres cez m^{rs} de delà les montz, qui ont une si particulière inclination à aymer et estimer ce grand autheur au dessus de tous les autres de l'antiquité profane'.

75 Peiresc to Grotius, 20 November 1629, no. 1447, ibid., IV, pp. 126–9. Comments on the *Eclogues* of Constantine Porphyrogenetus (905–959) follow in Grotius' letters of 6 September 1630 (no. 1539, *Briefwisseling*, IV, p. 255–62), 16 September 1630 (no. 1540, ibid., p. 262), and 23 March 1635 (no. 2022, ibid., p. 381). Peiresc's letters to the brothers Dupuy in the 1630s reflect his intense respect for Grotius' Greek scholarship.

76 Peiresc to Grotius 11 December 1636, no.2874, *Briefwisseling*, IV, p. 561 and reply, Grotius to Peiresc, 8 April 1637, no. 3016, ibid., V, p. 201; Peiresc to Grotius 20 April 1637, no.3037, ibid., VI, pp. 233–4.

77 Carp. Bibl. Inguimb., MS 1775 fols 110–39; marginalia at the top of fol. 110^r. In fact, Grotius' comments were limited to correcting sums and the observation that 'Ce discours a esté faict avant l'annee 1607 becaucoup de choses ont depuis change pour le faict du trafic & de la navigation.'

78 'l'edito contra il Sr Grotio l'habbiamo veduto e certo è cosa tyrannica e indegna di persone che hanno fatto tanto rumore per la ricuperatione della libertà di coscienza'. Peiresc to Cardinal Bagni, 3 February 1623, Carp. Bibl. Inguimb., MS 1872, fol. 59^r, quoted in Rizza, *Peiresc e l'Italia*, p. 69.

79 Rare among contemporary scholars, Peiresc had a special appreciation for English learned life. The absence of domestic wars and general abundance of things, especially books, meant that he often found rare Italian books in England that could not be had even in Italy (see Ernesta Caldarini, 'Notizia sul carteggio tra N.C. de Peiresc ed Elia Diodati', *Studi Urbinati*, 39, 1965, p. 439). He felt that the exceptional efforts of Englishmen like Arundel to seek out and acquire 'rare treasures of antiquity' had shown up the rest of 'more civilized' Europe (Peiresc to Holstenius, 27 April 1629, *Lettres de Peiresc*, V, p. 318). Pierre Dupuy, by contrast, thought that the English were 'so uncurious and so haughty that there was nothing to be hoped from them' (Pierre Dupuy to Peiresc, 17 December 1626, ibid., I, p. 788).

80 'Je vous supplie donc de vouloir faire exactement conferer ceste parole dans les anciennes Chartres et Registres du tems, et me mander s'il vous plaist, si les sieges tant des Prelats à main droite, que des Barons à la gauche du Roy, aux assemblées de grand Parlement d'Angleterre,

ne sont pas encores appelez ESTALLES, ou en language moderne, ou en ancien; et si les sieges des gens de justice, qui sont au milieu de la salle en telles assemblées ont aussi pareill denomination d'ESTALLES ou diverse.' Peiresc to Camden, 14 January 1622, *Lettres de Peiresc*, VII, p. 816.

81 'Je vouldrois bien scavoir par mesme moyen si dans l'adminstration de la justice faicte dans la province d'Angleterre, vous n'avez pas eu aultrefois, comme nous avons en ce Royaulme, certaines espèces de Parlements ambulatoires . . . Ce qui n'est plus en usage en cet estat icy . . . Vous avez si religieusement maintenu en voz quartiers les anciennes formes, que je tiens quasi pour asseuré que vous n'avez pas entierement aboly celle-là, ou pour le moings la mesmoire n'en sera pas entierement esteinte dans les Chartres et Registres du temps passé, desquelles je vouldrois apprendre comment estoient nommées telles Assises, si on ne se servoit poinct du mot d'*Estalles* ou aultre qui en approchast.' Peiresc to Camden, 14 January 1622, *Lettres de Peiresc*, VII, pp. 816–17.

82 '. . . car cela nous en donneroit une grande ouverture pour penetrer à d'aultres choses, qui nous sont bien inconnues pour ce jour d'huy, à faute de scavoir les etymologies et origine des mots qui sont demeurez des langues Septentrionales parmy la nostre'. Peiresc to Camden, ibid. This was a point made by other antiquaries in other contexts: Pietro della Valle, for example, explained to Jean Morin that the pronunciation of Samaritan might be better ascertained by looking at the pronunciation of Samaritan loan-words by Arabic speakers than by native Samaritan speakers because they were less exposed to change (see this author's 'A Philologist, a Traveller and an Antiquary Rediscover the Samaritans in Seventeenth-Century Paris, Rome, and Aix: Jean Morin, Pietro della Valle and N.-C. Fabri de Peiresc', *Gelehrsamkeit als Praxis: Arbeitsweisen, Funktionen, Grenzbereiche*, ed. Helmut Zedelmaier and Martin Mulsow, Max Niemeyer Verlag, forthcoming).

83 'Nec tantum suadent, sed ex operibus suis, re antiqua splendidis, saepe mihi ramum aureum ad tartareas istas regiones peragrandas, porrexerunt *Bignonius, Meursius, Lindenbrogius*; multis etiam veterum paginarum exemplaribus (ignotum me eximia colens amicitia) *Peireschius*' (Spelman, *Glossarium Archaeologicum*, London, 1687 [1626], sig.d'). For Spelman's relationship to Peiresc and the location of their letters see Linda van Norden, 'Peiresc and the English Scholars', *Huntington Library Quarterly*, 12 (1948–49), pp. 369–89 and p. 376, n. 46. Peiresc and his brother also served as chaperons when Spelman

sent his son to visit French learned circles. See the letters of 24 December 1619, BL Add. MSS 25, 384, fol. 6.

84 Pocock devoted a chapter to Spelman 'because he reveals in great detail the way in which the antiquarians set to work' (*Ancient Constitution*, p. 92) and explained more precisely that 'the range of his erudition is not so important as the comparative use he made of it' (ibid., p. 95). The same judgement could be applied to Peiresc. For a parallel presentation of Selden see now Paul Christianson, *Discourse on History, Law and Governance in the Public Career of John Selden, 1610–1635* (Toronto, 1997).

85 Peiresc to Spelman, 21 December 1622, Oxford, Bodleian Library, MS Tanner 89, fol. 13. In this same letter Peiresc announced that he was sending Spelman a medieval manuscript he had found in Rheims, 'ou il s'y trouve de bonne formules, des appretiations de monoyes, assez remarquables, et enfin tout plen de particularité qui ne semblent poinct mal convenables, a votre dessein du Glossaire pour l'intelligence de quelque mots ou barbares, ou abusivement tirez a des significations un peu esloignees'.

86 'l'autheur [Spelman] m'a envoyé les 20 premiers cahiers plus de dix ans y a, où j'ay apprins des merveilles de cez langues septentrionales et origines des mots anciens qui en sont descendus'. Peiresc to Camden, 11 September 1618, *Lettres de Peiresc*, VII, p. 790; Peiresc to Dupuy, 8 November 1629, ibid., II, p. 156.

87 Carp. Bibl. Inguimb., MS 1864, fols 310–24. The handwriting alone seems to date from the 1620s or 1630s.

88 Ibid., fols 311^{r-v}. Spelman's entry 'MALLUS' makes reference to Ole Worm's work on runes, reflecting the contents of their substantial correspondence between the two.

89 Ibid., fols 314^{r-v}; fol. 315^r.

90 Ibid., fols 316^v–317^v.

91 'Combien que les termes de Placitums, conventus, ou Judicium Parium vel Barronum, Regia Curia Francorum, et Curia Domni Regis soient plus conformes aux regles de la Langue Latine que les aultres, ils n'ont pas neantmoins tousiours esté estimez assez propres, ne si convenables que ceux de MALLUS, SERMO BARONUM, COLLOQUIUM, et CONSILIUM BARONUM lesquels ont esté recherchez, affectez, et employez pour exprimer la vraye energye du mot vulgaire de PARLEMENT, qui fut enfin Latinizé comme celuy de MALLUS, par la seule terminaison. Lorsque l'ignorance de siecle augmentant, diminüä le scrupule qu'on avoit en iusques de forger le mot de PARLAMENTUM'. 'La Vraye Origine des parlements', Carp. Bibl. Inguimb., MS 1864, fol. 318^r.

92 Ibid., fols 319^{r-v}; 321^v; 324^r.

93 'Parlamentum', Spelman, *Glossarium archaeologicum*, pp. 450, 452; 'Of the Ancient Government of England', *Reliquae Spelmannianae*, in *The English Works of Sir Henry Spelman* ed. Edmund Gibson (London, 1727, 2nd edn), p. 49.

94 'Parlamentum', Spelman, *Glossarium archaeologicum*, p. 451.

95 Ibid., p. 452. Spelman explained that his English essay 'Of Parliaments' was written after he had seen 'more Parliaments miscarry, yea suffer shipwreck, within these past sixteen years, than in many hundred heretofore' ('Of Parliaments', *Reliquiae Spelmannianae*, p. 57). Van Norden dates it between the Short and Long Parliaments ('Peiresc and the English Scholars', p. 371, n. 17).

96 Spelman, 'Of Parliaments', *Reliquae Spelmannianae*, p. 58.

97 Such as the harangue of the Chancellor Olivier before the King in *parlement* 2 July 1549 that Dupuy quotes in full and at length. It gives the King (Henri II) a brief history lesson on the authority of the *parlement* that suggests a more important contemporary role for the institution (Pierre Dupuy, *Du Parlement de Paris*, in *Traité de la maiorité de nos rois, et des regences du royaume*, Paris, 1655, pp. 574–85).

98 'Ce Parlement conserve en soy la dignité Royale, & si quelqu'un à chercher la Maiesté Royale en quelque lieu, il ne la peut rencontrer qu'en cette Compagnie . . . tellement que qui veut diminuer l'autorité du Roy & la dignité de cette Compagnie, ne le peut faire sans se rendre criminel, sans rabattre de l'autorité du Roy & la dignité de son Estat' (Dupuy, *Du Parlement de Paris*, p. 559). Compare this with Cotton's essays in *Cottoni Posthuma*, 'That the Kings of England have been pleased usually to consult with their Peers in the great Councell, and Commons in Parliament, of Marriage, Peace and War' and 'That the Soveraignes Person is required in the great Councells, or assemblies of the State, As well at the Consultations as at the Conclusions'.

99 'Depuis ces derniers siecles, nos Rois ont tenu leur lict de Iustice, pour publier des Edits pour la pluspart burseaux; mais leurs predecesseurs en usoient autrement.' Dupuy, *Du Parlement de Paris*, pp. 569–70.

100 'J'estime qu'en servant le Roy nous debvons faire le moings de bruict que nous pouvons & plustost chercher des remedes a nos desordres, que d'en publier la honte.' 'A messieurs de Parlement', Carp. Bibl. Inguimb., MS 1864, fol. 209^r.

101 Peiresc remonstrated that *parlement's* rejection of an appointment would 'tourne a la diminution de la dignité du parlement qui a interest que le chef de la justice soit en sa compagnie. Que cela diminue a son authorité car elle perd le moyen d'avoir communication des affaires de l'estat qu' elle ne peult esperer si non.' 'Pour la Iussion de mes letres [in cipher] au parlement', ibid., fol. 209ᵛ.

102 A document that he preserved, the 'Remonstrance faicte à la Royne Mere pendant la Regence lors des premiers mouvements de Peroune pour la dissipation des factions qui se formoient lors dans l'Estat, avant que monsieur le Prince se fust mis en Campagne' focuses on the consequences of the inability to subordinate self-interest to the common good. It emphasizes the need to prevent factions and alliances among the great. 'Toute Confederation, Ligue ou societé', it begins, 'qui se faict dans une Monarchie au desceu du souverain, principallement entre les Grands, soit par escript soit de parolle doibt estre punie comme un Crime de Leze Maᵗᵉ (Carp. Bibl. Inguimb., 1789 fols 227–9). The document outlines a series of measures worthy of a Machiavelli or Richelieu designed to keep malcontents divided and prevent the consolidation of a coherent opposition, such as sending away the most troublesome aristocrats to difficult positions of authority, buying the loyalty of critics, and augmenting the military defences of Paris (fols 227ᵛ–228ʳ). 'Authority' had to be preserved at all costs, and leagues of the sort that proliferated in the sixteenth century threatened to dissolve it and the kingdom little by little. 'L'Autorité est celle qui maintient les Estats, l'aneantissement de l'auctorité Royalle cause le mespris des loix, et les loix mesprisees causent la licence et desobeissance. La desobeissance la conspiration les caballes et les Ligues, lesquelles ont leurs pretextes specieux, ou la Religion, ou le bien public, ou service du souverain, ou feindre de se deffier de quelques ennemis puissans, le tout affin de s'unir en n'orant se choquer' (fol. 227ʳ). Leagues 'ne tendent qu'a empieter l'auctorité et le gouvernement des affaires pour apres se porter a leurs interetz soit de Religion, soit de pretention sur l'estat, soit de vengeance, ou la dissipation du Royᵐᵉ par parcelles, affin qu'un ieune Roy trouve aultant de Roys avec le temps, et de Souverain qu'il est le rendre compagnon' (fol. 227ᵛ).

103 '. . . y a eue grand peyne à r'acquoyser les esprits emeus et grandement alterez'. Peiresc to Dupuy, 19 December 1628, *Lettres de Peiresc*, I, p. 763.

104 'Puis donques que ny la force, ny l'ayde & faveur des Grands, ny le consentement des peuples ne nous peult soubstenir, Il fault recouvrir a d'autres moynes pour soubstenir l'estat . . . pour la Iussion de mes letres au parlement, fol. 210ʳ.

105 'Establir le gouvernement en sorte qu'il plaise a tous, ou pour le moins qui doibve plaire c'est a dire que les affaires soient gouvernez par gents qui soient en estime de gents de bien', ibid. 'Secondement que les Princes & Grands, soient du conseil, afin qu'ils soient interessez a faire executer les resolutions qui se prendroit & que leur respect faire ployer ceux qui doivent obeir . . . Il fault aussy administrer purement les finances, & neantmoins faire voir le fonds a tous en sorte que ceux qui ont apprendre de dons d'eux mesmes se tranchent, ou les remettent sur deux annees . . . Regarder quel est le fonds; acquitter les parties les plus pressants & plus necessaires a l'estat, & que le reste attende.' Ibid.

106 'Vous voyez la haine qui est desja contre le gouvernement, vous voyez des gents qui cherchent des pretextes, & vous leur donnez des vrayes causes' ('A La Royne sur un comptant de trois millions huict cents mille libvres'. Carp. Bibl. Inguimb., MS 1864, fol. 210ᵛ.

107 'Et pour cet effect resolvez vous en portant voz ballottes a suffrages de mettre à part & vous despouillez non seulement de voz passions, Jalousies & emulations s'il y en avoit aulcunes (ce que ie ne veux pas croire). Mais aussy toutes sortes d'Interestz, affections, ou preoccupations, & tous autres respectz & considerations particulieres' ('1628. Dernᵉ Sept. L'action que ie fis a l'hostel de ville a Aix president à l'assemblee generale convoque pour l'election des consuls', BN MS N.a.f. 5171, fol. 689ʳ). This text was published by Tamizey de Larroque (*Peiresc Orateur. Discours inédit*, Carpentras, 1897) but its source was not cited.

108 The calumny threatened 'la reputation que nous y avons acquise de gentz de bien, en servant un chascun quand nous l'avons peu, et principalement le public, pour lequel seul nous avons travaillé quasi toute nostre vie, sans vouloir quasi considerer noz intherestz [*sic*] particuliers, ayant jusques icy dirigé mes estudes et mes travaux principalement à ce qui pouvoit regarder l'honneur et l'advantage du païs, et la grande antiquité et justes fondementz de ses privilèges et libertez si legitimement acquises, et continuées de temps en temps, non seulement pour le corps du païs, mais pour les principales villes et lieux de la Province en particulier et pour l'honneur des personnes plus celebres en toutes professions qu'elle a produictes durant

quelques siècles tant j'ay esté soigneux des interestz d'aultruy, au lieu que la pluspart des gens de ma condition ayment mieux se mettre en peine *de pane lucrando*, comme on dict, et de faire leurs affaires particulieres que de prendre aulcun soing des publiques, lorsqu'il n'y a rien à gaigner, et c'est en celles-là principalement que nous n'avons espargné noz labeurs, ne noz petitz moyens, quand on a trouvé bon que nous nous en meslaissions . . . et creu que nostre fidelité inviolable et nostre vray zelle au bien du public paroistroit assez tost ou tard, et que Dieu protegeroist nostre innocence et nostre sincerité . . . si aulcune l'on nous peut reprocher, que d'avoir tasché tant que nous avons peu de servir tout le monde et particulierement les gentz d'honneur et de qualité, tant du dedans que du dehors du Royaulme indifferemment, sans aultre dessein que de faire honneur à la nation et à nostre bon païs.' Peiresc to Simon Corberan, 28 October 1630, *Lettres de Peiresc*, VII, pp. 967–8.

109 Peiresc to Dupuy, 19 December 1628, ibid., I, pp. 763–4: '. . . pourveu qu'il [Louis XIII] luy plais les laisser dans leur loix fondamentales, privileges, libertez et forme d'estats et de comitez qu'il ne pouvoient souffrir de voir abolir de voye de faict, sans edict et sans aulcun juste pretexte, contre les formes et ordres non seulement du pais, mais de tout le royaulme . . . Je ne veux pas excuser la violance, mais encores est-ce un grand creve-coeur à des peuples qui ont si longuement demeuré dans la fidelité et dans l'obeissance, lorsque tous les aultres se desmancheoient, de voir ainsi renvoyer toutes ses libertez, et tout l'ordre soubs [*sic*] lequel ils avoient vescu durant tant de siecles, et l'adveu de tant de grands roys.' On this crisis that turned out to be but the opening act of the more excruciating one of 1630 see René Pillorget, *Les Mouvements insurrectionnels de Provence entre 1596 et 1715* (Paris, 1975), pp. 318ff.

110 '. . . d'un nouvel establissement d'Esleus qui brescheroit les privileges et libertez de la province' (Peiresc to Menestrier, 7 November 1630, *Lettres de Peiresc*, V, p. 586). See René Pillorget, 'Les "Cascaveù": L'insurrection aixoise de l'automne 1630', *Dix-septième Siècle*, 64 (1964), pp. 3–30.

111 Peiresc to Dupuy, 18 November 1630, *Lettres de Peiresc*, II, p. 263.

112 Peiresc to Dupuy, 18 February 1631, ibid., II, p. 267.

113 For Peiresc's research aimed at rebutting Habsburg pretensions to the French Crown based on a fabricated medieval genealogy,

see Gassendi, *Mirrour*, year 1618, pp. 157–8. On this general theme see Anthony Grafton and Lisa Jardine, '"Studied for Action": How Gabriel Harvey Read his Livy', *Past and Present*, 129 (1990), pp. 30–78; William H. Sherman, *John Dee: The Politics of Reading and Writing in the English Renaissance* (Amherst, 1995).

114 He was disliked from the start: Peiresc reports that the 'ministers of the state' and of nearby provinces had 'mauvoises impressions' of him and his behaviour (Peiresc to Valavez, 12 July 1624, *Lettres de Peiresc*, VI, p. 37).

115 'Toute la ville, dit-on, est remplie de factions dont l'Evesque fait bonne part' (Dupuy to Peiresc, 12 October 1627, ibid., I, p. 872).

116 The letters from Rohan are printed in A. de Pontbriant, *Histoire de la principauté d'Orange suivie de lettres inédites des princes d'Orange* (Avignon, 1891), pp. 410–13. The discussion of Richelieu's plan is at p. 191. Peiresc, too, had got wind of Rohan's negotiations with Valckembourg (Peiresc to Dupuy, 22 April 1628, *Lettres de Peiresc*, I, p. 569).

117 Carp. Bibl. Inguimb., MS 1863, fols 219ʳ–220ᵛ. This might be the letter of 29 October 1628 that Peiresc referred to in his letter to Dupuy: 'Je vous renvoye avec mille remerciements la lettre de Valckembourg' (of 7 April 1629, *Lettres de Peiresc*, II, p. 64).

118 'en ce mesme temps là, il y avoit des commisaires du Prince d'Orange dans la ville qui faisoient je ne sçay quelles procedures'; 'mais pour le moings il n'a point encores faict de profession publique de la religion Catholique'. Peiresc to Dupuy, 2 March 1629, *Lettres de Peiresc*, II, p. 33.

119 Peiresc preserved a detailed narrative that remains an important first-hand account of these events: '*Veritable recit de ce qui s'est faict passé en la ville & Chasteau d'Aurange pour y restablir la service de Monsieur le Prince contre le sieur de falkembourg cy devant Gouverneur de ladicte place, lequel s'estoit rebelle è soubstraict de son obeissance*', Carp. Bibl. Inguimb., MS 1863, fols 223–36. The story is also told by Pontbriant, *Histoire de la principauté d'Orange*, pp. 191–5, relying in part on the material gathered by Peiresc. In a later letter from Paris, Jacques Dupuy informed Peiresc of the arrival of the new governor and the departure of Valckembourg's widow (20 September 1630, *Lettres de Peiresc*, II, p. 707).

120 '. . . les droits de nostre couronne et de nostre comté de Provence sur quelques occasions qui se sont présentées et traictées depuis peu en nostre Conseil'. Carp. Bibl. Inguimb., MS 1863, fol. 370ʳ.

121 'Nous vous mandons que vous aydez à faire exacte perquisition et recherche de toutes les papiers, livres, registres et memoires dont vous pourrez avoir notice sur ce sujet.' Ibid., fol. 363ʳ.

122 Peiresc to Louis XIII, 22 June 1628, ibid., fol. 373ʳ; Peiresc to d'Herbaut, 22 June 1628, ibid., fol. 375ʳ⁻ᵛ. In the surviving register of out-going correspondence Peiresc records sending, on 22 July, 'par une laquay de Mʳ d'Or. au Roy, a Mʳ d'Herbault avec la minute de la commission, a Mʳ l'Ev. d'Orange' (BN MS N.a.f. 5169, fol. 34ᵗ). On the flyleaf of the Bishop of Orange's letters of 15 July and 2 August Peiresc wrote 'avec la commission du Roy pour les Archifs'; this may have come from d'Herbault with his of 15 July (ibid., 365ᵗ), minuted on the reverse by Peiresc 'avec la commission du Roy pour les Archifs'.

123 Peiresc to Dupuy, 2 March 1629, Lettres de Peiresc, II, p. 33.

124 Carp. Bibl. Inguimb., MS 1863: the draft is fols 187–205 and the clean copy fols 145–86. One of these might be the memoir that Pierre Dupuy promised to return to Peiresc (Jacques Dupuy to Peiresc, 20 March 1629, Lettres de Peiresc, II, p. 687).

125 Carp. Bibl. Inguimb., MS 1863, fols 183ᵛ–186ᵛ.

126 From the first misstep, the decision of René of Anjou, the King of Sicily, to pay a ransom for his freedom to Louis de Chalon, Count of Baux, in exchange for the grant of sovereignty over Orange, an alienation that René was in no position to make (ibid., 158ᵛ–159), ignorance of details resulted in unforeseen, but always more complicated, consequences. And then again, in 1475, when Guillaume needed money and agreed to sell the Principality of Orange to Louis XI for the sum of 40,000 écus, he relied on the prior, illegal, agreement. 'Il suppose contre la verité que le Roy René eust vendu ses droicts à perpetuité audict Louys de Chalon; et sur ceste faulse supposition, Il vend au Roy Daulphin le droict de fief hommage' (ibid., fol. 160ᵛ).

127 '. . . les officiers de sa Majesté [Charles VIII] negligerent d'en faire la poursuite'. Carp. Bibl. Inguimb., MS 1863, fol. 162ᵛ.

128 'à cause qu'on negliger pour lors de s'instruire plus particulierement des droicts que le Roy y avoit'. Ibid., fol. 178ᵗ.

129 Spelman, 'Of Parliament', Reliquae Spelmannianae, p. 57.

130 Among Peiresc's contemporaries Pierre Charron (De la sagesse), Guez de Balzac (Socrate Chrestien), Robert Burton (Preface of Democritus

Junior to the Reader) and John Donne (Second Anniversary) all attacked the antiquary.

131 Gassendi, Mirrour, bk 6, p. 204. Of Spelman, the editor wrote, 'too much cannot be said in his Commendation: As who confuted that Aspersion which is generally cast on Antiquaries, that they are either supercilious or superstitious, either proud or popishly affected, such was his humble Carriage to all Persons and Sincerity in the Protestant Religion.' Villare Anglicum: or, a View of the Towns of England (1655), ed. 'R.H.', The English Works of Sir Henry Spelman . . . together with his Posthumous Works, ed. Edmund Gibson (London, 1727, 2nd edn), p. 193.

132 Vie de Peiresc, tr. Requier (Paris, 1770), pp. vii–viii.

133 Peiresc, for example, always complained of being short on time, as letters signed 'in haste' or 'late at night' bear witness. A young man who lived for eight months in Peiresc's household wrote that Peiresc never wasted even a quarter of an hour and that over the course of that period he only saw him take recreation once – going for a walk with Gassendi in the outskirts of Aix ('Le Témoignage d'un cour simple', L'Été Peiresc. Fioretti II. nouveaux mélanges, ed. Jacques Ferrier (Avignon, 1988), p. 95).

134 Gassendi, Mirrour, bk 6, pp. 200–1.

135 BN MS Dupuy 661, fol. 120ʳ. See the full account in C. A. Sapey, Études Biographiques pour servir à l'histoire de l'ancienne magistrature française (Paris, 1858), pp. 88–103.

136 'C'est pourquoy je n'estime pas que ceste inflexible rigidité, qui nous rend tout ce qui n'est pas bien insupportable, soit commode ni utile au bien de l'Estat, et quoyque je loue l'opinion de nostre bon amy si faut il confesser qu'il y a beaucoup de choses au gouvernment qu'il faut dissimuler pour éviter le pis, et mutata vela non semper eundem tenere cursum sed semper eundem petere portum.' Du Vair to de Thou, 26 February 1616, Lettres inédites de Guillaume du Vair, p. 28.

137 'Des affaires de deça, c'est tousjours une mesme chose. L'on voit le mal, et au lieu d'y apporter le remède, on le nourrist, ce qui est pis est on l'accroist tellement que je ne voy point d'autre port pour moi, sinon chercher ceste stoique insensibilité, mais je ne sçay si je la pourray trouver comme j'ay subjet de la desirer.' Du Vair to de Thou, undated, ibid., p. 24.

138 'J'ay eu grand desplaisir d'apprendre en ce voyage que le pauvre Seldenus soit prisonnier d'estat, pour avoir trop librement parlé dans la dernière assemblée du Grand Parlement

d'Angleterre.' Peiresc to Dupuy, 21 July 1629, *Lettres de Peiresc*, II, p. 138.

139 Rubens to Dupuy, 8 August 1629, *Rubens Correspondance*, v, p. 148. The translation, which I have modified, is by Ruth Saunders Magurn, *The Letters of Peter Paul Rubens* (Evanston, 1991 [1955]), p. 332.

140 'Il cui trattato de Diis Syris, V.S. aveva veduto stampato di nuovo, recensitum iterum et auctius, ma io vorrei che si limitasse negli termini de la vita contemplativa sensa intricarsi nelle rumori politichi per gli quali sta preso con alcuni altri accusati di contumacia contra il Re nel ultimo Parlamento' (Rubens to Peiresc, 9 August 1629, *Rubens Correspondance*, v, p. 152); Peiresc to Dupuy, 2 September 1629, *Lettres de Peiresc*, II, p. 175: 'Il m'escript de la debtention du pauvre Seldenus que je plains grandement . . .' In a letter to Grotius, who, it will be remembered, seemed to him (before Galileo) a hero of free thought, Peiresc observed that 'le pauvre mons^r Seldenus' would not be making any more contributions to the study of antiquities 'parcequ'il est debtenu prisonnier à mon trez grand regret pour le zelle de la patrie et du bien public, aussy que vous l'estiez autres foys' (Peiresc to Grotius, 20 November 1629, no. 1447, *Briefwisseling*, III, p. 127).

141 Rubens to Peiresc, 18 December 1634, *Letters of Peter Paul Rubens*, tr. and ed. Magurn, p. 392.

142 Peiresc to Dupuy, 23 July 1633, *Lettres de Peiresc*, II, p. 568: 'Mais s'il veult estre du monde, je n'improuve poinct son dessein, puis que la commodité du prix de cet office à 24 mille livres luy ouvre la porte à un si bel employ pour son filz . . . Mais il peult dire adieu aux Muses, s'il se met à cela.'

143 Peiresc to Naudé, 3 January 1635, *Lettres à Naudé*, ed. Wolfe, 1983, p. 32: 'C'est pourquoy le plus seur et le plus doulx est de jouyr le plus doucement qu'on peult et avec moins de bruict de la tranquillité que nous pouvons trouver en nostre condition et en nostre vacation par la comparaison des inquietudes et mortifications d'autruy. . .'

144 Peiresc to dal Pozzo, 3 October 1636, *Lettres à Cassiano dal Pozzo*, ed. Jean-François Lhote and Danielle Joyal (Clermont-Ferrand, 1989), p. 252: 'La quiete domestica gli poteva prolongar la vita molto più che la vita delle core con li disaggi che l'accompagnano'.

145 Gassendi, *Mirrour*, bk 6, p. 211. This is a perfect illustration of Arendt's claim that in Epictetus the classical notion of happiness was fundamentally altered from 'living well' to not being miserable (Hannah Arendt, *The Life of the Mind. Two: Willing*, New York, 1978, p. 74).

146 'Specimen animi bene compositi et vera philosophia imbuti', Rubens to Peiresc, early August 1630, *Rubens Correspondance*, v, p. 312; quoted by Jean-Jacques Bouchard, 'Prayse of Peireskius', in *Mirrour*, p. 255.

4 THE THEOLOGY OF A SCHOLAR

1 'Propono Domine cum divino tuo auxilio, hodie et deinceps peccata omnia vitare; consueta vitia, ea maxime ad quae propensior sum, deponere: Actiones & studia mea ad tuam gloriam referre, denique in virtutibus me exercere, ne dies hic, & vita mea sine bono opere transeat, Tu tantum non desis mihi gratia tua.' Carp. Bibl. Inguimb., MS 1815, fol. 601^r.

2 Peiresc was named abbé by Louis XIII in October 1618 and confirmed by the Pope in January of 1619. For Peiresc's appointment and subsequent effort to reform the Abbey see Ant. de Lantenay, *Peiresc abbé de Guistres* (Bordeaux, 1888). There is, to my mind, no reason to associate him with any form of contemporary *libertinage*, as did Pintard. Beyond admiration for, and identification with, the positive theology of Hugo Grotius, we can find no disrespect for Christianity or its rituals. Nor was Peiresc particularly close to the most scandalously sceptical figures in the circle of the Dupuys, such as François La Mothe le Vayer. Peiresc's confidant, Gassendi, the Canon of Digne, was certainly a Christian. Moreover, Peiresc's efforts to secure the conversion of Protestants such as Giulio Pace, Grotius, or Samuel Petit (though they never interfered with intellectual collaboration) are clearly the work of a believer.

3 Jean Clement, 'Peiresc et la monastère de Guitres', *Les fioretti du quadricentenaire de Fabri de Peiresc*, ed. Jacques Ferrier (Avignon, 1980), p. 79. Peiresc apparently kept for himself nothing of the 1,200 écus that were the Abbey's living but ploughed it back into the capital budget (BN MS N.a.f. 4217, fol. 6 quoted in 'Du Côté de chez Peiresc', *L'Été Peiresc. Fioretti II. nouveaux mélanges*, ed. Jacques Ferrier, Avignon, 1980, p. 93).

4 Peiresc explained to Gassendi that he hadn't heard the latest news in Aix 'tant je faictz peu de chemin hors de celuy du Palais et de l'Eglise'. Peiresc to Gassendi, 16 November 1633, *Lettres de Peiresc*, IV, p. 381. Bouchard's comment is found in his *Voyage de Paris à Rome*, reprinted with other biographical material in 'Du Côté de chez Peiresc' in *L'Été Peiresc. Fioretti II*, p. 60. For a survey of the

state of the question see Michel Feuillas, 'Le Catholicisme de Peiresc', *Peiresc ou la passion de connaître*, ed. Anne Reinbold (Paris, 1990), pp. 61–77.

5 Ruth Murphy, *Saint François de Sales et la civilité chrétienne* (Paris, 1964), p. 17. For de Sales' influence on the sociability of women see Ian Maclean, *Woman Triumphant. Feminism in French Literature 1610–1652* (Oxford, 1977), pp. 121–3. For a broader, comparative perspective, see Richard Strier, 'Sanctifying the Aristocracy: "Devout Humanism" in François de Sales, John Donne, and George Herbert', *The Journal of Religion*, 69 (1989), pp. 36–58.

6 Noel Forno, 'Messe anniversaire de 24 June 1987', *L'Été Peiresc. Fioretti II*, p. 15. Peiresc referred to her 'ferme et constante' desire to become a religious (Peiresc to Valavez, 26 April 1625, *Lettres de Peiresc*, VI, p. 151) and her 'constance', 'gravité', and 'joye apparente' (Peiresc to Valavez, 1 June 1626, ibid., VII, p. 536).

7 'Je n'avois lors rien en main de si propre ne si digne que cette piece là' (Peiresc to Dupuy, 8 December 1627, *Lettres de Peiresc*, I, p. 429).

8 Peiresc sent the manuscript to 'the Cardinal' (Francesco Barberini) on 26 November 1627 (BN MS N.a.f. 5169, fol. 29ʳ) and the printed book in March 1628 (Peiresc to Dupuy, 17 March 1628, *Lettres de Peiresc*, I, p. 562) – he apparently enjoyed it (Peiresc to Dupuy, 2 June 1628, ibid., p. 625); and to Thomas d'Arcos (Peiresc to d'Arcos, 22 March 1633, ibid., VII, p. 108).

9 Hugo Grotius, *True Religion Explained* (London, 1632), bk 2, ch. 13, p. 113.

10 Ibid., bk 1 chs 1–6.

11 Ibid., bk 2 ch. 13, pp. 111–12.

12 Grotius to Vossius, 1 January 1639, quoted in Jan Paul Heering, 'Hugo Grotius' *De veritate religionis Christianae*', *Hugo Grotius, Theologian: Essays in Honour of G. H. M. Posthumus Meyjes*, ed. Henk J. M. Nellen and Edwin Rabbie (Leiden, 1994), p. 50, n. 36.

13 Grotius, *Meletius sive de iis quae inter Christianos conveniunt epistola*, ed., tr. and intro. Guillaume H. M. Posthumus Meyjes (Leiden, 1988), p. 63. For a discussion of the tract's structure and content the reader is referred to Posthumus Meyjes' comprehensive and illuminating introduction.

14 *Meletius*, para. 2, p. 104.

15 Ibid., para. 4, p. 104.

16 Ibid., para. 5, p. 105. In his introduction, Posthumus Meyjes declared that this idea of consensus was 'the cornerstone of Grotius' concept of religion, and it recurs over and over

again in the works he wrote subsequently' (p. 51).

17 Ibid., para. 89, pp. 132–3.

18 Ibid., para. 91, pp. 133–4.

19 Edward Gibbon, *An Essay on the Study of Literature* (London, 1764), p. 14.

20 Grotius, *Meletius*, para. 90, p. 133; para. 51, p. 119.

21 Ben Jonson's *Epistle to Master John Selden* printed in Selden's *Titles of Honour* (1614) focuses on precisely this function: 'What fables have you vext! What truth redeem'd! / Antiquities search'd! Opinions disesteem'd! Impostures branded! And Authorities urg'd! / What blots and errours have you watch'd and purg'd / Records, and Authors of! How rectified / Times, manners, customes! Innovations spide! / Sought out the Fountaines, Sources, Creekes, paths, wayes / And not'd the beginnings and decayes!' (quoted in Adriana McCrea, *Constant Minds: Political Virtue and the Lipsian Paradigm in England, 1584–1650*, Buffalo, 1997, p. 147).

22 Quoted in Marc Fumaroli, *L'Age de l'Éloquence: rhétorique et 'res literaria' de la Renaissance au seuil de l'époque classique* (Geneva 1980), p. 554, n. 316.

23 See, for example, Grotius to Casaubon, 7 January 1612, *Briefwisseling*, I, pp. 191–3; 6 February, p. 196; 7 February, pp. 196–8; 5 March, pp. 200–1. For this episode see Hugh Trevor-Roper, 'Hugo Grotius and England', *From Counter-Reformation to Glorious Revolution* (Chicago and London, 1992), pp. 47–82, and for Grotius' wider ecumenical pursuits Hans Bots and Pierre Leroy, 'Hugo Grotius et la réunion des chrétiens', *XVIIᵉ Siècle*, 141 (1983), pp. 451–64.

24 Hugo Grotius, *Sophompaneas, or Ioseph. A Tragedy*, tr. Francis Goldsmith (London, 1652 [1635]). For background, see Arthur Eyffinger, '*La plus belle des histoires.* Grotius' Drama on Joseph in Egypt in the Tradition of the Theme', *Grotiana*, n.s. 8 (1987), pp. 80–90; idem, '*Amoena Gravitate Morum Spectabilis* – Justus Lipsius and Hugo Grotius', *Bulletin de l'Institut Historique Belge de Rome*, 68 (1998), p. 321.

25 For this see Jacqueline Lagrée, 'Grotius, Stoicisme et Religion Naturelle', *Grotiana*, n.s. 10 (1989), pp. 80–96.

26 Peiresc to Dupuy, 6 August 1635, *Lettres de Peiresc*, III, p. 354. Peiresc noted that opera – 'des comedies chantées à l'antique' – had not yet arrived in France (see Peiresc to Dupuy, 24 July 1635, ibid., p. 348).

27 For Grotius and Erasmus see G. H. M. Posthumus Meyjes, 'Hugo Grotius as an Irenicist', *The World of Hugo Grotius (1583–1645)*

(Amsterdam and Maarssen, 1984), esp. pp. 44–53; Jacqueline Lagrée, *La Raison ardente. Religion naturelle et raison au XVII⁽ siecle* (Paris, 1992), pp. 9 and 47–50; Johannes Trapman, 'Grotius and Erasmus', *Hugo Grotius, Theologian*, ed. Nellen and Rabbie, pp. 77–98. For the centrality of learning in Grotius' view of reformed religion, see Trevor-Roper, 'Hugo Grotius and England', p. 76. For contemporaries on the Grotius–Erasmus connection, see for example, John Selden, *Table-Talk* (London, 1689), section 7; Brian Walton, *The Considerator Considered: or, a Brief View of Certain Considerations upon the Biblia Polyglotta, The Prolegomena, and Appendix thereof* (London, 1659), in *Memoirs of the Life and Writings of the Right Rev. Brian Walton,* ed. Henry John Todd, 2 vols (London, 1821), I, p. 22.

28 Trapman, 'Grotius and Erasmus', pp. 92–4.

29 Erasmus, *Colloquies*, tr. and ed. Craig R. Thompson, *Collected Works of Erasmus* (Toronto, 1997), XXXIX, p. 194.

30 'Deum immortalem nosse omnia. Falli hunc ab homine non posse. Honestatem ab utilitate separandam non esse. Bonum unicum scientiam, malum unicum esse ignorantiam'. Daniel Heinsius, *Socrates; sive, de moribus & vita Socrates oratio* (Leiden, 1612), sig. Cii⁽.

31 For an important statement of the meaning of eirenicism in this circle, see G. H. M. Posthumus Meyjes, 'Protestant Irenicism in the Sixteenth and Seventeenth Centuries', *The End of Strife*, ed. David Loades (Edinburgh, 1984), pp. 77–93.

32 Gassendi, *Mirrour*, bk 6, pp. 208–9.

33 Carp. Bibl. Inguimb., MS 1865, fols 143–7, for example at fol. 145ᵛ. A listing of public prayers used in the *Ecclesia Arlatensi* is found in BN MS N.a.f. 5174, fols 17–18.

34 Gassendi, *Mirrour*, bk 6 p. 209. As Thomas Browne explained, 'as points indifferent, I observe according to the rules of my private reason, or the humour and fashion of my Devotion' (*Religio Medici and Other Writings*, London, 1947 [1905], p. 6).

35 'S'il eust usé au moings une foys du terme de parabole et rendu la raison pourquoy il estimoit que sans deroger à la foy qu'elles meritent on peust user du terme de fabellae, il eust fermé la bouche à cez frattoni . . . Encores faut-il quelques foys aux choses indifferants s'accommoder un peu à la mode' (Peiresc to Dupuy, 29 September 1627, *Lettres de Peiresc*, I, p. 389). This is exactly the advice that Aleandro gave Pierre Dupuy. Referring here to the censure of Grotius' *De iure belli ac pacis*, he explained that, as with Marino's *Adonis*, it might

still be possible to get the book printed regardless of the censure: 'Ma mi parevano anco cose, che si potessero tollerare, dovendosi chiuder gli occhi de alcuni diffettucci, quando nel rimanente il libro è buono e utile' (Aleandro to Dupuy, 2 August 1627, BN MS Dupuy 705, fol. 101ʳ).

36 See Enrico de Mas, 'Le edizioni italiane delle opere di Bacone nella prima metà del Seicento', *Sovranità politica e unità cristiana nel seicento anglo-veneto* (Ravenna, 1975), pp. 151–214.

37 'Car il vault beaucoup mieux que la religion ruine l'entendement es hommes que leur pieté et charité, ne se servant de la raison seulement que comme d'un instrument propre a forger malice et cruauté.' 'De la Religion', Carp. Bibl. Inguimb., MS 1789, fol. 44ʳ, Peiresc's filing title 'SAGGI MORALI del Verulamio'.

38 'L'Atheisme laisse a l'homme le sens, la philosophie, la pieté naturelle, les loix, la reputation, et tout ce qui peut servir de guide a la vertu quoiqu'il n'y eust poinct de religion: mais la superstition desmonte toutes ces choses, et erige une tirannie absolute en l'entendement des hommes.' 'De la Superstition', ibid., fol. 44ᵛ.

39 Peiresc 'could not with patience endure the boldness of such as would take upon them to prove there is no God, that God is injust, impotent, improvident, miserable, and the like.' Gassendi, *Mirrour*, bk 6, p. 209 – note, these are the negations of Grotius' simple definition of God (see note 10 above).

40 Ibid., p. 210.

41 '. . . à cause que les Chrestiens n'y sont tenus en guiere de respect, et casez comme les Juifs sont casez parmy nous aux lieux, où l'on les souffre.' Peiresc to Mersenne, 1 May 1634, *Mersenne Correspondance*, IV, p. 108.

42 Peiresc described himself as 'si scandalizé que je ne sçaurois exprimer le juste sentiment de deplaisir que j'en ay.' Peiresc to Aycard, 26 December 1632, *Lettres de Peiresc*, VII, p. 287. Peiresc expended a great deal of energy on winning over Grotius and Giulio Pace to Roman Catholicism (see Raymond Lebègue, *Les Correspondants de Peiresc dans l'ancien Pays Bas,* Brussels, 1943, pp. 65–9, and Peiresc's letters to Paolo Gualdo in *Lettere d'uomini Illustri che fiorino nel principio del secolo decimosettimo, non piu stampate*, Venice, 1744, respectively). Moreover, Peiresc applauded the proselytizing efforts of Holstenius (Peiresc to Holstenius, 9 April 1637, *Lettres de Peiresc*, V, p. 456). Protestantism, even that of friends, is described as 'pretendue pseudotheologie' (Peiresc to Holstenius, 6

August 1629, Ibid., p. 340). There is, however absolutely no evidence that Peiresc ever tried to persuade his friend Rabbi Salomon Azubi to abandon his faith.

43 'Un autre m'escrit que cest homme est tenu pour Turc entre les Turcs, pour juif entre les juifs, et pour chrestien entre les chrestiens; ou pour ne sçavoir qu'est ce qu'il est ou qu'il doibt estre; en quoy je le plains grandement.' Ibid., VII, p. 289.

44 Gassendi, *Mirrour*, 1628, p. 25. The book was begun by Joannes Bayerus and finished by Jules Schiller. For receipt of Schiller's *Caelum Stellatum Christianum* (1627), see Peiresc to Dupuy, 11 November 1627, *Lettres de Peiresc*, I, pp. 409–10.

45 'Je veux faire Dieu aydant un traicté ex professo, qui fera possible parler du tresor de St Denys en autres termes que l'on ne souloit faire et qui pourra rendre tous cez beaux vases precieux utiles au public et propres à d'autres usaiges [*sic*] dont on ne s'estoit point encore advisé de nostre temps (sans rien desroger à la sainte application qui s'en estoit faicte depuis le christianisme, et depuis qu'ilz sont dans le tresor St Denis), car l'examen que j'en faictz faire n'est point pour les profaner, ains à trez bonnes et trez innocentes fins.' Peiresc to Guillemin, 16 January 1633, *Lettres de Peiresc*, V, p. 99.

46 'L'ignorance qui est la vraye mere de toutes cez difficultez surabondantes que vous ont faict cez bons moynes.' Ibid., p. 106.

47 'L'ignorance est tousjous inseparable de l'arrogance et de la presomption de soy mesme' (Peiresc to Bishop of Orleans, 27 April 1627, ibid., VII, p. 245). See also Peiresc's comment on the Roman censure of Grotius' *De veritate* (Peiresc to Dupuy, 29 September 1627, ibid., I, p. 389).

48 'En effect, quoique cez grandes bibles ne semblent se faire à autre dessein que pour avoir toutes les diverses conceptions et interpretations que peuvent fournir diverses versions, je ne vois pas pourquoy on veuille avoir les unes et negliger les autres, principalement celles cy, qui se trouvent accompagnées de tant de circonstances notables et de tant de diversitez considerables et utiles' (Peiresc to Dupuy, 23 May 1631, ibid., II, p. 278).

49 '. . . dans l'Arabique il y a certaines petites diversités de paroles capables de fournir de tres belles conceptions à ceux qui y voudroient mediter, & rechercher l'energie des unes & des autres.' Peiresc to Jean Morin, 8 November 1631[2], *Antiquitates Ecclesiae Orientales* (London, 1682), pp. 186–7.

50 Peiresc to Jean Morin, 2 June 1637, ibid., p. 259.

51 Peiresc to de Loches, 13 February 1634, *Correspondance de Peiresc avec Capucins*, p. 19; 20 March 1634, ibid., p. 29.

52 Peiresc to de Loches, 1 October 1635, ibid., p. 196: 'd'empescher [que] des choses si nobles ne demeurent ensevelies avec tant de humilités et mortifications religieuses avec tant de prejudice au genre humain'.

53 In a letter to Holstenius of 1636 Peiresc explicitly indicated that the Church was wrong to make Galileo's case a sticking point. 'Car il seroit à desirer que ces bonnes gents qui se meslent de la censure y peussent tost ou tard gouster la facilité et vraisemblance, comme il faudra tost ou tard qu'ils s'accoustument à tollerer, quelque repugnance qu'ils y trouvent; comme firet autrefois ceulx qui trouvoient si estranges les propositions de la verité des Antipodes lesquels n'avoient pas moings de raison de trouver incompatible que ceulx qui avoient leurs pieds directement opposés aux nostres se peussent tenir debout sans tomber dans le fond du Ciel qui passe par dessoubs [*sic*] nous. Et toutefois les voyages des Indes ont guary nos faulces apparences et imaginations de ce costé-la.' Peiresc to Holstenius 2 July 1636, *Lettres de Peiresc*, IV, p. 434.

54 In a letter to Dupuy of 13 February 1634 Peiresc had made clear that it was difficult to get people to change their views, 'principalement quand ils y peuvent mesler quelque participation d'interest de religion.' Ibid., III, p. 33.

55 Mersenne to Rivet, 20 December 1638, *Mersenne Correspondance*, VIII, p. 239.

56 Anthony Grafton, 'The Strange Deaths of Hermes and the Sibyls', *Defenders of the Text. The Traditions of Scholarship in an Age of Science, 1450–1800* (Cambridge, Mass., 1991), p. 171.

57 For accommodation in antiquity see Robert Lamberton, *Homer the Theologian: Neoplatonist Allegorical Reading and the Growth of the Epic Tradition* (Berkeley and Los Angeles, 1988); John Dillon, *The Middle Platonists* (London, 1977); Carlo Ginzburg, 'Distance and Perspective: Reflections on Two Metaphors', *Jahrbuch des Wissenschaftskolleg zu Berlin-Institute for Advanced Study 1997* (Berlin, 1998), pp. 218–32. The essay is reprinted, in translation, in *Occhiacci di legno: nove riflessioni sulla distanza* (Milan, 1998), pp. 171–93; for the connection between late antiquity and the late Renaissance, see Sabine MacCormack, 'Limits of Understanding: Perceptions of Greco-Roman and Amerindian Paganism in Early Modern Europe', *America in*

European Consciousness 1493–1750, ed. Karen Ordahl Kupperman (Chapel Hill, N.C., 1995), pp. 79–129, esp. pp. 93–6 and 'Ubi Ecclesia? Perceptions of Medieval Europe in Spanish America', *Speculum*, 69 (1994), pp. 74–100.

58 Jean Jehasse, *La Renaissance de la critique: l'essor de l'Humanisme érudit de 1560 à 1614* (Saint-Etienne, 1976), pp. 259, 265, and 485. Léontine Zanta, in fact (*La Renaissance du stoicisme au XVI⁰ siècle*, Paris, 1913, p. 121), suggested that the early modern neo-Stoics adopted the method of the Church Fathers. On the connection between Lipsius' neo-Stoicism and theological *adiaphora*, Karl Alfred Blüher, *Seneca in Spanien: Untersuchungen zur Geschichte der Seneca-Rezeption in Spanien vom 13. bis 17. Jahrhundert* (Munich, 1969), p. 305. I am quoting R. J. W. Evans, *The Making of the Habsburg Monarchy 1550–1700. An Interpretation* (Oxford, 1991 [1979]), p. 113.

59 ' "Stoici nostro dogmati in plerisque concordant. Concordant? ita: et quod sequitur, occulte ad nostrum dogma et pietatem ducunt" ' (*Manductio*, bk 1, diss. 17, p. 101 quoted in Anthony Levi (*French Moralists. The Theory of the Passions 1585 to 1649*, Oxford, 1964, p. 68). Thomas James also refers his readers to Jerome in his translation of du Vair's *Moral Philosophie of the Stoicks* (1598): 'no kinde of philosophie is more profitable and neerer approaching unto Christianitie (as *S. Hierome* saith) than the philosophie of the Stoicks' (sig.A6ʳ). Levi, however, has pointed out that the Stoic revival needs to be defined 'in relative terms. There is a more frequent and more general recourse to the moral maxims and principles of the Stoics, a more systematic attempt to adapt them to orthodox Christian sentiment. But the Stoicism was not pure, and the adaptations often rested on a confusion of Stoic and scholastic meanings attaching to the same formulae.' Levi, *French Moralists*, p. 54.

60 In a letter of 1584 to Laevinus Torrentius, quoted by Levi, *French Moralists*, p. 67.

61 Julien Eymard d'Angers, 'Le Renouveau du stoicisme du XVI⁰ et au XVII⁰ siècles', *Recherches sur le stoicisme aux XVI⁰ et XVII⁰ siècles* ed. L. Antoine (Hildesheim, N.Y., 1976), p. 21.

62 This is not commented upon by those approaching the issue from the missionary fringe; see for example Michael T. Ryan, 'Assimilating New Worlds in the Sixteenth and Seventeenth Centuries', *Comparative Studies in Society and History*, 23 (1981), pp. 519–38.

63 William J. Bouwsma, 'The Two Faces of Renaissance Humanism: Stoicism and Augus-

tinianism in Renaissance Thought', *Itinerarium Italicum: Essays for Paul Oskar Kristeller*, ed. H. Oberman (Leiden, 1975), pp. 1–60.

64 See Ruth Murphy, *St François de Sales et la Civilité Chrétienne* (Paris, 1964), pp. 36–54 (on humility) and pp. 58–62 and 72–4 (on reason); also Julien Eymard d'Angers, *Pascal et ses precurseurs* (Paris, 1954), p. 152, and ch. 7 more generally.

65 Pascal, 'Entretien avec M. De Saci', *Oeuvres complètes*, ed. Jacques Chevallier (Paris, 1954), p. 571: 'Il me semble que la source des serreurs de ces deux sectes est de n'avoir pas su que l'état de l'homme à présent diffère de celui de sa création; de sorte que l'un remarquant quelques traces de sa première grandeur, et ignorant sa corruption, a traité la nature comme saine et sans besoin de réparateur, ce qui le mène au comble de la superbe; au lieu que l'autre, éprouvant la misère présente et ignorant la première dignité, traite la nature comme nécessairement infirme et irréparable, ce qui le précipite dans le désespoir d'arriver à un véritable bien, et de là dans une extrême lâcheté'. Still, Levi notes that in *De l'Usage des passions* (1641), by Pascal's contemporary, Jean-François Senault, 151 out of 370 Latin quotations were drawn from Seneca. He suggests that the Augustinian and Stoic elements combined so that 'the presuppositions are Augustinian but the tone is neostoic' (*French Moralists*, p. 214).

66 'Die Glaubenslehre konnte sich den Gehalt der stoischen Ethik nicht assimilieren, ohne damit die Grundlagen des dogmatisch-mittelalterlichen Systems zu erschüttern. Dieses System ruhte auf der Augustinischen Gnadenlehre, die zu dem stoischen Ideal der Souveränität und der unbedingten "Autarkie" des Willens in schroffstem Gegensatz steht' (Ernst Cassirer, *Descartes. Lehre–Persönlichkeit–Wirkung*, Stockholm, 1939, p. 228). Dilthey had drawn attention to the importance of anthropology in seventeenth-century thought in his 1904 essay, but believed that there was only one kind: 'Die Funktion *der Anthropologie in der Kultur des 16. und 17. Jahrhunderts'* (*Sitzungsberichte der Königlich Preussischen Akademie de Wissenschaften*, 1904, pp. 2–33).

67 Antoine Adam, in fact, chose Grotius' *De veritate* as an example of the theology to which the Augustinians were most completely opposed. *Sur le Problème religieux dans la première moitié du XVII⁰ siècle. The Zaharoff Lecture for 1959* (Oxford, 1959). p. 9. Grotius himself, in the *Ordinum Pietas* (1613) had cautioned against giving sole responsibility for salvation to either God or nature.

68   For discussions of du Vair's importance see Levi, *French Moralists*, pp. 74–94; Gunter Abel, *Stoizismus und frühe Neuzeit. Zur Entstehungsgeschichte modernen Denkens im Felde vom Ethik und Politik* (Berlin, 1978), ch. 5 'Neostoizismus als Denk- und Handlungsform (Guillaume du Vair)'. Elsewhere, as in Nannerl Keohane, *Philosophy and the State in France. The Renaissance to the Enlightenment* (Princeton, 1980), pp. 130–3, his work is generally treated as a slight variation on Lipsius' theme.

69   See Marc Fumaroli, *L'Age de l'eloquence*, pt III, ch. 2, section 2.

70   Levi suggests that 'it is possible that the neo-Stoic group of moralists are to be defined precisely in terms of their alliance of an ethical vocabulary taken from the Stoics with an inclination to scepticism in matters of speculation' (*French Moralists*, p. 56). The most important treatment of the convergence of Stoicism and scepticism in neo-Stoicism is Richard Tuck, *Philosophy and Government 1572–1651* (Cambridge, 1993), ch. 2. For presence of neo-Stoic works, both Lipsius' and du Vair's, in contemporary French libraries see the conclusions of Abel, *Stoizismus und frühe Neuzeit*, pp. 273–86.

71   Hippolyte Guillibert, *Portraits de Peiresc et du Vair par Finsonius* (Paris, 1909), p. 5.

72   'Comme i'ay veu à Rome les riches temples bastis par les Payens, à l'honneur de leurs Demons, avoir esté sainctement appliquez au service de nostre Dieu: ainsi en ce petit recueil i'ay pris peine de transferer à l'usage & instruction de nostre religion, les plus beaux traits des Philosophes Payens, que i'ay pensé s'y pouvoir commodement rapporter.' Du Vair, *La Saincte Philosophie. La philosophie des stoiques. Manuel d'Epictete. Exhortation à la vie civile. Et plusieures autres traictez de pieté* (Lyon, 1594) sig. A5^v.

73   'Lapides, caementa, calcem ex veteri et diu lapso aedificio illo philosophiae comportamus: ne invide hoc lucellum architecto et patiare materiam hanc substernat salem in fundamentis.' 'We take with us the stones, cement and mortar from this ancient and now fallen edifice of philosophy. Do not begrudge the architect this little profit and leave him this material; may he spread salt upon the foundations.' Quoted in René Radouant, *Guillaume du Vair. L'homme et l'orateur jusqu'à la fin des troubles de la Ligue (1556–1596)* (Geneva, 1970 [1907]).

74   In harmony with du Vair's vision of churches rising amidst the ruins of temples, John Eliot wrote that Seneca's teaching 'strikes a full *Diapason* to the concord of the Scriptures, & consents with that sweet harmony; o let us then applie it to our selves & make his wordes our workes' (*The Monarchie of Man*, ed. Alexander B. Grosart, 2 vols, n.p., 1872, II, p. 98).

75   Seneca appealed to men like du Vair, or Eliot, because he made frequent enough mention of God to enable them to see him as an ally to be pressed into the service of a rational Christianity. Seneca's distillation of his philosophy into 'one principle', '*Deum sequere*, be obedient unto God', enabled Eliot, for example, to hang his own anthropocentrism on an authoritative, if pagan, peg (*The Monarchie of Man*, p. 97).

76   Du Vair, *De la Saincte Philosophie*, in *Les Oeuvres du Monsieur du Vair* (Rouen, 1623), p. 911. The appeal of this philosophy *en calamitez publiques* persists. G. Michaut's edition of *La Sainte Philosophie* and *Philosophie morale des stoiques* was published in 1945 and dedicated to the memory of a son murdered in Buchenwald by the Nazis.

77   Du Vair, *De la Saincte Philosophie*, in *Oeuvres*, p. 915.

78   Ibid., p. 927.

79   'Or comme nous somme deiettez és tenebres de ce monde, és deserts de peché, & és abysmes de perdition, nous ne pouvons ni voir nostre but sans lumiere, ni trouver nostre chemin sans guide; ni nous soufleur & avancer sans appuy.' Ibid., p. 940.

80   'Voila Seigneur comme nous sommes coupables, et comme nous le confessons, et recognoissons ingenument que si vous ne nous pardonneez nous perirons et Justement.' Carp. Bibl. Inguimb., MS 1815, fol. 396^r.

81   Levi suggests that du Vair does not follow Lipsius and sharply separates reason and opinion and to that extent is more Neoplatonic than Stoic (*French Moralists*, p. 330).

82   'Il y a des choses qui sont en nostre puissance, les autres n'y sont pas. Approuver, entreprendre, desirer, & fuit, pour dite en un mot, ce qui ne dépend que de nous seuls, est en nostre puissance. Le corps, les biens, la reputation, l'authorité, & pour abreger ce que ne dépend point de nostre fait, n'est point en nostre puissance. Ce qui est en nostre puissance est naturellement libre & ne se peut defendre ni empescher. Ce qui n'y est pas, est infirme, serf, aisé à empescher & dépend d'autruy.' Du Vair, *Le Manuel d'Epictete*, in *Oeuvres*, p. 777.

83   The figure comes from F. E. Sutcliffe, *Guez de Balzac et son temps* (Paris, 1959), p. 114; see also Michel Spanneut, *Permanence du stoïcisme*

de Zénon à Malraux (Gembloux, 1979), p. 217.

84   Du Vair, *The Morall Philosophie of the Stoicks*, tr. Thomas James [1598], ed. and intro. Rudolf Kirk (New Brunswick, 1951), pp. 58, 59, 61, 68, and 69.

85   See Levi, *French Moralists*, p. 85.

86   'Now that which can best instruct us in this way, and teach us the inclination of a right spirit, and a will, governed by reason, is Prudence; which is the beginning and end of all Vertue. For that, making us exactly and truly to know the condition and quality of things objected to us, renders us fit to distinguish what is according to Nature, what is not; what we ought to pursue, and what we ought to fly.' Du Vair, *The Morall Philosophy of the Stoicks*, p. 13.

87   Du Vair, *The True Way to Vertue and Happinesse. Intreating specially of CONSTANCIE in publike Calamities, and private Afflictions* (London, 1623), p. 29.

88   Ibid., p. 20.

89   Du Vair, *Exhortation à la vie civile* (1594) in *Oeuvres*, p. 749; Montaigne, 'On Restraining Your Will', *Essays*, p. 1144.

90   Meyjes, 'Hugo Grotius as an Irenicist', p. 45, n. 10.

91   Du Vair, *The True Way to Vertue and Happinesse*, pp. 126–7. Was there something of an effort at self-exoneration here? Now a loyal servant of the King, du Vair had, nevertheless, remained in the Paris of the Sixteen that was besieged by Henri IV in 1590 while Montaigne had quit Paris with the old King on the 'Day of the Barricades' in May 1588.

92   'Je prise beaucoup la vie solitaire, je la prise beaucoup, je l'aime et peut-estre trop . . . La vie monastique n'a pas esté introduite ny en une saison troublée, ny pour ceux dont la prudence et la fidelité estoient nécessaires à la conduite et au gouvernement des affaires publiques.' Quoted in C. A. Sapey, *Études biographiques pour servir à l'histoire de l'ancienne Magistrature française* (Paris, 1858), pp. 159–60.

93   BN MS Dupuy 661 fol. 120ʳ. See the full account in Sapey, *Études biographiques*, pp. 88–103.

94   'Quant aux iniures particulieres que nous en recevons, où pouvons-nous mieux employer la charité & la patience?' Du Vair, *Oeuvres*, p. 752.

95   See S. C. Humphreys, 'Introduction: Let's Hear it for the Magpies', *Cultures of Scholarship*, ed. S. C. Humphreys (Ann Arbor, 1997), p. 11: 'the effect of studying culture contact (for us) is to highlight distinctions in European models

that were taken for granted and contradictions that were displaced'.

96   This relation to contemporary European thinking has been insufficiently considered. Neither Johannes Betray, *Die Akkommodationsmethode des P. Matteo Ricci in China* (Rome, 1955) nor Peter R. Bachmann's parallel study, *Roberto Nobili, ein missionsgeschichtlicher Beitrag zum christlichen Dialog mit Hinduismus* (Rome, 1972) mentions Epictetus, Seneca, nor scepticism. For insightful treatments of Ricci in a broader context see Howard L. Goodman and Anthony Grafton, 'Ricci, the Chinese, and the Toolkits of Textualists', *Asia Major*, 3 (1992), pp. 95–148 and Jonathan Spence's masterful, *The Memory Palace of Matteo Ricci* (New York, 1984).

97   'Io in tutto mi accomodai a loro, e, dove era bisogno, mutai alcuna cosa i detti e sententie de' philosophi nostri, [e] alcune cose presi di nostra casa.' Ricci to P. Girolamo Costa, quoted in Ricci, *Treatise on Friendship*, *Studia Missionalia*, 7 (1952), p. 463.

98   See Alan Charles Kors, *Atheism in France 1650–1729* (Princeton, 1990), pp. 172–3.

99   For a general account see Ricci's own history, *Storia dell'introduzione del cristianesimo in Cina*, ed. Pasquale M. d'Elia, *Fonti Ricciane*, 3 vols (Rome, 1942–49). For the *Treatise on Friendship* see I, pp. 368–70 and for the others bk 5, ch. 2.

100   Pasquale M. d'Elia has produced a marvellous edition: see *Studia Missionalia*, 7 (1952), pp. 425–515, updated in 'Further Notes on Matteo Ricci's *De Amicitia*', *Monumenta Serica*, 15 (1956), pp. 356–77. The dating is from *Storia* in *Fonti Ricciane*, I, p. 368.

101   Ricci, *Treatise on Friendship*, para. 86: 'Tibi potius quam cuivis sis amicus' (Seneca, *Epistulae morales*, IX).

102   For the parallel to merchant practice see ibid., paras 10, 24, 27, and 59; on the increasing prevalence of this style of friendship, see paras 34 and 57.

103   Ibid., paras 14 and 21.

104   Ibid., para. 70. The story of Phocion provided a fitting example and conclusion to the maxims. Alexander the Great had tried to buy his friendship but was rejected, showing that real friendship was subject neither to market forces nor to aspirations of grandeur. Ricci's Phocion rebuffed the advice of the great man because he was great, just as Charron's Phocion repudiated the applause of the many because it came from the many (ibid., para. 92).

105 *Storia* in *Fonti Ricciane*, ed. d'Elia, bk 5, ch. 2, section 707, II, p. 286.

106 Goodman and Grafton, 'Ricci, the Chinese, and the Toolkits of Textualists', p. 103.

107 Matteo Ricci, *Book of Twenty-Five Paragraphs*, in Christopher Spalatin, *Matteo Ricci's Use of Epictetus* (Waegwan, Korea, 1975), paras 13, 20, 23, and 24.

108 Ibid., para. 2, p. 26. Ricci's text is printed, in Spalatin's translation, alongside relevant passages from Epictetus' *Enchiridion* (pp. 26–50).

109 'Se l'oggetto della stima è fuori di sé, uno non potrà mai essere soddisfatto/ . . . /Gli autori antichi e I moderni tutti dànno questo consiglio: / A nulla giova andar fuori, / ma è utile restar in casa!' 'Il Pastorello che viaggia sulle Colline', in Pasquale M. d'Elia, 'Musica e canti italiani a Pechino', *Rivista degli Studi Orientali*, 30 (1955), p. 138.

110 Ricci, *Twenty-Five Paragraphs*, para. 16.

111 Ibid., para. 7.

112 Ibid., para. 11.

113 *The True Meaning of the Lord of Heaven* was complete in draft by 1596, the woodblocks were prepared for printing by 1603, and in 1604 a Latin summary was sent to Rome. All quotations are from *The True Meaning of the Lord of Heaven (T'ien-chu Shih-i)*, ed. Edward J. Malatesta, tr. with intro. and notes Douglas Lancashire and Peter Hu Kuo-Chen (St Louis, Miss., 1985).

114 *Storia* in *Fonti Ricciane*, ed. d'Elia, bk 5, ch. 2, section 709, II, pp. 292–3.

115 Ricci, *The True Meaning*, para. 13, p. 63.

116 Ibid., para. 468, p. 375.

117 Ibid., para. 16, p. 65. See p. 65, n. 2, *voce* 'Chün-tzu'.

118 Ibid., para. 432, p. 355.

119 Ibid., para. 24, p. 69.

120 Ibid., para. 157, p. 163.

121 'Therefore almost everything a man does during his lifetime he does as a slave to selfish desires' (ibid., para. 305, p. 271).

122 Ibid., para. 306, p. 271. The 'Western Scholar' describes the preparation for a life of virtue in terms very like Charron's when defending the value of suspension of judgement for missionaries who had first to undermine native beliefs before Christianity could be substituted in their place. 'I always compare this kind of task with the planting of vegetables: First one prepares the soil, pulls up the weeds, rids the ground of broken earthenware and stones, and guides accumulated water so that it flows into ditches. Only when all this has been done does one plant the seeds' (para. 461, p. 371).

123 Ibid., para. 420, p. 345.

124 Ibid., para. 122, p. 137.

125 Ibid., para. 123, p. 137.

126 Ibid., para. 455, p. 369.

127 Ibid., para. 304, p. 269.

128 Ibid., para. 310, p. 275.

129 Ibid., para. 459, p. 371.

130 Ibid., para. 159, p. 165. Ricci's contemporary St François de Sales also invoked Augustine's teaching of humility in an effort to balance the tendency to hubris that praise of reason might otherwise have encouraged. For de Sales, see Murphy, *Saint François de Sales*, pp. 36 and 55–60.

131 Ricci repeats the story that Charron had also told of the Mexicans who gathered at births to mourn another entry 'into this cruel world' and at deaths to rejoice for the escaping of suffering (*The True Meaning*, para. 126, p. 141; Pierre Charron, *De la Sagesse*, Paris, 1986 [1601], bk 1, ch. 39, p. 255).

132 Ricci, *The True Meaning*, para. 429, p. 353.

133 Ibid., para. 223, p. 215.

134 Ibid., para. 248, p. 229.

135 Ibid., para. 451, pp. 365–7.

136 Ibid., para. 248, p. 231.

137 Ibid., para. 287, p. 293.

138 'Per l'uomo, / conoscere sé stesso è difficile; / ingannare sé stesso, è facile. / . . . / Nel mondo pochi sono quelli che non hanno difetti; / e quelli i cui difetti sono leggieri, sono i savi. / Tu che speri che gli altri ti perdonino i gravi falli, non puoi forse perdonare ad essi i loro piccoli difetti.' D'Elia, 'Musica e canti italiari a Pechino', p. 143.

139 Ricci, *The True Meaning*, para. 303, p. 269.

140 Ricci, *Storia* in *Fonti Ricciane*, section 176, pp. 115–17.

141 Ibid., section 170, p. 110; para. 177, p. 118.

142 Ibid., section 180, p. 120.

143 '. . . che non è questa una legge formata, ma solo è propriamente una academia, instituita per il bon governo della republica. E così ben possono esser di questa academia e farsi christiani, posciachè nel suo essentiale non contiene niente contra l'essentia della Fede catholica, nè la Fede catholica impedisce niente, anzi agiuta molto alla quiete e pace della republica, che i suoi libri pretendono.' Ibid. section 181, p. 120.

144 'Ut quid ornamentum domus, ut quid

alia igni obnoxia attendimus? Fundamentum tentandum esse: dum illud constet, reliqua eant ut volent, igne probanda' (Sarpi to Casaubon, 22 June 1610, *Lettere ai Protestanti*, ed. Manlio Busnelli, 2 vols, Bari, 1931, II, pp. 217–18). David Wootton has suggested a parallel to themes expressed in the *Pensieri Medico-Morali*. (*Paolo Sarpi. Between Renaissance and Enlightenment* Cambridge, 1983, pp. 88–90).

145 'Insaniae erunt donec homines . . . Nemo sapiens publicos morbos corrigere parat. Satis tibi sit, si me emendaveris.' The text of this letter was first published as an appendix to Gaetano Cozzi, 'Paolo Sarpi tra il cattolico Philippe Canaye de Fresnes e il calvinista Isaac Casaubon', *Bollettino dell'Istituto di Storia della Società e dello Stato Veneziano*, I (1959), p. 162.

146 For le Vayer's place in the history of political thought, see Domenico Taranto, 'Sullo scetticismo politico di La Mothe le Vayer', *Il Pensiero Politico*, 20 (1987), pp. 179–99; A. M. Battista, 'Come giudicano la "politica" libertini e moralisti nella Francia del seicento', *Il libertinismo in Europa*, ed. Sergio Bertelli (Milan and Naples, 1980), pp. 32–6; Julien Eymard d'Angers, 'Stoicisme et "libertinage" dans l'oeuvre de François La Mothe le Vayer', *Revue des Sciences Humaines*, n.s. 65 (1954), pp. 259–84 [= *Recherches sur le stoicisme au XVIe et XVIIe siècles*, pp. 481–506].

147 I cite from *La Vertu des payens* in *Oeuvres de François la Mothe le Vayer*, 7 vols (Dresden, 1757), V, pt I. For the controversy over the salvation of pagans see George Hunston Williams, 'Erasmus and the Reformers on non-Christian Religions and *Salus Extra Ecclesiam*', *Action and Conviction in Early Modern Europe*, ed. Theodore K. Rabb and Jerrold E. Seigel (Princeton, 1969), pp. 319–70; Louis Capéran, *Le Problème du salut des infidèles*, 2 vols (Paris, 1912).

148 Le Mothe Le Vayer, *La Vertu des payens*, pp. 51–2.

149 Ibid., pp. 311–14.

150 Antoine Arnauld, *De la nécessité de la foi en Jesus Christ pour être sauvé*, in *Oeuvres de Messire Antoine Arnauld*, 43 vols (Paris, 1727), X, p. 66. For a summary of this debate see Louis Capéran, *Le Problème du salut des infidèles. Essai historique*, pp. 316–29 and Henri Busson, *La Pensée religieuse française de Charron a Pascal* (Paris, 1933), pp. 408–11.

151 Arnauld, *De la Nécessité de la foi*, X, p. 77.

152 Ibid., pp. 87–8.

153 Ibid., pp. 115 and 124.

154 Ibid., p. 69.

155 Ibid., p. 231.

156 Ibid., p. 115. See J. F. Senault, *L'Homme criminel* (1644) for a straightforward exposition of this point of view, and Arnauld, *La Nécessité de la foi*, p. 108.

157 Arnauld, *De la nécessité de la foi*, pp. 124–5.

158 For examples of the Stoics' likening of the philosopher to God, see Seneca's *Epistulae morales* XLVIII.11–12 and LXXI.6.

159 Arnauld, *De la nécessité de la foi*, pp. 328–36.

160 Ibid., p. 328.

161 See Jean Jehasse, *Guez de Balzac et le Génie Romain 1597–1654* (St Etienne, 1977); Julian Eymard d'Angers, 'Le Stoicisme dans l'oeuvre de J.-L. Guez de Balzac', *Recherches sur le stoicisme aux XVIe et XVIIe siècles*, ed. L. Antoine (Hildesheimer and New York, 1976), pp. 421–52; Roger Zuber, 'Guez de Balzac et les deux antiquités', *XVIIe Siècle*, 131 (1981), pp. 135–48; J. B. Sabrié, *Les Idées religieuses de J.-L. Guez de Balzac* (Paris, 1913), ch. 3.

162 In the *Apologie* Balzac declared that 'if we wish to imitate the Ancients, we would not imitate the Ancients' (*Oeuvres complètes*, Paris, 1665, Discourse II, p. 110). In the 'Dissertation a M. Conrart' in the *Socrate chrestien*, Balzac explicitly declared that it was necessary 'to accommodate oneself to the maxims accepted at the time' as true (ibid., II, p. 575). 'It is necessary to follow the usage of the Church of the times' and to pay more attention to contemporary prelates than to Tertullian, Origin, Justin or Clement. 'We could', he declared, 'be of the primitive Church by imitation of ancient virtue; but we must be of the present Church, by the practice of those things which it observes' (ibid., I, p. 1033). However, in Balzac's interpretation of the Erasmian imperative, the adaptation took on a wholly inward character. He reflected, writing to P. Vavasseur, that whereas the 'other' Ciceronians attend to external representations like comportment, Vavasseur possessed 'his heart, his spirit and his virtue' (ibid., I, p. 1050).

163 Balzac, *Socrate chrestien*, I, p. 21: 'The ignorant had persuaded the philosophers and the poor fisherman had become the teachers of kings and nations, catching in their nets orators and poets, jurisconsults and mathematicians.'

164 Ibid., III, p. 28.

165 Ibid., IV, p. 33.

166 Ibid., V, p. 36.

167 Ibid., XI, p. 102. By contrast, Selden contended that 'Lay-men have best interpreted the hard places in the Bible' (Selden, *Table-Talk*, section 6).

168   Ibid., p. 107.

169   Gassendi, *Mirrour*, bk 6, p. 211.

170   Susan James, *Passion and Action. The Emotions in Seventeenth-Century Philosophy* (Oxford, 1997), ch. 7, esp. pp. 160–3.

171   Justus Lipsius, *Two Books of Constancie*, ed. Rudolf Kirk (New Brunswick, N.J., 1939 [1594]), pp. 71–2.

172   '. . . ombre et image, mais vaine et fausse . . . mere de tous maux, confusion, desordres: d'elle viennent toutes les passions et les troubles.' Charron, *De la sagesse* (bk 1, ch. 18) quoted in Levi, *French Moralists* (p. 104).

173   Quoted here in Levi's words (*French Moralists*, p. 79). In *La Sainte Philosophie* (1945), p. 57. In this extraordinary Neoplatonic equation of felicity with light du Vair acknowledges that this perfection 'n'est rien de ce que nous connaissons par le sens' – exactly Senault's formulation.

174   'Car puis que la vie de l'homme n'est qu'une mer flottante continuellement en miseres, où les afflictions recoupent plus dur l'une sur l'autre, que ne font les ondes agitées par la tourmente, & où les calmes, si quelquesfois il s'y en trouve, ne sont pour la pluspart que presages de tempeste, dequoy se peuvent mieux equipper & freter ceux qui ont à faire ceste navigation, que de ceste divine patience & equanimité, qui sert d'ancre asseuré aux plus agitez esprits, & aux ames plus tourmentées?' Du Vair, *Oeuvres*, pp. 929–30.

175   Ricci, *The True Meaning*, paras 124 and 137. 'Chi possiede la tranquillità del cuore pondera tutto nella calma. / Nella gloria non si innalza troppo, e nell'umiliazione non si abbatte troppo / . . . / Venti gagliari fanno impeto contro di esso, / e le onde che si accavallano lo sommergono, / eppure non si muove' ('Equilibrio interiore', in d'Elia, 'Musica e canti italiani a Pechino', p. 141). For more on this metaphor see David Halsted, 'Ships, the Sea, and Constancy: A Classical Image in the Baroque Lyric', *Neophilologus*, 74 (1990), pp. 545–60.

176   Virgilio Malvezzi, *Stoa Triumphans* (London, 1651), p. 13. The English 'translator', one 'J.H.', attributes it to Virgilio Malvezzi; I have not yet found any indication of such a work by Malvezzi nor of a work of his from which it could have been excerpted.

177   Malvezzi, *Stoa Triumphans*, p. 14. The passage cited in the margins as a source is the same preface to Seneca's *Naturales Quaestiones* that the Jesuit Daniello Bartoli had used in *L'huomo di lettere difeso e emendato* (Bologna, 1646) to make the same point (p. 27). Ironically, we see here how Stoic anthropocentrism, in the

form of confidence in the power of reason, grounds an argument designed to ease mental pain by undermining anthropocentrism!

178   Izaak Walton, 'The Angler's Song', for two voices set by Henry Lawes, *The Compleat Angler*, in *The Compleat Walton*, ed. Geoffrey Keynes (London, 1929), pp. 148–9.

179   *Col. Henry Marten's Familiar Letters to his Lady of Delight* (London, 1663), letter 2, p. 6.

180   Ricci, *The True Meaning*, para. 24, p. 69.

181   Two of Julien Eymard d'Angers' essays emphasize the Stoic language of Senault's anti-Stoic argument: 'Le Stoicisme dans le traité *De l'usage des passions* de l'oratorien Senault (1641)' and 'Réfutation et utilisation augustiniennes de Senèque et du stoicisme dans *L'homme criminel* (1644) et *L'homme chrétien* (1648) de l'oratorien J.-F. Senault', both reprinted in *Recherches sur le stoicisme*, ed. Antoine.

182   Senault, *The Use of the Passions* (London, 1652), p. 18.

183   Ibid., pp. 75–6.

184   Ibid., p. 124.

185   Ibid., p. 114.

186   Ibid., p. 88

187   The quote is from Spenser, *The Faerie Queene*, bk 6, canto 1. Neither this nor any of the other sources cited pp. 126–9 are referred to by Ernst Gombrich in his classic study, 'The Subject of Poussin's *Orion*', *Burlington Magazine*, 84 (1944), pp. 37–41. Poussin was closely bound to the circle of Peiresc's Roman friend Cassiano dal Pozzo; for their common intellectual context see recent examinations of Poussin's intellectual life and cultural position by Elizabeth Cropper and Charles Dempsey, *Friendship and the Love of Painting* (Princeton, 1996) Sheila McTighe, *Poussin's Allegorical Landscapes* (Cambridge, 1996; and now Ingo Herklotz, *Cassiano dal Pozzo und die Archäologie ds 17. Jahrhunderts* (Munich, 1999). Peiresc knew Poussin and the two exchanged letters, though all that has survived (or yet been discovered) is printed in 'Lettre inédite de Peiresc à Nicolas Poussin 8 novembre 1632', *Nouvelles Archives de l'Art Français*, 3, ser. 8 (1892), pp. 293–5.

5   HISTORY AS PHILOSOPHY

1   Erwin Panofsky, *Hercules am Scheidewege und andere antike Bildstoffe in der neueren Kunst* (Berlin, 1930), p. 124. De Thou to Henry Savile, 27 July 1606, *Histoire universelle de Jacques-Auguste de Thou*, 12 vols (Basel, 1742), X, p. 406. For de Thou's letters see Anthony Grafton, *The Footnote. A Curious History* (Cambridge, Mass., 1997), pp. 140–1.

2   De Thou to Pierre Jeannin, 31 March 1611, *Sylloge scriptorum varii generis et argumenti, historiarum sui temporis* (London, 1732), VII, pt 2, p. 4; *Histoire universelle*, X, p. 376.

3   Casaubon to de Thou, 21 April 1611, *Sylloge scriptorum varii generis et argumenti, Historiarum sui Temporis*, VII, pt II, p. 12; *Histoire universelle*, X, p. 390.

4   'Quoiqu'il en soit, marchons toujours d'un pas ferme dans notre chemin, & opposons aux traits de la calomnie le bouclier de la patience'. Camden to de Thou, 11 June 1615, *Histoire universelle*, X, pp. 451–2.

5   'Nous navigeons l'un & l'autre sur la même mer. Nous sommes dans un danger égal: nous avons à luter contre les mêmes vents & contre les mêmes tempêtes. Nous sommes menacez des mêmes écueils . . . Mais pourquoi croirai-je que nous sommes malheureux l'un & l'autre? ne trouvons-nous pas dans notre philosophie des secours suffisans, pour soutenir, pour repousser même les efforts de nos ennemis, & des motifs puissans de constance & de courage? C'est ce que j'ai exprimé autrefois dans mon Poeme de Job . . . Le tems est enfin venu de mettre, l'un & l'autre, en usage les maximes de Philosophie, en nous vengeant des injures par le mépris, & en appellant au jugement de la posterité'. De Thou to Camden, 7 July 1615, ibid.

6   'And however difficult, however remote it may seem, the establishment of the philosophical basis of the latter [baroque philology] is absolutely indispensable' (Walter Benjamin, *The Origins of German Tragic Drama*, tr. John Osborne, London, 1992, p. 163). 'Throughout my life', Arnaldo Momigliano wrote, 'I have been fascinated by a type of man so near to my profession, so transparently sincere in his vocation, so understandable in his enthusiasms, and yet so deeply mysterious in his ultimate aims' (*The Classical Foundations of Modern Historiography*, Berkeley and Los Angeles, 1990, p. 54).

7   Gassendi, *Mirrour*, bk 6, p. 200. Peiresc to Dupuy, February 1627, *Lettres de Peiresc*, I, p. 139; Peiresc to Dupuy, 10 January 1633, ibid., p. 409. This same fascination with the practical benfits of learning was shared by Aubrey (Michael Hunter, *John Aubrey and the Realm of Learning*, London, 1975, p. 111).

8   Gassendi, *Mirrour*, year 1628, p. 27.

9   Hunter, *John Aubrey*, pp. 64–6.

10   Krzysztof Pomian, 'Le Cartésianisme, les érudits et l'histoire', in *Histoire. Philosophie. Religion* (Warsaw, 1966), pp. 175–204.

11   In fact, the very letter adduced by Pomian as proof of Peiresc's accumulation-driven

'Baconianism' (Peiresc to Dupuy, 16 December 1636, *Lettres de Peiresc*, III, p. 619) is to my mind one of the chief pieces of evidence for a motivation that more closely resembles Pomian's view of humanist historians. See below p. 218, n. 68.

12   Francis Bacon, *Advancement of Learning*, *Works*, III, bk. 1, p. 271. For Arnold's own defence of 'curious' learning and view of culture as 'a study in perfection', see *Culture and Anarchy*, ed. Stefan Collini (Cambridge, 1993), pp. 55 and 58–63. For a different view of the unsuitability of the antiquary to politics see George Steiner's reflection on the case of Anthony Blunt, 'A Cleric of Treason', *George Steiner. A Reader* (Oxford, 1984), pp. 197–8.

13   'Mais il me rebroua furieusement et me reprocha que je ne me vouloys rendre coulpable envers la posterité de luy avoir envié le fruict qu'elle pouvoit tirer de cez belles pieces. Qu'aultant vauldroit les jetter quasi dans la mer que de les donner à des gents de cette sorte . . . vous auriez quelque jour un grand remords de conscience d'avoir contribué voz soings et voz peines à faire perir un monument de l'Antiquité digne de memoire, quand vous luy pouviez de saulver la vie qu'il avoit si inesperement garentie jusques à vous' (Peiresc to Menestrier, 31 January 1636, *Lettres de Peiresc*, V, p. 791). 'Et de faict je croys bien qu'on n'y eusse possible jamais descouvert cez belles choses que j'y au trouvées avec ma patience et mon estude, lesquelles m'ont porté bien plus avant à d'autres descouvertes qui seroient pareillement demeurées incogneues' (ibid., p. 790).

14   This fear of losing or destroying something that had magically survived is invoked in a letter to d'Arcos explaining to him how to make casts of inscriptions so as not 'de faire courrir fortune à un si noble et ancient monument de perir tout à faict ou entre les mains des ouvriers, ou bien pour les chemins'. Peiresc to d'Arcos, 3 August 1634, ibid., VII, p. 134.

15   Henry to Borilly, 31 December 1654, printed in Gassendi, *Mirrour*, p. 294. This was also a lesson that Samuel Johnson took away from his reading of Peiresc's *Life* (the *Idler*, ed. W. J. Bate, John M. Bullitt, and L. F. Powell, in *The Yale Edition of the Works of Samuel Johnson*, 16 vols, New Haven and London, 1963, II, no. 65, 14 July 1759, p. 202). I thank Walter Kaiser for bringing this reference to my attention.

16   Erwin Panofsky, 'Father Time', *Studies in Iconology. Humanistic Themes in the Art of the Renaissance* (New York, 1962 [1939]), p. 92. For a survey of attitudes to time in seventeenth-century painting, see John Rupert Martin, *Baroque* (New York, 1977), ch. 6.

17 Time, Micanzio wrote on the last page of his *Life* of Sarpi, consumed stone and metal but was powerfuless against the memory of heroic virtue (Fulgenzio Micanzio, *Vita, del padre Paolo*, in Paolo Sarpi, *Istoria del Concilio Tridentino*, ed. Corrado Vivanti, 2 vols, Turin, 1974, II, p. 1412). And Izaak Walton's *Life* of Donne was praised as 'More faithful to him, than his Marble was: / Which eating age, nor fire, shall e're deface' (*The Compleat Walton*, ed. Geoffrey Keynes, London, 1929, p. 205).

18 Gassendi, *Mirrour*, sig. (a)^r. Gassendi explained his decision to undertake the biography of Brahe in similar terms (*Opera Omnia*, 6 vols, Leiden, 1658, IV, p. 366).

19 Gassendi, *Mirrour*, year 1614, p. 167.

20 Cyriac of Ancona, *Kyriaci Anconitani Itinerarium*, ed. L. Mehus (Florence, 1742), pp. 54–5. Karl August Neuhausen, 'Die vergessene *göttliche Kunst der Totenerweckung*. Cyriacus von Ancona als Begründer der Erforschung der Antike in der Renaissance', *Antiquarische Gelehrsamkeit und bildende Kunst: die Gegenwart der Antike in der Renaissance*, ed. Gunter Schweikhart (Bonn, 1996), pp. 51–68; Charles Mitchell, 'Archaeology and Romance in Renaissance Italy', in *Italian Renaissance Studies*, ed. E. F. Jacob (London, 1960), pp. 455–83. See now *Ciriaco d'Ancona e la cultura antiquaria dell'umanesimo. Atti del convegno internazionale di studio*, ed. Gianfranco Paci and Sergoi Sconocchia (Reggio Emilia, 1998).

21 John Donne, *Essays in Divinity*, ed. Evelyn M. Simpson (Oxford, 1952), p. 56: 'For naturally great wits affect the reading of obscure books, wrastle and sweat in the explication of prophesies, dig and thresh out the words of unlegible hands, resuscitate and bring to life again the mangled, and lame fragmentary images and characters in marbles and Medals, because they have a joy and complacency in the victory and atchievement thereof'; H. A. Cronne, 'The Study and Use of Charters by English Scholars in the Seventeenth Century: Sir Henry Spelman and Sir William Dugdale', in *English Historical Scholarship in the Sixteenth and Seventeenth Centuries*, ed. Levi Fox (Oxford, 1965), p. 75; Gassendi to Peiresc, 28 April 1633, *Lettres de Peiresc*, IV, pp. 249–50: 'Tant y a que la satisfaction me demeure de descouvrir tousjours quelque chose dans l'esprit de ces braves hommes du temps passé, dont peu de gens se prennent garde. Ce m'est de la peine de vray, mais le plaizir que je reçoy à n'apprendre rien à credit, et puiser moy-mesme dans les sources qui ont peu surmonter les injures du temps, ce que les anciens ont imaginé des choses, me paye avec tres grande usure tout le travail que j'y puis employer.'

22 Lorenzo Pignoria, 'Seconda parte delle imagini de i dei', in Vincenzo Cartari, *Imagini delli dei de gl'antichi* (Venice, 1647), p. 397: 'il Tempo, ottimo manifestatore di tutte le cose occulte'.

23 Of course, to the extent that neo-Stoicism served as a philosophy of consolation it could touch a strain of melancholy or piety that existed independently of any scholarly immersion in the past. This seems to be true of Spain in the seventeenth century, where neo-Stoicism flourished while antiquarian scholarship, perhaps because of Iberia's intellectual isolation during these decades, languished. But much more needs to be known about provincial and antiquarian erudition in early modern Spain before any definite claims can be made.

24 Nicole Dacos, 'Hermannus Posthumus. Rome, Manuta, Landshut', *Burlington Magazine*, 127 (1985), p. 438.

25 Ruth Olitsky Rubinstein, '*Tempus edax rerum*: a Newly Discovered Painting by Hermannus Posthumus', *Burlington Magazine*, 127 (1985), pp. 425–33 has identified around sixty objects and monuments. For a study of this moment in the history of antiquities in Rome, see Nicole Dacos, '*Roma Quanta Fuit*'. *Tre pittori fiammingi nella domus aurea* (Rome, 1995). Insofar as *Veritas filia temporis* is the reverse of *Tempus Edax Rerum* Carlo Ginzburg's discussion of historiography as the revealer of truth also reflects on Posthumus' message ('In margine al motto *Veritas Filia Temporis*', *Rivista Storica Italiana*, 88, 1966, pp. 969–73).

26 Edmund Spenser, *The Ruines of Rome: by Bellay*, in *The Yale Edition of the Shorter Poems of Edmund Spenser*, ed. William A. Oram et al. (New Haven and London, 1989), VII, p. 389; Joachim du Bellay, *Les Antiquitez de Rome. Les Regrets*, ed. Françoise Joukovsky (Paris, 1994), VII, p. 31: 'Et bien qu'au temps pour un temps facent guerre / Les bastiments, si est-ce que le temps / Oeuvres et noms finablement atterre.' 'Judge', he later demands of the reader, 'by these ample ruines view, the rest / The which injurious time hath quite outworne'. Spenser, *The Ruines of Rome*, XXVII, p. 401; du Bellay, *Les Antiquitez*, p. 40.

27 Spenser, *The Ruines of Rome*, III, pp. 386–7; du Bellay, *Les Antiquitez*, sonnet III, pp. 28–9.

28 Spenser, *The Ruines of Rome*, VIII, p. 390; du Bellay, *Les Antiquitez*, p. 31: 'Et que, si bien le temps destruit les Republiques, / Le temps ne mist si bas la Romaine hauteur.'

29 Spenser, *Two Cantos of Mutabilitie* in *The Faerie Queene*, ed. Thomas P. Roche Jr., (Harmondsworth, 1987), canto VI, stanza i, p. 1025. For surveys of this theme see George Williamson, 'Mutability, Decay, and Seventeenth-Century Melancholy', *English Literary History*, 2 (1935), pp. 121–50; Walter Rehm, *Europäische Romdichtung* (Munich, 1960 [1939]), esp. ch. 5.

30 For the story of the dig, and the prayer offered up by the Abbot in the best spirit of medieval accommodationism, see Thomas Wright, 'On Antiquarian Excavations and Researches in the Middle Ages', *Archaeologia*, 30 (1844), pp. 438–57.

31 Spenser, *The Ruines of Time*, in *The Yale Edition of the Shorter Poems*, p. 234, ll. 43–4.

32 Spenser, ibid., p. 235, ll. 50 and 56.

33 Ibid., pp. 239–40, ll. 162, 155 and 165–6.

34 Ibid., p. 240, ll. 166–76.

35 William Camden, *Britain, or a Chorographicall Description of the Most Flourishing Kingdoms, England, Scotland and Ireland*, trans. Philemon Holland (London, 1610), pp. 2^{r-v}, 3^{r}, 3^{v}. A less romantic account of Camden's method is found in a letter to Jacques-Auguste de Thou of 10 August 1612 printed in de Thou, *Histoire universelle*, x, p. 435. De Thou described his own efforts to amass the raw materials for his history in a letter to Pierre Jeanin of 31 March 1611 (ibid., p. 379).

36 Camden, 'Of Language', *Remaines Concerning Britain* (Toronto, Ontario, 1984), p. 27.

37 Richard Verstegan, 'Verses of the Authors concerning this his Work', *Restitution of Decayed Intelligence in Antiquities* (London, 1653 [1605]), sig. B3^{r}.

38 Francis Bacon, *De augmentis scientiarum*, *Works*, IV, bk 2, ch. 6, pp. 303–4. Bacon's words – and Cyriac of Ancona's thoughts – were echoed half a century later by John Aubrey: 'These Remaynes are *tanquam tabula naufragii* (like fragments of a Shipwreck) that after the Revolution of so many yeares and governments have escaped the teeth of Time and (which is more dangerous) the hands of mistaken zeale. So that the retrieving of these forgotten things from oblivion in some sort resembes the Art of a Conjuror who makes those walke and appeare that have layen in their graves many hundreds of yeares: and represents as it were to the eie, the places, customs and Fashions, that were of old Time. It is said of Antiquaries, they wipe off the mouldinesse they digge, and remove the rubbish' (quoted in Stan A. E. Mendyk, *'Speculum Britanniae'. Regional Study, Antiquarianism and Science in Britain to 1700*, Toronto, 1989, p. 174).

39 Bacon, *Advancement of Learning, Works*, III, bk 1, p. 318.

40 For Opitz' biography see Marian Szyrocki, *Martin Opitz* (Munich, 1974, 2nd edn); Klaus Garber 'Martin Opitz', *Deutsche Dichter des 17. Jahrhunderts*, ed. Harald Steinhagen and Benno von Wiese (Berlin, 1984).

41 For Opitz as a typical *Gelehrter*, see Joseph Fritz, 'Zu Martin Opitzens philologischen Studien', *Euphorion*, 26 (1925), pp. 102–8. For the Leiden years, see J. Bernhard Muth, *Über das Vernhältnis von Martin Opitz zu Daniel Heinsius* (Leipzig, 1872). For the visit to the Cabinet Dupuy, see Opitz to Lingelsheim, 31 May 1630, in *Quellen zur Geschichte des geistigen Lebens in Deutschland während des siebzehnten Jahrhunderts. I. Briefe G. M. Lingelsheims, M. Berneggers und ihrer Freunde*, ed. Alexander Reifferscheid (Heilbronn, 1889), no. 328, p. 398; for mention of Peiresc's loan to Grotius of a manuscript of Nicolas of Damascus see Grotius to Opitz, 1 March 1631, ibid. no. 371, p. 440 (for Grotius' discussion of the material see Grotius to Peiresc, 6 September 1630, *Briefwisseling*, IV (1964), no. 1539, pp. 256–60). For Opitz and Grotius see Christian Gellinek, 'Wettlauf um die Wahrheit du christlichen Religion. Martin Opitz und Christoph Köler als Vermittler zweier Schriften des Hugo Grotius über das Christentum (1631)', *Simpliciana*, 2 (1980), pp. 71–89 and idem, 'Politik und Literatur bei Grotius, Opitz und Milton. Ein Vergleich christlich-politischer Grundgedanken', in *Martin Opitz. Studien zu Werk und Person*, ed. Barbara Becker-Cantarino (Amsterdam, 1982) [= *Daphnis*, 11], pp. 201–32.

42 Bernegger announced that he was sending them to Grotius, along with a letter from Opitz, in a letter of 17 December 1628 (Grotius, *Briefwisseling*, III, p. 432) and Peiresc later wrote that 'J'ay prins grand plaisir de voir les inscriptions de Transylvanie de Mr Grottius' (Peiresc to Dupuy, 2 March 1629, *Lettres de Peiresc*, II, p. 35; the same identification in Peiresc to Dupuy, 16 March 1629, ibid., p. 54). See Jörg-Ulrich Fechner, 'Unbekannte Opitiana – Edition und Kommentar', *Daphnis*, 1 (1972), pp. 23–41.

43 Klaus Garber, 'Martin Opitz', p. 152.

44 Opitz' neo-Stoicism has been studied extensively. The best treatments are those of Kurt H. Wels, *Die patriotischen Strömungen in der deutschen Literatur des Dreissigjährigen Krieges* (Greifswald, 1913), pp. 51–2; idem, 'Opitz und die stoische Philosophie', *Euphorion*, 21 (1914), pp. 86–102, esp. 89–90 and 95–6; and William L.

Cunningham, *Martin Opitz. Poems of Consolation in Adversities of War* (Bonn, 1974), esp. chs 4 ('Stoicism') and 5 ('Justus Lipsius' *De constantia*). Especially trenchant is Leonard Forster, 'Lipsius and Renaissance Humanism', *Festschrift for Ralph Farrell*, ed. Anthony Stephens, H. L. Rogers and Brian Coghlan (Bern, Frankfurt am Main, and Las Vegas, 1977), pp. 212–13.

45 On this period, see Rolf Marmont, 'Martin Opitz in Weissenburg (1622–1623)', *Neue Literatur* (Bucharest), 22 (1971), pp. 98–105; Szyrocki, *Martin Opitz*, pp. 51–6.

46 On Lissabon, see the fascinating study by Leonard Forster, Gustav Gündisch and Paul Binder, 'Henricius Lisbona und Martin Opitz', *Archiv für das Studium der neueren Sprachen und Literaturen*, 130 (1978), pp. 21–32. For praise of life in Zlatna see ll. 125–455. For an interpretation that concentrates on the pastoral see G. Schulz-Behrend, 'Opitz' *Zlatna*', *Modern Language Notes*, 77 (1962), pp. 398–410.

47 'Und so viel schriefften sunst / Die keine macht der zeit / kein weter / keine brust / Zu dämpffen hat vermocht'. Opitz, *Zlatna, Oder von Ruhe des Gemüthes*, in *Opitz gesammelte Werke*, 4 vols ed. George Schulz-Behrend II (Stuttgart, 1978), ll. 68–9.

48 'Hier einen Todtentopff mit aschen volgefüllt / Wie nechst mir wiederfuhr / so wird mir eingebildt / Die eitelkeit der Welt'. *Zlatna*, ll. 75–7.

49 Panofsky, 'Et in Arcadia Ego', *Meaning in the Visual Arts* (Garden City, N.Y., 1955), p. 312. This particular argument does not appear in an earlier version of this essay, first published in *Philosophy and History. The Ernst Cassirer Festschrift*, ed. Raymond Klibansky and H. J. Paton (Oxford, 1936), p. 236.

50 'Wir lassen nichts hindan: Die ursach aller dinge / Worauß von wem und wie ein jeglich thun entspringe / Warumb die Erde steht der Himmel wird gewandt / Die wolcke Fewer giebt is sämbtlich uns bekandt'. *Zlatna*, ll. 501–4.

51 'Die edle Wissenschafft / Schmückt aus das gute Glück und gibt in Unglück Krafft: / Sie zeigt den rechten Weg bestendig außzuhalten / Und lest in keiner Noth di Hertzen nicht erkalten.' Opitz, *Trostgedichte in Widerwertigkeit des Krieges*, in *Gesammelte Werke*, ed. George Schulz-Behrend (Stuttgart, 1968), I, bk 4, ll. 63–6.

52 'Die also auff den lauff der Welt recht achtung geben / Erlernen der natur hierauß gemesse leben / Sie bawen auff den schein des schnöden wesens nicht / Das beydes nur die zeit gebieret und zubricht'. *Zlatna*, ll. 513–16.

53 'Sie werden durch den wahn / der wie ein blinder jrret / Im fall er die vernunfft wil meistern / nicht verwirret: / Sie wissen allen fall des Lebens zue bestehn / Und können unverzagt dem Tod' entgegen gehn'. Ibid., ll. 517–20.

54 'Das wolt' ich gleichfalls thun / und meines geistes kräfften / Versuch allezeit mit müssigen geschäfften; / Ich liesse nicht vorbey so viel man künste weiß / Und was man helt vor schwer erstieg' ich durch den fleiß. / Der Länder untergang / der alten Völker sitten / Ihr essen'jhre tracht / wie seltzsam sie gestritten / Wo diß und das geschehen / ja aller zeiten stand / Von anbegin der Welt macht' ich mir gantz bekand'. Ibid., ll. 521–8.

55 BN MS Dupuy 551, fol. 81.

56 '. . . la corruption des langues est subjette à des changements et deteriorations ou esloignements de leur principe' (Peiresc to de Loches, 13 February 1634, *Correspondance de Peiresc avec Capucins*, p. 20). This is one of Peiresc's hobby-horses and recurs frequently in his discussion of oriental languages; see, for example, Peiresc to Holstenius, 6 August 1629, *Lettres de Peiresc*, v, pp. 343–5.

57 '. . . ainsy qu'il se peut voir par la comparaison des vieux glossaires, où il se trouve bien des changements et quelque fois de la confusion selon que la diversité des pais, des nations et des siècles, destournoit à aultre sense que le plus ancien la signification de plusieurs motz, ainsy qu'il arrive encores aujourdhuy aux langages vulgaires . . .' (Peiresc to Dupuy, 4 July 1632, *Lettres de Peiresc*, II, p. 307). Peiresc even had access to a manuscript devoted to this very subject: 'Origines de plusieurs mots François & Observations sur les mots antiens de la lange Françoise' Paris, BN, (MS Dupuy 249, dated 1633).

58 Peiresc to Dupuy, 31 July 1632, *Lettres de Peiresc*, II, p. 321. Peiresc warned Jacques de Bie, then at work on a series of portraits of the kings of France, 'ne les point mesler avec des choses qui ne soyent bien compatibles avec ce qui estoit de l'usage et des habillements de leurs temps, aussy bien que de leurs vrayes images' (Peiresc to de Bie, 31 July 1632, ibid., VII, pp. 627–8). For law, see Peiresc to Bignon, 15 March 1637, ibid., p. 641; for heraldry, see Peiresc to Chifflet, 2 October 1620, ibid., p. 881.

59 'Sur quoy j'ay à vous dire qu'il se faut un peu plaindre au bon R. Azuby de quoy il a alteré la première page des dites tables, pour les r'apporter à nostre temps, plus tost que de la laisser comme l'autheur l'avoit escrite en la rapportant à son temps'. Gassendi to Peiresc, 28 December 1633, ibid., IV, p. 403.

60 '. . . mais je voudrois un peu de griffon-
nement de chacun à part non des enrichs-
sements d'or et de pierreries . . . car les
enchasseurs me sont inutiles, voire m'em-
peschent plus qu'elles ne me servent, attendu
que je n'y cherche que ce que les Anciens y
pouvoint avoir faict, et non ce que les
modernes
y ont ajouté qui ne fait que m'enchérir ce qu'il
y pourroit avoir d'Antique et m'oster le moyen
de l'achepter' (Peiresc to Alvares, 28 November
1633, ibid., VII, p. 33). The same historical
sensibility is revealed in an exchange with
Mersenne about the meaning of a mathemati-
cal symbol. When Mersenne denied that it had
any symbolic value, Peiresc answered in some
frustration, 'Mais je n'y cherche que de recog-
noistre ce que les Anciens en ont cru' (Peiresc
to Mersenne, 19 December 1634, *Mersenne
Correspondance*, IV, p. 415).

61 I follow the attribution to Posthumus
in Dacos, *'Roma Quanta Fuit'*, p. sl. Vincenzo
Golzio, *Raffaelo nei documenti nelle testimonianze
dei contemporanei e nella letteratura del suo secolo*
(Vatican City, 1936), p. 82.

62 Golzio, *Raffaelo*, p. 85, n. 7 citing from a
variant manuscript.

63 Ingrid Rowland, 'Raphael, Angelo
Colocci, and the Genesis of the Architectural
Orders', *Art Bulletin*, 76 (1994), p. 95.

64 'Les plus rares peinctures de Fontain-
bleau sont . . .', includes works by Michelangelo,
Raphael, Leonardo, Correggio, Pordenone,
Sebastiano del Piombo, Rosso, and Titian (BN
MS Lat. 8957, fol. 128). The Michelangelos
and Polydor da Caravaggios were among 100
engravings made by Cherubino del Borgo that
he purchased (BN MS N.a.f. 5169, fol. 34ᵛ; entry
for 23 July 1628). Peiresc's definition of opera
was 'un chant qui n'est quasi qu'un simple
parler en certain cadance, accompagné de l'harmonie des instruments qui delecte sans couvrir
et confondre la parolle. Ce qui n'est pas de
mesmes en nos airs et aultres façons de chanter,
où la parole ne peut quasi pas estre entendue
ou discerne' (Peiresc to Mersenne, 23 July 1635,
Mersenne Correspondance, V, p. 329; also p.
358).

65 Peiresc to Rubens, 23 December 1621,
Rubens Correspondance, II, p. 317.

66 Ibid., p. 318.

67 Peiresc to Dupuy, 15 December 1629,
Lettres de Peiresc, II, p. 209.

68 'J'advoue qu'il y a bien des faultes et des
besveues dans le Geographe Arabe, mais oultre
qu'il y a des notices qui ne se peuvent avoir
d'ailleurs, il me semble qu'il se peult tirer des
faultes mesmes qui y sont, et des plus lourdes,

le mesme fruit et le mesme plaisir que nous
pouvons avoir quand nous considerons combien
estoit petite la portion du monde habitable qui
estoit cogneue aux premiers temps, et depuis
d'en voir le progrez de siecle en siecle et
combien se mesuroit la cognoisance qui s'en
pouvoit prendre, et la mesme chose eschoit à
considerer les opinions dont se payoient encores
lors les peuples de l'Afrique meridienne, et dont
ils ne sont possible pas à cette heure guere plus
scavants . . . Enfin, de l'humeur dont je suis qui
n'est pas tant attachée à la perdrix que le boeuf
et le moutton ne puisse suffire à me rassasier,
je trouve partout de quoy glaner et proffitter
quelque chosette quoy qu'elles ne soient toutes
du plus hault goust'. Peiresc to Dupuy, 16
December 1636, ibid., III, pp. 619–20.

69 'C'est avoir faict bien du progrez en
la vie contemplative que d'y estre arrivé en
ce point de se contenter des viandes les plus
agrestes et les plus insipides et moings nutritives
et d'en pouvoir tirer aultant de bon aliment
qu'il en fault . . .' Peiresc to Beauclerc, 7
November 1617, ibid., VII, p. 530, n. 1.

70 'Già che talvolta l'opinioni che paiono
ridicole ad altrui (come sono per esempio
appresso I Mahometani quelle de Christiani et
al contrario quelle delli Mahomettani appresso
li Christiani), con la benigna interpretatione che
vi può occorrer passano per mysterii gravissimi
et di somma importanza frà li dottori principali
dell'una et l'altra legge'. Peiresc to Campanella,
3 July 1635, in *Fra Tommaso Campanella ne'
Castelli di Napoli in Roma ed in Parigi*, ed. Luigi
Amabile, 2 vols (Naples, 1887), II, p. 255.

71 'Car il seroit à desirer que ces bonnes
gents qui se meslent de la censure y peussent
tost ou tard gouster la facilité et vraisemblance,
comme il faudra tost ou tard qu'ils s'accoustument à tollerer, quelque repugnance qu'ils y
trouvent; comme firent aultrefois ceulx qui
trouvoient si estranges les propositions de la
verité des Antipodes lesquels n'avoient pas
moings de raison de trouver incompatible que
ceulx qui avoient leurs pieds directement
opposés aux nostres se peussent tenir debout
sans tomber dans le fond du Ciel qui passe par
dessoubs nous. Et toutefois les voyages des Indes
ont guary nos faulces apparences et imaginations de ce costé-là'. Peiresc to Holstenius, 2
July 1636, *Lettres de Peiresc*, V, p. 444.

72 'E così in materie philosophiche se
si esaminano gli vari concetti degli antiqui
philosophi greci, pochi ve ne sono che non
habbiano qualche cosa del mirabile, mentre si
guardano con charità humana e che vi si con-
sidera ciò che vi puol essere degno di lode,

lasciando ciò che non par tanto compatibile, et riducendo le cose alli termini dell'ignoranza de'tempi loro'. Peiresc to Campanella, 3 July 1635, in *Fra Tommaso Campanella*, II, p. 255.

73 'Scusimi di gratia. V.P.^ta et stabilisca la sua philosophia senza dimorare a persuadere che sia ridicola quella philosophia d'Epicuro, mentre se ne veggono pochissime risolutioni sparse di quà et di là senza ordine; gia che s'ella le havesse vedute ordinate, non le parebbono forzi tanto strane; ben che la dottrina de gli atomi non le piaccia, siccome ne anco à molti altri, ma non però è necessario di ridur subito di no, che non piace, massime quando non è conosciuto'. Ibid., p. 256.

74 'Io son d'un umore ch'io non gusto troppo le fatiche de que'ch'attendono à confutationi dell'altrui opinioni, giudicandovi ... la brevità della vita humana non comportando queste cose senza grave necessità. Et mi par molto più nobile di stabilire ciascheduno I suoi fondamenti con le miglior ragioni che ci può somministrare il proprio ingegno, senza rifutar altro che ciò che non si può vietare di necessità. Et così lasciando al Pittore la lode che può occorrere alla sua arte, et al Cantore quella della sua musica, et all'architetto quella delle sue fabriche, et così degli altri'. Peiresc to Campanella, 3 July 1635, in ibid., II, pp. 255–6.

75 'La debolezza del ingegno humano è troppo grande per poter in un tratto penetrare ogni secreto della natura. Vi vuol una gradatione che per diversi mezzi conduca allo scopo, et la brevità della vita humana non comporta che una sola persona basti: vi bisogna adoperare l'osservationi di buon numero d'altri de secoli passati et futuri per chiarirsi di ciò che conviene meglio, et vi bisogna un certo amore et venerationi dell'uno agli altri per cavarne l'ottato frutto, e più tosto l'interpretatione benigna che la sinistra'. Ibid., p. 256.

76 Peiresc to Mersenne, 18 June 1634, *Mersenne Correspondance*, IV, pp. 181–2.

77 Mersenne to Peiresc, 26 July 1634, ibid., p. 255 and 27 August, p. 328.

78 Peiresc to Mersenne, 5 May 1635, ibid. V, p. 171: 'Je trouvois estrange que des personnes d'honneur fussent mal traictées sans l'avoir merité à faulte de chercher des paroles plus doulces et moins aigres que celles qui viennent quelquefois les premières à la bouche, et qu'il est bon de revoir une seconde fois ce que l'on escript trop précipitamment pour l'examiner'.

79 Peiresc to Mersenne, 3 July 1635, ibid. p. 277; 23 July 1635, p. 332.

80 'Et sì come a Tertulliano, ad Origene e a tanti altri Padri, che si sono lasciati andare a qualche errore per semplicità o altramente, la Sta Chiesa come buona madre non ha lasciato di portare gran veneratione per gli altri concetti religiosi et indici della lor pietà et zelo al servicio divino, anzi sarebbe sinistramente interpetato et biasimato il zelo di chi gli havesse voluto castigare con la medesima severità che si castigano gli heretici ostinati, et esercitare sopra delle persone loro quelle pene che puonno cadere in persone ree di qualche grand'errore o furfantaria, stante l'infermità humana che gli poteva haver fatto cadere in qualche peccato, la cui fragilità non è sempre indegna di schusa o di perdono ... così pare chi secolo a venire potranno trovare stranno, che doppo la ritrattatione d'una opinione che ancora non era stata assolutamente prohibita in publico ... si usi tanto rigore ad un povero vecchio settuagenario di tenerlo in carcere ... et tante inventioni, le più nobili che si fussero scoperte in tanti secoli, non potranno meritar l'indulgenza d'un scherzo problematico, dove egli non ha mai affirmativamente asserito esser suo proprio parere quello che non s'è voluto approvare?' Peiresc to Francesco Barberini, 5 December 1634, *Le Opere di Galileo. Edizione Nazionale*, ed. Antonio Favaro, 20 vols (Florence, 1966 [1890]), XVI, p. 170.

81 'Je trouve que comme c'est une espece de participation aux actions divines que de faire plaisir et des bons offices à quelqu'un, ce n'en est pas une moings digne que de pardonner à ceux qui par infirmité ou aveuglement s'oublient de leur debvoir envers nous'. Peiresc to Holstenius [1637], *Lettres de Peiresc*, V, p. 486.

82 Christophe Dupuy to Peiresc, 29 February 1634, ibid., III, p. 697, citing Cicero, *Ad familiares*, III.ix.1 ('plenas humanitatis officii diligentiae').

83 Thomas Fuller, *The Holy State, and the Profane State* (London, 1841 [1642]), bk 2, ch. 6, pp. 64–6.

84 'Pour moy je n'y trouve pas moings de plaisir qu'à examiner la differance des maximes de cez anciens philosophes qui prenoient de si diverses routtes pour arriver à la cognoisçance de la nature et de si divers biaiz et raisonnements pour appuyer leurs conceptions et conjectures' (Peiresc to Dupuy, 16 December 1636, *Lettres de Peiresc*, III, p. 620). Perhaps this absence is less uncommon than it might seem; J. B. Sabrié notes that Mersenne never mentions Montaigne and that François de Sales treats him as only one source among many (*De l'Humanisme au rationalisme: Pierre Charron (1541–1603). L'homme, l'oeuvre, l'influence*, Paris, 1913, p. 492).

85 Montaigne, 'On Coaches', *The Complete Essays*, tr. M. A. Screech (Harmondsworth, 1991), p. 1028. On the place of this passage in the chiasmic structure of the essay, see Edwin M. Duval, 'Lessons of the New World: Design and Meaning in Montaigne's *Des cannibales* (1:31) and *Des coches* (III.6)', *Montaigne: Essays in Reading*, ed. Gérard Defaux (New Haven and London, 1983), pp. 95–112. Montaigne had explained that 'only a man who can picture in his mind the mighty idea of Mother Nature in her total majesty; who can read in her countenance a variety so general and so unchanging and then pick out therein not merely himself but an entire kingdom as a tiny, faint point: only he can reckon things at their real size . . . Such a variety of humours, schools of thought, opinions, laws and customs teach us to judge sanely of our own and teach our judgement to acknowledge its shortcomings and natural weakness' ('On Educating Children', *Essays*, I.26, p. 177).

86 Gassendi, *Mirrour*, bk 6, p. 202.

87 Ibid., p. 211.

88 'Il [the sage] est citoyen du monde, comme Socrates, il embrasse d'affection tout le genre humain, il se promène par tout comme chés soy, voyt comme un soleil, d'un regard égal, ferme et indifférent comme d'une hautte guette, tous les changemens, diversités et vicissitudes des choses, sans se varier et se tenant tousjours mesme à soy, qui est une livrée de la Divinité'. Pierre Charron, *De la sagesse* (Paris, 1986 [1601]), bk 2, ch. 2, p. 406. In a letter to Henri du Faur de Pibrac, Gassendi thanked him for sending a copy of Charron's *Discours chrestiens* but explained that the *Sagesse* pleased him more: 'Tu fais bien de me recommander d'emmener Charron dans ma solitude. Quel juge plus sûr? Surtout si on lui donne pour compagnons ceux dont il a lui-même fait son profit: Montaigne, Lipse, Sénèque, Plutarque, Cicéron'. Quoted in Henri Busson, *La Pensée religieuse française de Charron à Pascal* (Paris, 1933), p. 182.

89 Gassendi, *Mirrour*, bk 6, pp. 202–3.

90 Daniello Bartoli, *The Learned Man Defended and Reforme'd. A Discourse of Singular Politeness and Elocution; Seasonably Asserting the Right of the Muses; in Opposition to the Many Enemies which in this Age Learning Meets with, and More Especially those Two IGNORANCE and VICE*, tr. Thomas Salusbury (London, 1660), p. 73. The first Italian edition was published in 1645. For a brief reception history see Roger Chartier, 'The Man of Learning', *Enlightenment Portraits*, ed. Michel Vovelle (Chicago, 1997), pp. 169–70.

91 Bartoli, *The Learned Man*, pp. 42, 44, 53, and 68. Though Bartoli, like Flavio Querenghi, explicitly rejected the old Stoic insistence on the extirpation of all the passions (ibid., p. 68).

92 Ibid., p. 32.

93 Ibid., p. 146.

94 Ibid., p. 149.

95 Ibid., p. 150.

96 Ibid., pp. 153–4. In the circle of Peiresc, Galileo had occupied this place. Lorenzo Pignoria had told Galileo, not long after the discovery of the Medicean planets, that 'Credami V.S. che la memoria dei Colombi e dei Vespucci si rinnoverà in lei et ciò tanto più nobilmente quanto è più degno il cielo che la terra' (Letter of 4 March 1611 quoted in Cecilia Rizza, 'Galileo nella corrispondenza di Peiresc', *Studi Francesi*, 15, 1961, p. 449). For the comparison see Andrea Battistini, 'Cedat Columbus e *Vicisti, Galilaee*: due esploratori a confronto nell'immaginario barocco', *Annali d'Italianistica*, 10 (1992), pp. 116–32.

97 For other perspectives on this shift see Pierre Chaunu, 'Reflexions sur le tournant des années 1630–1650', *Cahiers d'histoire publiés par les Universités de Clermont–Lyon–Grenoble*, 12 (1967), pp. 249–68 and André Stegmann, *L'Héroïsme cornélien*, 2 vols (Paris, 1968), I, pp. 215–16.

98 Sir Thomas Browne, *Hydriotaphia*, in *The Religio Medici and Other Writings* (London, 1947), pp. 92–3.

99 Ibid., pp. 131–3. This is a theme touched on as well in Flavio Querenghi's semi-serious *Delle lucerne de' sepolchri antichi*, in *Discorsi morali politici e naturali* (Padua, 1644), p. 301.

100 Browne, *Hydriotaphia*, p. 134.

101 Sorbière to Hobbes, 2 January 1663, in Thomas Hobbes, *The Correspondence*, ed. Noel Malcolm, 2 vols (Oxford, 1994), II, pp. 540–3.

102 After viewing what survived of Peiresc's cabinet at the library of Saint-Geneviève he commented that 'nothing pleased me more than to have seen the remains of the cabinet of the noble Peiresc, the greatest and heartiest Maecenas, to his power, of learned men of any of this age'. Martin Lister, *A Journey to Paris in the Year 1698*, in *A General Collection of the Best and Most Interesting Voyages and Travels in all Parts of the World*, ed. John Pinkerton, 17 vols (London, 1809), IV, p. 39, also p. 20.

103 Walther Haage, *Kakteen von A bis Z* (Leipzig and Radebul, 1982), p. 611.

104 See, for example, J.-B. Argens, *Lettres juives* (The Hague, 1738), p. 331; J.-B. Jourdan, *Le Guerrier philosophe* (The Hague, 1744), p. 189;

and, of course, Riquier's French translation of Gassendi's *Vita*, published in 1770 with its dedication to the *parlementaires* of Provence.

105 'One thing I read, not without a groan, that the most venerable and divine Fabri de Peiresc took pains to have copied out from the Vatican, Royal, Imperial and other libraries all the authors, and especially the Greeks, who wrote on weights and measures in order to share them with men learned in these things. Where is the copy? From where did he get it? When was it made? What has become of this treasure? Or, truly, who can provide me with a copy?' ('Unum non sine gemitu legi, sanctissimum illum & divinum Fabricium Peirescium, auctores omnes & Graecos potissimum, qui de Ponderibus & mensuris scripserunt, per bibliothecas Vaticanam, Regiam, Augustanam, caeteras, exscribi curasse, ut cum hominibus istorum studiosis communicaret. Ubi talem? unde talem? quando talem? quo thesaurus iste devenit? aut quis ejus mihi copiam facturus est?') Johannes Federicus Gronovius, *De Sestertiis seu Subseciurom Pecuniae Veteris Graecae & Romanae* (Leiden, 1691), p. 183.

106 The continuation of Montfaucon's expression of indebtedness reads as follows: '. . . [and] hath commonly added short Explanations to these Monuments, which may be still seen in some of his Manuscripts and furnished all the learned Men of *Europe* with Materials. It is a great pity that his Manuscripts are either lost or dispersed in several places' (*Antiquity Explained and Represented in Sculptures*, tr. David Humphreys, 2 vols, London, 1721, I, sig. B2ᵛ). For more on this see E. S. Peck, 'Peiresc Manuscripts Aiding the Reconstruction of Lost Medieval Monuments,' Harvard University, unpubd Ph.D., 1963, p. 17. Du Bos, *Reflexions critiques sur la poésie et sur la peinture* (Paris, 1733), p. 225.

107 It contains mock-learned disquisitions on the *latus clavus* (bk 6, ch. 19), pseudo-Sorbonnic documents on *in utero* baptism (bk 1, ch. 20), Toby on the design of fortresses (bk 2, chs 3–4), the utterly successful parody of a humanist dialogue on 'The Nose'(bk 3, ch. 38), the 'Slawkenbergii Fabella' at the start of book 4, and the mention of Walter Shandy's manuscript 'Life of Socrates' and 'History of the Transmigration of Souls' (bk 5, chs 12–13).

108 Laurence Sterne, *Tristram Shandy*, ed. Howard Anderson (New York, 1980), II, ch. 14, p. 83. Uncle Toby praises the way 'Peireskius elegantly expresses' the speed of the wind-driven chariot, '*Tam citus erat, quam erat ventus*; which, unless I have forgot my Latin, is "that it was as swift as the wind itself"'.' This is Sterne's elegant translation; Rand's was 'that it would run swiftly with sails upon the land, as a ship does in the sea'. The account is in book 2 of the *Life*, year 1606, p. 104. Peiresc's friend, Grotius, was a passenger on the chariot's maiden voyage and commemorated the event in two Latin poems (see Edwin J. Van Kley, 'The Effect of Discoveries on Seventeenth-Century Dutch Popular Culture', *Terrae Incognitae*, 8, 1976, p. 29). Peiresc's next appearance is in the midst of an utterly farcical discussion about fast learners. Walter Shandy's 'What shall we say of the great *Piereskius*?' [*sic*] is answered by Uncle Toby who reminded his brother of their earlier talk about Stevinus' flying chariot. Gassendi's claim that Peiresc was appointed his brother's tutor while himself a child is one of a series of absurd claims for the early genius of learned men brought to a fitting end by the attribution to Lipsius of a book written on the day he was born! (Sterne, *Tristram Shandy*, VI, ch. 2, p. 288). This same anecdote of childhood was incorporated by Samuel Johnson in the 'virtuoso's' autobiography offered up in the *Rambler*, ed. W. J. Bate and Albrecht B. Strauss in *The Yale Edition of the Works of Samuel Johnson* (New Haven and London, 1969), IV, no. 82, p. 65.

109 A.-L. Thomas, *Essay sur les éloges* (1733), *Oeuvres complètes*, 6 vols (Paris, 1822), II, pp. 152–3.

110 'Peyresc cherche principalement l'histoire de l'Homme dans celles des peuples. Il le trouve partout le même; les mêmes vices & les mêmes vertus, les memes penchans forment par-tout le fond de son caractere. L'étranger qui arrive parmi nous, reconnoit aisément la même Nation, malgré la variété de nos usages, de nos modes & de nos habits, malgré la diversité de nos gouts & de nos occupations. Tel Peyresc, comparant les siecles & les peuples, ne trouve, pour ainsi dire, de difference entr'eux, que dans les manieres' (M. Paris, *Éloge de Nicolas-Claude Fabry de Peiresc, conseiller au Parlement de Provence*, n.p. [Marseille], n.d. [1783], pp. 20–1). This metaphorical link between the antiquary's knowledge of the deepest past and the traveller's of the most distant present had become something of an enlightenment commonplace. Jean-Nicolas Démeunier, in his encyclopaedic catalogue of world rituals (1776), explained that 'the most singular customs would appear simple if it were possible for the philosopher to examine them in place' (Jean-Nicolas Démeunier, *L'Esprit des usages et des coutumes des différants peuples*, 1776, quoted in Marie-Noëlle Bourguet, 'The Explorer', *Enlightenment Portraits*,

ed. Michel Vovelle, Chicago, 1997 [1992], p. 302). Joseph-Marie Dégerando, writing in advance of the French expedition to Australia in 1800, observed that 'the philosophical traveller, sailing to the ends of the earth, is in fact travelling in time; he is exploring the past; every step he makes is the passage of an age' (Joseph-Marie Dégerando, *The Observation of Savage Peoples*, tr. F. C. T. Moore, London, 1969, p. 63).

111 'Par-tout il apperçoit, depuis la naissance du monde, des erreurs remplacées ou fortifiées par de nouvelles erreurs, quelque vérités surnagent, d'abord saisies par hasard, longtemps exposées aux outrages de l'ignorance & dévelopées avec peine'. Paris, *Éloge de Nicolas-Claude Fabry de Peiresc*, p. 21.

112 'What a retrospect it is to a genius truly philosophical, to see the most absurd opinions received among the most enlightened people; to see barbarians on the other hand, arrive at the knowledge of the most sublime truths; to find true consequences falsely deduced from the most erroneous principles; admirable principles, bordering on the verge of truth, without ever conducting thither; languages formed on ideas, and yet those ideas corrected by such languages; the springs of morality universally the same; the opinions of contentious metaphysics universally varied, and generally extravagant, accurate only while superficial, but subtile, obscure and uncertain whenever they were profound'. Edward Gibbon, *Essay on the Study of Literature* (London, 1764), p. 93.

113 Quoted in Hanns Gross, *Rome in the Age of Enlightenment. The post-Tridentine Syndrome and the Ancien Régime* (Cambridge, 1985), p. 311.

114 'Dans l'instant où ses trésors arrivent, il ouvre avec une douce inquiétude, mêlée d'e-spérance, les caisses qui les renferment: il se flatte d'y trouver des choses rares & inconnues. Le moment de la découverte est pour lui une jouissance vive'. Comte de Caylus, *Recueil d'antiquités egyptiennes, etrusques, grecques et romanes*, 7 vols (Paris, 1759–65), II, p. ii). 'Il examine ces Monumens antiques; il les compare avec ceux qui sont déjà connus; il en recherche la différance ou la conformité; il réfléchit; il discute; il établit des conjectures, que les temps reculés & le silence des Auteurs ont rendues nécessaires. Si un de ces morceaux présente des idées sur une opération de l'Art, négligée, perdue ou refusée aux Modernes, le plaisir de faire des expériences, celui de les décrire, l'anime, flatte sont gout. Mais rien n'est comparable à la satisfaction de prévoir une utilité publique. Cette idée le pénètre; elle touche son

coeur; & le bonheur de réussir, le dédommage amplement de tous ses soins & de toutes ses peines. Voilà, je l'avoue, les motifs qui m'ont séduit'. Ibid.

115 '. . . l'Antiquaire cherche dans les temps anciens, & veut considérer les simples Particuliers, il ne démelera qu'avec peine quelques atomes dans l'immensité du vuide; ses recherches ne lui présenteront qu'un très-petit nombre d'hommes, dont les noms sont connus de la postérité, ou qui ont obtenu deux ou trois lignes d'une Inscription, dont souvent on ne comprehend plus le sens; ou s'il est possible de la lire, on apprend, en général, qu'un tel homme à vécu'. Ibid., v, p. xiv.

116 'J'avoue que cet examen particulier est le point essentiel, & l'object principal de ces réflexions, puisqu'il présente en effet le plus grand avantage de l'étude dont il est question, qu'il montre à l'Antiquaire des millions d'hommes, noyés dans l'abime du temps dont le tourbillon doit l'emporter lui-meme. Il appercoit un nombre considerable de Rois absolument ignorés, ou dont le nom est à peine connu . . . Enfin, supposé que l'on opposat à des exemples si convaincans, que plusieurs des Anciens ont été célébrés, & que l'on retrouve tous les jours des Monumens élevés à leur honneur, l'Antiquaire remarque sans peine que ceux qui sont parvenus à quelque distinction, sont nos voisins de siecles & de pays. Ce voisinage lui démonstre la raison physique qui met leur mémoire à portée de recevoir cette légère fumée; & le retour que ces exemples l'engagent à faire sur lui-meme, est peut-etre le moyen le plus efficace pour la destruction de l'*Egoisme*, ce grand ennemi des hommes, & le défaut le plus importun dans la societé'. Ibid., pp. xv–xvi. Kant's formulation was similar, though he emphasized the anthropological dimension of antiquarian scholarship rather than, as with Caylus, the archaeological: 'The opposite of egoism can only be pluralism, that is, the attitude of not being occupied with oneself as the whole world, but regarding and conducting oneself as a citizen of the world. – This much belongs to anthropology' (*Anthropology from a Pragmatic Point of View*, ed. and tr. Mary J. Gregor, The Hague, 1974, p. 12).

117 'J'ai voulu faire sentire que l'étude de l'Antiquité, c'est-a-dire, les réflexions auxquelles elle peut conduire, éclairent l'Antiquaire, & le mettent en état de connoitre les hommes, & de les estimer pour ce qu'ils valent'. Caylus, *Recueil*, v, p. xiii. Caylus' English admirer, Thomas Burgess, who incorporated a translation of

much of this preface into *An Essay upon the Study of Antiquities* (Oxford, 1782), pushed the argument one step further. He suggested that studying the past appealed to a fascination with 'the irreversible destiny of human nature' and induced 'a kind of pleasing melancholy' (pp. 26, 3).

118   'Je ne puis faire un certain cas de celui la qui l'on montre une pierre gravée et qui demande si elle est antique. Antique ou non, d'hier ou d'il y a trois mille ans, de Picher ou de . . . [*sic*], qu'importe si elle est belle?' Maurice Tourneux, 'Fragments inédits de Diderot', *Revue d'Histoire Littéraire de la France*, I, (1894), pp. 164–74, p. 173. By comparison, in his finely balanced 'virtuoso's curiosity justified' Samuel Johnson acknowledged that it was difficult 'to forbear some sallies of merriment, or expressions of pity' when confronted with someone so committed to study of things that seemed so unimportant, but noted, echoing Bartoli and Seneca, that because 'it is impossible to determine the limits of enquiry, or to foresee what consequences a new discovery may produce', these labours ought not to be mocked or condemned. Objects of 'small importance' (Peiresc's *goffa maestria*) offered testimony to the advance of 'human powers' and could 'sometimes unexpectedly contribute to the illustration of history' (*Rambler, The Yale Edition of the Works of Samuel Johnson*, IV, no. 83, pp. 70–3).

119   See Jean Seznec, *Essais sur Diderot et l'antiquité* (Oxford, 1957), ch. 5; Krzystof Pomian, 'Medailles / coquilles = érudition / philosophie' and 'Maffei et Caylus', in *Collectionneurs, amateurs et curieux. Paris, Venise: XVIe–XVIIIe siècles* (Paris, 1987), pp. 143–62 and 195–211.

120   Quoted in Pomian, *Collectionneurs, amateurs et curieux*, p. 158.

121   Keats to Benjamin Bailey, 22 November 1817, *The Letters of John Keats*, ed. Hyder Edward Rollins, 2 vols (Cambridge, Mass., 1958), I, p. 184; 'Ode on a Grecian Urn', *Complete Poems*, ed. Jack Stillinger (Cambridge, Mass., 1978), p. 283. I thank Harry Ballan for suggesting I look at Keats' *Letters*.

122   Keats to J. H. Reynolds, 19 February 1818, *Keats Letters*, I, pp. 231–2; Kant, *Anthropology*, p. 58.

123   Keats to James Rice, 24 March 1818, *Keats Letters*, I, pp. 254–5.

124   Keats to George and Georgina Keats, 31 December 1818, ibid., II, p. 18.

125   G. W. F. Hegel, *Phenomenology of Spirit*, tr. A.V. Miller (Oxford, 1977), para. 753, p. 455.

126   Ibid., p. 456.

127   Keats, 'Ode on a Grecian Urn', *Complete Poems*, pp. 282–3.

128   *The Poetical Works of Byron*, intro. Robert F. Gleckner (Boston, 1975), canto IV, lxxx, lxxxi, p. 67.

CONCLUSION

1   Raymond Lebègue, *Les Correspondants de Peiresc dans l'ancien Pays-Bas* (Brussels, 1943), p. 71. While acknowledging that 'nous ne trouvons rien du côté de l'un ni de l'autre qui nous fasse voir le fondement de leur connoissance mutuelle', A. Baillet in his *Vie de Monsieur Descartes* (Paris, 1691) suggests that it was Descartes' intention, before learning of his death, to send Peiresc a copy of the *Discourse* for him to bring to the attention of his friend, the great patron of learning Cardinal Francesco Barberini (p. 301).

2   For Pownall's antiquarian researches, see for example, 'A Description of the Sepulchral Monument at *New Grange*, near *Drogheda*, in the County of *Meath*, in *Ireland*' (1770), *Archaeologia*, 2 (1773), pp. 236–75; 'Description of the Carn Braich y Dinas, on the Summit of Pen-maen-mawr, in Caernarvonshire' (1771), 'Further Observations on Pen-maen-mawr' (1774), 'An Account of Irish Antiquities' (1774), *Archaeologia*, 3 (1786), pp. 303–9, 350–4 and 355–70; 'Observations arising from an Enquiry into the Nature of the Vases found on the *Mosquito* Shore in *South America*' (1778), *Archaeologia*, 5 (1779), pp. 318–24. For Pownall as a political thinker, see the author's *Defining the Common Good: Empire, Religion and Philosophy in Eighteenth-Century Britain* (Cambridge, 1994), pp. 202–39.

3   Joseph Addison, *A Dialogue upon Medals* (1726), *Collected Works*, 6 vols (London, 1804), V, pp. 4–6.

4   In a letter to the abbé Du Bos in 1738 explaining his preference for writing a cultural history that focused only on the geniuses who advanced the arts and philosophy (quoted in Anthony Grafton, *The Footnote. A Curious History*, Cambridge, Mass., 1997, p. 95).

5   Arnaldo Momigliano, 'Ancient History and the Antiquarian', *Contributo alla storia degli studi classici* (Rome, 1955), p. 102.

6   'Mr Naudé m'escript que le P. Scheyner escrivoit dez lors ex proffesso contre le pauvre Galilée, qu'il y travailloit puissament et avec grandissime animosité, à ce qu'on leur en mandoit de Rome; dont les effects n'ont que trop paru à mon grand regret et peult estre au

dezadvantage des arts liberaulx'. Peiresc to
Gassendi, 25 June 1633, *Lettres de Peiresc*, IV, p.
318.

7　Ralph Waldo Emerson, *The Uses of Great*
Men, in *The Collected Works of Ralph Waldo*
Emerson, ed. Wallace E. Williams and Douglas
Emory Wilson, 5 vols (Cambridge, Mass., 1987),
IV, p. 8.

INDEX